Ariadne's Clue

A GUIDE TO THE
SYMBOLS OF HUMANKIND

ANTHONY STEVENS

Ariadne's Clue

A GUIDE TO THE
SYMBOLS OF HUMANKIND

PRINCETON UNIVERSITY PRESS
PRINCETON, NEW JERSEY

Published in 1999 in the United States, Canada, and the
Philippine Islands by Princeton University Press, 41 William Street,
Princeton, New Jersey 08540

First published in the United Kingdom by
Allen Lane, the Penguin Press

Set in 11/14 pt PostScript Monotype Sabon
Typeset by Rowland Phototypesetting Ltd, Bury St Edmunds, Suffolk
Printed in Great Britain by The Bath Press, Bath

ISBN 0-691-00459-5

http://pup.princeton.edu

1 3 5 7 9 10 8 6 4 2

Contents

Acknowledgements

I must thank Routledge and the Princeton University Press for permission to quote from *The Collected Works of C. G. Jung*; Hamish Hamilton and Penguin UK for permitting me to use material relating to the serpent archetype which originally appeared in my *Private Myths: Dreams and Dreaming*; Routledge for allowing me to reproduce a schema for the classification of major disorders, originally published in *Evolutionary Psychiatry: A New Beginning*; the University of Toronto Press for permission to use Dr P. D. MacLean's diagram of the triune brain; and Phillida Gili for permission to use Reynolds Stone's engraving of a waterfall in Chapter 1.

I am immensely grateful to 'Lynda' and 'Jonathan' for their generous permission to publish their dreams on pages 5 and 78–9; to Norma Luscombe for word-processing numerous drafts of this book with her usual combination of high professionalism and inexhaustible goodwill; and to Mary Omond for copy-editing the final product with enviable patience and sensitivity.

About This Book

This is a book for browsing in, but it is also designed to be read from cover to cover. It is intended as a guide for those wishing to deepen their understanding of symbolism, as well as a work of reference in which individual symbols can be looked up. I have chosen to present the reference part in the form of a thesaurus, rather than the more usual form of a dictionary, because I believe that all dictionaries of symbols, of which there are many, share a common drawback: they give the impression that symbols are susceptible to arbitrary interpretation, as if their meanings were indelibly fixed. What dictionaries do, with varying degrees of success, is describe individual symbols in terms of meanings that have been historically attributed to them (for example, Becker, Chevalier and Gheerbrant, Cirlot, Cooper, Leach and Fried, De Vries); but they make no attempt to explain how or why we create the symbols that we do.

Symbologists compiling dictionaries are rather like children collecting birds' eggs: they extract their contents and arrange them in neatly ordered ranks for our inspection. But they give scant attention to the possibility that in the process they could be killing something live. For symbols are *living entities* with a life-cycle of their own; they are born, flourish for a while, then dwindle and die. New symbols come into existence all the time, but not in an arbitrary or unrelated way. They bear a family resemblance to each other and to their ancestors, in the sense that they are imaginal forms which possess a dynastic relationship to symbols that have preceded them.

On the whole, dictionaries are more appropriate for the description of intellectual concepts formulated in words than the interpretation of intuitive concepts represented by symbols. Where the logic of language dissects, divides, and breaks things down into packages of meaning, the symbol assembles concepts into integrated *Gestalts*. A book of symbols is of limited use if it can tell you merely what a symbol 'stands for'. What it should seek to create is an allusive field of meanings within which the significance of a symbol can be appreciated. It is for this reason that the present volume aims to explain the meaning of symbols in terms of their psychodynamic importance, as well as their evolutionary or prehistoric origins.

To explore a symbol, to trace it to its archetypal roots, is to follow it back through time till its universal configurations and its psychobiological foundations stand revealed. Why are the great cathedrals of Europe adorned with images of eagles, lions, and oxen? Do they indicate that medieval Christians worshipped animals? That would be a plausible supposition if we knew nothing of Christian iconography. Our perception is changed, however, once we learn that these creatures symbolize three of the four Evangelists and that the symbols are derived from a vision received by the prophet Ezekiel. Our understanding is deepened by the discovery that they are analogous to the four sons of the Egyptian sun god Horus. Still further investigation carries us back to the most ancient of symbolic configurations: the quaternity, the mandala, the cross – all symbols of totality. These in turn owe their origins to the neuropsychic capacity to conceive coordinates – North–South, East–West, up–down, left–right – a capacity which is indispensable to orientation in the real world of phenomena and inseparable from the earliest beginnings of our conscious perception of the world and our appreciation of the miracle of existence.

The purpose of this book is not, therefore, to provide an interpretative system which can be arbitrarily imposed on symbolic images, but to grant access to the enormous reservoir of human symbolic talent so that readers may cultivate a more fruitful understanding of the symbols that come to their attention.

Finally, I must confess that I am not an expert in semiotics but a psychiatrist and analyst who has spent his professional life working with people on the meaning of their symptoms, their fantasies, and their dreams. This has induced in me so deep an admiration for the symbolic genius at work in every human personality that writing this has been as much an act of homage as a personal adventure.

THE STRUCTURE OF THE BOOK

Part I seeks to provide an explanatory introduction to the evolution and psychology of symbolism. It has been written to satisfy a personal need which I suspect many readers will share. Since childhood I have loved and collected symbols, and, like all lovers, have wanted to learn everything I can about their past, to know where they come from, and to understand why we produce and respond to them the way we do. How do we bring them into being and why do we find it necessary to create them in the first place? The first chapters, in addition to providing a general orientation to the study of symbolism, are attempts to find answers to these endlessly intriguing questions. However, it is not necessary to read them in order to use the Thesaurus, and readers who are uninterested in the theoretical background may prefer to turn directly to the Thesaurus itself.

Part II, the Thesaurus proper, is divided into four sections, each of which deals with symbols relating to:

1 The Physical Environment
2 Culture and Psyche
3 People, Animals, and Plants
4 The Body.

Each section is broken up into a number of subsections in which individual symbols are examined in detail. In order to investigate the psychological implications of a certain symbol, the reader should first consult the Symbol Index, then look up the pages and read the sections in which the symbol is discussed.

A WARNING TO THE READER

All symbols, even the most ancient of them, are experienced in a manner unique to the person who produces them; and this book is not intended to be a substitute for the toil of working on your symbols for yourself. So, before rushing to look up a symbol in the Symbol Index, you are strongly advised to reflect for a few minutes on *what the symbol means to you*. What ideas, feelings, and memories does it bring up *for you*, and where do you stand in relation to them? If you do this, you will be better prepared for what the text has to convey, for then the work of conscious and unconscious integration can proceed in a way that is intrinsically more satisfying and psychologically more productive.

PART I

SYMBOLISM, EVOLUTION, AND PSYCHOLOGY

I

Ariadne's Clue

Those entering the study of symbolism for the first time can be forgiven for feeling overwhelmed by the vast array of cultural information that anthropology, history, and psychology have amassed, and for wondering how on earth it may be possible to make some sense of it all. The German philosopher Ernst Cassirer (1874–1945) understood this very well. Discussing advances in the psychology of symbolism, he wrote: 'Our technical instruments for observation and experimentation have been immensely improved and our analyses have become sharper and more penetrating. We appear, nevertheless, not yet to have found a method for the mastery and organization of this material . . . unless we succeed in finding a clue of Ariadne to lead us out of this labyrinth we can have no real insight into the general character of human culture; we shall remain lost in a mass of disconnected and disintegrated data which seem to lack all conceptual unity.'

Are we any closer to finding the clue of Ariadne than we were when these words were written in 1944? I believe we are, as I hope to demonstrate in Part 1. Our word 'clue' is derived from the Anglo-Saxon *clew*, meaning a 'ball of thread'. The most famous ball of thread in Western culture belonged to Ariadne, the beautiful daughter of King Minos of Crete, who fell in love with Theseus when he arrived from Athens as part of the tribute of youths and maidens sent to the great Labyrinth of Knossos to be sacrificed to the Minotaur. Theseus promised to marry Ariadne if she would help him to kill the Minotaur and escape. Accordingly, she gave him her clue of thread to be paid out as he entered the Labyrinth so that, once he had dispatched the Minotaur, he could find his way out again. The deed done, Theseus carried her off to Naxos, where he abandoned her, and she eventually married Dionysus.

Theseus's daring expedition into the Labyrinth resembles the journey of other heroes such as Orpheus and Aeneas into the Underworld, the realm of dead ancestors and the unconscious. Indeed, Virgil tells us that Aeneas found a representation of a labyrinth on the gates of the Temple of Cumae which stood at the entrance to the Underworld. In medieval churches the same labyrinthine image was to become a Christian symbol of Hell.

The thread has been rich in symbolic significance ever since women discovered the arts of spinning and weaving – activities as distinctively feminine as ploughing is masculine. For both women and men weaving and ploughing provide the means of participating in the work of creation, and, as a consequence, they have acquired worldwide religious and ritual significance. In the Upanishads, for example, the thread (*sūtra*) is described as linking 'this world to the other world and all beings'. The thread is both *ātman* (self) and *prāna* (breath) and is linked to the central point in the cosmos, the sun. It is written that the thread must 'in all things be followed back to its source' (Chevalier and Gheerbrant). Similarly, the word *tantra* is also derived from the notion of thread and weaving and indicates the interdependence of all things. The warp and the woof, and the forward and backward movement of the shuttle across the loom, represent the notion of time and space interacting in the perpetual cosmic dance of creation, diastole and systole, inhalation and exhalation, evolution and involution, light and darkness, life and death. Penelope unravels every night the shroud she has woven the previous day.

The symbolism both of the thread and of the labyrinth gives expression to the notion of fate guiding the passage through life, but nowhere more completely than in Greek myth and legend. The distaff is an attribute of Clotho, the youngest of the Three Fates: Clotho prepares the thread of life, which Lachesis spins, and Atropos cuts off. The thread and the labyrinth come together in the symbolism of the spider's web – a mandala reconciling the opposites of creation and destruction, with its creator sitting at the centre.

The thread, therefore, may be understood as an archetypal symbol of the life principle stretching through time as a means of conscious orientation and a guide to understanding.

LYNDA'S DREAM

A rich source of clues as to the nature and function of symbols is provided every night in our dreams, and an example will help to demonstrate what I mean.

Lynda Clayton was an attractive young woman in her late twenties. In the three years since her husband left her alone with their 18-month-old daughter, Jennifer, Lynda had been struggling, with a sense of mounting desperation, to deal with a series of problems which seemed to her insoluble. When she found herself thinking up ways in which she might kill Jennifer and herself, she realized the time had come to seek professional help.

After her first analytic session she had the following dream:

She was trudging across a barren, snake-infested plain. The going was rough and, in places, swampy. Two mountains dominated the landscape. The taller of these was particularly stark and threatening, its peak shrouded in black clouds from which came an occasional peal of thunder. Then she was no longer on the plain but on a lightly wooded mountainside, sitting at the edge of a stream. She was hot, tired, and very thirsty. Gradually she lowered herself into the torrent. The water gushed over her body, and it seemed to gush through *her too, in a way that she found wonderfully refreshing. For the first time since early in her marriage, she experienced optimism and hope.*

Initial dreams are often important. They may not only symbolize the patient's situation but may also be prognostic as to its outcome. What are the main symbols here? The *plain, snakes, mountains, clouds, thunder,* a *wood,* and *water* (the *swamp* and the *stream*). For the moment, let us confine our attention to one of them: the *water.*

From the purely practical standpoint we can agree that water is a fluid, with a molecular structure of two hydrogen atoms bonded with a single atom of oxygen which, under the influence of gravity, will tend to seek its own level – hence the existence of mountain streams. If you place yourself in the way of such a flow of water, it is reasonable to assume that it will gush over you and, if you are hot, tired, and weary, that you will experience the sensation as agreeable. So much is clear. But such a common-sense account of the dream would leave out one significant but unrealistic feature: the water not only gushed *over* the dreamer but *through* her as well. What is more, the experience was accompanied by powerful emotions which, under the burden of all her anxieties, she had not known for a long time, and she awoke to find her situation transformed: she had a sense of new confidence and hope. Evidently, the dream water embodied meanings and feelings beyond those implicit in the actual water of a mountain stream. This is because it is *psychological* water, or, as we more usually express it, *symbolic* water.

So a distinction has to be made between a thing and its symbolic value. A thing is a thing. Its symbolic value is derived from the

meanings and emotions it evokes in us. In other words, a thing becomes a symbol when something has been added to it. This does not alter its nature or its practical significance: it loads it with an increased weight of meaning. If, for example, a spade is called a phallus (as it is in some Australian aborigine languages), or when sowing seed in the earth is likened to sexual intercourse (as it has been all over the world), it does not follow that the practical agricultural implications of digging, ploughing, and sowing are being discounted but that a dimension of symbolic significance has been added to them.

To understand the implications of Lynda's dream, therefore, we have to discover the meanings with which the snakes, mountains, swamps, and the stream have been endowed. Where do these meanings come from? From the dreamer's personal experience of her life, certainly. From the meanings attributed to such things by the culture in which she grew up, no doubt. But could snakes, mountains, swamps, and streams carry *implicit meanings for all members of our species*, codified in our brains and psyches as a consequence of having evolved in the environmental circumstances typical of this planet? As we shall see, there is a growing body of evidence to suggest that this third fascinating possibility may well be so.

During the first session which preceded the dream, Lynda had described her bitter feelings of rejection when her husband left home to go and live with another woman. These feelings were, she at once acknowledged, a recapitulation of the misery she had suffered when she was twelve, at the time that her parents split up and eventually divorced. She adored her father, despite his dark moods and flashes of furious temper, and never got over the sense of betrayal and personal inadequacy his departure produced in her. He mother had been little comfort because she was too preoccupied with her own grief to give much attention to her daughter. Could it be that the mountains represented her parents; the taller of the two her father; the dark clouds and thunder rolling round its peak symbolizing his moods and temper? Quite possibly. And what about the mountain stream? As a child, she had gone on holiday with her parents to Scotland and to Switzerland. Her father, a strong, handsome man, was a keen angler. One memory she treasured was of him lounging on the bank of a wide stream, shirtless in the sunlight. He reminded her of the statue of a river god she had seen reclining by a fountain on a visit to some stately home. Then, two months later, he was gone, leaving her with nothing but her memories and an anguished sense of loss.

Could the relief of finding a male therapist, who impressed her as kind and understanding, have restored to her a glimpse of the happiness she had known before her father (and her husband) abandoned her? And what of the snakes on the plain? Could these sinister 'phallic' creatures represent some lethal form of masculine threat to her security? Quite possibly again. But here we run into a major difficulty of symbolic interpretation: it is an intuitive process which is heavily influenced by the theoretical biases of the interpreter. A Freudian, for example, might concentrate on the orgasmic implications of the water gushing *through* the woman and see this as an indication of a powerful erotic transference on to the person of the analyst. A Jungian would not be unreceptive to such implications, but would consider that to stress these over and above all the other meanings in the dream would be to run the risk of fixing the woman in an erotic transference instead of helping her to transcend her problems and to promote her individuation (her development towards wholeness).

THEORETICAL CLUES

At the end of the nineteenth century when he published *The Interpretation of Dreams*, Freud was convinced that he had got the *clew* firmly in his grasp. Symbol production, he asserted, was essentially a *private* process which was directly reducible to already experienced events or wishes of a predominantly sexual nature. He also believed symbols to be *pathological*, because he persuaded himself that only *repressed* material was symbolized. That Freud should adopt so pessimistic a view of so rich a human faculty was perhaps due to his daily involvement with neurotic and 'hysterical' patients on whose behaviour his theoretical formulations were based. Since symbols were private, Freud believed that the meaning attributed to them could be derived only from the 'free associations' and the personal history of the subject producing them. That they were reducible to already known events and objects was, Freud insisted, because they were 'substituted formations' whose function was to disguise the true meaning of the ideas they represented – a subterfuge made necessary if a symbolic image was not to offend the moral propriety of dreamers and shock them out of their slumbers. For the function of dream symbolism was to preserve the sleep of the dreamer: 'Dreams,' said Freud, 'are the GUARDIANS of sleep.' Thus, a sword appearing in a dream was a symbol of the penis, its sheath a symbol of the vagina, and thrusting the sword into the sheath would be symbolical of sexual intercourse.

This reduction of the symbol to individually repressed psychopathology was a cultural misfortune which, because of Freud's intellectual stature, may have contributed to what many have seen as the spiritual bankruptcy of our times. We now know that Freud's view was a narrow travesty of the creative and adaptive functions of symbolism. It was an error as gross as arguing that white blood corpuscles must be agents of disease because they are found in pus or that beds must be lethally dangerous because people die in them. The Freudian fallacy persisted, however, for the great part of this century, uncorrected by other theoretical orientations. For example, the academic psychologists' doctrinal commitment to behaviourism encouraged them to view symbolic behaviour, like all other forms of behaviour, as being acquired through learning and personal experience. The philosophers' espousal of logical positivism resulted in a further devaluation of symbolism to the status of an 'inferior' form of intellectual activity. And the influential French developmental psychologist Jean Piaget made matters worse by arguing that symbolic thinking was fundamentally 'autistic' – that it was wholly subjective and 'not adapted to reality'.

A more congenial view was adopted by anthropologists, with their appreciation of the important social implications of symbolism. Unfortunately, they regarded all symbolic meanings as culturally relative – that they were to be understood as wholly derived from the social context in which they had arisen. This anthropological position, together with various Freudian admixtures, has been embraced by most compilers of dictionaries and encyclopaedias of symbols up to the present time.

Recent years, however, have witnessed a growing interest in the idea, originally mooted by C. G. Jung in the first decade of the century, that we possess an innate symbol-forming propensity which exists as a healthy, creative, and integral part of our total psychic equipment. Although possessing a flexible capacity for local variations, this symbolizing ability proceeds on an archetypal basis which gives rise to characteristic symbolic manifestations (Jung and Von Franz, 1964; Kast, 1992; Stevens, 1993).

That previous works on symbolism have taken little account of Jung's archetypal theory is because of the hostility that has prevailed against it among the majority of behavioural scientists who flatly rejected the idea that biology made any significant contribution to the structure and function of the human mind. Instead, they clung to a *tabula rasa* view of mind as a general-purpose learning mechanism which was free of all content other than what 'culture' put into it. This obsolete view is now crumbling before the onslaught of evolutionary psychologists like Leda Cosmides and John Tooby (1989), evolutionary archaeologists like Steven Mithen (1996), and evolutionary psychiatrists like John Price and myself (1996), who hold that the human mind evolved the capacity to think, use symbols, develop explanations, and create myths as the result of selection pressures encountered by our species in the course of its evolutionary history.

According to this view, the mental apparatus is made up of numerous 'modules', or archetypes, which have evolved through natural selection to meet specific adaptive problems confronted by our hunter-gatherer ancestors in the past. These modules not only provide the rules to be followed but much of the necessary information as well. This view, which has now entered the mainstream of behavioural science, is entirely compatible with Jung's later formulation of his archetypal theory, namely, that it is the archetype-as-such which is inherited as an innate predisposition rather than the archetypal images, symbols, and patterns of behaviour that the archetype-as-such gives rise to. What becomes fixed in the genetic structure is the *predisposition* to develop certain kinds of perception, ideation, or action, and not the actual percepts, ideas, and actions themselves.

Any attempt to account for the ubiquitous themes and symbols of the human imagination must, therefore, look beyond the recent Sumerian, Egyptian, Greek, or Roman past to the hunter-gatherer existence for which our psyches were formed.

It is this evolutionary insight that provides us with Ariadne's clue capable of guiding us through the vast labyrinthine complexity of the human capacity to symbolize. For instead of seeing symbols as a vast array of discrete entities, each with a meaning arbitrarily designated to it by historical tradition, the evolutionary perspective provides a profound and integrated view of the adaptive role that archetypal symbols have performed in the survival and success of our species.

The practical value of a thesaurus of this kind is that it can help to amplify, to use Jung's term, the meaning of any symbol that one may encounter. Readers may like to test this by looking up in the Symbol Index each of the symbols in Lynda's dream and reading the relevant passages in the text. This will provide greater intuitive understanding of her total psychic situation at the time of the dream.

2

What is a Symbol?

A symbol is an image or a thing which acquires its symbolic value through the meanings and emotions it evokes in us. Among the various theoretical accounts of how this process may occur, Jung's theory of archetypes conceived as adaptive structures which we have acquired in the course of our evolution as a species is, in my view, the most satisfactory explanation.

Viewed from this perspective a symbol is not something that can be consciously invented or specified by convention (like a mathematical, algebraic, or chemical symbol) but something which comes into existence spontaneously as, in Jung's phrase, 'the best possible formulation of a relatively *unknown* thing, which cannot for that reason be more clearly or characteristically represented'. Jung argued that the rational, deductive applications of verbal language are not adequate to meet this task because the unknown aspect of the thing to be expressed *points to something more than consciousness can know*. This specifically Jungian concept of symbolism accords well with the etymological roots from which the word *symbol* is derived.

The Greek noun *symbolon* referred to a token or tally which could be used as a verification of identity. An object, such as a bone, would be broken into two halves and each given separately to two people (for example, members of the same sect or secret society) who could then identify each other by producing both halves and checking that they fitted together. Each tally-holder knew his own half to be genuine. If perfect fit occurred between the two halves of the *symbolon*, a *Gestalt* was suddenly created out of the familiar (known) and the strange (unknown) parts and the *bona fides* of each individual was established as sharing the same allegiance. The conjunction of *sym* (together) and *ballein* (to throw) emphasizes the idea that the strange must be 'thrown together' with the familiar to construct a bridge of meaning between the known and unknown. In psychological terms, something unconscious is connected with consciousness, resulting in the experience of new meaning.

This bridge-building capacity of the psyche, uniting known with unknown elements in one symbolic form, is what Jung called its *transcendent function*. The transcendent function itself frequently appears as a symbol: one of the most evocative is the caduceus, the magic staff of the Greek god Hermes (the Roman god Mercury), with its two intertwined snakes. It is significant that Hermes, the psychopomp, messenger of the gods, conveyor of souls, was the mediator between the upper world and the Underworld (the conscious and unconscious realms). More significantly still, it was believed that when Hermes touched men or women with his caduceus they fell asleep and entered the world of dreams.

That a symbol signifies, in Jung's phrase, 'something more and other than itself which eludes our present knowledge' is what endows it with fascination and power. As its conscious (known) and unconscious (unknown) elements are bridged, it is as if creative energy flows between them, releasing a sudden perception of meaning or flash of insight: 'Aha!' There are many instances of this eureka! experience in the history of scientific discovery, perhaps the most famous being Kekulé's revelation of the molecular structure of benzene. Having worked on the problem for years, Kekulé had begun to despair of ever finding a solution. Then, sometime in 1865, he had a waking dream, or hypnagogic experience, in which he saw chains of carbon and hydrogen atoms turning themselves into circles, like snakes biting their tails. This was a completely spontaneous manifestation of the ancient symbol of the uroboros. He was startled into full wakefulness, Kekulé says, 'as if struck by lightning'. He understood at once that the benzene molecule must be composed of six carbon atoms bound to one another in a ring. With this realization, all the facts of organic chemistry known up to that time fell directly into place, and the foundation of modern structural theory was laid.

Having perceived the symbol (the snake biting its tail) and understood its meaning in the light of his previously accumulated knowledge of organic chemistry, Kekulé was able to communicate his insight in words (a scientific hypothesis). He recognized, in the process, that he had made a psychological as well as an organic discovery, and when he reported his findings at a scientific conference he said: 'Let us learn to dream, gentlemen, and then we may perhaps find the truth.' This is a good example of how an archetypal symbol can be activated by a conscious situation (that is, having to find a solution to a weighty problem) with which one may be grappling at the time.

SYMBOLS, NATURAL AND UNNATURAL

The critical issue for symbolism – the nature of the relationship between a symbol and what it represents (its *significatum* or 'referent') – has led many authorities to draw a distinction between what they term 'natural' and 'cultural' symbols. In his important review of this literature up to 1973, Raymond Firth draws attention to the work of Robertson Smith (1889), Mary Douglas (1970), S. F. Nadel (1951), and Paul Ricoeur (1970). Robertson Smith, a nineteenth-century ethnographer, claimed as 'natural' what he regarded as symbols of divinity, such as rocks, trees, bushes, and waterfalls, whose existence was independent and unaltered by man. Mary Douglas, on the other hand, in her book *Natural Symbols*, derived such symbols not from the physical environment but, like the psychoanalyst Melanie Klein, from the human body (for example, from flesh, blood, breath, orifices, ingestion, excretion, and so on).

To the anthropologist S. F. Nadel natural symbols were those that betrayed an obvious 'correspondence' between the symbol and that which was symbolized, as in the image of a woman draped in black to indicate mourning. This is close to the position developed by Paul Ricoeur in *The Symbolism of Evil*, where he discusses defilement and pollution. Ricoeur argues persuasively that all humanity understands about becoming dirty through exposure to the natural environment or to the products of the human body, and that to become physically cleansed is a natural human need. In the religious realm of experience, the fact of physical uncleanliness is linked to the spiritual sense of being defiled or impure, for 'cleanliness is next to Godliness'.

According to the distinction favoured by Jay Appleton (1990), cultural symbols have their origin in some human act of attribution (for example, the dove is a symbol of peace, the lily is a symbol of purity), whereas natural symbols are the result of evolutionary pressures (for example, the green head of the mallard drake which excites the amorous propensities of the mallard duck, or the claustrophobia induced by interiors drawn by Giovanni Battista Piranesi, reminiscent of prisons from which no escape is possible). Yet this distinction cannot be absolute. Although the dove of peace is established in received iconography and is, consequently, a cultural symbol, it is, nevertheless, a cultural elaboration of a natural symbol (a dove is an unpredatory, peaceable sort of bird known for billing and cooing). Similarly, the lily, in its white perfection, is, in a sense, a natural symbol of purity. My point is that cultural symbols, when one examines them, are often not the products of arbitrary attribution. They owe their origins to a recognition of their natural significance. In the Jungian view, all archetypal symbols are natural because they originate from deep structures in the human psyche (the collective unconscious of the species). Similarly, by speaking of 'the logic of symbols', Mircea Eliade (1958) implied that if we inquire into the meaning of related symbols we will discover an intuitive logic at work in their formation. It is this latter view that comes closest to the evolutionary perspective.

To accept Eliade's term 'the logic of symbols' is not to imply that symbol-creation is a rational exercise, in the sense of science, mathematics, or deductive logic, but merely that the symbol-forming psyche, like the heart, has its reasons – archetypal reasons – which are, *au fond*, biological and adaptive, though we experience the consequences as spiritual, emotional, and intuitive.

If the phylogenetic psyche provides the basic hardware, then culture produces much of the software; and symbol-formation, as in dreaming, is the product of their function. As a result of dreaming, and the integration of new symbols in the course of ontogeny (personal development), the software is itself reconverted into hardware as selected items of experience are taken from short-term circuits and made permanent in the long-term memory store. This process incorporates what Turner and Pöppel (1983) call a 'cultural loop' into the human neuropsychic circuitry. The actual neurophysiological mechanisms involved are still, however, far from being understood.

WHAT USE ARE SYMBOLS?

Through evolution we have acquired the capacity to use symbols to connote concepts, and this development has had psychological consequences of incalculable importance. For, once we have formed a concept of a thing or a process, we can play with it in the imagination: the object of our thinking no longer needs to be present; we can reflect on it in its absence. What is more, we can relate one concept to another and, through their interplay, create myths, arts, and religions and make new scientific discoveries. Like all psychobiological capacities, symbol formation has an *adaptive* function: it promotes our grasp on reality. It enables us not just to adapt passively to reality but to master it, to adjust reality to our needs.

Of no symbolic activity is this adaptive function more apparent than in dreaming, the biological significance of which may be deduced from the fact that it evolved over 130 million years ago and creatures have been dreaming on this planet ever since. Human dreams are spontaneous, involuntary events which generate symbols every night of our lives. In dreams, no less than in consciousness, we use symbols to try out ideas in the light of past experience and to formulate new concepts as they burst through the threshold of consciousness. Far from being pathological phenomena, symbols are instruments of mental health: one of their most important contributions is to correct deficient modes of psychological functioning. A good therapeutic rationale exists, therefore, for working analytically with dreams, for it is a process which can open up the personality to new symbolic meanings rich in implications for the life of the dreamer and possessing potentially enormous transformative power.

The influences which coalesce in the formation of a symbol, therefore, have complex origins: these are personal, cultural, and phylogenetic. The personal determinants of a symbol cannot be found in a book, but only from the biography of its originator. The cultural and phylogenetic determinants, on the other hand, are matters of collective interest, and valuable information about them can be gathered from the comparative study of myths, religions, folklore, and the arts, from the analysis of contemporary dreams, and from study of the evolutionary history of our species. It is on these sources that the data presented in this book are based.

A NATURAL ESPERANTO

Since long before history began, we humans have expressed our main preoccupations in myths, stories, religions, and dreams, and in the images and objects we have always loved to create. The eternally recurring themes of childhood and youth, love and sex, hunting and warfare, sickness and healing, death and rebirth, fertility and sacrifice – everything that constitutes a core experience of human life – has been put into symbols and tales which, for all their manifold variety, often share striking resemblances to one another, wherever on this planet they have been brought into being. Symbolism is a language that transcends race, geography, and time. It is the natural Esperanto of humanity.

Moreover, the critical events of each personal journey from the cradle to the grave have been symbolized as occurring within a grander transpersonal or religious context, providing a sense that the archetypal patterns of human existence are granted to us as pre-existing

17

forms, determined as it were by an imperturbable fate whose vast realm extends to regions out of our control and beyond our understanding. Attempts to formulate our awareness of these, the ultimate issues of life, have taken symbolic forms because symbolism is the most fundamental and most ancient means of communication available to us. As a result, the study of symbols has for many centuries preoccupied philosophers, antiquarians, and theologians, as well as psychologists, anthropologists, and historians: the implications of symbolism for the human arts, sciences, and religions being seemingly infinite in their ramifications.

One of the most industrious of these researchers was the nineteenth-century ethnographer Adolf Bastian (1826–1905). Travelling all over the world to study the myths, folklore, and customs of widely differing peoples, Bastian was impressed by the similarity he noted between the themes, motifs, symbols, and rituals he encountered wherever he went. He noticed, however, that these universal themes, which he called *Elementargedanken* (elementary ideas), invariably manifested themselves in local forms, peculiar to the group of people he happened to be studying at the time. These he called *Völkgedanken* (ethnic ideas) (Koepping, 1983).

Jung formulated his theory of archetypes functioning as components of a collective unconscious on much the same grounds as Bastian inferred the existence of *Elementargedanken*. Jung's decisive insights came from the study of comparative religion, mythology, and alchemy, as well as from the material produced by his patients and himself. Like Bastian, he was struck by the way in which analogous motifs cropped up in the most diverse cultures, as far removed from each other in geography as they were in historical time. In other words, he noted that mythological and religious themes were, as the evolutionary biologists say, 'environmentally stable'. The points of similarity between the myths of the Babylonians, Egyptians, Greeks, and Romans, the peoples of China, India, and Oceania, the Teutons, Norsemen, Celts, and Amerindians are so marked as to defy explanation in terms of coincidence, and scholars wedded to the *tabula rasa* view of human development have been hard pressed to account for them.

Until recently, the prevalent theory held that cultures borrowed myths and stories from each other through such contacts as those induced by migration, war, and trade. But this explanation is plausible only for nations like Babylonia and Egypt, or Greece and Rome, whose relatively close proximity made frequent contacts between them possible.

While Jung acknowledged that similarities could be brought about by the combined operation of migration, tradition, and trade, he nevertheless argued that some form of transmission through heredity must also occur since he was able to discover instances where such motifs arose spontaneously, without any previous encounter with them on the part of the subject. Jung, therefore, concluded that these motifs must correspond to 'typical dispositions', 'dominants' or 'nodal points' within the structure of the psyche itself. Since then, data have been collected from a variety of different sources supportive of the position adopted by Bastian and Jung. All cultures, it seems, display a large number of traits which are in themselves diagnostic of a specifically human culture. These have been independently catalogued by George P. Murdock (1945) and Robin Fox (1975). According to them, no human culture is known which lacked laws about the ownership, inheritance, and disposal of property; procedures of set-tling disputes; rules governing courtship, marriage, adultery, and the adornment of women; taboos relating to food and incest; ceremonies of initiation for young men; the manufacture of tools and weapons; cooperative labour, athletic sports, gambling, trade; rules of etiquette prescribing forms of greeting, modes of address, use of personal names, visiting, feasting, hospitality, gift-giving, and the performance of funeral rites; status differentiation on the basis of some kind of hierarchical structure; superstition, belief in the supernatural, religious rituals, soul concepts, myths and legends; dancing, homicide, suicide, homosexuality, mental illness, faith-healing, dream interpretation, medicine, surgery, obstetrics, and meteorology.

This list is far from exhaustive. In a recent publication Walter Burkert (1996) has emphasized worldwide similarities in religious phenomena: 'they include formalized ritual behaviour appropriate for veneration: the practice of offerings, sacrifices, vows, and prayers with reference to superior beings; and songs, tales, teachings, and explanations about these beings and the worship they demand'. A religion, Burkert argues, is a system of symbols incorporating ideas and beliefs which are emphatically accepted as true even though they cannot be verified empirically. They are confirmed, however, through meditation, trance, and ecstatic experiences which purport to establish a direct encounter with supernatural forces. These universal and prehistoric phenomena cannot be explained or derived from any single cultural system maintains Burkert: 'The search for the source of religion calls for a more general perspective, beyond individual civilizations, which must take account of the vast process of human evolution within the more general evolutionary process of life ... Cultural studies must merge with general anthropology, which is ultimately integrated into biology.' The results of cross-cultural studies indicate that analogous symbolisms, whether of religion, myth, or folk tale, are so consistently and universally apparent that it is hard to escape the conclusion that the propensity to create them is implicit in the mind-brain of humanity.

THE LOGIC OF SYMBOLS

The leading authority on the symbolism of different cultures who consistently adopted a position similar to Jung's was Mircea Eliade. Eliade maintained that a symbol does not depend for its existence on being understood, known, or even recognized, since it preserves its inherent structure long after it has been forgotten. Thus, myths and rituals involving immersion in water (baptism), purification (lustration), the deluge (the flood), the submersion of lost continents (Atlantis), the dissolution of the old order and the precipitation of the new (the stories of Noah and of Deucalion, or of Armageddon and the Apocalypse), all fit together so as to 'make up a *symbolic system which in a sense pre-existed them all*' (Eliade, 1958; italics added). As a result, symbolism, myth, and ritual proceed through an inherent order, Eliade's 'the logic of symbols'. This logic holds good not only in the enormous ethnographic compilations of magico-religious symbology but in the spontaneous productions of individuals in fantasies, delusions, visions, hallucinations, and dreams.

To penetrate the occult meanings of abstract and animal images on the walls of palaeolithic caves, the vegetation and solar symbolism of Mesopotamian agriculturalists, and the religious artefacts of early civilizations, is to expose the archetypal propensities which underlie all human thought and action. The same symbolic capacities that enable us to use verbal language and mathematical language also enable us to express our ideas and intentions in fantasies and dreams. In one of the most influential books on symbols ever published, *The Symbolism of Dreams* (1814), Gotthilf von Schubert (1780–1860) argued that when we fall asleep our minds begin to think in 'dream picture language' (*Traumbildsprache*), in contrast to the verbal language of conscious thought. This 'hieroglyphic language', which enables us to forge concepts into pictures, is universal, in that it yields similar symbols in the dreams and myths of peoples throughout the world. *Traumbildsprache* is, Schubert maintained, 'a higher kind of algebra'.

Empirical evidence strongly supportive of this insight was gathered in the 1950s and 1960s by the American psychologist Calvin S. Hall. Together with his colleague Vernon J. Nordby, Hall collected dreams from a large number of subjects from various parts of the world. On the basis of their examination of over 50,000 dreams, they concluded that a number of typical themes are symbolically represented over and over again: 'These *typical dreams*, as we shall call them, are experienced by virtually every dreamer,' they wrote (1972). The typical dreams reported involved predatory animals, flying, falling, being pursued by hostile strangers, landscapes, sex, getting married and having children, taking examinations or undergoing some similar ordeal, travelling (whether on foot, horseback, car, aeroplane, or ship), swimming or being in the water, watching fires, and being confined in an underground place. They concluded: 'These typical dreams express the shared concerns, preoccupations and interests of all dreamers. They may be said to constitute the universal constants of the human psyche.' They thus provide copious evidence in support of Jung's hypothesis of a collective unconscious, although they do not themselves make this connection. What is more, their findings are in keeping with the overall perspective of evolutionary theory. We are now in a position to carry symbology beyond a Jungian context into the post-Darwinian realm of psychobiology: we can celebrate man as *Homo symbolicum*.

3

The Evolution of Meaning

Semeiosis, communication through signs and symbols, occurred on this planet long before the emergence of *Homo sapiens*. It is one of the earliest archetypal propensities to have evolved. Essentially, archetypes are genome-bound units of information which programme the individual member of a species to perceive, respond, and behave in ways which are adapted to the circumstances prevailing in the environment at any given time. That archetypes should give rise to characteristic images or configurations in living organisms is not nearly so outlandish an idea as it seemed to most psychologists when Jung proposed it. Indeed, it is one which has long been entertained by biologists when considering, for example, the extraordinarily complex operations performed by a bird engaged in building a nest: the bird may not have a clear 'idea', in the human sense, of precisely what it is doing, but it must have some kind of 'image' of what the nest – the (arche)typical nest of the species – should be like when completed. The nest-image may not be 'conscious', as we understand the term, but clearly there is some central mechanism that 'knows' how the nest should be built and how to coordinate the energies of the bird as it builds it.

That the capacity to retain and reproduce such images is implicit in the genome of the species is apparent, for example, in the predator image encoded in the central nervous system of ground-nesting birds. If a goose or a heron, or any other bird with a long neck, flies over a clutch of newly hatched chicks, they continue scrabbling and pecking quite undisturbed. But if a hawk or a raven or a bird with a short neck flies overhead, the chicks either crouch down against the ground or scuttle for cover. This is a defensive response against predatory birds and it is innate (McFarland, 1987). Generations of chicks can be raised in artificial circumstances where they are never exposed to a predator without extinguishing the response. But the moment a real or model hawk is exposed to members of the ninth or tenth generation, then they cringe or scuttle. An archetypal image or pattern of behaviour, once it has evolved as a characteristic of a given species, breeds true as long as the species exists, and does not disappear with disuse.

An astonishing example of this was observed when thirty caged finches were sent from the Galapagos Islands to California in 1939. These were direct descendants of the same finches that had provided Charles Darwin with crucial evidence for the principle of evolution by natural selection when he visited the Galapagos Islands just over a century earlier. The reason why finches flourished in the Galapagos – they had been there long enough for fourteen different species to evolve from an original mainland species, now extinct – was because the Islands possessed no large birds of prey. For hundreds of thousands of years, these finches had no cause to cringe in alarm because *symbols of predatory danger* (large short-necked birds overhead) had not been encountered. Yet when the finches were put in new cages open to the sky on their arrival in California, to everybody's amazement they cringed and emitted cries of alarm whenever a hawk came in sight. The *archetypal image of the predator* had lain dormant in the 'collective unconscious' of these birds for something approaching a million years. Yet the moment the appropriate stimulus was encountered in the environment, the archetype was at once activated, with its related patterns of behaviour and, we may infer, with the experience of fear. Thus, image, behaviour, and emotion appear to be constellated round an archetypal core existing as an innate predisposition in the central nervous system of the species.

For the first half of this century, Jung was one of the very few psychologists of stature who considered that such innate predispositions could exist in human beings. Then, in the 1950s, the British psychiatrist John Bowlby (1958) shocked the academic establishment by proposing that such innate predispositions not only existed in humans but that they were responsible for initiating and coordinating the crucial relationships of human life. The patterns of behaviour, wrote Bowlby in 1969, 'often very intensely motivated, that result in mating, in the care of babies and young children, and the attachment of young to parents are found in almost all members of the human race and seem best considered as expressions of *some common plan* . . .' (italics added). Bowlby compared this behaviour with that studied by ethologists in other animal species, concluding that it was 'released' in mothers and children and in lovers in response to patterns of stimuli which each partner in the relationship represented to the other. 'In all cases, we must suppose,' declared Bowlby, 'the individual has *a copy of that pattern in its CNS* [central nervous system] and is structured to react in special kinds of ways when it perceives a matching pattern in the environment' (italics added).

This process of 'matching' is analogous to the encounter of two members of a Greek sect presenting each other with their own halves of a *symbolon*, and, clearly, the innate ability to perceive, recognize, and process patterns or configurations must be involved in all forms of symbolizing at whatever level in the phylogenetic scale. But where does the all important factor of *meaning* come into the evolutionary picture? Perception of specific external stimuli may serve to 'release' certain characteristic behaviours – as when a male robin perceives another robin with a red breast encroaching on his territory and attacks him – but some added cognitive process must be involved to appreciate the significance of the stimuli (that is, to recognize their meaning) and to assess those behaviours 'prepared for' in the archetypal programme so that the most appropriate option can be selected and put into effect.

Previously, it was thought that only human beings possessed the intellectual equipment to perceive meaning, but this is no longer the case. All animals have to be able to recognize and classify incoming sensory information so as to build up an adequate model of the world. The capacity to make generalizations about complex sensory information from a variety of different sources is, in the view of the American neuroscientist Gerald Edelman (1989), the basis of psychic development. It can achieve a remarkable degree of effectiveness in all mammals and even in relatively primitive animals like birds, which, Edelman believes, possess 'primary consciousness' – 'the state of being mentally aware of the world' without having any developed concept of personal identity as an individual with a history and a future. Edelman argues that animals are exploring organisms always seeking to impose meaning on events. The symbolic systems on which consciousness is based are constructed out of meanings.

Edelman's ideas are part of a wider scientific movement to put the mind back into nature. In the past, researchers in neuroscience and in artificial intelligence have maintained the fallacy that forms of intelligence could be devised on the basis of pure logic without having to postulate anything so messy as 'meaning'. The realization has now dawned that this cannot be the case and scientists are increasingly accepting meaning as a fundamental concept in biology. Meaning, it seems, is something that nature cannot do without. And the capacity to create and respond appropriately to signs and symbols is indispensable to the apperception of meaningfulness. That an image becomes a symbol precisely when it is endowed with meaning is apparent in the German word for symbol, *Sinnbild* (*Sinn* = sense, meaning; *Bild* = image).

SYMBOL, SIGN, AND RITUAL

When a domestic cock wishes to attract a hen, he adopts the same strategy as a hen wishing to gather her chicks round her. Pecking the ground, while at the same time emitting calling sounds, he picks up a morsel of food and lets it drop again. Sometimes he only pretends to find food; he may, in fact, pick up and drop a small stone, but this symbolic enticement with symbolic food can just as readily lead to success. As the ethologist Irenäus Eibl-Eibesfeldt (1971) has commented, once the feeding of young has evolved within an animal group, then it is likely that this cherishing behaviour will be generally adopted as a friendly gesture, a sign of appeasement, or a means of attracting a mate. Thus among many species of birds, courting females will beg food from a male as a necessary part of the courtship ritual, mimicking the begging behaviour of a chick in the nest. Such examples illustrate the importance of *ritualization* in the evolution of communication of signs and symbols.

Ritualization is the term given to the evolutionary process by which innately determined behaviour patterns become modified so as to promote communication between individuals. Ritualization of certain forms of behaviour is often associated with the evolution of special markings so as to make the behaviour pattern more conspicuous and to enhance its reliability as a means of communication. Patterns such as intention movements, feeding, and conflict behaviours become ritualized in this way because they symbolize a particular motivational state. If it is of advantage to an animal that its motivational state should be perceived and appreciated by another, then there is a chance that a gesture indicative of that state will be transformed into a *sign* or *signal* by natural selection.

Thus, numerous instances have been recorded of flight or avoidance movements being ritualized into gestures of appeasement. A sand lizard defeated in a 'ritual agonistic conflict' over territory with another will acknowledge defeat to the victor by lying flat on the ground and making paddling movements with its legs. This 'fleeing on the spot' signals defeat through an indication of readiness to withdraw expeditiously from the field of battle.

The point is that communication between animals is originally *iconic* in the sense that an animal will imitate the action that is intended or the object that is desired. Just as the nestling begs food from its parents by opening its beak and thrusting its head upwards, so a male rhesus monkey will threaten another by staring aggressively at him and slapping his hands on the ground. As more sophisticated signals emerged through ritualization, so the ritualized gestures often lost their original function and became more conspicuous and more stereotyped. Thus, an African chameleon will defend its territory not by a direct physical attack on its adversary but by performing an alarming display of exaggerated respiratory movements and ritualized thrusts of the head. Some species of rhesus monkey display semiotic capacities far more advanced than was previously supposed; when approached by a predator, they have distinctly recognizable signals to warn one another whether it is a leopard, a snake, or an eagle (Cheney and Seyfarth, 1990).

That a vervet monkey in Kenya can emit specific alarm calls for different predators, and release an appropriate flight response in other members of its troop, demonstrates that these primates can make use of a common code or 'language' to refer to biologically significant features of the external world. What they cannot do, of course, is communicate to one another the content of their private fantasies or dreams. It is, nevertheless, from such beginnings as these that our own linguistic and symbolic capacities probably evolved. Psycho-linguists have convincingly argued that language originated by the ritualization of movements of the mouth and tongue to make primitive sounds of increasing complexity and significance. These sounds were originally iconic, but, with time, words emerged which lost their mimetic component and became progressively ritualized into more sophisticated forms of speech.

Much human communication has evidently been ritualized in the same manner as in other species. Kissing between human adults, for example, is thought to be ritualized feeding behaviour (chimpanzee mothers and human mothers in many societies wean their young by feeding them chewed up morsels by mouth). The laying of hands by one person on the head of another as a act of consecration or a gesture of comfort is probably ritualized grooming behaviour (removing para-sites from hair). When a girl blushes she is signalling her embarrass-ment in a manner we can instantly recognize, and when a man strikes a table with his clenched fist we know that he is angry. These are all behaviours linked with biologically motivated states which have become ritualized into symbolic vehicles of communication.

Our capacities to create words and symbols and our ability to communicate by means of them developed through the rapid evolution of the human brain as a result of increased selection pressures coming from a largely hostile environment – ice ages, the presence of deter-mined and skilful predators, scarce food resources, droughts, floods, etc. Such pressures not only promoted our capacities to adapt to them but heightened our ability to compensate for them through the discovery of how to make and control fire, turn stone and wood into weapons, communicate and cooperate on the hunt, understand the progression of the seasons and make appropriate plans to accommo-date to them – all of which contributed to the cultural canon of every human society.

The mental traits and capacities that were naturally selected in the course of our evolution were, like our physical traits, randomly generated. Every component of the human brain, like each gene responsible for its construction, is there for one reason: it enabled our ancestors to survive long enough in the ancestral environment to pass their genes on to the next generation. All our archetypal patterns of thought, feeling, symbolism, and behaviour are present and expressed in us because of the contribution they made to the fitness of past generations.

WORDS AND SYMBOLS:
TWO WAYS OF THINKING

Before the advent of modern psycholinguistics, it used to be thought that every language had a vocabulary and syntax unique to itself; but it is now realized that all languages are but sets of variations on basic linguistic themes: a universal syntax exists dependent upon deep structures embedded in the human brain. If this is true of verbal language, it is even more evident in the hieroglyphic language of symbols. Viewed from the biological standpoint, it is true to say that the evolution of our capacity to decipher visual meanings occurred much earlier than our capacity to use language; as a result, symbols, being imagistic rather than verbal, are more directly linked to their deep structures (archetypes) than are words. This would account for the great immediacy of symbols, their universality, and their ability to communicate at a more primitive, more emotive level. What the dictionaries and encyclopaedias of symbols have hitherto failed to recognize is that symbolism has its roots in neurology and the evolutionary history of our species as much as in the ancient religious and artistic traditions of human culture.

Symbols and words have one thing in common: that they are all sensory expressions of thought. Thoughts which are invisible and inaudible in themselves are made visible and audible in images and sounds. Every discipline conceptualizes this transformation in its own terms: just as Noam Chomsky (1965) maintains that the deep structures of language find expression in surface structures, namely words, so Freud held that the *latent content* ('the latent dream thoughts') became the *manifest content* of dreams, Jung that the archetype-as-such became the archetypal image, and Niko Tinbergen (1951) that innate releasing mechanisms built into the central nervous system of animals manifested themselves into patterns of behaviour typical of the species. Just how something so essentially occult and private as thoughts can become manifest and public in symbols, words, and deeds is a profound mystery which psychology and neuroscience still have to unravel.

Individual workers have made the discovery – or rediscovery – that words and symbols derive from different forms of thinking. In *Symbols of Transformation* (CW5), for example, Jung distinguished between directed thinking and fantasy thinking, which is a rephrasing of Freud's distinction between primary process thinking (which manifests itself in symbols, symptoms, and the transference) and secondary process thinking (which is orientated to reality and functions rationally and logically). In *Mind: An Essay on Human Feeling* (1967), Suzanne Langer distinguished discursive, representational symbolism (that of language and mathematics, where meaning resides in designated words and signs) from non-discursive, presentational symbolism (which is apparent in dreams and the expressive arts, where meaning resides in the felt qualities of the medium). Parallel to all such distinctions is that made by linguistics between metonymic and metaphoric modes of speech. In metonymic speech words are linked together to form phrases and sentences to transmit literal statements, whereas metaphoric speech conveys meaning through the use of analogy, similarity, or resemblance. All these distinctions may ultimately be attributable to the different functions of the two cerebral hemispheres of the human brain: the left hemisphere being predominantly concerned with the metonymic, discursive symbolism of mathematics and speech; the right hemisphere more with the metaphoric, non-discursive symbolism of dreams and the arts.

The value of such distinctions as these is that they help us to explain the phenomenological differences between symbols and words. Both enable us to formulate and communicate our thoughts and feelings, but symbols can combine many disparate elements into a unitary expression, while numerous words are needed to deal with one thought at a time. Symbols tolerate paradox and can combine contradictory ideas; words are about one thing or another. Symbols awake intimations; words explain. Like musical compositions, symbolic forms are psychologically more athletic than words: they leap across national barriers. Hence the long historical existence of Christendom which, for all the different linguistic and cultural differences it embraced, and despite all the secular and religious conflicts it generated across the war-ravaged plains of Europe, endured for nearly two thousand years. It is often forgotten that the perception of meaning is not solely an intellectual or cognitive activity, it is visceral as well. Every symbol has an aesthetic quality: its meaning is *felt* as well as understood. As a result we experience symbols as *powers* as well as communications.

Mathematical symbols also transcend linguistic barriers and codify thoughts and sequences of reasoned argument in a way which seems both more precise and more universal than words. Hence Galileo's conviction that the language best suited to a description of the laws of nature was mathematics and Descartes' belief that mathematics would make possible the Science of Everything. But the symbolism of dreams and the arts touches an altogether more intuitive, more allusive realm of communicable experience.

The point to remember, however, is not that directed thinking in words and metaphoric thinking in symbols are separate or independent modes of cognition, but that both modalities are perennially available to us: when they interact, logical and 'magical' modes complement one another, their natural medium being the myth or the dream. But language as we use it in everyday communication is itself rich in imagery, metaphor, and symbol.

EVOLUTION OF THE ARCHETYPAL SERPENT

As an example of an archetypal symbol whose natural origins can be traced to evolutionary pressures it is hard to better that of the serpent. I have already subjected this symbol to an evolutionary analysis in *Private Myths: Dreams and Dreaming* (1996), but it provides so persuasive an example that I should like to repeat it here.

That the serpent is indeed an archetypal image can be deduced from its ubiquity and its power to release the emotions of awe, fascination, and dread. Why should this exist as an inherited propensity within the human psyche? Presumably because many dangerous snakes inhabited, and still inhabit, those regions of Africa in which our species evolved. Having become established in the human genome at that time, some sense of the danger implicit in serpentine imagery has apparently persisted as archetypal potential in the unconscious of us all, which explains why we are still fearful of snakes (which are of no danger to us), while experiencing no corresponding fear of modern artefacts such as motor cars or cigarettes (which most certainly are). How could this archetypal propensity have been acquired and passed down to us? Not by being 'engraved' on the psyche by repetition through the millennia of human existence, as Jung proposed (*CW*9i, para. 99), but through the time-hallowed rituals of natural selection. What is inherited is not an archetypal image of the snake *per se*, but an archetypal *predisposition* to perceive danger in a configuration of snakelike characteristics – something long, sinuous, and slithery, with fangs, and forked and flicking tongue.

Every species evolves in its typical environment and, in the course of its life-cycle, encounters typical situations. As a result of genetic mutations, which occur spontaneously and at random, an individual member of a species will acquire a characteristic which makes it better adapted than its fellows to respond appropriately to a certain typical situation – such as, for example, greater awareness to the danger of serpentine forms. This individual will tend to survive and pass its new genetic material to members of subsequent generations who, possessing the desirable characteristic, will compete more effectively in the struggle for existence and enjoy greater reproductive success. As a result, the new attribute eventually becomes established as a standard component in the genetic structure of the species.

In this manner our archetypal propensities have become adapted to the typical situations encountered in the ancestral environment. The repeated selection of fortuitous mutations, occurring through thousands of generations and over hundreds of thousands of years, has resulted in the present genotype or archetypal structure of the human species. And this expresses itself as surely in the structure of the psyche as it does in the anatomy of the human physique.

Accordingly, we are predisposed and prepared to encounter archetypal figures (for example, mother, child, father, mate), archetypal events (for example, birth, death, separation from parents, courting), and archetypal objects (for example, water, sun, fish, predatory animals, snakes). Each is part of the total endowment granted us by evolution in order to equip us for life in the ancestral environment. Each finds expression in the psyche in dreams, in behaviour, and in myths.

That we all inherit a propensity to respond emotionally to snakelike configurations and to create snakelike images in our dreams suggests that some capacity for generic recognition is built into our brains. Thus the inherent propensity to recognize the category 'snake', which is apparently shared by all primates, is paralleled by other propensities such as the human infant's capacity to recognize the generic category 'face' long before it can recognize the particular configuration of a face belonging to a special person to whom it is attached. Indeed, there is now evidence for 'face-detecting' cells in the cerebral cortex. These must in some way be involved in creating the extraordinarily detailed and character-filled faces one can observe in hypnogogic images as one falls asleep. It is not unlikely that there are 'snake-detecting' cells as well.

How is it, then, that a simple alarm system designed to protect our ancestors from dangerous reptiles has become generalized into a symbolic canon so rich as that surrounding the serpent? That one symbol can express so many different meanings must be because the sinuous, slithery schema is susceptible to contamination by other archetypal schemata – for example, those concerned with sex, evil, healing, etc. The Self constructs its images by mixing the schemata at its disposal as the artist mixes paints of different colour. For example, on 9 March 1868, John Ruskin, who was prone to recurrent sexual nightmares, dreamt *he was showing a snake to his young cousin Joan and making her feel its scales*: '*Then she made me feel it, and it became a fat thing, like a leech, and adhered to my hands, so that I could hardly pull it off*' (Rosenberg, 1963). In this dream the snake is clearly a phallic symbol expressing guilt, disgust, and horror as well as sexuality. In Kekulé's dream cavorting snakes offered a playful uroboric solution to a scientific conundrum, while in the Garden of Eden the snake symbolized sexual temptation, evil, and rebellion against the will of God. In all these instances, length and sinuosity were basic characteristics to which other meanings were added.

Essentially, the serpent symbolizes the chthonic, most primitive form of energy and power both inside and outside ourselves. The characteristic morphology of the snake, corresponding as it does to the human brain stem and spinal cord, represents the reptilian stage of our evolution. The uroboric snake slumbering in the unconscious, coiled up in the lowest chakra of kundalini ascent, is the reptilian life still lurking in the nuclei of the nervous system. By the practice of spiritual disciplines, so the yogis believe, the serpent can be induced to uncoil itself and move upwards via the six chakras (wheels of life) until it reaches the seventh, unnamed chakra situated in the forehead (Shiva's third eye). This is yet another metaphor of the individuation process: the elevation of psychic energies and potentials from their lowest origins to their highest modes of expression. Interestingly, the stages are commonly held to be seven in number – the seven terraces of the ziggurat, the seven rungs of the ladder in Mesopotamian tombs, the seven metals of the Mithraic ritual, the seven steps to the alchemical bath, etc. The symbolism of seven links up with the seven planets and the seven deadly sins (together with the seven virtues which compensate for them). Not infrequently, the monsters of myth and legend have seven heads, and to vanquish them is to conquer the evil aspects of planetary influence. Seven seems to owe its particular importance to the fact that it is a ternary plus a quaternary, but the phyletic significance of this has yet to be determined.

Closely associated with the snake is another symbol of individuation, the Cosmic Tree. That the tree should represent individuation and the heightening of consciousness cannot be unconnected with our ancestors' practice of climbing trees in order to use them as look-out points. But here the symbolism is again complex. In one sense the tree is phallic, erect, and masculine, while the serpent entwined about it is sinuous, dependent, and feminine. In this instance the serpent is Lilith, the temptress of Adam and Eve, Eve herself being related to an archaic Phoenician goddess of the Underworld. Like all symbols, these are ordered in the imagination by the archetypal propensity to dichotomize phenomena into opposites: the tree is the Good Tree of Life encircled by the serpent principle of Evil. The serpent is itself similarly dichotomized: the Asklepian staff is encircled by the principle of sickness and healing, while the two intertwining snakes of the caduceus of Hermes/Mercury symbolize good and evil, health and sickness. The snake is sacred to many different healing traditions: it can kill *and* cure. The same principle is evident in the practice of homeopathy: administration of the agent that caused the disease is believed to produce the cure.

As with all archetypal symbols, different cultures relate to the serpent in their own characteristic ways. While it represented evil, temptation, and sexual passion to the Hebrews, to the Hindus it is Shakti, cosmic power, Nature. However, the capacity of the serpent to inspire awe, dread, and wariness is common to all human communities, and its ability to shed its old skin and replace it with a new one has led to its universal association with the ideas of resurrection, immortality, and the continuance of life.

The serpent is thus a symbol of great interest, for it links phylogeny with symbology in a way that not only gives support to Jung's archetypal hypothesis but makes its mode of functioning both comprehensible and hermeneutically useful in the study of dreams. From the neurological standpoint, symbolism, such as that associated with the serpent, keeps open the lines of communication between the neocortex and the limbic system, enabling the dialogue between recent (more conscious) and ancient (more unconscious) functions to occur. Not possessing the gift of speech, the old brain has no recourse but to phrase its communication in symbols, which provide a kind of

Esperanto that both brains can understand. The symbol is the medium which is the message. The forebrain, which has speech as well as a gift for telling stories, collaborates by transforming these symbolic messages into narrative form. The result is what we call a dream. Or a myth.

4

How Do Symbols Work?

Truly one of the most miraculous achievements of the human psyche is its genius for fabricating images imbued with emotional and cognitive significance. How is it that an otherwise incomprehensible archetypal imperative can be fulfilled through an imaginary representation such as a lion, a hero, a steeple, or a bridge? It remains a profoundly intriguing mystery. Despite the extensive research of the last two hundred years, all we have to show are the records of this baffling phenomenon as manifested by different peoples from round the world. Again and again it is reported that members of human cultures communicate with one another, with the spirits of their ancestors, and with their gods through the process of symbolization – that is to say, through the innovative association of an image or an object with a complex of emotions and ideas.

Symbol formation is evidently related to *reification* – a parallel propensity by which an idea or an abstraction is transformed into something tangible, such as a deity (for example, Eros, God of Love; Mars, God of War; and Gaia, Mother Earth). So it is that the archetypal relationship between masculine and feminine principles may be symbolized by the frank image of a man and woman in the sexual act, by a sword fitting into its scabbard, a train going into a tunnel, the illumination of the moon by the sun, the marriage of a prince and princess, or by the highly sophisticated symbolism of ancient China enshrined in the dynamic interaction of Yin and Yang. The archetypal conflict between good and evil, or between light and darkness, is dramatized in the ubiquitous motif of the hero's tournament with the dragon or sea-monster. The course of the human life-cycle is represented by the rising, zenith, and setting of the sun, while the trials and tribulations of existence are ritualized in the negotiation of a maze or labyrinth. These images abound not only in the myths, legends, and fairy tales recorded by ethnographers but also in the dreams of modern men, women, and children.

Symbols can thus be understood as metaphors for archetypal needs and intentions or expressions of basic archetypal patterns. Every individual, every family, every community, and every nation will produce symbols appropriate to its circumstances but, for all their apparent variety, they are based on similar structural configurations which are ultimately inherent in the human mind-brain.

SYMBOL CREATION

Although we know little of the neurophysiology of symbol creation, the psychic processes involved are better understood. Essentially, these involve three principles: resemblance, condensation, and the microcosmic principle.

The first of these was initially worked out in connection with rhetorical figures of speech (for example, the use of simile, metaphor, hyperbole, etc.), Both simile and metaphor work on the principle of **resemblance**, while hyperbole depends on resemblance and exaggeration. It is on the basis of resemblance that a snake can be symbolically equated with the phallus, fertilizing rain with semen, and ploughing the soil with sexual intercourse. Metaphoric statements such as 'Jack is a black sheep' or 'Jill is a snake in the grass' may be employed quite literally in dream symbolism where Jack or Jill may appear in these guises. Dream symbolism also commonly makes use of simile: for example, 'Man is like the flower of the field' – that is, here today and gone tomorrow. While hyperbolic statements such as 'Tom is a towering giant among men' readily lend themselves to symbolic representation.

Symbolism makes effective use of these principles through analogy. Just as the rising sun banishes darkness from the world, so the mythic hero emerges from the stomach of the whale, the ego struggles free from the grip of the unconscious, the boy liberates himself from his emotional dependency on his mother. Just as the sun climbs up the heavens to achieve its zenith, so the hero triumphs in his battle with the monster and wins the treasure hard to attain (the princess and the kingdom), good triumphs over evil, young people marry and find their role in life. The Egyptians believed fire to be a living creature, so Herodotus tells us, which devoured whatever it got hold of and, when it had eaten enough, died with the food it fed on (*The Histories*, 3, 16, p. 210).

These analogies are experienced as meaningful not because they are logical but because they represent parallel ideas: they satisfy what J. E. Cirlot (1971) calls 'the principle of sufficient identity'. The different images coincide and 'reveal their allegiance in one essence'. Though different existentially they unite symbolically: what is objectively a *distinctio*, in the parlance of the alchemists, becomes subjectively a *coniunctio*, and the union releases a rush of psychic energy and insight: 'Aha!' It was on account of this experience that Jung conceived of symbols as coming from the wellsprings of psychic life, in that they stream out of the unconscious as from a fountain.

It was Freud (1900) who drew attention to the manner in which dream symbols are 'overdetermined', in that their formation makes use of the process he termed **condensation**, whereby many meanings are drawn together into one configuration. When interpreting a symbol one puts the process of condensation into reverse, unpacking the meanings which have been wrapped up in it. Thus, in China, the pearl was held to be the embodiment of Yin, incorporating the symbolisms of moon, water, birth, and femininity. As a consequence, to the Chinese imagination the pearl came to carry magical, gynaecological, and medical implications since it was recognized that natural rhythms such as tides, rains, floods, and menses appeared to be under the influence of the moon.

The third and, perhaps, most crucial principle for symbol creation – particularly the creation of sacred symbols – is the **microcosmic** principle, whereby the macrocosm is felt to be in the microcosm. To the unconscious psyche, it seems that symbol and nature are inseparable. A tree can become the Cosmic Tree because all cosmic forces are embodied in that tree: life, rebirth, and the cosmos are not merely *represented by* the tree; they *exist in* the tree. Therefore, it is felt to be entirely appropriate to worship them *in* the tree.

A symbol is a transitory embodiment of all that is analogous and associated with it. Its magical quality lies in its capacity to speak to many levels of experience at once. This miraculous power demands reverence if it is not to be extinguished. Psychic impoverishment is inflicted by over-restrictive definitions. Thus, in attributing objective meaning to symbols, and in compiling symbolic treasuries, one must exercise extreme caution lest one overgeneralize, officiously categorize, and kill. Even the most widely dispersed, most indestructible symbols will have different shades of meaning for each psyche in which they appear, for symbols, like the dreams of which they are part, are *polyvalent*: they have more than one meaning. Thus a serpent would imply different things to a San Bushman, a phobic patient, an analyst, and a zoologist. A tree will carry different symbolic overtones for a rain forest pygmy and for a bedouin tribesman. Cultural associations as well as personal associations are always of importance. Skill in the art of interpretation lies not only in a knowledge of symbolic origins but in laying due stress on the symbol's subjective impact: a tree may well be the World Axis, the Cosmic Tree, but it is also a subjective manifestation of a psychological process in the person producing it – an image of the Self, perhaps – and only contributes to personal growth and healing if it is experienced as such.

SACRED TECHNOLOGY

Sophisticated symbolic complexes like those surrounding the pearl, the serpent, or the tree are by no means confined to advanced civilizations like the Chinese or Indo-European. Ethnographic studies of pre-civilized societies, such as the Dogon people of Mali, the Yoruba of Nigeria, and the Aboriginal peoples of Australia, have demonstrated a ubiquitous human capacity for producing elaborate theories and coherent symbols based on cosmological, theological and protoscientific principles. These symbolic systems invariably (1) celebrated the interdependence of like phenomena and (2) developed the 'sacred technology' necessary (3) to facilitate human participation in natural phenomena and (4) to mobilize helpful assistance from the gods:

(1) **Interdependence of like phenomena**: here the principle of

resemblance is felt to be self-evident: not only does the fertility of women affect the fertility of the fields, but a rich harvest enhances the likelihood of women conceiving. The dead have to be buried like seeds; then the regeneration of life in the spring will guarantee the after-life of their departed spirits.

(2) **Sacred technology**: this involves the use of dance, shamanic trance, the induction of ecstatic mental states, and the use of ritual so as to increase the power of the symbolic processes involved. Eliade has drawn attention to the frequency with which success in a variety of endeavours, such as healing, rain-making, initiating young men and women, sowing and harvesting crops, depends on *a ritual repetition of the Creation* which took place 'at the beginning' (*in illo tempore*, to use Eliade's favourite phrase). To regenerate the vegetative force necessary for the growth of crops, a victim must be sacrificed so as to repeat the act of creation which brought grain into existence in the first place. For every important eventuality a ritual must be performed: 'We must do what the gods did in the beginning' (Eliade, 1958).

(3) **Human participation in natural phenomena**: because rhythmic regeneration is too important a matter to be allowed to function of its own accord, it must be assisted by human rituals, sacrifices, and actions. Thus, a Pueblo chief whom Jung (1963) met on a visit to New Mexico during the winter of 1924–5 told him: 'We are the people who live on the roof of the world; we are the sons of Father Sun, and with our religion we daily help our Father go across the sky. We do this not only for ourselves, but for the whole world. If we were to cease practising our religion, in ten years the sun would no longer rise. Then it would be night for ever.' The Dogon believe that every child is born with both male and female characteristics. If they are to become mature members of their own sex they must undergo circumcision if they are boys and clitoridectomy if they are girls, for if they were permitted to languish in their natural androgynous state they would never develop the desire or the capacity for procreation.

(4) **Mobilizing the power of the gods:** to the pre-civilized mind all creation is a sacred mystery. The only means of relating to it effectively is through ritual propitiation of the spirits, gods, and divine forces of nature and by eliciting their goodwill and cooperation. This is the ultimate purpose of much 'sacred technology' and, as a result, the

majority of symbolic artefacts recorded by ethnology are fundamentally religious in nature.

Western science and technology may be more immediately successful in achieving desired results than these symbolic, protoscientific
ways of proceeding, but they do so at great cost to the environment
as well as to the modern psyche. For we have lost our sense of the
sacred nature of things and have become removed from the mythic
world 'in which we were once at home by right of birth' (Jung, 1963).

THE SYMBOLIC IMPERATIVE

'Symbolization,' declared Suzanne Langer (1967), 'is a natural state
of mind, not a defensive manoeuvre designed to conceal meaning.'
Freud attempted to reduce all dream symbolism to disguised variants
of one archetypal propensity, namely sex, while ignoring the other
archetypal propensities that evolution has programmed into the phylogenetic psyche of our species. Contemporary researchers, on the whole,
agree that dream symbols do indeed present dream thoughts as Freud
maintained, but no longer accept his assertion that they are distorted
through the intervention of a censor so as to preserve sleep (Hobson,
1990). Symbols are viewed as the natural language of dreams because
the dreaming brain makes use of image and dramas rather than words
(probably for good neurological and evolutionary reasons).

A question of great psychological interest is how the personal
symbols of dreams and the collective symbols of myths, religions, and
folk tales are related to one another. The general consensus is that
the relationship is very close. As Otto Rank put it, 'The myth is the
collective dream of the people.' If people everywhere tend to dream of
similar themes and produce common symbols, then cultural traditions
help shape these symbols and give them their particular ethnic quality;
and the archetypal propensity to produce symbols of this generic type
will go on as long as human beings survive, whatever their cultural
circumstances. Joseph Campbell (1990) summed up this line of thought
in his brilliant aphorism: 'A myth is a public dream, a dream is a
private myth.' All symbols are the product of interaction between
phylogenetically prepared propensities and personal experiences. For

this reason, collective symbols transcend geography and history, while personal symbols relate to the here and now. It would be wholly artificial, however, to attempt a clear distinction between the two forms, since all symbols are the product of both collective and personal influences. What may be said with a degree of certainty is that some symbols are more personally inflected than others: the more archaic the symbol, the more phylogenetically ancient its origins, the more collective or universal it will be; the more differentiated the symbol, the more coloured it is by the ontological peculiarities of the individual producing it.

Many of the symbolic rituals devised by our ancestors arose out of the anxieties that inevitably afflicted human beings living in the environmental circumstances in which our species evolved and lived for most of its existence. Fears that the vegetative forces of regeneration might wear out and the crops fail gave rise to the fertility rituals, sacrifices of animals and the first fruits, etc., practised by human communities all over the world. Fears that the winter solstice might not mark the end of the sun's withdrawal over the horizon and the beginning of its return explain the ubiquitous existence of solstice rituals, saturnalia, orgies, and so on. Omnipresent fears of predatory animals and hostile tribal neighbours generated the supernatural strength and magical powers of myriad heroes and hero-gods, enabling them to triumph over the monsters, snake-haired medusas, ogres, ghouls, and terrible chimeras which have horrified the imagination since the beginning of anthropological time. While the fear of sickness, spells, bad magic, demons, and jealous ancestral spirits generated the need for shamans, wizards, medicine men, white witches, and wise women, with their amulets, masks, drums, ecstatic trances, and magic flights necessary to counter the evils lying in constant wait for us.

Our capacity to find symbolical means of dealing with these fears is one of the most striking characteristics of humankind. When in need, we seek symbolical expression as well as practical fulfilment of those needs. One convenient method of classifying symbols, therefore, would be to relate them to the archetypal needs from which they have arisen. For example, our need to discover meanings, to know the nature of things, to explain origins, has given rise to the universal production of cosmologies with their symbols of chaotic waters, primordial animals, sky gods, earth mothers, cosmic trees, titans, original men and women, and so on. The struggle for power, rank, status, esteem, social recognition and acceptance yields the symbolisms of ascent and descent (ladder, steps, tree, mountain, ziggurat, Heaven and Hell), of dominance and submission (initiation, bondage, the whip), status symbolism, and so on.

The need to meet death, to postpone or overcome it, yields the symbolism of suffering, death, and resurrection (Jesus, Osiris, Dionysus), and of alchemy (the quest for the elixir of life, the Philosopher's Stone). The need for law and order to ensure group cohesion, economic efficiency, and competence in defence gives rise to symbolic embodiments of divine authority (Jahweh, Jehovah, Moses, Zeus, the Patriarch), morality (the Ten Commandments) and justice (the scales, the Last Judgement).

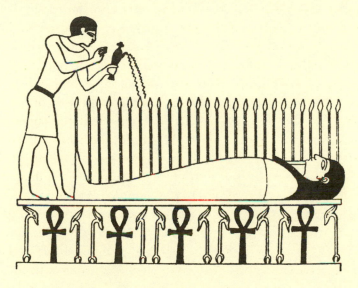

The list of archetypal needs and the symbols that these needs generate could be extended to many pages, and very boring it would be. Our present archetypal need, therefore, is to impose some order on this profusion. There are many ways in which this could be achieved, but the method I have found most satisfactory is the one already outlined, where I suggest we may best review the meanings of symbols in the Thesaurus if we assemble them into four groups, namely, symbols relating to (1) the physical environment, (2) culture and psyche, (3) people, animals, and plants, and (4) the body. In these sections, and their subsections, the cultural as well as the personal and archetypal implications of each symbol will be respected, since culture provides the traditional canon to which archetypal patterns, and to a large extent personal patterns, are assimilated. But it must be stressed once more that personal, archetypal, and cultural influences all coalesce in the production of any symbol at any time or place in history and that it is not possible to make a clear distinction between its constituent parts.

5

Basic Symbolic Themes

In *Archetype: A Natural History of the Self* (1982), I argued that Jungian psychology and ethology (the new science of behavioural biology) were studying the same archetypal phenomena from opposite ends: Jungian psychology focused on their introverted psychic manifestations while ethology examined their extraverted behavioural expression. I attempted to demonstrate how these two approaches complemented one another in such fundamental areas as bonding between parents and children, sex and gender differences, courtship and mating, cooperation and hostility between individuals and groups, and the development of the individual through the course of the human life-cycle. Since then, this dual introverted/extraverted methodology has been united in the rapidly developing science of evolutionary psychology, which studies both the psychological and behavioural manifestations of innately determined predispositions as they are activated in the course of human development.

Two areas have received particular attention, and these have to do with **affiliation** and **rank**. These are archetypal propensities which have hitherto received little attention from Jungians on account of the fundamentally introverted orientation of Jung himself, but affiliation and rank are, as we shall now see, of crucial significance for the psychology of symbols. In addition to their role in organizing the day-to-day interactions between people, the archetypes of affiliation and rank provide much of the core symbolism of myths, folk tales, religions, and dreams.

The myth of Orpheus, for example, is packed with archetypal symbols. It touches, of course, on the basic religious themes of life, death, and resurrection, but the fundamental symbolism of the myth has to do with love, separation, reunion, and loss on the one hand (affiliation/attachment), and with ascent and descent on the other (which are inextricably linked to notions of rank, status, achievement, success, and failure). In a sense, the story of Orpheus is the story of all heroes. Yet, at the same time, it is unique. This is true of any tale that has the power to take hold of the imagination: the special details of the story move us through their particular evocation of universal archetypal themes.

THE LOVING DESCENT OF ORPHEUS

The first and most striking thing about Orpheus is how much he differs from other heroes of classical or pre-classical antiquity: he is no Hercules. His fame is not won through bloody victory with the sword but through supreme virtuosity on the lyre. Though an indifferent warrior, he was a musician of such transcendent genius that wild beasts came running to hear him and trees uprooted themselves to follow him and be ravished by his songs.

The major events in Orpheus's life were his part in the expedition of the Argonauts to Iolcus in pursuit of the Golden Fleece and his marriage to the fair nymph Eurydice. Because he was not as tough as the other heroes aboard the *Argo*, they made him coxswain rather than an oarsman. Indeed, it is doubtful if they would have taken him along with them at all had he not been a king of Thrace and capable of putting his voice to such miraculous effect. At the mere sound of his singing, for instance, the *Argo*, stranded high up on a beach, descended to the sea; storm-lashed waves were calmed, the Symplegades ceased clashing together so that the *Argo* could slip between them unharmed, and the Sirens themselves were charmed into silence so that the Argonauts escaped their dreadful seductions.

Even the infernal deities could not resist the spell of Orpheus's lyre, as he was to discover when tragedy struck his wife Eurydice, whom he loved with a passion beyond all mortal bounds. Her beauty was so great that it made her particularly vulnerable to masculine predation. One day while walking beside a river in Thrace, she was espied by Aristaeus, the beekeeper, who attempted to seduce her. She ran away from him but, in her flight, trod on a snake in the grass which bit her and she died.

Frantic with despair at her loss, Orpheus resolved on an incredibly reckless deed: he would descend into the Underworld to recover her. There he is confronted by the terrible beasts and deities of the infernal depths. But with his lyre he makes such music as to entrance them and all others who languish there. Ixion's wheel stops turning, the stone of Sisyphus remains poised on the rim of the hill, the Danaids cease filling their sieve, and even Tantalus for a moment forgets his everlasting thirst. With such talent at his disposal, it is not surprising that even Hades and Persephone are beguiled. Succumbing to Orpheus's entreaties, they restore Eurydice to him. But they do so on one condition: during the couple's ascent from the realm of darkness to the upper world, Orpheus must go before Eurydice and must not turn back to look at her. They proceed uneventfully on their upward journey until, nearing the very exit from the Underworld, Orpheus is overwhelmed by an impulse to see and embrace his beloved. He turns towards her. Instantly, she becomes a shade and vanishes for ever.

Orpheus is inconsolable. So deep is his despair that, so one tradition has it, he kills himself. According to another version, the women of Thrace attempt to console him, but are so infuriated by the intransigence of his grief that they set upon him, tear him limb from limb, and fling his head and his lyre into the River Hebrus. The current carries them to Lesbos. Hence the Lesbians' ability to make fine music, which they continue to enjoy to this day. Orpheus's soul is carried to the Elysian Fields, where it sings to the eternal delight of the blessed ones (*Larousse*, 1959; Tripp, 1970).

For centuries it was thought that the journey to the Underworld (also made by Odysseus/Ulysses, Hermes/Mercury, Herakles/Hercules, Psyche and Aeneas) was peculiar to the classical tradition. But then in the nineteenth century ethnographers began to discover similar stories originating from many different parts of the world. In Polynesia and Central Asia, for example, the hero who dares to enter the dark subterranean regions actually succeeds in bringing his wife back to the world, while in the North American myths, as in the myth of Orpheus, he fails. All these instances resemble another universally repeated journey into the Underworld, that of shamans to recover the lost souls of their patients. All of them, despite individual differences in the actual circumstances and details of the tale, are variations on basic archetypal themes. In addition to those linked to the archetypes of affiliation and rank, there are also the themes of life, death, and resurrection (the religious archetype), and the trial and ordeal (the initiation archetype). We will consider each of these archetypal components in turn, for each of them will recur many times in the Thesaurus.

LOVE, LOST AND FOUND

As a species we are predisposed to form bonds of attachment to crucial figures in our lives. Bonds are formed not only between parents and children, but also between heterosexual and homosexual couples, between members of a peer group, and between members of an extended family or a small hunter-gatherer-type community. Indeed it is our capacity to form bonds of attachment and to display loyalty, affection, and altruism towards one another that makes it possible for us to love in cohesive, cooperative groups. As John Bowlby (1969, 1973) demonstrated, the success (or failure) of our attachment bonds has profound consequences for our emotional lives. Fear that an attachment bond may be under threat can result in anger and aggression, as well as anxiety, while loss of an attachment figure is associated with grief, despair, depression, and, sometimes, suicide. Renewal of an attachment bond, on the other hand, or reunion after a period of separation, can be experienced as a source of profound joy.

The symbolic association of union with the notion of wholeness and joy, and of separation with division, loss, and longing is beautifully represented in Plato's myth of the original human beings. These were round, their back and sides forming a circle, and they had four arms and four legs. Some were male, some were female, and some incorporated both male and female within themselves. 'Terrible was their might and strength,' Plato tells us, 'and the thoughts of their hearts were great, and they made an attack upon the gods.' But 'the gods could not suffer their insolence to go unrestrained' and so they cut each of them in half and separated the halves from each other.

Ever since, we have all been seeking to be reunited with our 'other half', whether this be a heterosexual or a homosexual union. Once the other half has been found, it follows that to lose her or him again is a recapitulation of the original anguish of division, and a primordial longing to be reunited is rekindled in our hearts.

The oldest and most sophisticated division between masculine and feminine principles, conceived as an everlasting struggle to achieve balance in relation to one another, is that of the ancient Chinese Taoists, with their concepts of Yin and Yang, those fundamental forces held to permeate all reality and to be present and active in both men and women. As with Plato's primordial human being, both masculine and feminine are incorporated within a circle, the *T'ai Chi*, with its interlocking elements of light and dark, Yang and Yin. Yang, energetic and assertive, embodies the light of heaven and the spirit; Yin, passive and containing, embodies the darkness of the womb, the cave, and the earth. In the Orpheus myth, and its countless variations, the Yang descends into the dark world of the Yin, and returns to its own sunlit realm again, but languishing in isolation, bereft of its other half.

DESCENT AND ASCENT

Vertical movement between all three cosmic levels of Heaven, Earth, and Underworld recurs in mythical traditions from the earliest times up to the present day. The shaman's descent to the Centre of the World to commune with the spirits of the dead and his ascent to Heaven (via the Cosmic Tree) to parley with the gods is paralleled by Christ's descent into Hell and his ascension (via the Cross) to Heaven to sit at the right hand of God. Immediately after the ascension of Christ, the disciples witness the descent of the Holy Spirit at Pentecost in the form of wind and fire and begin 'speaking in tongues'. This Christian symbolism of levels, linking Heaven, Earth, and Hell, through descent, ascension, and Pentecost, celebrates the mystic union of God and man: the Holy Spirit becomes incarnate, and the living Temple of God is created.

Parallels occur in other religious contexts. The Sanskrit word for descent is *avatar*, and in Hinduism avatar refers to a god's incarnation – that is to say, his descent from the heavens to achieve embodiment on earth in human or animal form. The Ascension, the central dogma of Christianity, is itself a manifestation of the Hellenistic tradition of *apotheosis* – the deification of an outstanding leader or 'culture hero'. Psychologically, this refers to the capacity of an archetype, such as that of the guru, hero-saviour, or wise old man, to inspire individuals personally and to move them collectively, especially when it is activated through religious ritual.

When Aeneas descends into the Underworld, accompanied by the Cumaean Sibyl, he takes with him, according to Virgil, a golden bough as a present for Persephone, and visits the shade of Dido, who has died for love of him. As Aeneas and the Sibyl ascend to the upper world, they leave via the Ivory Gate, through which false dreams are sent to mortals. The part of Virgil's great poem that describes these events has the lines: 'Roman, let your concern be to command the nations; your skills shall be these: to impose the rule of peace, to spare the submissive, and to crush the proud.'

Virgil's lines are a direct evocation of the rank archetype. This ancient and most powerful propensity is responsible for sustaining the social hierarchy in human and animal groups, for coordinating all manifestations of dominance, deference, and submission, and all related symbolisms of status. Heaven and Hell stand at opposite poles of the archetype. Heaven is as high as humans can ascend; Hell is as low as they can fall. The symbolism of level, says Cirlot, 'so deeply rooted in the psyche of man, equates all that is on a low level spatially with what is low in a spiritual, negative, destructive, and hence fatal, sense'. For a hero possessing the highest rank to descend to the lower depths to recover a loved one who has been carried there is a supreme act of sacrifice displaying the greatest altruism, paralleled by the act of Christ, descending into Hell after his crucifixion to accomplish the salvation of Adam – and all humankind.

LIFE, DEATH, AND RESURRECTION

Orpheus's murder and dismemberment by the Thracian women, his head and lyre being thrown into the river and conveyed by the current to Lesbos, recall the Egyptian myth of Osiris's murder and subsequent dismemberment by his brother Set, his body having been thrown into the Nile and conveyed in its wooden coffin to Byblos. Both achieve eternal life: Orpheus in the Elysian Fields and Osiris through the ritual of embalmment performed by his sister-wife Isis. These, like the dismemberment of Dionysus and other 'dying gods' of the Greek mysteries, are prefigurations of the Crucifixion and Resurrection of Christ. The torture, death, and resurrection of countless corn gods have punctuated critical stages of the agricultural cycle since the earliest days of sowing and harvesting in Mesopotamia. They are all echoed in the initiatory torments of shamans in Siberia, Africa, and North America, and by the ritual dismemberment, beatings, mutilations, 'death' and 'resurrection' of neophytes in male initiation rites as practised in primordial societies throughout the world. The same symbolism manifests itself in the dreams of modern people, as well as in the experiences of visionaries such as the alchemist Zosimos who was of such interest to Jung.

TRIALS AND ORDEALS:
THE INITIATION ARCHETYPE

That hero myths all have a great deal in common was vividly demonstrated by Joseph Campbell in *The Hero with a Thousand Faces* (1949). No sooner does the hero set out on his adventures than he is confronted with a series of trials and ordeals, such as a fight with a dragon, an encounter with a monster, or a descent into the Underworld. Ultimate success is rewarded with the treasure hard to attain – as often as not the throne of a kingdom or a beautiful princess as a bride. The purpose of the trials and ordeals is to enable the hero to prove his metal, that he is truly worthy of the treasure.

In Orpheus's case, the hero fails and the treasure is lost. We are prepared for this failure by the fact that Orpheus is not as tough, powerful, and manly as the other heroes on board the *Argo*, and that he has to compensate for this by using his musical gifts. He gets by very successfully until the ultimate challenge comes – the 'supreme ordeal' – when his lack of masculine strength and determination lets him down, he succumbs to a silly impulse, and he loses everything. It is a tragic story of love, loss, and heroic failure, which moves us more than conventional heroic sagas, where all goes more or less according to plan. As a consequence, the Orpheus myth has inspired some sublime works of art, such as paintings by Poussin, Claude, and Corot, as well as the enchanting opera by Gluck.

So total is Orpheus's sense of loss and despair that, in the absence of Eurydice, he becomes wedded to his grief. Such behaviour can indeed seem maddeningly stubborn to those who want the afflicted person to recover and commit himself once more to the business of living. To tear him to pieces on account of it is, perhaps, a little extreme, but it does dramatically symbolize how one can feel in these circumstances. The determinedly grief-stricken can so try the patience of others as to put themselves beyond the Pale. Such intransigence amounts to an abrogation of one's social responsibilities and can be harshly judged by one's fellows, especially at times of collective danger or need, and may result in rejection, ostracism, and worse. For it is perceived as a threat to the cohesion of the group.

GROUP COHESION: INDIVIDUAL COMPETITION
AND SELFISH GENES

As a social animal, our personal survival depends on being accepted as a member of a successful, well-organized, and reasonably cooperative human group. It is in order to guarantee the long-term cohesion of such groups that initiation rituals evolved, as well as the mythic-religious context which sanctions all such rituals and grants the tribal elders their spiritual authority and political power. Biologically this is the most crucial function of religion. Not only does it ensure group cohesion but provides the justification, the means and the motives, to induce individual members of the group to sacrifice their narrow self-interests to the wider interests of the community as a whole.

This is a reinforcement of a natural biological process. Since the 1960s it has been recognized that the Darwinian struggle for survival is not essentially between organisms or groups but between genes. According to this view, we are the means that our genes make use of to satisfy their own selfish ends – namely, to get into the next generation. If this is so, how can selfish genes produce unselfish people? The answer is, say the neo-Darwinists, that our genes see to it that we behave altruistically because it is to their advantage that we should do so. Our cooperativeness is driven by self-interest. The grocer sells vegetables to make a living, not to help us. We buy his vegetables to live, not to help him. But the result is that both sides benefit from the exchange. That we live in societies is because societies make it possible for us to exchange favours: they enable us to pursue selfish goals through cooperation. Thus, it is of advantage to our genes – and, *inter alia*, to ourselves – that societies should have a hierarchical structure and a moral code which is sanctioned by religion. Such a set-up greatly facilitates the wheeler-dealer propensities which are encoded in our genes (Axelrod, 1984; Ridley, 1994).

So although we are cooperative creatures, we are also fundamentally competitive: we compete with one another for love, resources, and rank. The dramas generated by this intractable rivalry are the very essence of human social existence, and it seems that they are derived from the two fundamental archetypal systems described at the beginning of this chapter: that concerned with attachment, affiliation, care-giving, care-receiving, and altruism; and that concerned with rank, status, discipline, law and order, territory, and possessions. These two archetypal systems (and the contrasting forms of social organization that they give rise to) find numerous parallels in the history of ideas. One example is Empedocles's distinction between love and strife, from which Freud derived his Eros and Thanatos instincts; other examples are Aristotle's distinction between the hedonic and political life, and Tonnies's classical sociological distinction between *Gemeinschaft* and *Gesellschaft*. The evolutionary importance of the first archetypal system has been established, as we have seen, by Bowlby and his followers. The second has only recently come under intense scrutiny.

The phylogenetic history of competitiveness began over three hundred million years ago, when our ancestors competed for resources (food, territory, and mates) on an individual basis, as many vertebrates continue to do to this day. Then, as group living became established and territory began to be shared, individuals ceased competing directly for territory and instead started to compete for rank. Once acquired, high rank brought with it access to the resources that were desired. Competition for rank took the form of threat displays and physical combat in tournaments, which behavioural biologists refer to as 'ritual agonistic behaviour' or RAB. Success in such tournaments provides a measure of an individual's 'resource holding power' or RHP. Repeated successes in ritual agonistic conflicts result in high RHP and access to prime breeding sites and prime mates, both of which contribute to increased reproductive fitness. Defeat, on the other hand, results in a lowering of RHP and radically alters the animal's physical and behavioural state. Lizards, for example, lose their colour in these circumstances and may die.

The human equivalent of resource holding power is self-esteem, and defeat can have similar effects on both the behaviour and self-esteem of human beings as it has on the behaviour and RHP of reptiles, mammals, and primates. An essential aspect of high self-esteem is the subjective awareness of being able to control desired social outcomes, while low self-esteem is the awareness of not being able to control such desirable assets, and is associated with submissive or subordinate forms of behaviour, as well as with a liability to anxiety, depression, or social withdrawal.

In all social animals, threat from a conspecific perceived as having higher resource holding power results in two alternative kinds of defensive behaviour: submission or escape. Submission differs from escape precisely because the animal stays put. The dominant individual will tolerate the continued presence of the defeated individual and cease to threaten him provided he puts on a postural display which symbolizes submission. Human patterns of dominance and submission are elaborations of these basic forms.

INTIMIDATION VERSUS ATTRACTION: THE AGONIC AND HEDONIC MODES

Some time in the last ten million years, a new form of social competition has arisen: instead of trying to intimidate rivals, the competitor seeks to attract them. This form of competition is apparent, for example, among chimpanzees, and its significance was first recognized by Michael Chance (Chance and Jolly, 1970). In addition to threat display, male chimpanzees indulge in a form of display that is not threatening at all and does not demand the submission of a subordinate. Rather it is a form of social solicitation, which, Chance noted, results in affiliative behaviour 'in which there is a continuing interaction between individuals, such as grooming, play, sexual or mothering behaviour with the displayer'.

In the course of extensive observations on social groups of primates, Chance recognized that they had two quite distinct modes of functioning, which he termed 'agonic' and 'hedonic'. The agonic mode is characteristic of hierarchically organized societies where individuals are concerned with warding off threats to their status and inhibiting overt expressions of aggressive conflict; while the hedonic mode is associated with affiliative behaviour in more egalitarian social organizations where agonic tensions are absent. In the agonic mode, Chance observed that the social balance between dominant and subdominant individuals is maintained by a process which he called 'equilibration': the group is held together by the threat of attack from dominant individuals, and any attempt on the part of a subdominant to escape from the group elicits attack. But should the subdominant approach the implicit boundary of the group, then a mere gaze from a dominant will usually be enough to slow him, stop him, and revert both his path and his attention to the centre. This phenomenon, which Chance termed 'reverted escape' is typical of the agonic mode. It contrasts with the freedom of individuals to drift apart within the group, and even to leave it for a time, which is possible in the hedonic.

It was the evolutionary replacement of intimidation by attraction that allowed the hedonic mode to emerge. In the hedonic mode, the competitor seeks to disarm potential rivals and attract potential mates as well as achieving status in the eyes of other members of the group. This was the technique used by Orpheus, when he charmed everyone with the beauty of his voice. Attractive people are granted prestige. They can assume leadership roles and have access to more resources than their less successful competitors. Their reproductive fitness thereby increases.

Unfortunately, the old kind of agonistic competition has not been eradicated from human nature. It has, after all, been present and evolving on this planet for three hundred million years, and it is deeply embedded in the human genome; whereas hedonic competition has only been in existence about one-thirtieth of that time.

Essentially, the possible outcomes of competition through physical threat (RAB to gain RHP) or competition through attraction (self-display for group approbation) are four in number:

    (1) social cooperation and integration
    (2) dominance
    (3) submission
    (4) withdrawal and social isolation

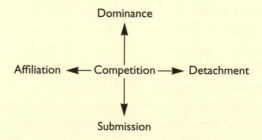

These can be represented orthogonally: (1) physical competition for dominance on the vertical axis, and (2) competition by attraction for approval and social integration on the horizontal axis.

The horizontal dimension may also be labelled closeness–distance, approach–withdrawal, ingroup–outgroup orientation, extraversion–introversion, and so on. In other words, the horizontal dimension is concerned with attachment, the vertical dimension with power. This schema carries significance not only for symbolism but also for the symptoms of psychiatric illness.

SYMBOLS AND SYMPTOMS AS ADAPTIVE MECHANISMS

In our book *Evolutionary Psychiatry: A New Beginning* (1996), John Price and I have proposed links between the basic dimensions of love and power and the different forms of psychopathology encountered in psychiatric practice. These may be summarized as follows:

(1) successful affiliation tends to be associated with social adjustment and mental health

(2) dominance tends to be associated with high self-esteem and hypomania

(3) submission tends to be associated with low self-esteem, feelings of shame and humiliation, dependent or anxious personality disorders, and depression

(4) failure in affiliation tends to be associated with schizoid personality disorder, an introverted, inner-directed mode of personality adjustment, and schizophrenia.

A crucial factor is whether or not the individual continues to feel himself or herself to be an 'insider' (a member of the ingroup, a committed member of the community, whether loved or unloved, of high status or low), or an 'outsider' (not a member of the ingroup, not a committed member of the community, not involved in attachment relationships or status conflicts). If an 'insider' develops a psychiatric disorder, it will tend to be a *disorder of attachment and rank* (a neurotic or manic-depressive disorder), whereas an 'outsider' will tend to develop a *spacing disorder* (a schizoid personality disorder or schizophrenia). Individuals who are uncertain as to their allegiance and who hover uneasily on the cusp between 'insider' and 'outsider' status will, if they develop a psychiatric disorder, tend to present with a *borderline state* (a borderline or schizotypal personality disorder). This means of reclassifying the major psychiatric disorders is summarized in Figure 1.

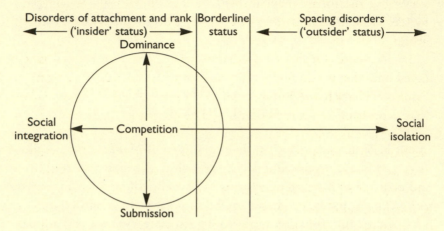

Figure 1 A schema for the classification of major disorders

The significance of these two archetypal systems is as great for the study of symbolism as it is for the diagnosis and treatment of psychiatric disorders. The symbolisms of tragedy, loss, demotion, and despair, like the psychiatry of bereavement and depression, are expressions of natural and universal experiences which human beings share with other mammalian species. They are manifestations of adaptive mechanisms that, in the ancestral environment in which we evolved, contributed to survival. Thus, depression (and all the symbolism it gives rise to) is an adaptive reaction to loss or deprivation. The loss in question may be loss of a loved one (the affiliative archetype) or loss of status (the rank archetype) or both. The adaptive function of the depressive reaction is to enable individuals so afflicted to adjust to their loss. By becoming depressed and displaying behaviour which symbolizes defeat, the demoted individual is forced, *faute de mieux*, to adapt passively to his lower status and, at the same time, to avoid further attack from the more powerful individual who has displaced him. Depression (and its symbolism of descent, oppression, and loss) is thus linked to the ubiquitous mammalian tactic of submission; while its opposite, mania (and its symbolism of ascent, triumph, and gain), is linked with the tactic of dominance. We may conclude, therefore, that manic-depression, and its non-pathological manifestations in elation and despair, as well as all the symbolism that these states give rise to, are inextricably linked to our evolved propensities to seek affiliation and rank within the context of a stable human group.

In one sense, Orpheus experiences what happens to us all when loved ones die: we do not want to accept their death and we want to bring them back to life, but we cannot. Evolutionary psychiatry teaches that depression is a means of adapting to loss and that a depression will last just as long as it takes us to give up what has been lost. Once we have really accepted the loss, and truly acknowledged to ourselves that we can *never* have it back again, then the depression will lift and one will be free to engage once more in the business of life. That Orpheus cannot and will not give up what he has lost means that his despair persists and results in his death either from suicide or dismemberment by those driven to distraction by his intransigent grief.

LOVE, RANK, AND RELIGION

Just as the two major archetypal systems of affiliation and rank rule our social relations with one another, they also rule our religious relationship with God. In the present century, the hierarchy archetype has lost some of its salience under the impact of an egalitarian consensus, but in the past we treated God with the same reverence we displayed to our rulers. 'Great and manifold were the blessings, most dread Sovereign,' begins the Dedication of the King James Bible, 'which Almighty God, the Father of all mercies, bestowed upon the people of *England* when first he sent Your Majesty's Royal Person to rule and reign over us.'

God is in the supremely dominant position: we are enjoined by the Church Fathers to love, fear, and obey Him. 'The fear of God is the beginning of wisdom' (Proverbs 1:7). From His throne in Heaven He rules the universe; we kneel before Him and throw ourselves at His feet in loving worship: 'Not my will but Thine, O Lord, be done.' We are miserable sinners who confess our guilt to Him, with the humble plea that in His Almighty wisdom He may forgive us and continue to grant us His Holy protection and love. Subordination is the *sine qua non* of religious life: 'Fear God, and keep his commandments, for this is the whole duty of man' (Ecclesiastes 12:13).

In the religious life of humanity, the attachment and rank archetypes have been *sanctified*, just as in sado-masochism they are *eroticized* (Stevens and Price, 1996). They provide the deep structures on which religious and sado-masochistic practices are built. In some expressions of Christianity – the making of saints and martyrs, the mortification of the flesh, the penitential self-mutilation of the *flagellentes*, etc. – religion and sado-masochism are combined. By adopting the symbolism of subordination in the presence of the Almighty, displaying both our love and fear, we participate in a sanctified ritual of 'reverted escape' which permits us to remain within the confines of the Church and in the continued presence of God. The alternative to such subordination to the Almighty will is banishment: excommunication, expulsion from the Garden of Eden, the Fall from Grace, the eternal agony of hell-fire. 'And fear not them which kill the body, but are not able to kill the soul,' warns Jesus, darkly, 'but rather fear him which is able to destroy both soul and body in hell' (Matthew 10:28).

Provided we dutifully acknowledge our dependence, subordination, and submission to this unseen superior, then He, like a monarch or great chief, will acknowledge His reciprocal obligation to us, by ensuring our care, nourishment, and protection. That is the covenant. And it is based on the archetypes of love and rank – particularly the latter.

These matters, which are so fundamental to the symbolic canons of all human cultures, will be examined in much greater depth in the relevant sections of the Thesaurus.

6

The Conjunction of
Heaven and Earth

In the fifteenth century the Swiss mystic Brother Klaus had a vision which changed his life. He called it 'The Vision of Threefoldness' and the experience was so terrible that his whole face was changed by it, and people were horrified when they saw him in church or in the street. His earliest biographer Heinrich Wölflin, born in 1470, recorded: 'All who came to see him were filled with terror at the first glance. As to the cause of this, he himself used to say that he had seen a piercing light resembling a human face. At the sight of it he feared that his heart would burst into little pieces. Overcome with terror, he instantly turned his face away and fell to the ground. And that was the reason his face was now terrible to others' (Jung, CW11, para. 478).

After years of contemplation, Brother Klaus came to the conclusion that what he had gazed upon was the Holy Trinity itself, and he recorded the vision in a painting on the wall of his cell. The painting, which is preserved in the parish church of Sachseln, is a mandala divided into six parts, in the centre of which is the crowned countenance of God. Thus Brother Klaus came to terms with his awe-inspiring experience by assimilating it into the dogma of his religion, and this may have saved him from going mad or being burned as a heretic.

The spontaneous eruption of a symbol in a vision or a dream is quite literally a hair-raising experience since it induces a psychophysical state of immense biological antiquity – one that biologists call arousal and theologians call numinous. The latter term was most famously used by Rudolf Otto in his book *Das Heilige* (*The Idea of the Holy*) published in 1917. Otto used it to describe what he regarded as the fundamental experience common to all religions – namely, the sense of awe and exaltation generated by the feeling of being in the presence of the Creator, an experience which Otto also designated the *mysterium tremendum et fascinans.*

Arousal is remarkably similar in a number of emotional conditions: sexual desire, anger, fear, and numinous excitement are all associated with increased heart rate, raised blood pressure, increased muscular tension, characteristic changes in the amplitude and frequency of the brain waves as recorded by the EEG, diminished electrical resistance of the skin, piloerection (the hair stands on end), dilatation of the pupil of the eye, respiratory changes, and so on. These changes typify arousal. And they give rise to a challenging question: if the physical signs of anger, fear, sexual desire, and numinous experience are all broadly similar, what distinguishes one from the other? The answer can only lie in the psychological perception of what is being experienced and this is determined by the actual circumstances that are being responded to.

A symbol is experienced as numinous if it refers to something tremendous (the *mysterium tremendum*) and is perceived as sacred in the sense that it relates to something infinitely greater than oneself. Numinosity coincides with an awareness that behind our personal intelligence a deeper intelligence is at work which guides, nourishes, and informs our daily existence. Whether this deeper intelligence is in fact 'God', or whether it is the evolved intelligence (the 'collective unconscious') of our species, makes no difference to the phenomenology of the experience.

Jung, who has contributed most to our understanding of the numinous, explained it in terms of the psychodynamics of what he called the Self – the nucleus at the core of the personality which incorporates the entire archetypal potential of the collective unconscious. The central importance of the Self, its powerful autonomy in sustaining and coordinating our psychic existence, would explain the ease with which we humans have ubiquitously identified it with (or projected it on to) a Supreme Being, or God, conceived as a transpersonal entity outside ourselves and responsible for everything that happens to us. All religions, all churches, all theologies are a metaphysical consequence of this projection of the Self and its enormous psychological potential. In the past, theologians have remained determinedly unconscious of this projection, persecuting as heretics anyone who drew attention to it. The Gnostics were hounded out of existence for it 1,800 years ago. One of them, Monoïmus, wrote a letter to his friend Theophrastus in the second century AD which is a model of psychological understanding, displaying deep insight into the dynamics of the Self. The ultimate secret, declared Monoïmus, is not to seek God *outside* in the universe but *inside* oneself. Then all is made clear: one learns 'whence is sorrow and joy, and love and hate, and waking though one would not, and sleeping though one would not, and getting angry though one would not, and falling in love though one would not' (Mead, 1931).

It is probably true to say that most people nowadays have far less psychological understanding than Monoïmus for the reason that they identify their psyche entirely with what lies within the confines of their conscious mind. This effectively closes them off from an experience of the numinous, unless it suddenly erupts in a dream, nightmare, or life-threatening event. Only at such moments as these, says Jung, do you begin to recognize that 'you are not master in your own house, you are not living alone in your room – there are spooks about. But if you understand it rightly, this recognition of the psychogenic factor is the first recognition of the Perusha – the Lord, the Master, the Christ within, the personified symbol of that archetype of archetypes, that Supreme Being in the collective unconscious – *The Self*.' The Self is thus the living embodiment in each and every one of us of the numinous power that has always and everywhere been attributed to 'God'.

Because the activity of the collective unconscious is experienced as both autonomous and transpersonal, Jung often referred to it as the *objective psyche*. To open oneself to the sacred is to mobilize the powerful energy of the objective psyche and to throw oneself on its mercy. As a result, the sacred is something that human beings have always approached in fear and trembling, surrounding it with taboos and prohibitions, and occasionally treating it with humour. What appears sacred to a member of one culture appears profane to a member of another. For this reason there is no such thing as a false religion: all religions are true for those who believe in them.

In the present century the sacred has become a lost continent. Like Atlantis, it has disappeared. But it has not ceased to exist. It is still there, not visible, but submerged in the oceanic depths of the unconscious. Some would deny its existence altogether, insisting that the sacred is and always has been an illusory phenomenon, a collective delusion. Such denial does not, however, account for the psychological facts. Belief in Zeus, Astarte, or Hathor may have been delusory when viewed from our twentieth-century standpoint, but the numinous experience induced by such belief was not. The goose pimples, the sense of awe in the presence of the *mysterium tremendum* experienced by believers entering a precinct sacred to one of these Supreme Beings, were *real*. This is why the phenomenological study of the sacred is so important, for it provides us with psychological insight into the symbolic and ritual practices that human beings have developed as a means of gaining access to the numinous powers of the Self.

What is perceived as sacred is invariably something that has been selected, chosen, picked out. A common object like a stone can be picked out from all other stones and rendered sacred. Such selective distinction has been traditionally attributed by religion, and the chosen object made hallowed through ritual, but it can also be performed by the arts. 'Art' means to make special. The selection is experienced as a hierophany (from the Greek *hieros*, meaning sacred and *phanien*, to reveal; a hierophany is thus a sacred revelation). From the psychodynamic standpoint, the important factor is that through hierophantic choice, *collective attention is focused on an object* and as a result of a group concentration of feeling, a group attribution of meaning, the object is rendered sacred. Though such group selection is traditionally divinely inspired, it may also occur when a creative genius selects a subject and renders it numinous through the miracle of art: the Mona Lisa's smile, Dürer's hare, and Van Gogh's chair somehow manage to express the sacred essence of the thing represented, and this would explain why people flock to pay homage to them. This tells us something fundamental about our nature as a species: we are *Homo artifex* as well as *Homo religiosus*.

Much of what can be said about numinous symbolism applies, therefore, to the arts as well as to religion – particularly to painting and to music, both of which were initially sacred in the sense that they were created as religious acts. Indeed, for many of us, art galleries and concert halls have replaced churches as the buildings we enter in search of the divine or sacred – of what strikes us as beautiful and eternally valid on the transpersonal plane. Wagner said of music that it must express the eternal, the infinite, the ideal. It should not concern itself with the passion, love, or longing of a particular person on a particular occasion, but with Passion, Love, and Longing in itself (Storr, 1992). Equally, the painting or sculpture of a Madonna and Child must not be limited to the portrayal of a particular mother and child: if it is to qualify as high art it must be transpersonal and convey something of the essence of maternal love itself. Then we are made aware of the 'divine' element in maternal tenderness flowing from the eternal archetypal pattern of the mother–child bond upon which all the variations of individual mother–child relationships have been repeated since our species began. For the unfailing characteristic of the symbolism of great art is that it leads us into the archetypal realm so as to reveal the eternal in the transitory, the universal in the particular. Whenever art achieves this it keys us into the *phrike* which the Greeks recognized as the hair-raising shudder, the sacred spine-tingling shiver of excitement, awe, and dread that is the quintessence of numinous excitement. It arises from the unconscious dynamics of the Self; it is not something that we can induce through conscious exercise of the will.

In his book *Music and the Mind* (1992), Anthony Storr argues that great music, like all great art, invariably has something beyond the personal about it because it depends upon an inner ordering process which is largely unconscious in the sense that it is not deliberately willed by the composer. It is this inner ordering process that is at work in dreams and the formation of symbols, as well as the creation of art. 'The greatest artists,' writes Storr, 'are able to plumb their own depths, and bring to the surface aspects of those basic emotions which are common to all mankind.'

A MATTER OF CHOICE

In *Patterns in Comparative Religion* (1958), Mircea Eliade says that we cannot be sure that there is anything that has not at the same time in human history been somewhere transformed into a holy object imbued with sacred power: 'Anything that man has ever handled, felt, come in contact with or loved *can* become a hierophany.' The truth of this was also apparent to the alchemists who held that the material necessary for making the Philosopher's Stone was readily available for all to see, but that people failed to recognize it: 'This Matter lies before the eyes of all; everybody sees it, touches, . . . loves it, but knows it not', says an alchemical text (*Hermetic Museum*, 1:13).

What is the trick? How is the common made special? How does the sacred symbol come into being? If you put these questions to people belonging to different cultures from all over the world, they will tell you that their holy symbols are sacred because 'the gods' made them so. Viewed from inside any tradition, that is how it seems. The Blessed Sacrament is holy because God ordained it. Viewed from outside the tradition, however, this answer fails to satisfy. For other peoples' holy symbols strike us not as products of divine ordinance but of human attribution. In other words, they result from the psychological mechanism of *projection*. How then does the projection come about? What triggers it?

As already suggested, the answer is that the object selected for the sacred treatment has to become the subject of collective attention and become special by general consent: it must be chosen. As it happens, this is the meaning of the word intelligence, which is derived from the Latin *legere*, to choose, to pick out. From being able to choose or pick out the right letters came the meaning of *legere*, to read. What is legible is that which can be picked out. What ought to be read is a legend (from the Latin gerundive, *legenda*). To choose from or between (*inter*) things is to display intelligence, *inter-legere*, from which we also derive *intellectum*, intellect. Now, all religions perceive a transpersonal intelligence behind the universe which chooses to bring the world and the tribe into existence and which chooses what is sacred. The Jews are far from being the only people who have believed themselves to be specially chosen. The very word 'ecclesiastic' (pertaining to the Church) is derived from the Greek word meaning chosen or called. In other words, all religions are symbolic explanations and symbolic systems of practice which are dependent upon the principle of divine choice. Psychologically, we can equate this divinity which chooses with the Self. We must, therefore, move the question onwards: what causes the Self to select one object to be imbued with numinous power rather than another? What can anthropology reveal of the processes involved?

It used to be thought that only advanced civilizations conceived of a divine Supreme Being. But it now appears that perhaps all primitive peoples believed in an omnipotent creator, dwelling in the heavens and being manifested in *epiphanies* (divine relations) of the sky and natural elements. The Konde of Tanzania, for example, believe in a Supreme Being called Kyala. Any great or impressive object or event is the temporary abode of Kyala. Frazer refers to this in *The Worship of Nature* (1926): 'When a great storm lashes the lake into fury, God is walking on the face of the waters; when the roar of the waterfall is louder than usual, it is the voice of God. The earthquake is caused by His mighty footstep, and the lightning is . . . God coming down in anger. God sometimes comes also in the body of a lion or a snake, and it is in that form he walks about among men to behold their doings.'

Such anthropological observations provide us with a valuable clue as to what it is that is capable of activating perception of the sacred: anything powerful, monstrous, extraordinary, or startling – what Eliade calls a *kratophany* (From the Greek *kratos*, meaning power, and *phanein*, a revelation – a revelation through power). This is perfectly understandable. Anything that is unaccustomed or extraordinary possesses the capacity to arrest our attention, inspire awe and fascination, or provoke fear and withdrawal – not only in ourselves but in all mammals to a greater or lesser extent. This is one aspect of the process by which things become sacred and set apart – the *mysterium tremendum et fascinans*. Anything exceptional can inspire this response: great height, great strength, loud noise, bright light, great beauty, or great ugliness. Shamans, sorcerers, and medicine men are often hideous and frightening – recruited from the eccentric, the mad, the ugly, and the deformed. These are the stigmata that mark them out as special and chosen. Ritual confirmation in the role of the shaman is merely a collective affirmation of a sacred choice that has already been made by a suprapersonal power. Such individuals are highly charismatic. They are sacred.

How are we to understand this?

THE SACRED ORIENTATION

To be alert in response to the unusual, the strange or uncanny, is a universal response apparent throughout the animal kingdom – an example of what biologists call *the orientation response*. Pavlov thought of it as a reflex; he called it the 'what is it?' reflex. The orientation response is displayed by a cat watching a mouse and preparing to pounce on it or by a rabbit confronted by a snake. All movement ceases. All attention, every scrap of energy, is focused on the perceived object. We display the same behaviour when we are fascinated by something – or terrified by it. It is not difficult to understand, therefore, how a manifestation of the extraordinary can be perceived and experienced as a disturbing revelation of the sacred. Such occurrences seem to indicate the presence of something *other* than natural – that is to say something *super*natural: they have *greatness*. In the traditional Melanesian view, such manifestations are held to possess mana. Mana is inherent magico-religious power. If people or things possess mana it is because they have been singled out and granted it by Higher Beings. Mana is sacred, god-given power. Mana is the mobilized energy of the Self.

Although mana is not a universal concept, it is very common and we can understand intuitively exactly what it means, even though it is foreign to our tradition. Many people have a similar concept. The Sioux Indians, for example, call it *wakan*; the Iroquois use the term *orenda*. To the Hurons it is *oki*, to the West Indians *zemi*, and to the African Pygmies (the Bambuti) it is *megbe*. It exists everywhere, preferring to manifest itself in extraordinary phenomena – such as the sun, the moon, thunder, lightning, the wind, and in certain animals and people. Not everyone is endowed with it, and some people and some animals possess more of it than others. Very capable people become eminent simply because they are well endowed with *megbe*, *orenda*, mana. Special individuals like sorcerers, kings, queens, and chieftains have a great deal. We still experience royalty and celebrities in the same way. They command our attention. They elicit the orientation response, which, we begin to see, is indispensable to perception and experience of the sacred.

The Monarch, the President, and the Pope all carry mana by virtue of their institutionalized role. The Great Leader possesses his power through constellation of the hero-saviour archetype, which can become linked to the sacred archetype. The history of Western civilization is not short of examples: Alexander the Great, Jesus Christ, Julius Caesar, Hannibal, Joan of Arc, Napoleon, Elizabeth I, the Duke of Wellington, Abraham Lincoln, Hitler, Mussolini, Winston Churchill, General de Gaulle, Mother Teresa, Margaret Thatcher, Nelson Mandela. In our democratic times, which are hostile to all forms of greatness, celebrities like pop stars and television personalities seem able to constellate this power. They are usually not particularly impressive people – often the reverse – but they acquire mana because of the media attention they receive. They become numinous and inspire awe, even hysteria. People become tongue-tied in their presence, flushed or pale, trembling as if in the ambience of the *mysterium tremendum et fascinans*. They display all the signs of arousal as well as the orientation response.

SACRED DANGER

Once a person, no less than an object, becomes imbued with mana, with sacred power, he becomes dangerous, for he can put it to destructive as well as to creative ends. Such ambivalence is recognized by all religious traditions: it is dangerous to come near any consecrated object in the profane state, without undergoing the proper ritual preparation necessary to enter the sacred state. Hence the Polynesian notion of 'taboo'. A thing or person or a place is taboo or forbidden precisely because it is both holy and dangerous. It is the Ark of the Covenant capable of striking dead all those who would defile it. 'Thou canst not see my face,' says God in the Old Testament, 'for there shall no man see my face and live' (Exodus 33:20).

Contact with the sacred can produce upheaval on the ordinary, everyday level of existence and could prove fatal either for the individual or the collective. Therefore, sacred things must be hedged round with prohibitions and ritual formalities. This is particularly true when they are out of the ordinary, large in scale, or novel – that is to say, anything perceived as *great* and capable of eliciting the orientation response as well as the physiological state of arousal.

THE SACRED CENTRE

But supernormal stimuli are not in themselves sufficient to activate the archetypal propensity for numinous experience. Something more is needed. Something crucial. And that is story, narrative, myth. Were it not for the indispensable element of myth, anything startling, strange, or dangerous would automatically be perceived as sacred. But it isn't. What picks out or selects a stimulus as possessing the numinosity of the sacred is the behaviour of a Supreme Being or a tribal hero recorded in a myth as occurring in the remote past, *in illo tempore*, in that time when the world began – what Aborigines call the Dreaming Time. Typically, the place and time at which the sacred events are believed to have occurred are the centre of the cosmos at the moment of the Creation. To Christians the centre of the world was at Golgotha. Golgotha means literally 'the place of the skull'. This may have been because the hill on which the Crucifixion occurred was shaped like a skull, but legend insisted that it was also the place where Adam was created and his skull was buried. It was the centre of the world where the two most important religious events occurred: Adam's Fall and our Saviour's redemption of his sin. By being crucified on Golgotha, Christ redeemed Adam directly with His blood. The image of Christ being crucified on Adam's grave is represented in a mosaic in the narthex of a church in Phocis, Greece, and in a carving on the door of Strasburg Cathedral.

For Christians, Golgotha, Jerusalem, and the Holy Land have always been sacred places for pilgrimages and crusades. For all of us, believers or non-believers, sacred places continue to exercise their powerful attraction. Why do the great cathedrals of Europe – which Nietzsche called the tombs and monuments of the dead Christian God – still have the capacity to move us with their numinous intensity? How is it that even the most godless among us will spend large sums visiting holy sites of antiquity in Greece, Rome, Sicily, Egypt, and

Asia Minor, the Hindu shrines of India, the Buddhist shrines of Thailand, Cambodia, and Japan? Apparently most of us still acknowledge a need to place ourselves in direct communication with a 'centre' imbued with sacred power. Such places are sources of spiritual vitality which can be renewed by the mere act of going there.

Sacred places are the most ancient and best preserved artefacts of every civilization, for they are their *raison d'être*. Their incredible durability even survives radical changes of religion. The rocks, caves, woods, and springs venerated from the earliest times in Greece have been taken over by Christian saints and are still venerated to this day. This is evidence of what Eliade (1958) calls 'the autonomy of hierophanies'. He says that 'the sacred expresses itself according to the laws of its own dialectic and this expression comes to man *from without.*' To the psychologist it does not come from without but from *within* – through activation of the archetype, experienced as autonomous, which, through projection, seems to be dependent on influences coming from without. The projection is, of course, unconscious. If people felt that they themselves could choose their own sacred places and bring them into existence as a mere act of will, then it is unlikely that such continuity would persist. But it is not possible to synthesize the sacred through the ego, for such conscious manipulation of space will not endure, and it will not be perceived by future generations to be sacred. The sacred nature of a place, such as Lourdes, has to be experienced as revealed, independent of all ego choice, as a hierophantic realization. It has to come in the form of what used to be called 'grace'.

One place of crucial religious significance to preliterate peoples was their totem centre. It was the ultimate sacred spot, designated by mythic beings who lived at the beginning of time and revealed to their people what foods to eat, what gods to worship, what rituals to perform. It was the original place of creation, the cradle of the ancestors, the centre of the earth. The rites performed there were an imitation and reproduction of things done there *in illo tempore* and these very rites guaranteed and perpetuated the sacred power of the place. Repeating the primeval hierophany ensures that sacredness continues there, so that it can be experienced as a tangible presence.

It is this sense that we can still get by going to Chartres, Notre Dame, Canterbury, or Delphi.

Not only is the actual location of a sacred place usually determined by a hierophany *in illo tempore* but the actual form, structure, nature of the place – whether temple, sanctuary, or altar – is likewise determined. The whole construction is necessarily based on 'a primordial revelation which disclosed the archetype of the sacred space *in illo tempore*, an archetype which was then indefinitely copied and copied again with the erection of every new altar, temple or sanctuary'. It is 'the sacred place where all impurity was done away with and the union of heaven and earth made possible' (Eliade, 1958).

HEAVEN AND EARTH CONJOINED

What other stimulus configurations are associated with numinous experience? In addition to the circle with its centre (the omphalos), the navel of the earth and the centre of the universe, there are such widely occurring symbols as the Cosmic Mountain, the *axis mundi*, and the Cosmic Tree. The Cosmic Mountain is invariably conceived as being at the centre of the world, as is the Cosmic Tree, and both, like the *axis mundi*, are at the point of junction between Heaven, Earth, and Hell.

Every sacred space, every holy city, every temple, every sanctuary, every altar, is an assimilation of these symbolic constellations of the sacred archetype. They represent the whole universe in a symbol and are ultimate, suprapersonal representations of the Self, in which all opposites and all possibilities exist *in potentia*. Thus, temples are cosmic mountains built over the omphalos at the *axis mundi*, their floorplan almost invariably representing a mandala. 'All these sacred constructions,' says Eliade, 'represent the whole universe in a symbol.' The Mesopotamian ziggurat is a cosmic mountain, joining Heaven to Hell. Each terrace represents a different cosmic level. As the pilgrims climb, they are coming closer to the centre of the cosmos. As they reach the highest point, they break through into the ultimately sacred sphere, transcending everything profane.

REVELATION OF THE ARCHETYPAL ORDER

As one reads of ancient cosmologies, one realizes that the latest scientific theories of the origins of the universe are primordial religious ideas in modern dress. The theory of the Big Bang, which holds that the entire universe was created from one minute centre of immense potential energy existing in timeless non-space, is prefigured by the Buddhist belief that the universe grew from a 'centre' when the Buddha entered a timeless moment just before the world was created. This links up with Jung's idea that all reality proceeds on an archetypal basis – both the universe and the psyche that perceives it, both the laws of nature and the psyche that can formulate those laws in scientific hypotheses. Here, too, an awareness of the sacred dimension becomes paramount through the perception of some absolute, pre-existent order manifesting itself in psychic forms, such as mathematics, music or philosophy, as well as scientific laws. It has been well said by Edward Young that 'the undevout astronomer is mad'. A fundamental question has been raised by Anthony Storr (1992): are mathematicians, composers, and scientists really uncovering truths which are, in fact, already 'there'? Is it possible that through their work they are analysing 'the mind of God'? Does Bach's 'Musical Offering' or his 'Art of Fugue' carry us into a world that exists beyond ordinary profane existence, a supraordinate world where music, mathematics, philosophy, and science are all one?

A major difference between the religious and scientific approaches to reality is not purely one of methodology but one of technology. Science can tell us how things are and how they came into being, but it can tell us nothing about their meaning or purpose, or why the vast cosmic experiment was set up and started off in the first place. Only myth and religion address these basic issues in the face of which science remains speechless. That is why, despite all the successes of science, myths and religions will continue to be needed and, when appropriate, re-created.

The attempt to envisage the infinite, the eternal, the absolute, is something that starts for many of us in childhood. In my own case, I recall, it used to make me so dizzy I felt sick. 'Where was I before I was born?' 'What lies beyond the universe?' 'What was here before the universe began?' These are questions with which children everywhere perplex their parents. Later on they give rise to the conjectures, fantasies, and intuitions which induce the symbolic–aesthetic attitude that Leibniz called 'the perennial philosophy'. Albert Einstein described it as 'the most beautiful emotion' which arises when one contemplates what must lie beyond our immediate sensory perceptions: 'To know that what is impenetrable to us really exists, manifesting itself as the highest wisdom and the most radiant beauty, which our full faculties can comprehend only in their most primitive forms – this knowledge, this feeling, is at the center of true religiousness' (quoted by Wilber, 1983).

The fantasy that 'what is impenetrable to us really exists', and that it is possible to 'know' it, lies behind all scientific inquiry and all religious symbolism. The 'most beautiful emotion' which accompanies the experience of genuine scientific insight or intense religious experience occurs when, however momentarily, the impenetrable becomes penetrable and 'the truth' is glimpsed. At such moments one steps outside Plato's cave of shadows and encounters the phenomenon of transcendence, *satori* (enlightenment). When such experience is communicated to others it may become a scientific hypothesis or religious dogma which will stand or fall with the test of time.

So great is the value attributed to such insights that those who are gifted at attaining them are venerated as scholars, saints, prophets, gurus, Nobel Laureates, messiahs, shamans, and mystics. They are seers who perceive more than is vouchsafed to the rest of humanity and are credited with a higher level of being: it is as if the archetypal substrate of the *unus mundus* is accessible to them. As a result, they are recognized as mana personalities, endowed with special powers.

As we have seen, a fundamental aspect of the phenomenology of the sacred or numinous experience is the act of giving close attention to something, selecting it as central to the focus of consciousness. It is both an application of the orientation response and the repetition of an archetypal pattern, linked in the ancient biological phenomenon of arousal. Attention confers reality on something, gives it substance; it brings out the figure from the ground. To perceive something as sacred is to give it what Eliade calls 'outstanding reality'. Only the sacred, to the primordial mind, really is. The sacred makes things absolute.

7

Living the Symbolic Life

To feel the power of a symbol is to enter a world of make-believe. For the devout Catholic, at the moment of consecration, the bread and the wine *become* the body and blood of Christ. When in a primitive ritual, a man puts on the mask of a god, then, for the duration of the ritual, he *is* the god. The profane object is transformed – or even transubstantiated – into the sacred object through a culturally sanctioned act of imagination. We have all experienced similar transformations, at a more simple, more personal level, as children at play. 'I'm Gene Autrey,' my cousin would announce as he came galloping along the hall. 'And me Big Chief Running Water,' I'd declare, fitting an arrow in my bow.

The non-believer can, of course, refuse to participate, and then the magic does not work. He stands outside it and scoffs. For him there is no transformation for he declines to have anything to do with the whole charade: he eschews the imaginal realm that the others have entered. Other people's religious beliefs have always seemed absurd, incomprehensible, risible even, to those who do not share them: 'Like those wicked Turks,' says Mrs Shewton in *Dombey and Son*, 'there is no What's-his-name but Thingummy, and What-you-may-call-it is his prophet!'

To play a part in a game or ritual, to enter a sanctuary as a participant in a rite, is to enter an altered state of consciousness, a different frame of mind, not dissimilar to a trance or a dream. You can experience something like it when gripped by a book, a play, or a film. You know that the plot and characters are imaginary, not real; yet you find yourself enthralled, committed, involved: you have to know what happens next. If it is frightening or horrible, you may have to remind yourself that 'it's only a film' in order to endure it – or, if really scared, bury your head in your neighbour's lap.

Animals at play, like children, demonstrate this make-believe quality: 'I'm attacking you, but not really!' The 'play face' of the wrestling chimpanzee, the wagging tail of the growling puppy, the exaggerated, clowning movements of all young animals at play, are examples of the same behavioural duality: 'Let's pretend!'

Much symbol formation occurs when the psyche is in playful mode, either waking or asleep. The idea that dreams could be a form of entertainment was expressed by Brian, a thirteen-year-old, who said: 'We dream so that we don't get fed up while we are asleep' (Mallon, 1989) – a sentiment expressed by the poet Novalis over a century earlier: 'Dreams are a shield against the humdrum monotony of life; they set imagination free from its chains so that it may throw into confusion all the pictures of everyday existence and break into the unceasing gravity of grown men with the joyful play of a child.' Play is a vital activity: by ensuring that young creatures play, nature provides the means of training behavioural systems that are vital to life – social intimacy, cooperation and conflict, ranking behaviour, sexuality, the control of aggression, and so on. Observing the play of animals and young children, one is aware that something is at work which transcends the behaviour and experience of each one of them.

The same truth becomes apparent when one examines a series of dreams from one person. Hence Jung's view of the transcendent function of symbols – that they are an expression of natural, biological intent, part of the autonomous developmental principle operating throughout life, which he called *individuation*. 'Individuation,' wrote Jung, 'is an expression of that biological process – simple or complicated as the case may be – by which every living thing becomes what it was destined to become from the beginning' (*CW*11, para. 144). 'Individuation means becoming a single, homogeneous being, and, insofar as "individuality" embraces our innermost, last, and incomparable uniqueness, it also implies becoming one's own self. We could, therefore, translate individuation as "coming to selfhood" or "self-realization"' (*CW*7, para. 266).

It was Jung's empirical discovery that 'living the symbolic life' – that is, being constantly alive to the symbolic meaning of events both in waking and dreaming reality – greatly enhances realization of the Self. All of us can experience the symbols created by our dreams, if we open ourselves up to them, as inner springs teeming with those archetypal energies that have inspired the human spirit since we emerged from the primeval forests and began to walk on two legs.

JONATHAN'S DREAM

When I neared this point in writing the present chapter, I had to break off to see a patient, a highly intelligent man in his mid thirties. At this session he reported the following dream, which he had had on the morning that he was to undergo the ordeal of the oral examination for his doctorate:

I was dark skinned and somehow like a primitive, rather innocent, original man. I was with a coloured girl who was a little younger than me and who had wiry, curly, dark hair. Her teeth were shiny but there was a gap between the front ones. She was a lot of fun and I wanted her as my partner and consort. I had to see the King of the tribe and I was somewhat fearful about telling him about my girl and my wish to be with her.

As I went forward to greet him, she hid behind some huts and I blew her a kiss as she went into some bushes on the left. She was like a brilliant, shining black jewel of total innocence and childlike simplicity. Not a malicious or scheming thought had ever entered her mind. Everything for her was clear and bright and her trust was total.

It was warm and the sun was shining. It seemed like early morning. There were many others of the tribe there. The King greeted me with a smile as he held out his hand to me. I did not know what I was going to say but I knew that I had to tell him that I wanted to be with the young girl. As the King came forward I saw that he had a snake in his hand. It was a huge cobra with a wide head and the markings of a tiger, beautiful stripes of orange and black. I was initially fearful and apprehensive.

Then I saw the snake curl its tail round up behind itself and then over its head, and I watched as it took its tail into its mouth to make a perfect circle. It was glorious and regal. Then I noticed that it was looking at me intently, with a smiling glint in its eye, looking straight at me, fixing me with its stare and trying to get me to understand something.

I walked towards the King and the snake and as I did so I realized that the snake was trying to get me to understand that there was nothing to fear and that it was communicating clearly to me that all was well. Then from the middle of its back, from inside the middle of the circle, a basket emerged; it was a wicker basket and I saw lilies and white flowers, like lotus and magnolia, emerge from within it. The flowers were a gift for me and a sign that great richness awaited and that the king approved of my choice of girl. There was nothing to fear. I had done what was necessary and he wanted me to know that he welcomed me and initiated me into the tribe as a man.

At that moment I realized the import of this vision and sensed myself coming up at high speed. I realized I had received an enormous sign. All the power and knowledge that the snake symbolized was complete and a major transition had occurred. As I came to, I knew with certainty that the oral examination would be all right and the sense of peace and completeness I felt was extraordinary.

Dreams rich in archetypal symbolism are particularly likely to occur at times of stress or challenge, when one feels one has one's back to the wall. Jonathan had been dreading the *viva voce* examination because he feared that one of his examiners would prove hostile. This situation evoked in him the transpersonal drama of the archetypal initiation necessary for the hero to win the princess and the kingdom. The treasure hard to attain is often guarded by a dangerous snake but, in this instance, the snake tips Jonathan the wink that all will be well and that the treasure is his for the taking. The symbolic meanings of the uroboros and the lotus are discussed in the Thesaurus. Suffice it to say here that they are implicated in many cultures through the expression of ideas of spiritual development comparable to Jung's 'individuation of the Self'. As Jonathan was able to tell me, the *viva* went extremely well and, at the end, the examiner whose negative judgement he feared told him unofficially that the doctorate was his. The dream both predicted the good outcome of the ordeal and provided the dreamer with the strength to meet it; at the same time, it promoted the individuation of the dreamer. That life should provide such a good example of the power of archetypal symbolism at the precise moment that I needed it for this chapter is an instance of what Jung called *synchronicity* – the occurrence of a meaningful yet acausally related event.

SYMBOLIC VITALITY

Analytic experience thus confirms Jung's assertion that living symbols have a life-enhancing effect. When is a symbol living and when is it dead? 'The symbol is alive only so long as it is pregnant with meaning,' wrote Jung. 'But once its meaning has been born out of it, once that expression is found which formulates the thing sought, expected, or divined better than the hitherto accepted symbol, then the symbol is dead.' A dead symbol is at best a conventional sign. 'It is, therefore, quite impossible to create [that is, consciously invent] a living symbol, i.e., one that is pregnant with meaning, from known associations. For what is thus produced never contains more than was put into it.' Symbols pass through their life-cycle at both the personal and the collective level. Those possessing great vitality in childhood often lose their magic as they grow older. So it is with cultural symbols: the crucifix, for example, which once had the power to unite Christendom, and send the faithful off on perilous pilgrimages and crusades, has lost its ability to inspire reverent piety in the majority of our contemporaries. 'A symbol really lives only when it is the best and highest expression for something divined but not yet known to the observer. It then compels his unconscious participation and has a life-giving and life-enhancing effect' (CW6, para. 819).

The property of symbols which Jung repeatedly stressed was their power – the psychic energy, which is stored up in them and which can be released in subjects who render themselves susceptible to the impact of symbols and their meanings. 'Symbols are not merely representational forms which serve our cognition,' wrote Jung, 'but rather *they are highly potent powers*' (quoted by Whitmont, 1969; italics added). In other words, symbolism is thinking in energized images, and this encapsulated energy-with-meaning gives the symbol its capacity to influence consciousness. The vitality of a symbol depends on the conscious attitude with which it is received. In themselves, images are meaningless; they acquire energy-with-meaning only when we grant it to them, by laying ourselves open to their influence. As this paradox demonstrates, the symbol functions as a psychic mirror in which we perceive our human energies reflected, and, by recognizing their significance, take personal possession of them. Once started, this projective—reflective dialectic gathers its own momentum, proceeding on the labyrinthine progress which Jung called individuation. 'The soul,' said Heraclitus, 'has its own *logos*, which grows according to its needs.'

To access the meaningful energy of a symbol it is necessary to realize its appositeness – to perceive that it contributes adaptive meaning to some situation that one happens to be confronting. Instantly, the symbol is charged with meaning; and the situation is, to a greater or lesser extent, transformed. For this reason, Jung sometimes referred to symbols as *transformers*. People who are, for whatever reason, cut off from their influence, he regarded as ill, in need of a symbol transfusion. Therapy, he said, is less a matter of treatment than of developing the creative, symbolic talents latent in the patient. Creative vitality, he discovered, was best served when the patient's symbols were amplified through the discovery of cultural and archetypal parallels, rather than analysing them reductively in the Freudian manner and attributing them to already experienced events. It is this amplifactory process that the present Thesaurus is intended to assist.

NEW SYMBOLS FOR OLD: REVOLUTION VERSUS THE *STATUS QUO*

Archetypal symbols are products of biocultural evolution – an evolutionary process in which genes and culture interact. The thesis of gene encounters the antithesis of culture to produce the synthesis of archetypal symbolism. The prevailing prejudice for most of this century has insisted that symbols are simply manifestations of the culture generating them, but this one-sided view is both misguided and out-dated. Like language and religion, symbols are a hybrid of culture and genes. The symbolism of religion probably arose early in the existence of *Homo sapiens*, for religious behaviour is essentially ritual behaviour: it consists of fixed, repetitive patterns of thoughts and actions which may antedate the use of fluent speech. Judging from the ceremonial burial of the dead practised by the Neanderthalers, it is clear that religious ideas were current at least one hundred thousand years ago. Neanderthal man may well have possessed the vocal and cerebral apparatus required for sophisticated speech and if *Homo religiosus* and *Homo symbolicum* preceded the emergence of *Homo loquens* it was probably not by a large margin.

Or, to rephrase this in modern computerspeak, genes provide the cerebral hardware, while religion, language, and symbolism provide the necessary software. Through the genome of our species we inherit the archetypal predispositions of our ancestors, and it is on these basic, universal, and persistently active themes that individual cultures work out their sets of variations and transmit them from generation to generation. When Jung referred to this archetypal hardware as 'the natural mind' or the 'two-million-year-old human being who exists in us all', he was coining a metaphor for the age-old dynamic at the core of human existence, there by virtue of our evolutionary history and still active in our symbols, dreams, and adaptive strategies, endeavouring to promote our survival and reproductive success in the often alienating conditions of the modern world.

Since the cultural software perishes with the hardware each time a member of the community dies, the software has to be reproduced in every generation. The early-nineteenth-century biologist Jean-Baptiste Lamarck did not understand this: he believed that what was learned or acquired by individuals in the course of their lifetime could be directly inherited by their progeny. We now know this to be untrue. Only the genes preserve and transmit information. Culture, on the other hand, transcends the individual life-cycle by codifying in symbolic and linguistic terms the information to be passed from one generation to the next. In human beings culture does what instinct does for less advanced creatures: culture is the memory store which exists outside the human brain. It represents an accumulated treasury of tested experience; and it is a gift which each generation has to acquire, earn, and deserve. Hence the worldwide occurrence of initiation rites, the means by which the past is reincarnated in the present and handed on to the future.

Cultural wisdom would soon become stultified, however, were it handed on automatically, as in societies of ants. The information has to be renewed, added to, and kept perennially alive. But this inevitably gives rise to conflict between the old and the new. 'In all human activities we find a fundamental polarity,' wrote the philosopher Ernst Cassirer (1944). '. . . We may speak of a tension between stabilization and evolution, between a tendency that leads to fixed and stable forms of life and another tendency to break up this rigid scheme. Man is torn between these two tendencies, one which seeks to preserve old forms whereas the other strives to produce new ones. There is a ceaseless struggle between tradition and innovation . . .'

Just as traditional symbols are necessary to ensure cultural coherence and the assimilation of successive generations, so it is our innate ability to think symbolically that enables us to reshape our universe. 'Language, myth, art and religion are parts of this universe,' says Cassirer. 'They are the varied threads which weave the symbolic net, the tangled web of human experience . . . instead of dealing with things themselves man is in a sense constantly conversing with himself. He has so enveloped himself in linguistic forms, in artistic images, in mythical symbols or religious rites that he cannot see or know anything except by the interposition of this artificial medium.' What Cassirer does not add, being a philosopher rather than a psychologist, is that human beings are also constantly engaged in a dialogue with their own unconscious psyches as well as with their cultural symbols. Through the remarkable phenomenon of human consciousness, the species is constantly reflecting on its condition and talking to itself – especially in dreams, which are the 'pillow talk' of the ego with the Self. In the course of this conversation, new versions of old symbols are constantly introduced.

Biology has decreed that the very continuance of life is dependent on the ability of organisms to replicate and regulate themselves. Replication and regulation proceed at both the personal and the cultural level, and it is religion that provides the link between them.

As enduring and forceful regulators of the social order, the gods ensure that a balance is maintained between the traditional forces of conservation and the progressive forces of change: they enshrine the principle of homeostasis. In the recurring conflict between the generations, it is crucial that there should be no outright winner. A complete break with tradition brought about by the total victory of the youthful progressives would imperil the survival of the social order as much as the triumph of conservative inflexibility imposed by the elders.

The dangerous moment for any society comes when the next generation of youths reaches puberty. Konrad Lorenz (1970) called this moment 'the moult', saying that it is as hazardous a time for society as it is for the newly moulted soft-shelled crab! He described the pubertal moult as 'the open door through which new ideas gain entrance'. But these new ideas have to be compatible with the old and have to achieve balance with them: the arrogance of youth has to be countered by the wisdom of collective experience, as the young themselves come to appreciate when they get older. This is where the gods come in with their divinely authorized rites of initiation.

THE LIMINOID STATE

Major insights into the function of symbols in organizing social life came from the American anthropologist Victor Turner (1969). Turner concluded that symbolic forms and rituals belonged to one of two categories: those serving the roles, rules, and regulations which sustain the established social order; and those permitting the emergence of subgroups, each sharing common convictions and organizing themselves in ways that differ from the larger social group – as in cults, millennial movements, elite regiments, counter-cultures, monastic orders, and so on.

Together with his wife Edith, Victor Turner (1978) went on to examine the conditions motivating pilgrims to go off on religious quests. Again, a similar distinction seemed to apply, for they found evidence that pilgrims characteristically participate in two categories of ritual processes and symbolic forms: 'liminal' rituals which remain within the ordered social structure; and 'liminoid' rituals which tend to go beyond or even break the pattern of the parent structure.

These two dynamics are indispensable to group splitting. Human groups, like all groups of social animals, possess an inherent dynamic to thrive and multiply until they reach a critical size at which the resources at their disposal are no longer adequate for their needs. Then they become unstable and split. When the split occurs, the group divides into two opposing factions, and all the mechanisms which previously served to promote group solidarity are put into reverse so as to drive the two subgroups apart. At this point, the issue of leadership becomes crucial for survival, because the leader has to inspire the departing group with its sense of mission and purpose, so that it can win through against all odds and find its own Promised Land. Such a leader needs the sort of charisma traditionally granted by divine will and maintained through direct communion with the gods. Leaders of this kind are thrown up at crucial moments in the history of all societies and many of them, on close examination, prove to have been of a schizoid, paranoid, or schizotypal disposition.

Independent investigations of gurus (Anthony Storr, 1996) and of charismatic leaders (Charles Lindholm, 1990), have demonstrated how figures such as David Koresh, Jim Jones, Charles Manson, and Adolf Hitler inspired incredible loyalty in the followers who gathered round them. Yet to others unaffected by their personalities, they appear half mad, 'driven', as Charles Lindholm observes, 'by violent rages and fears that would seem to make them repellent rather than attractive, while their messages look, from the perspective of the outsider, to be absurd *mélanges* of half-digested ideas, personal fantasies and paranoid delusions'. The most striking thing about them is their shamanic quality. (The Tungus noun *saman* means one who is excited, moved, raised. As a verb it means to know in an ecstatic manner.) Ethnological studies of shamans in Siberia, Africa, and North America reveal them to be close to the borderline of psychosis, but not over it: they are schizotypal not schizophrenic; they have ready access to the liminoid (half-conscious, half-unconscious) state.

As with all charismatic leaders, their influence arises from their apparent ability to put themselves in close touch with the unconscious and to articulate its archetypal contents in a way that convinces their followers that they are divinely inspired. The inspired figure is always one who stands apart, completely focused on his inner vision. This sets him on a level above that of ordinary humanity. He is seen to be in the liminoid state, halfway between Heaven and Earth. It means that he speaks with the conviction of higher authority, which puts his followers in awe of him. They adore him and long to place themselves under his influence, for he can heal their fears of separation by giving them direction and welcoming them into the arms of the charismatic group.

With time, this union, even in the most secular movement, assumes an unmistakably religious form, as the new group is bound together in its faith and rituals. Thus Nazism had its Messiah (Hitler), its Holy Book (*Mein Kampf*), its cross (the swastika), its religious processions (the Nuremberg Rally), its ritual (the Beer Hall Putsch Remembrance Parade), its anointed elite (the SS), its hymn (the 'Horst Wessel Lied'), excommunication for heretics (the concentration camps), its devils (the Jews), its millennial promise (the Thousand-Year Reich), and its Promised Land (the East).

In the history of Nazi Germany we see how a new religion may be born out of social disintegration and the compensatory emergence of a charismatic leader – although in Hitler's case, instead of leading a subgroup, he took over the host group, completely displacing the old guard, and then proceeded to mastermind the split in German society between the Aryans and the Jews. Having stigmatized the Jews as 'subhuman', he expelled those who could leave and exterminated those who could not, while leading his own people off into the Promised Land of the East. This demonstrates the power of liminoid symbolism arising from the unconscious of a charismatic leader to inspire his people to collective action with incalculable consequences.

HOW NEW SYMBOLIC CANONS DEVELOP

We are now in a position to adapt Figure 1 on p. 58 to illustrate how in ancestral societies 'borderline' personalities in the liminoid state could facilitate the formation of a daughter group from the parent group, with the production of new religious, mythological, ritual, and symbolic variations on ancient archetypal themes.

Each group codifies its social organization within a religious envelope which may be conceived as consisting of two layers, which we may call the transcendent and the sacred, both of which are experienced as being placed in a realm beyond that of ordinary mundane existence (Figure 2).

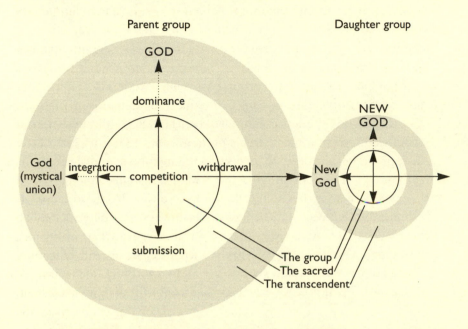

Figure 2 Group splitting: the religious dimension

The transcendent layer represents the abode of God (or the gods and goddesses). Members of the parent group relate symbolically to this transcendent figure (or figures) through the traditionally established symbols and rituals, which are believed to have been the result of the hierophany *in illo tempore*. This symbolic relationship may occur along both the vertical (agonic) or horizontal (hedonic) axis. On the vertical axis, God is experienced as being at the peak of the hierarchy, while His faithful followers declare their total submission to His will towards the lower end of the hierarchy (the officials of the religion, the archbishops, bishops, priests, mullahs, and rabbis, as well as kings, nobles, and generals, enjoy somewhat higher status – but experience themselves nevertheless as subordinate to God). On the horizontal axis, God is experienced as a figure with whom it is possible to form close bonds of affiliation culminating in a sense of mystical union, or from whom one may become alienated and feel impelled to withdraw in order to seek a substitute elsewhere.

The sacred layer is intermediate between the transcendent and the mundane: it represents the moral values, religious beliefs, numinous symbols, and sacred rituals which sanctify the structure, life, and identity of the group, and provide it with its means of communication with the transcendent figure(s).

When membership of the group passes beyond the critical size that the resources of the group can maintain, a charismatic or liminoid individual (who experiences himself as being on the borderline between membership and non-membership of the group) will begin to articulate the fears and aspirations of its disaffected members, and through his mythopoietic fantasies provide them with a vision of the salvation that awaits them if they will follow him into the 'Promised Land'. If his initiative succeeds and he and his followers are able to establish themselves in a new territory geographically separated from the old, the leader's schizotypal 'gifts' – his hallucinatory voices and delusional convictions, ecstatic mood swings, verbal pyrotechnics, and inventive neologisms – will promote the establishment of a new group which,

if it survives, will create a new language, a new culture, and a new religion with its associated dogmas, symbols, and sacred rituals which will endure until the size of the group again reaches critical dimensions, when the process of splitting and new group formation under a new charismatic leader will recur. The new myths and symbols which emerge will be sets of variations on the archetypal themes described in the sections of the explanatory Thesaurus which follows.

PART II

THE EXPLANATORY THESAURUS

The Explanatory Thesaurus

This Thesaurus is a compendium of common symbols which are amplified in terms of their archetypal significance. No such treasury can ever hope to be exhaustive, since the variety of symbols arising in dreams, religions, and works of art is infinite. Nor does this Thesaurus offer a form of 'dream book' where ready-made meanings to symbols can be looked up. Our imagination makes use of common symbols, it is true, but these must always be examined within the context of the life of the person producing them. A knowledge of common symbols may assist one to relate better to one's dreams, for example, but can never deputize for the work involved in befriending them. For possible ways of achieving this, the reader may refer to Chapters 8 and 9 of my book, *Private Myths: Dreams and Dreaming* (1996). To live the symbolic life is to adopt an open, undogmatic state of mind, receptive to hints of metaphor and analogy. Nothing should be taken literally, 'for the letter killeth, but the spirit giveth life' (2 Corinthians 3:6). The symbolic life is about gaining access to the liminoid state in oneself, and it should always be treated with the respect it deserves.

As has already been seen in Part I, we can derive some idea of the meanings attributed to common symbols by studying their manifestations in the myths, fairy tales, religions, and the arts of peoples living all over the world, not only at the present time but, more importantly, in the past. The extraordinary degree of similarity between these symbolic manifestations and the agreement about what they signify across history and across the planet points to their archetypal roots in the phylogenetic psyche (the collective unconscious) of humanity. Common symbols are listed, described, and amplified under four categories:

1 The Physical Environment
2 Culture and Psyche
3 People, Animals and Plants
4 The Body

Each section is broken up into a number of descriptive subsections in which individual symbols are examined in detail. In order to investigate the psychological implications of a certain symbol, the reader should first consult the Symbol Index, then look up the pages and read the sections in which the symbol is discussed.

SECTION I

THE PHYSICAL ENVIRONMENT

I

The Physical Environment

In the introduction to his classic text *A Dictionary of Symbols* (1971), J. E. Cirlot describes the symbolic implications of environmental objects in a way that cannot be bettered: 'All natural and cultural objects may be invested with a symbolic function which emphasizes their essential qualities in such a way that they lend themselves to spiritual interpretation. So, for example, rocks, mountains and all topographical features; trees and vegetables, flowers and fruit, animals, works of architecture and the utilities, the members of the body and the four elements. But it should be remembered that this catalogue of objects becomes much shorter when the objects become possessed of certain symbolic potentials, when they are strung together, as it were, along one line of meaning. For example, within the symbolism of levels and of the relation between heaven and earth, the mountain, the tree, the temple and steps can often be equated. On occasions, such a relationship appears to be created by, or at least to bear the imprint of, one principal symbol.'

Because of our primordial animism, which persists in the unconscious – as is evidenced by our dreams – we attribute psychological value, power, and meaning to all these natural objects. 'It is not the world as we know it that speaks out of [the] unconscious,' wrote Jung, 'but the unknown world of the psyche, of which we know that it mirrors our empirical world only in part, and that, for the other part, it moulds this empirical world in accordance with its own psychic assumptions. The archetype does not proceed from physical facts, but describes how the psyche experiences the physical fact, and in so doing the psyche often behaves so autocratically that it denies tangible reality or makes statements that fly in the face of it' (*CW* 9, para. 260).

Isaiah Berlin (1980) has argued that speech was predominantly metaphorical before it became abstract or metanymic, pointing out that this is still apparent in the *Iliad*: 'Ploughs actually appeared to have teeth; rivers, which for them were semi-animate, had mouths; land was endowed with necks and tongues, metals and minerals with veins, the earth had bowels, oaks had hearts, skies smiled and frowned, winds raged, the whole of nature was alive and active.' Australian Aborigines traditionally believed that their spirits inhabited the trees and rocks around them, and that when they moved from one place to another that they actually left parts of themselves behind.

The way in which a place, a stone, or a tree becomes sacred provides clear insights into the process of symbol formation. The object becomes sacred, as we saw in Chapter 6, when it is singled out by a hierophany (an event causing arousal, the orientation response, and the constellation of an archetype), which reveals it to possess a reality and a power greater than itself. 'No tree,' says Eliade (1958), 'was ever adored for itself only, but always for what was revealed through it, for what it implied and signified.'

A natural object, such as a tree, becomes a sacred symbol through the intervention of the three principles described in Chapter 4:

(1) **The principle of resemblance** whereby the range of meanings implied by the symbol are recognized as existing in the object symbolizing them: 'If the tree is charged with sacred forces, it is because it is vertical, it grows, it loses its leaves and regains them and is thus regenerated (it "dies" and "rises" again) time without number' (Eliade, 1958). As Samuel Taylor Coleridge put it: 'A symbol partakes of the reality which it renders intelligible.'

(2) **Condensation** whereby the same tree becomes a symbol of life, of resurrection, of the cosmos, the centre of the world, and the support of the universe. All these meanings are packed into one special tree, which is perceived as sacred.

(3) **The microcosmic principle** through which the whole is recognized as existing in each of its parts – that is, life, resurrection, and the cosmos are not merely *represented by* the tree: they *exist in* the tree. The symbolism of the centre comes into its own here, for the centre is that microcosmic point in which the macrocosm is concentrated. This is the essence of all sacred phenomena. The tree–stone–

altar, which occurs early in the emergence of religious life, is an example of this: a whole landscape becomes implicit in a sacred clearing, where there stands a triptych of tree, altar, and stone. Such a sacred place reproduces the landscape in microcosm: it is the sacred embodiment of the quintessence of the whole.

i Landscape

Landscape is often experienced as more numinous in dreams than in waking reality for in dreams we seem to get closer to what Jung called the 'natural mind', the 'two-million-year-old human being in us all'. The intense emotions released by dream landscapes are commonly associated with the seasonal changes which betoken fertility, ripeness, or death, and these powerfully charged images lend weight to the argument that theologies, mythologies, and rituals are extensions of dreams. It is as if we identify our symbolic life with the same creative and destructive processes that we observe outside ourselves in nature. This would help to explain why peoples all over the world have performed religious rites designed to ensure that the crops grow and the sun rises, while ignoring the truth that the crops would continue to grow and the sun would continue to rise whether they did these rituals or not.

Much of our knowledge of landscape symbolism is now empirically based, since there has been a growing research interest in the adaptive significance of human responses to the physical environment. Studies of picture preferences among people from widely differing backgrounds, for example, have confirmed not only that natural as opposed to man-made environments are consistently preferred (Kaplan, 1992) but also that savannah-like landscapes are liked better than all others, particularly by young children (Balling and Falk, 1982). On the whole, people prefer environments that have large trees, semi-open spaces, hills and valleys, streams, rivers, lakes, and estuaries, and a distant view of the horizon. They also like there to be an element of ambiguity or mystery which invites further exploration – for example, roads or paths that lead out of sight round hills, or the representation of partially blocked views which hint at interesting but hidden possibilities. All such research findings indicate that parallels exist between what people prefer and the environmental circumstances in which humans evolved. It seems increasingly likely that our aesthetic responses to landscape have been derived, at least in part, from evolved propensities that functioned to help hunter-gatherers make such crucial decisions as when to give up one location and move on to another, where to settle and what kind of places to avoid (Orians and Heerwagen, 1992).

Environmental adaptation depends on the perception of natural cues, the recognition of their significance, and the capacity to react appropriately when their significance has been recognized. This is as true of humans as of any other animal. We assess things in terms of their significance for us and the behavioural opportunities they provide according to the motivational or psychological state we happen to be in at the time. A tree is not just a tree but something one can climb if one is in need of a vantage point from which to view the land ahead or if one is in need of a refuge from a hostile stranger or a predator. A river will provide water if we are thirsty, fish if we are hungry, and a means of washing if we are dirty; the same river will present an obstacle if we wish to cross it, and a means of transport if there is no road. Like any object capable of becoming a symbol, a tree can convey many meanings: it is polyvalent. A tree which appears to provide a refuge may also become a symbol of danger if it hides a poisonous snake or a man with a spear.

Clearly, habitat selection is of profound significance for the survival and reproductive success of every organism, and, in our own case, our perceptual, cognitive, emotional, and behavioural responses to environmental cues have been under powerful selection pressure for hundreds of thousands of years. While the survival requirements of contemporary human beings differ in many ways from those of our ancestors, the story has not changed all that dramatically. We still have to orientate ourselves to the physical environment, obey the archetypal imperative to explore our surroundings and construct inner cognitive maps; we have to assess lurking threats and dangers as well as to locate promising resources, and afterwards we have to find our way safely home again. Indeed, many of the phobias from which our contemporaries suffer (agoraphobia, arachnophobia, acrophobia, claustrophobia, etc.) are exaggerated responses to environmental cues that signalled actual danger in the surroundings in which we evolved (Stevens and Price, 1996). Biological sources of danger include potentially hostile strangers, spiders, snakes, predatory animals, heights, confined spaces from which there is no escape, parasites, poisonous foods, and so on. These dangers can, of course, be reduced by not venturing out into the environment (the strategy adopted by agoraphobics), but the price of such timidity is the forfeit of access to information and resources that enhance survival and reproductive success.

In their invaluable paper 'Evolved Responses to Landscapes' (1992) Gordon Orians and Judith Heerwagen suggest that, when on the move, our hunter-gatherer ancestors selected suitable habitats in three stages:

Stage 1: Assessment of a new and unfamiliar landscape, which occurs rapidly: the responses are strongly emotional and based on innate propensities as well as previous experience.

Stage 2: If the response to Stage 1 is positive, then the environment is explored to assess its resource potential. Here again, evolved responses guide investigation and focus attention on those aspects of the habitat which are relevant to survival and reproductive success.

Stage 3: The decision is taken whether to settle in the environment or to move on.

All these stages are influenced by factors additional to the landscape *per se* – for example, by weather changes, the presence of predators, prey or enemies, the possibility of finding a mate, etc. There are good biological reasons why behavioural response patterns should have evolved to guide these decisions. As Orians and Heerwagen point out, time is important, and automatic responses leave the brain free to focus on those aspects of behaviour that urgently require attention. Thus, an open environment, devoid of protective cover, is perceived as undesirable, as is a dense forest within which movement and visual surveillance are difficult. Both such environments can be inhabited by people, but they require more extensive experience and learning for their inhabitants to survive in them.

Personal experience as well as objective research indicates that landscape and weather are invariably interlinked in aesthetic responses, and this would account for the close attention given by artists to the sky as well as the morphology of the terrain in landscape painting. Light intensities indicating weather fluctuations and changes in the time of day and alterations in cloud patterns are cues that trigger emotional responses in us all. Landscape painters became expert in manipulating these cues from Claude Lorrain (1600–1682) onwards. John Constable's particular gift, for example, was capturing sudden changes in the weather: as a result, he is a painter especially close to English hearts.

Seasonal changes also carry powerful symbolic overtones: the germination and sprouting of seeds, buds, and the sudden appearance of new leaves, the greening and browning of grass, the golds and reds of deciduous trees in autumn – all evoke emotional responses in us and all signify changes in resource availability.

One fascinating application of evolutionary theory is that of Jay Appleton (1990) in his aesthetic analysis of landscape painting. Appleton employs three categories which he calls *prospect* (the visual information provided about the landscape in view), *refuge* (the availability of cover, shelter, or protection), and *hazard* (the possibility of threat or menace which prompts evasive action such as hiding or escaping, or aggressive behaviour designed to eliminate the danger). Generally, people prefer places that enable them to see without being seen, namely, spaces with overhead cover, protection at the rear and on the flanks. Part of the appeal of landscape painting lies in its frame, since it grants the illusion that one is viewing the landscape from a refuge. Different pictures, like different dreams, evoke different stages of the habitat-selection process. For example, landscapes that encourage exploration by providing a sense of security and suggesting the presence of abundant resources evoke Stage 2 while pictures that draw one into the landscape, inducing feelings of peace and pleasure, evoke Stage 3.

We are, says Appleton, an exploratory animal with a need to discover where things are and to decipher the symbolic information they have to convey. In orientating ourselves to a landscape, the horizontal and vertical coordinates are crucial. A picture which draws us into it raises questions in our minds about what lies beyond the horizon. 'The capacity to anticipate what we have not yet attained is a fundamental part of successful behaviour.' A creature needs to be able to predict what may happen in a situation it has not yet encountered on the basis of its experience of preceding events and this is one adaptive function that dream symbolism has come to perform (Stevens, 1996).

Vertical projections from the horizontal – for example, mountain peaks, steeples, and pyramids – carry the eye upwards to the top. Such eminences, Appleton remarks, have strategic as well as aesthetic significance. As Gordon Orians points out, cliffs and bluffs attract us more than flat plains and fill us with the desire to scale them, even in contemporary circumstances when we are well fed and un-threatened, and when our exertions to get to the top will grant us no advantages in terms of detecting game or enemies. People travel from all over the world to climb the Eiffel Tower in Paris, the Monument in London, the spire of St Stephen's Cathedral in Vienna, and the Empire State Building in New York. All they get in return is the prospect, the view.

Natural hazards have also been exploited by landscape painters in order to thrill the public. The canvases of Turner and John Martin, for example, are replete with mountain precipices, tumultuous waves, lightning, threatening clouds, landslides, and barren immensities of space – each capable, in natural circumstances, of meeting Eliade's definition of a kratophany.

Individual features of a landscape which carry special symbolic significance are presented in the rest of this section. They are caves, deserts, forests, hills, the horizon, lakes, the land, light, metals, mountains, rivers, savannahs, the sea, stones, and valleys.

Cave A symbol of venerable antiquity, linked to the general symbolism of containment, enclosure, and concealment, the cave also participates in the symbolism of Mother Earth, the entrance and exit to the Maternal Womb as well as to the unconscious, the dark place beyond consciousness, the Underworld, Hades, Hell (the German word for cave, *Höhle* is related to *Holle*, Hell). The cave is thus a paradoxical symbol relating both to the realm of life (the womb) and death (the Underworld). For this reason, caves have commonly been regarded as sacred and as places for initiation. They were revered as the birthplace of gods and heroes, as well as dwellings of the spirits of the dead. Mithras, who was 'born from a rock', was worshipped in churches deliberately constructed to resemble caves. In Orthodox iconography, the birth of Christ is represented in a cave, as is His resting place after the Crucifixion and before His descent into Hell in preparation for His ascension into Heaven. In Amerindian creation myths, such as those of the Zuni and the Hopi, the original men and women were created and brought to birth in the bowels of the earth and climbed up to the daylight, emerging through a cave.

Although we cannot be certain, it seems highly probable that the caves so beautifully decorated by palaeolithic artists between 30,000 and 10,000 years ago were sacred shrines of some kind. These masterpieces owe the very fact of their survival to their inaccessibility: it required a dangerous and frightening pilgrimage to get to them. Unlike other undecorated palaeolithic caves, no animal remains have been found in them, which proves that people did not live and eat there. As Richard Leakey (1981) has shrewdly commented, it is unlikely that palaeolithic people made this hazardous journey into the bowels of the earth merely to exercise their artistic skills. Several of these caves, such as those at Montespan and Le Tuc, have rivers running through them, and, as we shall see, people everywhere have attributed spiritual powers to springs, streams, rivers, and lakes. The famous image of the 'Sorcerer of Trois Frères' would also lend weight to the idea that cave art afforded a ritual means of relating to the 'animal powers' (*see also* pp. 167 and 299). Robin Fox (1989) goes so far as to compare the ceremonial complex at Lascaux 'with its great halls, tunnels and side chapels, its crypts and vestries' to the cathedrals of Notre Dame in Chartres and Paris. What are these vast Gothic edifices, he asks rhetorically, but 'huge, dimly lighted caves erected above ground, with crypts, tunnels, side chapels and wall decorations; erected at huge expense of money, time and labour, and more often than not to honour the Great Mother – Notre Dame – who is Nature?'

Being a place of dread and darkness, the cave has a terrifying quality as the fearful abyss where monsters dwell. It is the dangerous home of miners, of serpents, and of gnomes who guard buried treasure there. Plato described the lot of ignorant, uneducated men as like living in a cave, their legs and necks fettered from childhood, so that they can only look at the cave wall before them, their fetters preventing them from turning their heads. All they can see are images flickering on the wall, cast as shadows by the light coming from the cave entrance behind them. The only escape is through meditation and ascent to the seat of the intellect to contemplate the real world of ideas. The notion of ascent from the depths as the ultimate goal is again apparent in this symbolism.

The symbolism of the cave is commonly associated with that of the **mountain**. Indian rock temples are hollowed out of mountainsides and contain a stupa and a cella. According to Thai legend, the waters of the world pour into a cavern at the foot of the Cosmic Mountain and emerge from its peak to form the Celestial River. This cavern is penetrated by the World Axis which runs down the centre of the mountain. In temples where the cella contains a lingam it is erected directly on the vertical of the World Axis. Similarly, the omphalos, the navel of the earth, at Delphi is directly above the tomb of the serpent, Python, and over the chasm down which the waters of Deucalion's flood had poured. At Teotihuacan in Mexico, the Pyramid of the Sun (built about 100 BC and destroyed about AD 750) was constructed over a subterranean cave which had the shape of a four-petalled flower, indicating the four cardinal points. The peak of the pyramid was directly above the centre of the cave.

Clouds These are considered under **Celestial Bodies**, p. 140.

Desert A symbol comprising both negative and positive implications: it is a place of temptation by demons (e.g. of Christ and St Anthony) but also a place in which God may appear with numinous intensity (e.g. the column of fire and cloud with which God led the Israelites through the desert). It is, therefore, a place where one may suffer abandonment and separation from God or special union with Him. The desert without God is barrenness, futility, sterility, despair; with God it is fruitfulness, hope, completion, grace. The scorching dryness of the desert, baked by the golden sun, and parched of all moisture and corruption, carries connotations of moral purity and holiness. To counter the agrarian religions based on fertility rites and orgies, the Biblical prophets stressed theirs as the purest religion revealed to the Israelites when they were in the wilderness. The desert is a world of abstraction and aesthetic contemplation far removed from the profane world of venal existence, and, for this reason, it is close to God; and monotheism is the 'religion of the desert' (Cirlot).

Forest Because it is dark, mysterious, and often impenetrable, the forest is a place readily filled with unconscious projections. For many different peoples, it has been a frightening though sacred realm inhabited by gods, spirits, monsters, demons, wild men, witches, fairies, wood nymphs, giants, pygmies, and gnomes. Like the desert, it is removed from profane reality, a place beyond civilization and unsusceptible to control, a law unto itself, a refuge for outlaws, and a retreat for hermits and *sānnyasin*. Its timeless quality makes the forest a place for events occurring *in illo tempore* and in fairy tales ('Once upon a time . . .'). Jung wrote: 'As at the beginning of many dreams something is said about the scene of the dream action, so the fairytale mentions the forest as the place of the magic happening. The forest, dark and impenetrable to the eye, like deep water and the sea, is the container of the unknown and the mysterious. It is an appropriate synonym for the unconscious . . . Trees, like fishes in the water, represent the living contents of the unconscious' (CW13, para. 241).

The forest is a common place of exile. Snow White escapes to the forest from the wicked queen. Rama, the hero of the Indian epic Ramayana, is banished to the jungle by his father, King Dasaratha. Parsifal grows up in the forest with his mother, who has retreated there from the evil influences of civilization. In all such tales, the period of exile appears to be a necessary phase in the hero's or heroine's individuation. Having retreated to the forest and achieved some crucial degree of self-awareness there, they return to the world to achieve fulfilment of their destiny.

Hill A muted form of the mountain symbol.

Horizon Both the limit and the extent of one's point of view; thus a metaphor of consciousness: the higher one's standpoint, the wider one's horizons, the more elevated and extensive one's degree of consciousness. In practical terms, the horizon always acts as a magnet to the eye and a stimulus to the imagination: it encourages one to explore and to fantasize what lies beyond it. Hence the attraction of hills, mountains, and tall trees, which provide vantage points from which the full extent of the landscape can be surveyed. Clear light and the absence of haze enable one to see further and with greater clarity and, therefore, also carry connotations for consciousness. From the desire to explore and extend horizons comes the desire for learning, migration, adventure, and tourism.

Lake More than the sea, the lake provides a mirror for self-reflection and self-consciousness: while its depths, when one can see through the surface of the mirror, are identified with projected unconscious components and fantasies. Thus, water in lakes alludes to the 'connection between the superficial and the profound' (Cirlot). The belief that the Land of the Dead is at the bottom of a lake or a sea (e.g. among Celts, such as the Irish and the Bretons) may be derived from watching the sun set over water and from the association of death with the setting of the sun. In many traditions, lakes are the abode of gods, nymphs, monsters, witches, and sirens, who lure humans to their deaths. Lakes can also symbolize the Earth's eye, through which those in the Underworld may observe the activities of those of us fortunate enough still to live above.

Land Land is of great emotional and symbolic significance: human beings become profoundly attached to it, especially their homeland, or land to which they possess a legal entitlement. In this sense, we are territorial species. Such behaviour has an immensely long evolutionary history, for territorial species have existed on this planet for over 300 million years, ever since reptiles began battling for possession of a patch of land (ritual agonistic behaviour or RAB). Not all human beings display territorial behaviour, of course, just as not all women give birth to babies or all men go to war, but the potentiality for such behaviour is present in us all: it depends on circumstances prevailing at the time whether or not it is activated in us.

To possess a piece of land, however small, grants status, self-esteem, and security, as well as food, a site for a home, and a tangible link between oneself, one's ancestors, and one's progeny. It is understandable, therefore, that land has been regarded as sacred and has excited veneration for earth goddesses such as Gaia, Mother Earth. It is this passionate attachment to the land that makes people ready to die rather than give it up. The kulaks died in their millions rather than give up their land to the Soviet commissars. Soldiers invariably fight with more bitter dedication and ruthlessness when fighting over their own land rather than other people's.

The Holy Land, Promised Land, Land of the Blessed, Earthly Paradise, Pure Land, all refer to the sacred land which each tradition regards as the centre of the earth, granted to the people by divine decree *in illo tempore*. 'A sacred place is what it is because of the permanent nature of the hierophany that first consecrated it,' wrote Lévy-Bruhl (quoted by Eliade, 1958). Pilgrimages to such holy plots produce spiritual regeneration, a return to the taproot of one's people.

Light Studies of the orientation response have demonstrated that people respond acutely to changes in stimulus intensity, and this explains why changes in brightness of light, which indicate weather fluctuations or changes in the time of day, excite emotional responses in us all. By association, these come to assume symbolic significance, so that dawn and dusk, which share similar light intensities, carry different symbolic connotations (e.g. beginning and ending, youth and age). Stark contrasts, as between daylight and darkness, noon and midnight, evoke more powerful symbolic meanings, and these are discussed in **Celestial Bodies**, pp. 134–45.

Metal The presence of metal deposits in a landscape did not become of significance to our ancestors until they discovered smelting. The invention of the furnace made it possible to harden the metal by bringing it to white heat. Only then did metallurgy and its associated symbolism come to assume importance for the human imagination. The miraculous ability to change the modality of matter through the application of knowledge and heat meant that people could embark on a quasi-religious endeavour to achieve its transmutation into something perfect. To these archaic artisans, minerals were imbued with the sacredness of Mother Earth, and their transformation into weapons and tools carried religious as well as obstetric implications. Ores were thought to be conceived in the belly of Mother Earth and grew there like embryos. Miners and metal workers were the midwives who collaborated with Nature in bringing the precious ores to birth (Eliade, 1971). As with the alchemists who followed, matter held a numinous intensity for them, and both metallurgy and alchemy stand as allegories of the symbol-forming process.

Through the mixture of 'male' and 'female' ores, smelting was itself conceived as a sacred sexual union, and the fire which caused their fusion to occur was symbolically equated with the sexual impulse. By extension, this notion led to the further symbolic idea of the furnace itself as a womb in which the hardened and purified metal was brought to birth.

The mine from which the ore was extracted was also a sacred precinct which it was taboo to enter without preliminary ablutions, purification rituals, fasting, meditation, and prayers; for the mine was an awesome subterranean world ruled by the spirits responsible for regulating the mysteries of mineral gestation in the womb of the Great Mother. This numinous underworld of tunnels, caves, and rivers was a sanctuary, like the caves which enshrine the stupendous images of palaeolithic art.

Mountain This belongs beyond all doubt to the symbolism of levels as: a means of ascent to a higher level spiritually, morally, socially, or consciously; a bridge between Heaven and Earth; a marker of the navel or the centre of the world; and the *axis mundi*, which integrates all three of the above associations.

As indicated in Chapter 5, 'height' possesses its own hierophantic power. The mountain peak is the nearest one can get to the sky god and practically every mythology has its sacred mountain. Invariably, they form the central point in the cosmos where Earth and Heaven meet. Mount Olympus and Mount Zion are the examples best known to us. In the Norse Edda, Himingbjorg (Celestial Mountain) provides the peak from which the rainbow Bifrost touches the dome of Heaven. Cosmic mountains also exist in China and India, as well as in pre-Columbian America in the form of Mayan temple pyramids – which were not tombs as in Egypt, but true temples like the ziggurats of Mesopotamia. In all such instances, the Cosmic Mountain is not merely the dwelling-place of the gods but also the navel of the world, the centre from which all life emanated.

The central role of the mountain as linking Heaven and Earth is evident in Japanese as well as Sumerian creation myths. Japanese hanging scrolls depict Mount Fuji as at the centre of the cosmos, uniting all the elements. To create the mountain, the earth rises from the waters through the air to the sky, realm of the moon and the fiery sun. Since ascent is the quintessential symbol of transcendence, to climb the mountain is to go through the ritual stages of ascent to the goal of enlightenment.

Parallel symbolism is manifested in the architecture of Hindu temples sacred to Shiva (e.g., the Khandariya Mahadeva Temple at Chandella in India) which resemble the rising peaks of a range of mountains. The highest tower is placed directly over the central shrine or 'womb chamber', representing Shakti (the divine feminine energy of God), which contains the Lingam (the erect phallus of Shiva), the creative principle at the centre of the universe, identical with the *axis mundi*. The Lingam is approached in three stages through ritual circumambulations. To achieve the highest goal of release from the endless cycle of the transmigration of souls, it is necessary to experience *moksa* (a Sanskrit word meaning liberation), a spiritual ascent up the *axis mundi* into a state of perfect freedom (Moon, 1991).

The famous Ziggurat at Ur represented the primordial mountain that existed before creation and which had arisen out of the great primeval sea. It was sacred to the Sumerian moon god Nanna, father of Inanna, goddess of love and war. In the Sumerian creation myth, the Cosmic Mountain which rose out of the primordial seas was made up of Heaven and Earth before they were separated. Their union produced Enlil, god of the air, who separated his parents, pushing his father up into the sky. He then begat Nanna, and, together with his mother Ki (Earth Mother), Enlil proceeded to create order, people, and civilization. In the Ziggurat, an architectural ladder leads from Earth to Heaven and is surmounted by a shrine at its pinnacle. The four corners of the Ziggurat are set at the cardinal points.

The Sumerian word 'ziggurat' literally means pinnacle. The Ur Ziggurat was Nanna's dwelling place on earth, and the city was ruled by Nanna's deputy, the High Priest. Similarly, Mount Zion in Jerusalem was God's home, where he lived among his people. Some of the earliest mountain-top sanctuaries were, in fact, Minoan (e.g. Mount Ida, Mount Dikte, and Mount Juktas in Crete), but Zeus himself, of course, preferred to live on Mount Olympus.

River Self-evidently, rivers share in the general symbolism of water. Because of their critical significance for siting human habitations, for the practice of agriculture, the provision of nourishment (fish), and a means of transport (on rafts, coracles, and ships), rivers have been regarded as sacred and worshipped as deities, particularly as masculine river gods who fertilize the lands through which they pass. The confluence of rivers into the sea symbolizes the union of the individual with the absolute (e.g. in Hinduism and Buddhism), while the course of the river, from its origin in a spring, its development into brook, stream, and river, and its final discharge into the ocean, is an evocative symbol of human life and death. The river is also an obstacle to migration, something that has to be bridged or forded to reach the opposite bank. It is also a formidable territorial boundary, separating one tribe or community from another. This division permits shadow projection to occur, so that each community attributes evil designs to the other. Jung liked the story of a visitor to a Swiss canton who discovered two peasants fighting on a river bank. When the visitor asked one of the protagonists why he was fighting, he replied, with patient logic, 'Because he's from the other side of the river.'

The river, as a symbol of life, fertilizes the imagination of scientists no less than poets and priests: 'The river of DNA,' says Richard

Dawkins, 'has been flowing through our ancestors in an unbroken line that spans not less than three thousand million years' (*River out of Eden*, 1995). The significance of specific rivers, such as the Styx, the Nile, or the Four Rivers of Eden, is discussed elsewhere (*see* Symbol Index).

Savannah The primordial landscape of our kind and, consequently, the sort of environment in which we feel most at home. Biomass and the availability of meat are much higher in savannahs than, for example, in forests, and, as a result, they provide an attractive environment for large terrestrial, omnivorous primates like ourselves. Savannahs provide distant views, grassy ground cover favourable to nomadic life, trees which offer protection from the sun and refuge from predators, and plentiful sources of food. These facts are in line with experimental findings that habitats resembling the African savannah (in which we evolved) induce positive aesthetic responses in people. Water is one resource that is relatively scarce in this environment and this could explain the great sensitivity of people worldwide to water symbolism (Orians and Heerwagen, 1992).

One fascinating experimental finding is that participants in experiments on landscape preferences were usually unable to explain or justify the choices that they made; yet they made them readily and with conviction, providing results which were regular, repeatable, and predictable. 'When questioning participants about the bases of their preferences,' reports Kaplan (1992), 'we have found that they are usually quite unaware of the variables that proved so effective in predicting what they would prefer . . . Perhaps there is an evolved bias in humans favouring preference for certain kinds of environments, just as there is an evolved bias favouring reproductive activities. In the case of sexual behaviour we do not expect people to be able to explain their inclinations on adaptive grounds, although such inclinations must ultimately derive from an adaptive basis.'

Further evidence for the savannah hypothesis came from a study by Orians (1985) of tree forms preferred by Japanese gardeners. Orians found that both selection and pruning practices favoured the shapes characteristic of trees in the savannah.

Sea or **Ocean** As in English, *thalassa and okeanos* were used inter-changeably in Greek, though *okeanos* was reserved for the sea that was believed to encircle the known world. This might help to explain why Americans tend to use 'ocean' (because their land is bounded by the Pacific and the Atlantic), where the British prefer 'sea' (their shores being washed by more domestic waters: the Irish Sea, North Sea, and English Channel).

Because they are so vast in comparison with the puny human frame, seas and oceans symbolize the primal undifferentiated state, the mysterious immensity from which all things arose and to which all things will return. The sun rises from the ocean in the East, sets in the ocean in the West, and passes beneath the ocean to complete the night sea journey during the hours of darkness, to rise once more, triumphantly, in the East, *sol invictus*. 'The sun also ariseth, and the sun goeth down, and hasteth to his place where he arose' (Ecclesiastes 1:5).

Similarly, the waters rise into the heavens from the sea, fall in fertilizing rain on the hills and plains, collect in the valleys, and return in rivers whence they came. 'All the rivers run into the sea; yet the sea is not full; unto the place from whence the rivers come, thither they return again' (Ecclesiastes 1:7).

As the source of life, the sea is equated with the mother and the unconscious psyche. Unconscious components emerge as water creatures, such as fish, sea-monsters, mermaids, and mermen (e.g. Oannes, the Babylonian fish god). The association between sea and mother archetype is apparent not only in dreams but also in many languages: *mère, mer* (Fr.); *madre, mare* (It.). This association stresses the life-generating potential of the unconscious. Ancient cosmological conceptions of the sea as the source of life are echoed in the modern scientific view of the role played by the oceans early in the history of our planet as providing a 'primordial soup' in which molecules developed the capacity to replicate themselves and produce life.

Stone 'The stone is the archetypal image of absolute and indestructible reality' (Eliade, 1958). The widespread belief that the first men were born of stones links with the no less widespread belief that mineral ores are stones which gestate in the womb of Mother Earth. The numerous mythic accounts of gods being born from the *petra genitrix* are analogous to those of gods born from the Great Goddess, the *matrix mundi*. The stone parentage of the first men is a theme which recurs in the civilizations of Central America (Inca and Mayan), among the Semites, the Greeks, and from Asia Minor and the Caucasus as far as Oceania. The idea that stones can give birth to people may be linked to the observation that the frozen earth of winter gives birth to the flowers of spring, as well as to the apparently universal notion that stones are 'the bones of Mother Earth'. Not only does the latter idea occur among nomadic and hunting peoples from America through Asia to Oceana but also among the ancient Greeks. After the flood, for example, Deucalion and Pyrrha ask how they may repopulate the earth. Zeus advises them: 'Cover your heads and throw the bones of your mother behind you.' They understand this at once to mean stones. They do as Zeus says, and from the stones thrown by Deucalion men come into existence and from those thrown by Pyrrha, women.

Tall, standing, upright stones, columns, and pillars, while unmistakably phallic, also represent the *axis mundi* and the omphalos, and often embody the souls of ancestors. Whether they are Indian lingams, Egyptian Djed pillars, Greek herms, or Breton menhirs, the symbolism is broadly the same. This symbolism recurs in modern dreams, as in the first dream Jung (1963) could remember from his childhood of a phallic god in an underground chamber. Conical stones and cairns share in the same symbolism: one of Hermes' epithets was 'God of Stones', and was represented throughout Greece by heaps of stones. Stones heaped into cairns are also evocations of the central mountain, and together the integrated symbolism of the stone—mountain—tree links the noösphere, the biosphere, and the lithosphere – that is to say, the psychic, the organic, and the inorganic dimensions of existence. The broken stone or column symbolizes death.

Cubic stones signify perfect stability and are used as the foundation stone of sacred buildings. Such a stone may be conceived both as the centre of the earth and the supporter of the world, as it was at the Temple of Jerusalem. The Black Stone of the *Ka'aba* in Mecca is both cubic and an omphalos. It is also a prime example of a baetylic stone (a sacred meteorite), as was the Black Stone of Pessinus, the aniconic embodiment of the Phrygian Great Mother Goddess, which was brought to Rome in 204 BC, to be erected with great ceremony on the Palatine Hill. Baetylic stones, generally, denote a place of indwelling divinity, the sacred meeting place between Heaven and Earth. They may also possess the power of prophecy as 'speaking stones' from which comes the voice of a divine oracle, the best known example being the omphalos at Delphi.

The alchemists regarded the common stone from which the Philosopher's Stone was to be created as the *prima materia* in which slept the spirit of Mercurius, the round square, the homunculus, Tom Thumb, and the Anthropos, all in one. The key-stone of an arch, which ensures its lasting stability, symbolizes the completion and crowning of a work. It is also a symbol of Christ: 'the stone which the builders rejected is become the head of the corner' (Psalm 118).

Stones have always performed an important role in initiation and healing rites, as when passing through the hole in a rock in a simulation of birth or when women rub themselves up against a standing stone as a cure for barrenness.

Though the stone and the tree may share a common symbolism, as in the lingam or Djed pillar, they are, nevertheless, to be differentiated: the stone is an eternal symbol of static existence, while the tree is subject to the cycle of life and death and is a symbol of dynamic regeneration.

Valley Being the geophysical obverse of the hill or mountain, the valley carries the opposite connotations: instead of representing aspiration to the heights and the gods, it represents descent to the fertile realm of the Earth Goddess, where the waters of Heaven come together with the soil of the Earth to produce rich harvests to nourish animals and humanity.

ii The Psychic Compass

Early in the development of human consciousness, the psyche evidently acquired the propensity to orientate itself to the physical environment through a tetradic arrangement of paired opposites: above and below, North and South are paired opposites in the vertical plane; left and right, West and East are paired opposites in the horizontal plane; when assembled they make up the indispensable tetrads:

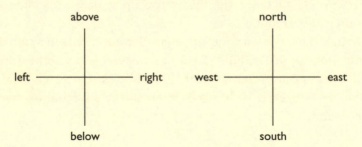

The point where the vertical and horizontal coordinates cross is the centre, where the conscious, orientating individual feels himself or herself to be. In a great many traditions, the centre is conceived as the dwelling place both of the gods and humankind, especially the original man, the Anthropos.

'The brain is a map-making device. It constructs from sensory inputs an internal virtual world, which we respond to as if it were the real one – a private, internal kind of symbolism. There is nothing unusual about this; it is what brains are for . . . Our ordinary cognitive map is organism-centred, its co-ordinates measured from the here-and-now of individual experience' (Knight, 1996).

We orientate ourselves in time in much the same way as we orientate in space. We experience ourselves from moment to moment as being here, now, in the present (in the centre), and we feel the past to be behind us and the future to lie ahead. Whatever is occurring synchronously with the present is felt to be proceeding in parallel beside us on the left and the right.

·It was Jung's empirical discovery that the psyche expresses itself as a complete entity of balanced oppositions through the spontaneous production of a circular and tetradic configuration known in Sanskrit as the **mandala**. This was a modern rediscovery of an extremely ancient and apparently universal propensity. The best known examples occur in Tantric art and in the rose windows of churches and cathedrals.

Everywhere the notion of wholeness seems to be satisfied by the representation of a quaternity, especially if the quaternity is integrated within a circle. Squaring the circle or circling the square is uniting the sacred and the profane, Heaven with Earth, the eternal with the here and now. In Chinese philosophy, the masculine Yang is represented by a white circle (Heaven) and the feminine Yin by a black square (Earth). The octagon, intermediate between square and circle, is represented by the *Ti-Te-Chi* surrounded by the eight trigrams of the *I Ching* within the circumference of a circle. In Greek Orthodox churches, the square, the cross, and the circle are combined in one sublime configuration to represent the union of all things in Heaven and Earth through the greatness of God.

Further division of the four quarters of the circle into twelve units has long provided the means of orientation to time, hence the twelve hours of the clock, twelve months of the year, and twelve signs of the zodiac. The great circular archetypal symbol of the **uroboros** (the snake eating its tail) represents the eternal cycles of self-propagation and auto-consumption which are inescapable features of organic existence on this planet.

The prevalence of the FOUR, the QUATERNITY, the tetrad, and the all-encompassing circle in organizing human thought and behaviour is everywhere apparent, and many instances occur in this Thesaurus. One example that has been of enormous influence in Western theorizing has been that devised by the Greek philosopher Empedocles in the fifth century BC. Empedocles taught that the whole world consisted of a tetrad of distinct elements – earth, air, fire, and water – which mixed and separated in accordance with the dictates of the ruling pair of archetypal opposites, Love and Strife. At about the same time, four primary qualities were defined – hot, cold, wet, and dry – which arrange themselves in a tetrad of paired oppositions, each identified with the four elements. Since fire was hot and dry, air hot and wet, water cold and wet, and earth cold and dry, it followed that fire and water formed a pair of opposites as did earth and air.

The four humours of Hippocrates – blood, phlegm, dark bile, and light bile – fitted in well with this scheme of things, it being affirmed by Galen in the second century AD that when the four elements were ingested into the body in the form of food and drink, they were transformed into the four humours by the heat of digestion.

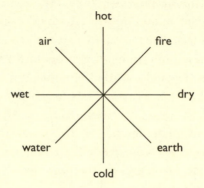

Already by Graeco-Roman times, many other tetradic concepts had developed round the CARDINAL POINTS of the compass: the four winds blowing from the four corners of the Earth, the zodiacal signs arranged in four groups of three (corresponding to the four seasons and the four ages of man), the four rivers of Paradise, the four Gospels, the four living creatures round the throne of God, the four Evangelists, the four cardinal virtues – bravery (*Fortitudo*), justice (*Justitia*), prudence (*Prudentia*), and temperance (*Temporantia*), the four generations of peoples (Adam to Noah, Noah to Abraham, Abraham to Moses, Moses to Christ), and so on. 'Matthew, Mark, Luke, and John, Bless the bed that I lie on; Four corners to my bed, Four angels round my head, One to watch and one to pray, And two to bear my soul away' – this used to be one of the best-known children's prayers.

Similar prayers beseeching all-round protection have existed since Babylonian times.

In Scandinavian mythology, four dwarfs, each named after one of the cardinal points, were responsible for holding up the sky. Throughout the Middle Ages it was usual to link the macrocosmic quaternities (the elements and seasons) with the microcosmic quaternities (the humours and ages of man), thus expressing the medieval conviction that man was a small world and the world a great man. One commentator, Remigius of Auxerre, who died in AD 908, summed it up by declaring: 'For just as the world is composed of four elements and four seasons, so man is composed of four humours and four seasons.'

These cosmological theories were incorporated in complex mandalas which were very popular: impressive examples were compiled by Isadore of Seville in his *Liber de Natura Rerum*, which came to be known as the *Book of Wheels*. The powerful approach of such configurations to the human psyche becomes apparent if one takes time to examine them. Excellent examples are provided by Elizabeth Sears in her book *The Ages of Man: Mediaeval Interpretations of the Life Cycle* (1986).

Jung has been attacked by his critics for displaying a mystical attachment to the number four, as if there existed no empirical grounds for seeing the quaternity as an archetypal configuration both in nature and the psyche. The notion of four entities as providing the basis of existence recurs again and again, not only in mythology, cosmology, religion, folk tales, and dreams, but in the course of evolution itself. As Jung says, with enviable good humour: 'In all these cases I am as little responsible for the number four as I am for all the other alchemical, Gnostic, and mythological quaternities. My critics seem to have the funny idea that I have a special liking for the number four and therefore find it everywhere . . . The number four, like the squaring of the circle, is not accidental, which is why – to take an example known even to my critics – there are not three or, for that matter, five directions but precisely four' (CW13, paras. 329–30).

Examples exist from the earliest times: of the ninety-two naturally occurring elements, only four are basic to the structure of all living organisms as the ancients supposed, although we now know that these are not earth, air, fire, and water, but hydrogen, oxygen, nitrogen, and carbon. When life began on this planet, the essential raw materials available on the earth's surface were again four in number: water, carbon dioxide, methane, and ammonia, which together made up the 'primordial soup' of the primitive seas (in which molecules began to replicate themselves to form the vital nucleic acids which provide the building blocks for living organisms).

In each cell of every organism there exists a highly specific blueprint composed of a further quaternary of substances, the nucleotides – adenine, thymine, cytosine, and guanine – which together make up the DNA of the genes. The genetic code, comments Richard Dawkins (1995), is not a binary code like a computer but a quaternary code comprising four basic symbols. DNA is a very long piece of text, written in a four-letter alphabet: 'The letters have been scrupulously copied from our ancestors with remarkable fidelity.' Combined in assorted pairs, these indispensable compounds compose the symbolic language through which matter communicates with matter in a perpetual renewal of the miracle we call life.

Our conscious discovery of the four cardinal points is a comparatively recent realization of a phylogenetically ancient navigational principle. Bees use the same points as a basis for a nectar-locating compass divided into eight quadrants, much like our own: N, NE, E, SE, S, SW, W, NW.

There is, therefore, something truly fundamental about the fourfold configuration in all biological phenomena and this would seem to be reflected in the archetypal structures basic to symbol formation in the human psyche, as this Thesaurus repeatedly demonstrates.

The Centre Numerous traditions attribute the origin of the cosmos to a central point (a navel) from which everything which exists spreads out in four cardinal directions. To place oneself at this centre is to be at the 'point of departure' and at the 'beginning of time'. Such ideas are the mythic precursors of the Big Bang theory. Accordingly, the cosmic perspective of religion invariably demands a centre, an **omphalos,** a privileged temenos where it is possible to contact the divine. The more threatening the surrounding environment, the more diabolical the times, the more crucial this divinely protected centre is felt to be. It is here that rituals must be performed, sacrifices made, prayers offered up, if catastrophe is to be averted and all is to remain well with the world.

All territorial species experience the centre of their territory as the place of maximum security. The further an animal moves from the centre towards the periphery, the less secure it appears to be. On the margin of the territory it is torn between the emotions of aggression and anxiety. The territorial proprietor is invincible if attacked on his own territory, particularly near the centre. In humans, agoraphobia (literally fear of the market place) is the fear of going off the home range into potentially hostile territory. The heroic quest for promised lands has inspired humans to overcome these fears in certain circumstances, but they can still operate very powerfully in phobic patients, keeping them securely imprisoned within the confines of their home.

The feeling that one's tribe is of central importance and that one's home and one's Self are at the centre of the universe is an illusion shared by all humanity. In ancient China, Shao Yung declared: 'I am happy because I am a human and not an animal; a male and not a female; a Chinese and not a barbarian; and because I live in Loyang, the most wonderful city in the world' (quoted by Sinclair, 1991).

Right and **Left**   The symbolism of sidedness is not as rich as the symbolism of levels, but it does, nevertheless, relate to religious, moral, and social issues in similar ways. This is apparent in the various meanings different languages attach to their words for right and left. For example, in English, right also means correct, to have justice on one's side. The French *droit* not only means right, but straight, untwisted, justice, and law; *gauche* means crooked, clumsy, awkward, uncouth, and ungainly as well as left. The Greek word for left, *aristerós*, similarly means clumsy as well as erring and crazy. The Latin word for left, *sinister*, is synonymous with dark and evil doings. In Russian, *na levo*, on the left, also means on the side or under the counter (i.e. black market dealings). This usage is clearly related to the phenomenon of handedness which depends on the cross-over of cerebral function, the left cerebral hemisphere controlling the right side of the body and the right hemisphere controlling the left; since in the great majority of people the left hemisphere is dominant, most of us are right-handed. The right side is our competent, effective side;

our left side is clumsy, awkward, *gauche*, and this has probably been the case since protohominid times.

This practical, cerebrally induced distinction between right and left has come to assume added symbolical impressions which hold good across a large number of cultures – so much so that they can be summarized in a table:

Table 1 Symbolic implications of left and right

LEFT	RIGHT
Moon	Sun
Feminine	Masculine
Night	Day
Winter	Summer
Unconscious	Conscious
Profane	Sacred
Death	Life
Illness	Health
Evil	Good
Hell	Heaven

These cross-cultural distinctions can be augmented by numerous specific examples. The alchemists associated the right with Mars and the King, the left with Venus and the Queen. In Islamic societies, and many others, the right hand is used for eating and making religious offerings while the left is reserved for cleaning the anus after defecation. In the Black Mass the sign of the cross was made with the left hand, and the first step towards the altar is taken with the left foot. There is an Islamic folk belief still current in Turkey that a recording angel sits on both shoulders: the angel on the right shoulder records one's good deeds, the angel on the left one's evil deeds. The Bagobo people of Malaysia believe that everyone has two souls, a good soul on the right and a bad soul on the left. The funeral custom of the Dogon is to bury men lying on their right side and women on their left. In Christian theology, Christ sits on the right hand of God and at Calvary it was the good thief who was crucified on Jesus's right. At the Last

Judgement the elect will turn to the right in the direction of Heaven, the damned will go to the left in the direction of Hell.

Mexican Compass Stone

iii The Four Elements

As we have noted in the previous subsection, the Greek division of the physical universe into the four 'elements', earth, air, fire, and water, associated with the four 'qualities', hot, cold, wet, and dry, corresponds to archetypal intuitions which are still active in us, although we no longer subscribe intellectually to the physical doctrines of Greek philosophy. The Greek humoral theory of disease may have developed from the Ayurvedic system of medicine, and it still influences the way in which doctors and patients converse with one another in the West, despite the large amount of medical information put out by the media. In a paper entitled 'Feed a Cold; Starve a Fever' (1978), Dr C. G. Helman reported that his mostly well-educated, middle-class patients described their symptoms in terms of the basic polarities hot and cold, dry and wet. Thus, wet conditions involved the production of fluid (phlegm, sputum, vomit, urine, diarrhoea), while hot and dry conditions were responsible for fever. Chills and colds, as their names imply, were due to the penetration of cold into the body. Night air was thought to be particularly dangerous.

The four elements and their symbols are still apparent in the dreams dreamt by modern dreamers. In view of the persistent relevance of this symbolism, therefore, each of the elements is examined in this subsection in terms of its universal symbolism and not in terms of the strict meanings applied to it by the Greeks. That the four-element theory should have arisen in the first place is not altogether surprising: our whole psychophysical organism presupposes an environment in which there is earth, air, and water. These are basic substances indispensable to life. The control of fire and the discovery of its transformative power in cooking and heating was the first blow against the oligarchy of the gods and the first step in the direction of technology and science.

Earth The supportive foundation of life, which we take for granted, like mother love, the community we are born into, its values, gods, and rituals. As a symbol of fundamental reality, the earth represents something that one comes down to or is brought down to: it is the basic representation of the way things are. As a result it is also a symbol of permanence: 'One generation passeth away, and another generation cometh: but the earth abideth for ever' (Ecclesiastes 1:4). In the vast majority of mythologies the earth is feminine and the sky masculine (Egyptian mythology is one of the few exceptions). In numerous cosmologies Heaven and Earth are the World Parents from which all life sprang. Originally, Father Sky lay so heavily on Mother Earth that no light could get between them, but they gave birth to a hero, who one day gave such an enormous shove to Father Sky that he flew up into the Heavens. Since then light has covered Mother Earth, who continues to perform her maternal duties. She is a symbol of birth, fertility, life, and regeneration, as well as a symbol of finality, the tomb of the Underworld to which we return at the end. The ancient burial practice of placing the dead in a foetal position stresses this dual function of the earth as both womb and tomb. As Job throws himself on the ground, he cries 'naked I came out of my mother's womb, and naked shall I return thither' (Job 1:21).

Before Isaac Newton announced his theory of gravity, it was impossible to imagine how the earth and the planets could exist in space and move about unless they were physically connected to one another. In the Western world picture, the universe was spherical, with the earth at the centre, surrounded by various heavens in concentric layers like an onion, each being named after a planet. The outermost sphere, or *archon*, was called Saturn. To the Chinese, the earth was square, presumably because it is bounded by the four points of the compass. The Chinese Empire was conceived of as a square, made up of smaller squares, with the Forbidden City at its centre. Similarly, the Chinese universe was a Great Square with a series of smaller squares contained within one another. Again, it is not hard to understand why the sphere, circle, and square have become symbols of wholeness, totality, and completeness.

The earth provides the means for human creativity. When mixed with water, the resulting clay can be moulded and then fired to create pottery, a basic artefact of all civilizations. When worked diligently and intelligently by man, the result is agriculture, permitting human transformation from the hunter-gatherer to the civilized state. The earth may be richly fertile when water is plentiful or a barren desert when it is absent. It is also the primal substance, the *prima materia*, of alchemy, the prototype of all physical sciences. Because of its caves, underworld demons and spirits, the earth is a potent symbol of the unconscious psyche. Often, in creation myths, the original man, the Anthropos, is formed out of earth, as is the case with Adam, whose name is derived from *adamah*, earth.

Earthquake Symbol of fundamental crisis and change.

Air The element symbolically linked with breath, wind, and the spirit. In Arabic, for example, the word *ruh* means both breath and spirit; the ancient Greeks associated the psyche with respiration and the diaphragm (hence, schizophrenia = split diaphragm). While earth is feminine and material, air is felt to be masculine as well as spiritual. To be 'up in the air' is the opposite of being 'down to earth'; **flying** in the air represents freedom, escape from the earth, from reality, and from mother; flying high in the air can also symbolize mania and hubris (the foolhardiness of Icarus). Dissolution into thin air, dematerialization, carries the idea of immortality, eternity, infinity.

WIND represents the creative spirit 'that bloweth where it listeth'. Winds feature in numerous creation myths; that winds are related to the cardinal points (the four winds blowing from the four corners of the earth), and also to the zodiac points to the cosmological significance they are felt to possess. 'The wind goeth toward the south, and turneth about unto the north; it whirleth about continually, and the wind returneth again according to his circuits' (Ecclesiastes 1:6). The WINGS necessary to fly in the air symbolize spirituality, imagination, thought, fantasy, and enlightenment. Both Love and Victory are winged figures, as are the angels of Christian iconography. The desire of men to emulate these figures by acquiring wings and the capacity to fly is a symbol of hubris inviting nemesis (Icarus again). The ability to levitate is a symbol of advanced spirituality.

Fire The Promethian capacity to control fire has been crucial to the final stages of our evolution as a species and our geographical spread into remote areas of the planet where it would not otherwise have been possible for a furless or hairless creature to live. Fire is dangerous, however, because it can get out of control and consume all that lies in its path, especially if it is driven by the wind (the dangerous combination of two 'elements', fire and air). That is why it is dangerous 'to play with fire' and why it is easy 'to get one's fingers burnt'. Human passions, particularly sex and fury, are exactly analogous to fire in this sense: one can be consumed by them and driven to irrational behaviour which may bring catastrophe to oneself or to others. One may be forewarned of such disasters in dreams of fire.

The tremendous discovery of how to kindle fire gave humanity an incalculable advantage over other animals. Not only did fire provide warmth, protection from predators, and illumination during the hours of darkness, but its transformative power enabled us to discover the arts of cooking, pottery, and forging metals (metallurgy). The symbolic implications of fire are thus enormous.

There is no evidence for domestic fire until about 250,000 years ago (such evidence is completely lacking in the Olduvai Gorge in Tanzania, the probable locus of our evolution). Before fire could be kindled at will, some member of the community, possibly an older woman, would have to have remained behind to tend a permanent fire while others went off on foraging expeditions. The HEARTH as symbol of home, mother, wife, must be very old.

The discovery of how to kindle fire would have liberated hunters to some extent from the need to remain close to home, for they could light their own fire and camp out overnight while on the hunt. This would have provided them with psychological as well as physical security, for, as a species, we have a primordial fear of the dark, which is still very apparent in our children. Jung reports that the Elgonyi people, whom he visited on the slopes of Mount Elgon in Kenya in the 1920s, were normally cheerful and optimistic during the day. 'Their optimistic mood was, however, always in abeyance between six o'clock in the evening and six o'clock in the morning, during which time it was replaced by fear, for in the night the dark being Ayik has his dominion – the "Maker of Fear". During the daytime there were no monster snakes in the vicinity, but in the night they were lurking on every path. At night the whole of mythology was let loose' (CW9i, para. 288).

The equation of firelight with consciousness and the banishment of fears lurking in the unconscious must be as ancient as its link with the hearth. This symbolism would account for the wide distribution of fire festivals, which have survived in such modern Western forms as firework celebrations, bonfire nights, and the lights on the Christmas tree. These celebrate the primordial animistic conception of fire as a demiurge, the earthly representative of the sun. Fire festivals guarantee the resurrection of the sun's heat and light each morning and each New Year, and celebrate the triumph of light over darkness, good over evil.

The transformative symbolism of fire accounts for its central role in the alchemical *opus* and its rites of initiation, where 'to pass through the fire' is to leave one's old self behind and to become refined and purified. Baptism with fire is regarded as a higher form of initiation than baptism with water. 'I indeed baptize you with water unto repentance,' said St John the Baptist, 'but he that cometh after me is mightier than I, whose shoes I am not worthy to bear: he shall baptize you with the Holy Ghost, and with fire' (Matthew 3:11).

The dual aspect of fire as both good (providing heat, light, the means for transformation) and bad (destructive, harmful, disastrous) is nowhere more apparent than in religious symbolism, where it represents both pure spiritual power and dangerous erotic passion: the 'tongues of fire' in which the Holy Spirit descended on the disciples at Pentecost, and the hell-fire which everlastingly torments the souls of the damned. This duality is also present in alchemy, where 'mercurial fire' is both the revelatory light of nature and the fire of Hell. 'Hell-fire,' comments Jung, 'the true energic principle of evil, appears here as the manifest counterpart of the spiritual and the good, and as essentially identical with it in substance. After that, it can surely cause no offence when another treatise says that the mercurial fire is the "fire in which God Himself burns in divine love"' (CW13, para. 257).

Fire is the one 'element' which can have no creatures native to it. This deficiency has been made good, however, by the human imagination, which has created fantastic creatures such as the **phoenix** (symbol of regeneration, death, and rebirth, of Christ consumed by the fires of the Passion, who rises again on the third day), the **salamander** (symbol of chastity, it plays innocently in the flames and is not harmed by the fires of temptation) and the **dragon** (the winged serpent which combines spirit with matter, conceived in the East to be a benevolent supernatural power but in the West to represent untamed nature which is seen as destructive and potentially evil; in alchemy it represents volatility).

The act of kindling fire lends itself to the symbolism of sex. The Indian equivalent of Prometheus is the fire-bringer Matarisvan, and Indian sacred texts invariably refer to the activity of fire-making by the verb *manthāmi*, to rub, to bring forth by rubbing. 'The *parmantha*, or instrument of the *manthāna* (fire-sacrifice), is conceived under a purely sexual aspect in India,' comments Jung. 'The fire-stick being the phallus or man, and the bored wood underneath the vulva or woman. The fire that results from the boring is the child, the divine son Agni' (*CW*5, para. 210). The Sanskrit word for fire is *agnis*. The Latin equivalent is *ignis*, from which we derive ignition. In the worship of Agni, the god of fire, the fire obtained by boring is a symbol of the regeneration of life.

Water There is a logic in the ancient concept of water as being a primary 'element' of nature, since it is as indispensable to life on this planet as is air. Throughout the entire course of our evolution, we have been water-dependent primates, the fossil record revealing a distinct hominid preference for rivers and lakes (the early Olduvan hominids have been called the People of the Lake). The Rift Valley of East Africa ideally provided the well-watered, variegated habitat necessary for hominid subsistence. Since humans sweat profusely in hot climates, they need to replace precious body fluids by copious drinking. If they are not to suffer pangs of thirst, or worse, they must ensure that water is always within reach. Water is also necessary for bathing and staying cool as well as providing sustenance in the form of fish, molluscs, etc. When migrating, foraging, or on the move, therefore, the natural routes to follow are along river banks, and lake and sea shores. Away from these benevolent locations, the well, the spring, or the oasis become natural symbols of spiritual refreshment and salvation. The cult of water, particularly of springs, is extremely ancient and seems to have persisted from Neolithic times up to the present, despite many attempts on the part of the Church to suppress it. Hence the Neolithic and Roman ex-votos found in the hot springs of Grisy (Saint Synphorien-de-Marmagne) and the Spring of Saint Sauveur (Compiègne Forest) in France.

Eliade (1958) has demonstrated how water and its symbolism have featured in the cosmologies of different peoples all over the world: 'Water symbolizes the whole of potentiality: it is the *fons et origo*, the source of all possible existence . . . Water symbolizes the primal substance from which all forms come and to which they will return.' In China, water is *Wu-Chi*, chaos, primordial amorphousness: 'the wide waters had no shores', say the Taoists. In India, the same idea prevails: 'all was water', say the Hindus. The Upper Waters (potentiality without form) and the Lower Waters (potentiality with form) are antimonies which are represented in *The Book of Enoch* as sexual opposites and elsewhere as a double spiral – like the double helix of DNA. This is not an altogether fanciful comparison for the mythic cosmology of water as the *fons et origo* of all creation has received scientific recapitulation in the Darwinian cosmology of the 'primal soup', where molecules hit on the knack of self-replication, the point at which all life began.

As an agent of purification before entering a sacred temenos, to worship or make sacrifice, the universal symbolism of ablution is readily understandable. Dirt dissolves in water and is washed away. Immersion in water, therefore, removes contamination; it cleanses and renders pure. The symbolism holds at the individual level (baptism, lustration, the sprinkling of holy water) and at the collective level (cataclysmic deluge and flood). As a result of such events, old sins are washed away and new life (and new faith) begins: 'Then will I sprinkle clean water upon you, and ye shall be clean: from all your filthiness, and from all your idols, I will cleanse you' (Ezekiel 36:25).

The same ambivalence applies to water as to fire symbolism. Just as water is indispensable to life, it can also be devastating in its effects. In all the **deluge** stories which feature in the world's literary and religious traditions (Cohn, 1996), an older, more sinful, more fallible humanity is overwhelmed by the waters of life from which it sprung. A new era is then inaugurated, marking the emergence of a more perfect humanity. Here, yet again, is the symbolism of death and resurrection. Water's cyclic autonomy determines a cosmic rhythm of annihilation and renewal which forms the background to all mythic cataclysms and apocalypses (e.g. Atlantis, Noah's flood, Deucalion, etc.). It is not only in the Judaeo-Christian tradition that humanity perishes for its sins: in the myths of the Pacific area, the cataclysm invariably occurs on account of some ritual misdemeanour. Not all perish; a privileged few survive and start the new order. 'The deluge myth,' observes Eliade (1958), 'with all that it implies, shows what human life may be worth to a "mind" other than a human mind.'

The devastating floods which feature in the myths of many peoples may often have their basis in historical fact. Between 10,000 and 7,000 years ago the seas rose fairly rapidly, and then more slowly until the present level was reached about 5,000 years ago. During this period about one seventh of the land mass of Greater Australia was inundated and many Aboriginal myths appear to reflect these events. According to Chris Knight (1996), the Yarra and Western Port tribes recollected a time when the present Hobson's Bay was a kangaroo hunting ground, and the Aborigines possessed this information long before the Europeans knew anything about the rise in sea levels which accompanied the end of the Ice Age. 'Likewise the separation of Kangaroo Island from South Australia, which is now known to have occurred about 10,000 years ago, is remembered in the legend of Ngurunderi drowning his wives as they fled across on foot . . . Support for the notion that myths can preserve genuine historical memories comes from an extraordinary finding – Aborigines in many coastal regions allegedly possess mythologically encoded *accurate mental maps* of territorial contours which were submerged as the world's sea levels began rising between 10 and 15,000 years ago.'

HYDROMANCY, the use of water in prophecy, has been found in many parts of the world. The oceans as well as pools and lakes have been regarded as a source of wisdom as well as physical nourishment. Sea divinities, like the Babylonian Oannes (half man, half fish), arose from the Persian Gulf and created culture, writing, and astrology. Thetis, Proteus, Glaucos, Nereus, and Triton all have the bodies of monsters of the deep or the tails of fish and all are Neptunian or Poseidonian deities. The sisters of Thetis, the Nereids, were called the Oceaniades by Hesiod. The sacred, prophetic, or magical powers of water are enhanced by the sea serpents, monsters, and dragons believed to lurk in the deep: 'Lying quietly in lakes or swimming across rivers, they bring rain, moisture, and floods, thus governing the fertility of the world. Dragons dwell in the clouds and lakes . . . The worship of serpents and serpent genies in India and elsewhere, in whatever setting we find it, always preserves its magico-religious bond with water' (Eliade, 1958).

All these features stress the symbolic identity of water with the unconscious psyche: 'Water is the commonest symbol for the unconscious,' says Jung. 'Water is the "valley spirit", the water dragon of Tao, whose nature resembles water – a *yang* embraced in the *yin*' (*CW*9i, para. 40). Water is 'psychic energy' with unconscious or as yet unrealized psychological potential.

iv Alchemy

A protoscience which anticipated psychology as much as chemistry, alchemy was essentially a symbolic exercise by which the alchemist projected his fantasies into matter. The rationale behind alchemical theory was based on the notion of primary matter – the belief that the world originated from a single substance, which separated out into the four 'elements', earth, air, fire, and water, and then recombined in various proportions to make up all the physical objects of the world. Aristotle was responsible for refining this idea, teaching that primary matter first existed as pure potentiality, which then acquired form when it was actualized in reality. This view anticipated to some extent Jung's theory of archetypes and modern Big Bang cosmology.

The objective of the alchemical quest was to isolate primary matter (the *prima materia* or *massa confusa*), separate it out into two or more reagents, and then, through practice of 'the art', achieve a recombination of these reagents to produce a miraculous new substance, variously called the Philosopher's Stone (the *lapis philosophorum*), the elixir of life, and so on. The alchemists held an animistic view of nature, believing in a kind of panpsychism – that all objects possessed spirits that, like the human spirit, were perfectible, in that they were capable of being transformed from lower into higher forms (yet another example of the archetypal symbolism of levels).

If one accepts these premises, the alchemical exercise begins to make a certain amount of sense. If all substances are composed of the same four elements, it should be possible to change one substance into another (e.g. lead into gold) by performing a *solutio*, a *separatio* or a *sublimatio* to reduce the substance to the original elements, rearranging their relative proportions, and then performing a *coagulatio* or a *coniunctio* to bring the new substance into being. And if the spirit of all entities is perfectible, there should be no insurmountable difficulty about transforming base matter into gold. The secret must lie in establishing the necessary stages through which the chemical operations had to pass and also in discovering a miraculous agent (what today we might call a catalyst) capable of promoting the necessary transformations. Many alchemists agreed on the appropriate stages necessary, but the miraculous agent proved more elusive.

That alchemy, as an elaborate discipline, was based on *projection* was an insight derived by Jung from the empirical observation that one becomes aware of new meanings arising from the unconscious psyche by seeing them mirrored in outer reality. The Rorschach ink blot test is based on this fact. Like nature itself, the psyche abhors a vacuum, and when confronted with a situation about which it knows nothing, it makes good the deficiency through use of the imagination. The arcane wisdom of astrology is largely based on the same process. For this reason, Jung advocated the study of alchemy and astrology as a means to discover more about the archetypal components of the human psyche which many generations of intelligent and articulate human beings had projected into them.

Jung did not deny that alchemists and astrologers applied their conscious minds to the practical implications of their work, but insisted that this would not impede the process of unconscious projection: 'For wherever the mind of the investigator departs from exact observation of the facts before it and goes its own way, the unconscious *spiritus rector* will take over the reins and lead the mind back to the unchangeable, underlying archetypes, which are then forced into projection by this regression' (*CW* 16, para. 405).

Because projection is of its very nature unconscious, alchemists and astrologers were unaware that their experiences and formulations had little to do with the chemical changes in their retorts or the movements of planets in the heavens. They experienced their projections as a property of matter or the influence of celestial bodies, but what they were really experiencing were symbolic processes at work in their own unconscious psyches. As they did so, Jung argued, they were working on their individuation. In attempting to liberate gold from the *prima materia*, they were bringing the Self to consciousness from the *massa confusa* (the unconscious). Making gold is bringing the Self to full realization, becoming as complete a human being as it is possible to be. The actual stages of the alchemical *opus* are described in **Individuation and Transcendence** pp. 235–56.

v Celestial Bodies

All cosmologies and mythologies distinguish between upper and lower realms of being (the symbolism of levels): (1) the heavens, the realm of the sky gods (and occasionally goddesses such as the Egyptian sky goddess Nut, who fertilizes the earth with her milky rain); (2) the earth, the realm of earth goddesses, humanity, and the animal kingdom; and (3) the Underworld, the realm of demons and the dead. Heaven and

Earth also represent spirit and matter (nous and physis). Heaven is the ultimate expression of aboveness: reaching up to the skies, flying, ascending mountains, etc. – all represent aspiration or the desire for social, spiritual or political ascendancy, and power. It can also be associated with ego-inflation, hypomanic 'flight of ideas', fantasies, castles in the air, lofty notions, and the magic flight of the shaman.

That the sky is the residence of gods and goddesses naturally accounts for awe-inspiring natural phenomena such as thunder, lightning, thunderbolts, rainbows, comets, and meteorites. In the great majority of mythologies, the sky is masculine and identified with the Father, while the earth is feminine and identified with the Mother. As already noted, in numerous creation myths Father Sky lies on top of Mother Earth in darkness until they give birth to a hero, who pushes them apart, thus bringing light into the world. Inevitably implicated in the symbolism of the heavens, the archetype of hierarchy gives rise to the common notion that there are several heavens on top of one another arranged in a series of concentric spheres, each being the abode of spiritual beings of ascending rank and importance. Heaven is thus the ultimate expression of transcendence, suprahuman power, and all that is sacred, for it is as high as anyone can reach. As a consequence, what happens in Heaven becomes a model for what happens on Earth. An alchemical text celebrates this:

> Heaven above
> Heaven below
> Stars above
> Stars below
> All that is above
> Also is below
> Grasp this
> And rejoice.

The Great Seal of Genghis Khan bore the inscription: 'One God in Heaven and the Khan on Earth, Seal of the Master of the World'.

Sun The supreme cosmic power, carrying the connotations of divinity, splendour, royalty: 'There is no visible thing, in all the world, more worthy to serve as a symbol of God than the sun, which illuminates with visible life, first itself, then all the celestial and mundane bodies' (Dante). The sun, like the heavens, is naturally associated with warmth, light, goodness, healing, and everlasting life; while its opposite, the stygian depths of the Underworld, with cold, darkness, evil, sickness, and death. In most cultures the sun is masculine and linked to the Father, the moon feminine and associated with the Mother, though in a minority of traditions the roles are reversed. In Slav symbolism sun and moon can even change sexes.

The course of the sun through the heavens is an age-old symbol of the human life-cycle. In Egypt the rising sun was linked with Horus, the zenith with Ra, and its setting with Osiris. The setting of the sun, its disappearance in the night, and its rising again in the morning links it irrevocably with the archetypal symbolism of death and rebirth.

Symbols of the sun are the disc, circle, wheel, eye, swastika, chariot, solar gods (Apollo, Helios), solar birds (eagle, phoenix), and solar animals (white or golden horses, winged serpents, dragons); sun rays, either straight or undulating, represent heat and light.

Vestiges of sun worship are apparent in all major religious traditions. In Christianity the sun represents God the Father, maker of heaven and earth, giver of all things, radiating light, love, and justice. Christ is both Son of God and 'sun of righteousness'. The nimbus round the head of Christ and the haloes of the saints are clear references to sun-worship in ecclesiastical art. Because the twelve apostles were likened to the twelve signs of the zodiac each is often represented with a star over his head.

Moon Our primordial clock. Both the symbol and measure of cyclic time, it governs tides, rains, floods, and the menstrual cycle. Being passive, reflective, and dependent on the sun for its luminosity, it is conceived as feminine in our tradition, as it is in most traditions, and commonly identified with the Mother archetype, the Queen of Heaven. Mysterious, beautiful, and wistful, her gentle light illuminates the darkness of night, and thus represents the consciousness that comes to us in dreams. 'Lunar consciousness' is inner *gnosis*, knowledge revealed by the reflected light of the divine sun mirrored in the soul. In folklore, myth, and fairy tale the moon is identified with nocturnal animals, the rabbit, hare, fox, and cat, and also with aquatic animals such as the frog and toad. Often these creatures are represented as having only three legs, betokening the three phases of the moon; birth, life, and death; past, present, and future; beginning, middle, and end. The waxing and waning of the moon links us inevitably with the archetypal notions of death, rebirth, and eternity. In traditional Chinese philosophy, the moon is the very essence of Yin, the eternal feminine in its transient cycles as well as its immortality; the hare who lives in the moon is perennially busy mixing the elixir of eternal life.

Together, the sun and moon represent the archetypal Father and Mother, the Heavenly Parents, united in the *hieros gamos*, the sacred marriage of Heaven and Earth, the *coniunctio Solis et Lunae*, king and queen, gold and silver. Depicted at the Crucifixion, sun and moon represent the dual aspect of Christ, God and man, soul and body, mortal and immortal. Yoga originates in the marriage of Sun (*ha*) and Moon (*tha*), hence Hatha-yoga, symbolizing breath and semen, fire and water respectively. Where sun and moon stand for the eyes of Heaven, the sun is usually the right eye, the moon the left. This distinction finds physical expression in the exogamic arrangements of the Omaha Indians: their tents were divided into two semi-circles, one belonging to the sun and associated with masculinity, the 'higher', the day, the north, the right side, and religion; the other belonging to the moon and associated with femininity, the 'lower', the night, the south, the left side, and politics.

Planets Since our original conceptions of external reality were formed long before the invention of the telescope, the planets were considered to be seven in number and to constitute the controlling influences of the cosmos. In fact, there were only five of them (Mercury, Venus, Mars, Jupiter, and Saturn). The other two were made up by the Sun and the Moon. Each of the seven was identified with a god, whose nature and characteristics were known to all: each was associated with one of the seven days of the week and one of the seven metals of alchemy. Since the soul is conceived as coming from the celestial spheres and as returning there at death, the planets have always been associated with death, rebirth, and eternity. The planetary gods are often portrayed as pouring their qualities into the bath of rebirth.

Since the celestial bodies are so distant and, before the invention of radio telescopes and space probes, we could know nothing about them, they stimulated our seemingly infinite capacities for fantasy. Astrology was a systematic attempt to discipline this imaginative exuberance and has greatly influenced planetary symbolism. By dint of naming each planet after gods in the Greco-Roman pantheon, the astrologers were able to attribute to them the characteristics of each god. This nomenclature provided a tradition in our culture which still flourishes, not only in the astrology columns of the daily press but in the names we use for the seven days of the week. These associations are presented in Table 2.

Table 2 Astrological association of planets with gods and days of the week

PLANET	QUALITIES	DAYS (in English and Italian)	
Sun	Will	Sunday	domenica
Moon	Imagination	Monday	lunedi
Mars	Action and destruction	Tuesday	martedi
Mercury	Intuition and movement	Wednesday	mercoledi
Jupiter	Judgement and command	Thursday	giovedi
Venus	Love and relationships	Friday	venerdi
Saturn	Endurance	Saturday	sabato

The vertical and horizontal coordinates indispensable to conscious orientation in space (*see* **Psychic Compass**, pp. 116–23) have inevitably influenced our conceptions of the relationship between the heavenly bodies, as in the notion that there are seven directions of space: these are made up of an inner group of three 'planets' on the vertical axis, and an outer group of four, forming the cardinal points, on the horizontal.

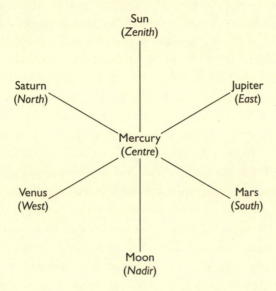

The figure combining these seven directions looks flat and two-dimensional at first, but the archetypal structures guiding the imagination quickly transform it into a three-dimensional figure, so that it begins to look like a weathercock: the cock being the sun, and the line joining Mercury to the moon being the pole on which the weather-vane stands.

In some systems, the triad sun–Mercury–moon is represented as a triangle and the tetrad Mars–Jupiter–Venus–Saturn as a square. The triad symbolizes psychic dynamism (active masculine sun, passive feminine moon, and neuter hermaphroditic Mercury), whereas the quaternity (Mars, Jupiter, Venus, Saturn) represents wholeness, completion. This linkage was of particular interest to Jung. In *Psychology and Alchemy*, he quotes the following passage from an alchemical treatise: 'You shall take seven pieces of metal, of each and every metal as they are named after the planets, and shall stamp on each the character of the planet in the house of the same planet, and every piece shall be as large and thick as a rose noble [a fifteenth-century

English gold coin]. But of Mercury only the fourth part of an ounce by weight and nothing stamped upon it.

'Then put them after the order in which they stand in the heavens into a crucible, and make all windows fast in the chamber that it may be quite dark within, then melt them altogether in the midst of the chamber and drop in seven drops of the blessed Stone, and forthwith a flame of fire will come out of the crucible and spread itself over the whole chamber (fear no harm), and will light up the whole chamber more brightly than sun and moon, and over your heads you shall behold the whole firmament as it is in the starry heavens above, and the planets shall hold to their appointed courses as in the sky. Let it cease of itself, in a quarter of an hour everything will be in its own place' (CW12, para. 348).

Here again the hierarchy archetype is evident: the seven stages of the alchemical *opus* correspond to 'an ascent through the planets from the dark, cold, distant Saturn to the sun. To the alchemists the connection between individual temperament and the positions of the planets was self-evident, for these elementary astrological consider-ations were the common property of any educated person in the Middle Ages as well as in antiquity. The ascent through the planetary spheres therefore meant something like a shedding of the characterol-ogical qualities indicated by the horoscope . . .' The journey through the planetary houses, like the crossing of the great halls of the Egyptian Underworld, 'signifies the overcoming of a psychic obstacle, or of an autonomous complex, suitably represented by a planetary god or demon. Anyone who has passed through all the spheres is free from compulsion; he has won the crown of victory and become like a god' (CW14, para. 308).

Jung concluded that what the alchemists meant by the ascent and descent was 'the freeing of the soul of the shackles of darkness, or unconsciousness; its ascent to heaven, the widening of consciousness; and finally its return to earth, to hard reality, in the form of the tincture or healing drink, endowed with the powers of the Above' (CW14, para. 297). For this reason the alchemists referred to their art as 'earthly astrology', maintaining that the *opus* was 'not of this world' (CW13, para. 355).

Clouds As harbingers of rain they are fertility symbols, condensations of the 'Upper Waters'. Halfway between Heaven and Earth they cloak the gods from our view, as do the clouds that lurk round the peak of Mount Olympus. In Islam, clouds are symbols of God's inscrutability before the Creation. In China, their dissipation in the sky symbolizes the transformation the wise man must undergo in order to merge with the infinite. Like mists, clouds are a fusion of the 'elements' air and water, a combination of form and formlessness, undergoing perpetual metamorphosis, like the human imagination which readily projects different images on to them.

Comet Universally regarded as bad news. Its appearance is a sign from the gods of imminent war, famine, pestilence, flood, the death of kings. To the Bantu-speaking peoples of the Kasai River it foretells great disaster. A comet appeared before the assassination of Julius Caesar. Another warned the Incas and Aztecs of the arrival of the Spaniards and the destruction of their world. That comets should be interpreted as omens of catastrophe is presumably because, like most disasters, their arrival is sudden and unexpected – except, of course, by astronomers.

Light and **Darkness** The general tendency of the human psyche to categorize phenomena in antithetical pairs may well owe its origins to the natural opposition between day and night. Light and darkness are, after all, fundamental data of existence on this planet. They must have been among the first phenomena of which consciousness became aware. It is not surprising, therefore, that light should have become a universal symbol of both consciousness and divinity, and that darkness – the time when we are most vulnerable to natural predators and conspecific attacks – should be symbolically equated with unconsciousness, fearful mystery, and evil. Only very recently has it been possible to banish darkness by artificial means, and, because darkness has constituted a threat throughout the evolutionary history of our species, it is still a source of dread to children and many adults.

Light and darkness symbolism has shaped the mythologies, cosmologies, and religions of all peoples of the earth, darkness being equated with an original chaos, light with the bringing of order: 'In the beginning God created the heaven and the earth. And the earth was without form, and void; and darkness was upon the face of the deep. And the Spirit of God moved upon the face of the waters. And God said, Let there be light: and there was light. And God saw the light, that it was good: and God divided the light from the darkness. And God called the light Day, and the darkness He called Night. And the evening and the morning were the first day' (Genesis 1:1–5). The dawning light of new day is a primordial symbol of psychological awareness, spiritual transformation, new life, and inspiration; the failing light of dusk, on the other hand, symbolizes contracting awareness, spiritual decline, death, and despair. All art, all narrative, all poetry, all theology, make use of this symbolism. In our own Christian version of it, Christ is the 'Light of the World'; 'God is Spirit, God is Love, God is Light', whose grace heals the 'dark night of the soul'. Indeed, this complementary yet antithetical dynamic is at the heart of all archetypal phenomena as is represented by the *T'ai Chi*, the binary symbol of Yin and Yang. The *Codex Marcianus* uroboros (second century AD), its top half black and lower half white (the inversion of the anticipated configuration), exploits the symbolic implications of the snake eating its tail – the eternal alternation between the opposites of life and death, light and darkness, good and evil, appearance and disappearance, typical of existence on this planet (Figure 3).

Like the black and white halves of the uroboros, day and night are *antinomies* – though opposites, they complement one another as two parts of the same cyclic whole – and would be meaningless without one another, as is true of all other pairs of opposites (hot and cold, peace and war, above and below, heaven and hell, life and death, left and right). This fundamental antinomy characterizing all archetypal phenomena is expressed in the symbolism of twins – e.g. the Dioscuri (Greek, *Dios kuroi* = sons of the sky god), Castor and Pollux, and the Gemini. Castor and Pollux, one light and the other dark, wear on their heads the domed caps which represent the two halves of the Cosmic Egg, from which they were born as sons of Leda: Castor is fathered by Leda's husband Tyndareus; Pollux by her lover Zeus.

Figure 3 The *Codex Marcianus* uroboros

Castor is therefore mortal, Pollux immortal. In Jungian terms, Castor represents the ego and Pollux the Self; the close bond that links them is the ego–Self axis.

The Gemini, which constitutes the third sign of the zodiac, are both complementary and antithetical, in that one is mortal, the other immortal; one is white, the other black; one creates and the other destroys; and both participate in the Wheel of Transformation. The sun passes the sign between 21 May and 21 June, at the end of spring and on the brink of summer, when the creative force of Aries and Taurus is split in two, one representing ascent, the other descent, the separation reaching its completion at the solstice on midsummer night. The pillars of Hermes and of Hercules participate in the same symbolism, as do the Jachin and Boaz columns of the Kabala. The Mithraic twins, Cautes and Caupartes, hold torches in their hands, one turned up towards heaven, the other pointing down to the earth. The Hero Twins of the Pueblo Indians in Mexico are gods of the dawn and dusk; like all heroes, they are monster-slayers and transformers of the old into the new.

TWINS in numerous folk cosmologies are cast in morally opposing roles, reflecting the evolutionary ascent and involutionary descent of the sun: the good twin is represented as white, the bad one as black; one creates civilization, the other destroys it; and they are locked in everlasting struggle. This archetypal symbolism probably reflects (and contributes to) colour prejudices among people, both white and black. Romulus and Remus from classical antiquity are typical examples of twins at war with one another. The Biblical brothers Cain and Abel, Jacob and Esau, take on the same symbolism, as do Osiris and Set in Egyptian mythology.

This symbolism has grown out of humanity's primordial awareness that day is paired with night, light with darkness, summer with winter, and that all such oppositions have to do with the perceived motion of the sun.

Meteorites These inspire awe because they have been cast down from the sacred realm of Heaven. Australian Aborigines believe that the heavenly vault is composed of rock crystal and that God's throne is made of quartz. The symbolic logic underpinning this belief must be that since meteorites come from Heaven, Heaven must be made of stone. When they fall to earth, therefore, aeroliths are charged with celestial sanctity: they are deemed worthy of worship because they are imbued with deity. The most famous example is the *Ka'aba*, the Black Stone in Mecca, which was sacred to the pre-Islamic Arabs long before the birth of Mohammed (about AD 570). Another example is the Black Stone of Pessinus, an epiphany of Cybele, the Great Mother of the Phrygians, which ended up in Rome during the last of the Punic wars. This meteorite embodied the Goddess herself; she had been pursued through the heavens by a thunder god and as she fell through the sky she left a hole through which communication became possible between Earth and Heaven.

Long before human beings learnt how to smelt ferrous ores, they worked with iron from meteorites, using silicic hammers to shape them into tools and weapons. The Eskimos of Greenland fashioned knives in this way. The Sumerian word AN.BAR, the oldest word known for iron, is composed of pictograms meaning sky and fire. The Greek word *sideros* is derived from *sidus, eris* meaning star. When Cortez asked the Aztec chiefs where their weapons came from, they simply pointed to the sky.

The celestial linkage of male deity, lightning, thunder, and meteorites leads by a short step to the notion of thunderbolts, the instruments of divine wrath.

Rain The fertilizing agent that descends from Heaven – the gift from the gods on which all life depends. For this reason, rain-making rituals are universal, even in normally well-watered countries, rain being too valuable a commodity to be taken for granted. In the cosmologies of agrarian peoples, rain is commonly equated with the divine semen which made fruitful the sacred marriage, the *hieros gamos*, between Heaven and Earth. Though usually considered to be the gift of a sky god, there are exceptions: the Egyptians worshipped a sky goddess Nut, and celebrated rainfall as milk descending from her divine breasts.

Rainbow The beauty, wonder, and intangible transparency of rainbows, together with their imprecise location, cause them universally to be expressions of divinity, providing a bridge or pathway between Heaven and Earth. In Norse legend the rainbow bridge is called Byfrost, and, in Japanese, the 'floating bridge of Heaven'. The Buddha's staircase, down which he makes his return from Heaven, is a rainbow of seven colours. To Muslim mystics, the seven colours of the rainbow are an image of the godhead, the sun reflected in the rain.

In many traditions the rainbow is associated with the mystic serpent, an image of power and generative vitality. In both Australia and South America, among populations that can have had no contact with one another for tens of thousands of years, there is widespread belief in a large water serpent, who takes the form of a rainbow and is responsible for controlling the menstruation of women. This must again derive from the archetypal notion that fertility is a divine gift from Heaven.

Thunder and **lightning** Kratophanous phenomena symbolizing the awesome power, and, usually, the displeasure, of the gods. The idea that lightning symbolizes God's virility is widespread. The Australian Aborigines, for example, equate lightning with the divine phallus, and the rain, which generally accompanies it, with the divine ejaculate which fertilizes the earth. Indra, the god of the thunderbolt, not only brought rain to the fields, but guaranteed the fertility of women and animals. Everywhere this potent combination of fire with water carries both positive and negative implications: it can be both fertilizing and destructive (causing catastrophic fires or floods, which are widely regarded as punishments sent by God). The idea of illumination from Heaven, the divine Logos piercing the darkness, is a symbol of enlightenment and sudden intellectual insight: the eureka! experience.

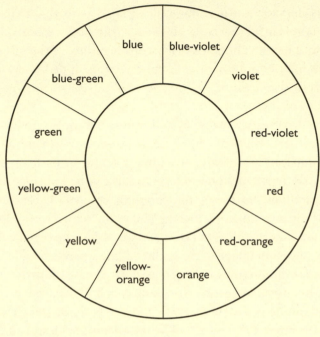

vi Colours

The capacity of the brain and eye to perceive the different colours of the spectrum is phylogenetically very ancient, and each colour is linked to a web of cognitive and affective associations. Hence *synaesthesia*, which lends a certain felt meaning to each colour or can give different days of the week, different musical tones, etc., a different hue in the minds of susceptible individuals. The subjective intensity of one's response to colour might seem to defy all attempts at objective classification in the study of colour symbolism. Yet, when we compare our subjective experiences with one another, areas of common agreement begin to emerge. For example, artists and interior decorators agree in classifying colours as warm or cold: those which are 'advancing' colours in that they give back light (red, orange, yellow, and by extension, white) are classified as warm and active, while those which are 'retreating' colours in that they absorb light (blue, indigo, violet, and by extension, black) are classified as cold and passive. Green stands on its own between the warm and cold colours as a transitional or intermediary colour, neither active nor passive but potentially both. This classification is in accord with the general tendency of the human psyche to place phenomena in antithetical pairs, particularly the antitheses positive (light) and negative (darkness). As noted in the entry for light and darkness, these antinomial pairs are presented in the myth of the Gemini. They are also represented in countless tales of struggle, as between White and Black Knights.

The spectrum represents all the colours of which white light is composed, and these are commonly described as seven in number, as is the case in rainbow symbolism. These seven colours are symbolically linked with the seven notes of the musical scale, the seven vowels of the Greek alphabet, the seven faculties of the soul, the seven virtues, the seven deadly sins, the seven days of the week, the seven planets, and so on. The correspondences are not unique to our culture: for example, the Zuni Indians of western America make an annual offering of 'corn of seven colours', each colour being associated with a planetary god (Cirlot, 1971).

Artists develop their own vocabulary of colour, as do dreamers, and it would be fallacious to attribute fixed meanings to different hues. The following comments are offered merely as a guide to values which have been traditionally associated with them. As will be seen, these attributions often possess a certain inherent logic.

Black As the colour of the primordial void before the coming of light, black is universally associated with darkness, death, sickness, and evil. Black represents the initial germinal state of many processes, as it does in numerous cosmologies and in alchemy. The *nigredo*, the initial stage of the alchemical *opus*, was known as the 'germination in darkness', and is paralleled by the 'dark night of the soul' of St John of the Cross. In the Christian tradition black is the colour of the Prince of Darkness, of despair, humiliation, death, sorrow, and mourning. It therefore readily symbolizes the 'shadow' aspect of the unconscious psyche.

White Associated with the light, sun, air, holiness, perfection, and innocence. Paradoxically, white can be associated with death as well as life for, when worn at a funeral, as it is in the East and was in ancient Greece and Rome, it represents birth into the new life beyond the grave. Even when worn at weddings it represents death to the old single unmarried life and birth into the new – as well as symbolizing the chastity and purity of the bride (though nowadays this symbolism is more honoured in the breach than the observance). When used to make a flag, white denotes truce, surrender, friendship, and good-will.

Red Associated with the sun, masculinity, fire, passion, energy, blood, and war; the attribute of Ares/Mars; in alchemy the zenith colour representing the third stage of the *opus*. Christianity associates it with the blood of Christ and the redemption of humankind. Since it is the colour of martyrdom, saints' days have always been inscribed in red – 'red letter days'. It is also the colour of rage, of 'seeing red'.

Red symbolism is often associated with that of black and white. In medieval Christian art, for example, black represents penitence, white purity, and red charity and love. Not only was black a symbol of spiritual darkness and of the Devil but also of witchcraft – the black art. Red, on the other hand, associated with white, represents the Resurrection and Transfiguration respectively. Victor Turner has demonstrated how Ndembu symbolism focuses on a white–black–red triad, which he links to archetypal symbols denoting pleasure and pain. In the Ndembu system, white stands for milk, purity, health, and good luck; while black stands for faeces and other dirty and disagreeable things. Red, on the other hand, stands for blood, male-ness, danger, and assertion – all means of transcending the black–white opposites. Similarly in Christianity, red, standing for the blood and the love of Christ, provides a way of transcending the conflict between good and evil.

In Andamanese colour symbolism, red was the colour of blood (representing life and the warmth of the body) and fire (activity and mental excitement). A. R. Radcliffe-Brown (1922), the authority on the Andaman Islanders, reported that red paint was applied to sick people (for healing) and to murderers (for purification). He maintained that the symbolism of redness, blood, and fire was universal and not restricted to the Andaman Islanders.

Gold Also associated with the sun and the masculine principle; the colour of all sun gods, corn gods and goddesses, and divine power. As the attribute of Apollo, it symbolizes intuition, illumination, consciousness, reason, and intellect.

Brown The colour of the earth, the soil, potential fertility, and nature's womb. Paradoxically, it is also the colour of vegetative death and autumn melancholy. In Ancient Rome and in the Catholic Church, brown symbolizes humility (*humus* = earth) and poverty (hence the brown habit worn by monks and nuns). Freudian psychology has made much of the excremental symbolism of the colour brown, linking it to anal sadism (as exemplified by Hitler's Brownshirts).

Green As with brown, this colour is associated with both life and death – the fresh green of new shoots as well as the livid green of putrefaction. As the colour of Venus and Mercury, the pair of lovers, it represents spring, reproduction, new life, abundance, gladness. It also carries implications of unripeness, naivety, being 'green' (immature and inexperienced) like the young corn god before he turns gold. The Green Knight, on the other hand, represents death, and a green flag represents a wreck at sea. In Christianity, green is the colour of hope and immortality, the triumph of spring over winter, as well as being the colour of Satan, evil, and death. In modern parlance, to be 'green' is not so much to be naive as to be ecologically aware. It is also associated with the emotions of envy and jealousy. Green is a mystic colour because it is compounded from blue and yellow, the colours of Heaven and Earth, and is, therefore, the fruit of their union.

Blue The colour of the sky and the sea; it therefore shares in their symbolism, their translucency, their vastness, their infinity, and their coolness. Because their extent so far exceeds the human condition, their colour represents both the ultimate and the eternal, the Beyond and Fate. Together with white (purity), blue is the colour of the Virgin Mary, Queen of Heaven.

Violet The archetypal complex violet—violate—violent is under **flowers** (pp. 381—2). Violet is also associated with religious devotion and grief; it is the colour of St Mary Magdalene. Derived from equal proportions of red and blue, violet stands for passion balanced by reason, the temporal by the external. During His Passion, Christ is depicted in a violet robe to stress the paradox of his incarnation as Son of Man and his divinity as Son of God. In Taoism, violet marks the transition from active to passive, from Yang to Yin. In Tantrism, it bears sexual connotations: blue stimulating female sexuality and red the sexuality of the male.

Purple Pomp, royalty, majesty, imperial and ecclesiastical power; the colour of Zeus/Jupiter.

vii Buildings

Human beings have built SHELTERS from the earliest times, bringing to the task a ready combination of improvisation and ingenuity, adapted to the prevailing climate and the materials available. Though we do not possess a nest-building instinct with the specificity of swallows, we do nevertheless demonstrate a worldwide propensity for creating habitations with a roof and walls (either circular, square, or rectangular), whatever materials are used in their construction. The satisfaction we all derive from making such structures begins in childhood, when cardboard boxes, deckchairs, garden tools, towels, and old curtains are happily put to architectural purposes. Tree houses are particularly popular at that age. The snug feeling of sitting in the house one has created is something many people can remember with pleasure. Homemaking and home maintenance continue to be major creative activities throughout the human life-cycle.

Different types of habitation carry their own connotations: the humble COTTAGE in a forest, the great PALACE in a famous city; the CHURCH representing the house of God, the body of Christ, and mother Church, protecting and sheltering all her children; the HOTEL or INN as temporary home, resting place on the journey of life, an abode of transition between one stage and the next; public buildings carry the connotations of their function: law courts, legislatures, banks, shops, bureaucratic departments, theatres, art galleries, sports stadia, barracks, prisons, etc.

Church or **Temple** A church or temple is a sacred place which is quite separate from the profane space around it. Indeed, this precisely defines the meaning of the word profane, which is derived from the Latin *pro*, meaning before or outside, and *fanum* a temple: *profanus*, therefore, means outside the temple. The earliest known forms of sanctuary were enclosures made by a circle of stones, and all such were consecrated by a theophany or kratophany of some kind (i.e. they were situated where there had been some form of divine revelation through a holy man or charismatic leader, through a bolt of lightning, or through consecration of a place where men had a violent end in battle or through some other catastrophe).

The wall round a sanctuary has the dual function of protecting it from profane influences from outside and of protecting people still in the profane state from the danger to themselves which could result from entering without first making the necessary gestures of approach (e.g. removing the shoes, undergoing purification rituals, kneeling, crossing oneself, etc.). Hence the importance of the threshold that must be crossed in order to gain entrance. The same function is provided by the gateway in a city wall. Such places of transition from outside to inside are symbols of the liminal state, the altered state of consciousness necessary for a transition to occur from one psychological orientation to another.

The shape and construction of all churches, temples, and sanctuaries closely follows an archetypal pattern which is based on a sacred revelation granted *in illo tempore*, and it is copied again and again with every new construction. The classic Greek or Roman temple, the Christian cathedral, and the Greek Orthodox church are all examples of such archetypally based and divinely ordained structures. The Orthodox church is a sublime example of an architectural mandala, combining the cross, the square, and a circle, created round a central axis linking Heaven and Earth. The DOME, constructed above the altar, represents the vault of Heaven and is usually painted blue as a background to the image of Christos Pantocrator. It is usually erected on four pillars, each at the corner of a square, representing the four corners of the earth and the four Evangelists.

This basic configuration is extremely widespread. It links with the ancient Chinese view that the earth is a square supporting the round domed sky, and with the symbolism of the Buddhist stupa and Muslim *Ka'aba*. The stupa is usually set on a square base with four portals of entry set at the cardinal points. The groins which meet at the top of the dome are identical with the curved poles of a Mongolian yurt. The eye at the very top is directly aligned with the World Axis and is known as the 'Gateway of the Sun'. The central pole which protrudes through the top of the stupa is the World Axis proceeding on its way to the heavens.

According to legend, the Buddha himself demonstrated how a stupa should be built. He took off his robe, folded it in a square, and put it on the ground to represent the platform. On this he placed his upturned alms bowl (the hemispheric dome) and stood his staff on the top of it (the *axis mundi*). The Great Stupa of Sauci in India (*circa* the first century BC) contained within its *garba* (womb) a reliquary 'at the centre of the world', in which it was believed were placed the ashes of Siddharta Gautama, the historical Buddha (563–483 BC).

When the prophet Mohammed returned from Heaven, he described it as a mother-of-pearl dome supported by four pillars. The Dome of the Rock (completed AD 492) in Jerusalem marks the site from which

Mohammed is believed to have made his ascent. It is an octagonal building with four doors set at the cardinal points. It has two concentric ambulatories round the central area containing the Rock, above which is the Dome. This, the earliest surviving example of Islamic architecture, is built on the same Mount on which, centuries earlier, God had commanded Solomon to build his Temple (built about 968 BC and destroyed in AD 70), with its central Holy of Holies, the Ark of the Covenant, containing the Tablets of the Law. That Jerusalem should be sacred to Muslims and Jews, as well as to Christians, demonstrates the truth that the sacredness of a place can persist independently of different religious traditions.

Indo-Tibetan temples, built according to Tantric doctrine, are similarly based on a mandala which incorporates the hierarchical archetype and the symbolism of levels: each floor or terrace of the temple represents a heaven, a step on the ladder of ascent. The Cosmic Mountain is the quintessence of this archetypal configuration, the ziggurat or pyramid built 'at the centre of the world'. Thus, the symbolism of the centre is crucial to the creation of all sacred structures, towns, cities, palaces, and houses. Every consecrated place, says Eliade (1958), is a centre, 'where there exists the possibility of breaking through from the level of earth to the level of heaven'. It is a place through which the *axis mundi* passes.

House Since houses grant a sense of containment and enclosure, providing warmth and protection from the elements, a place of domesticity, intimacy, and nurturance, they are extensions of the Mother archetype and of the symbolism of the womb. Home is the centre of one's existence, one's security, one's bolt hole: 'Home is the place where, when you have to go there/They have to take you in' (Robert Frost).

Symbolically, buildings are an extension or projection of the human psyche. Different parts of the house carry their special connotations: the KITCHEN, associated with the transformation of raw materials into digestible forms of nourishment; the BEDROOM, with sex, birth, sickness, and death; the BATHROOM, with purification and regeneration, the shedding of old sins and associations and preparation for a new day; the DRAWING-ROOM, with social intercourse, gossip, intrigue, the *va et vient* of the world; the DINING-ROOM, with good fellowship, hospitality, assimilation, and integration; the BASEMENT or CELLAR, with the unconscious, with stores of living potential; the FOUNDATIONS, the basic configuration determining the shape, size, and structure of the house represents the phylogenetic psyche (the collective unconscious); the ATTIC, associated with secrets carried over from the past; STAIRS with the notion of descent and ascent, and, in Freudian psychology, with sexual intercourse; DOORS, either shut or open, are excluding or welcoming, as the case may be; while the FAÇADE stands for the *persona*, the aspect of oneself one displays to the world. The house may thus symbolize the Self in both its physical and psychological entirety.

viii Migration

Fossils of hominids much older than *Homo sapiens* (*Homo erectus*) have been found outside as well as inside Africa. We, *Homo sapiens sapiens*, are the descendants of migrants who left Africa within the last 250,000 years, what Dawkins (1995) calls the 'second African diaspora'. There was an earlier exodus about a million and a half years ago, when *Homo erectus* moved out of Africa to colonize parts of the Middle East and Asia. If one goes back two million years, we are all Africans.

The facts of human migration down the Nile Valley into Eurasia, along the shores of the Indian Ocean to accomplish the daunting sixty-mile sea crossing between Timor and Greater Australia, would indicate something of the phyletic background to the mythic theme of the water/river/sea crossing to the Promised Land. Rivers, lakes, seas, and oceans, like mountain ranges and dense forests, are obstacles to migration, making barriers between peoples of different culture, language, and religion, encouraging mutual incomprehension and shadow projection between them. Crossing such barriers is a symbol of transcendence, both of obstacles in outer reality and of divisions in oneself, in the furtherance of forward impetus from one stage of life to the next and towards the goal of individuation.

Human beings have ever been great travellers, our bipedal mode of progression leaving our hands free to carry weapons, food, and possessions, our quick, adaptable brains enabling us not only to cross natural hazards, make shelters, clothes, and fires, but to spread out over the planet to take up residence in widely differing climates and physical environments, thus outwitting every other species on earth. There is a sense in which we are never more truly ourselves than when we are travelling, and this would explain why we spend so much time, ingenuity, and money in devising, developing, and using ever more efficient means of transport.

Different forms of transport carry their own connotations for the modern psyche (*see* **Transport**, pp. 291–7). Travel on horseback, bicycle, or motor-bike emphasizes one's solitary journey towards individuation; travel by car stresses one's family associations and responsibilities (it is important to note who is driving); while travel by public transport (bus, train, or aeroplane), underlines collective aspects of one's journey through life. In *The Selfish Gene* (1976), Richard Dawkins argues that we are all vehicles carrying our genes until they are ready to move on into the next generation. This is undoubtedly true. As far as our genes are concerned we are mere vehicles placed, for our lifetime, at their disposal. But what Dawkins and the sociobiologists sometimes overlook is that we are *sentient* vehicles. We are conscious: our egos knowingly go along for the ride. To the genes, which we inherited from the generations that went before us, our personal life and death is of no consequence: we are like horses they change at posting stages on the way. But to us, as self-reflective individuals, it is the *journey* that matters.

The journey The journey is the great allegory of life, leaving the familiar past behind and progressing into the unknown future. It is inextricably linked to the idea of meaning and purpose, the quest, and the goal. It may also represent flight, exodus, escape from natural or man-made disasters to a place of retreat, sanctuary, or greater security. Heroes in myths, folklore, and fairy tales invariably set out on a journey encountering trials and ordeals which test their strength and ingenuity as they proceed on their quest for some great prize: the bride, the kingdom, the treasure hard to attain. The journey is thus rich in initiation symbolism, and initiation rituals frequently involve symbolic journeys: a descent into the stygian depths of the Underworld (the Mother, the unconscious, the kingdom of the dead) and an ascent towards the light of Heaven (the Father, consciousness, the realm of everlasting life); or the circumambulation of a maze, leading the initiate ever closer to the centre of all things, the sacred mystery of life, and then out again to the profane world of contemporary reality. Classic examples of such journeys are the descent into Hades of Odysseus, Aeneas, Orpheus, Psyche, and Dante, the pilgrimage to the Holy Land, to Compostella, to Canterbury, or to Mecca, and the night sea journey of the solar hero. We shall return to these great archetypal themes in the next section.

Bridge The bridge is not an invention of civilization; men have been bridging rivers, streams, and canyons by means of branches, fronds, and creepers bound into ropes, etc., since the beginnings of time. Bridges represent the triumph of human ingenuity over the abyss, the raging torrent, the obstacle to progress and migration. A bridge not only joins opposite sides of a gap, but bridges over ('overcomes') what is in the gap.

In many cultures, the bridge provides a connection between the known and the unknown, the perceived and the imperceptible (conscious and unconscious), between Earth and Heaven, between man and god, and is commonly identified with the rainbow – the bridge that Zeus flung between the two worlds and down which came Iris, messenger of the gods, and conveyor of good tidings.

The humped-back nature of many old bridges, especially in the East, stresses the symbolic connection with the rainbow. In Latin *pontifex* means builder of bridges. The Pope as Pontiff is the bridge between humanity and the Lord of Creation. The rainbow is a natural symbol of the pontificate.

Bridges are dangerous: one may fall off them or they may give way. Hence the common superstition that it is unlucky to be the first to cross a new bridge (an animal is usually driven across; sometimes it is sacrificed to assuage the fury of the river god for having his power 'overcome'). In some traditions (e.g. Islamic and Zoroastrian) the bridge between Earth and Heaven is thinner than a hair and sharper than a knife: it is suspended over Hell, and the wicked fall off it. In Venice, the Bridge of Sighs connected the place of judgement with the place of execution. Initiation into Chinese secret societies was marked by the crossing of a bridge.

The bridge thus marks the threshold between one psychological state and another. Though dangerous, the bridge must be crossed: to turn back is a regression, a refusal to embark on the next stage of life (which, paradoxically, could be death).

Path From nomadic times, and probably long before, a symbol of human life, as being a passage from the cradle to the grave; in religious life, a symbol of The Way.

SECTION 2

CULTURE AND PSYCHE

2

Culture and Psyche

Symbols relating to culture and the psyche are grouped together in this section because culture and psyche are not opposed entities but two aspects of the same psychobiological process – the actualization of innate archetypal propensities. We live in societies because we are social animals; and our predisposition to create culture resides in our biology as a species. We come into the world as unfulfilled potential, with a long evolutionary past and a comparatively brief social future: we need culture to complete us.

But culture is itself the product of a long and complicated interaction between natural selection and cultural innovation (Boyd and Richerson, 1985; Davies *et al.*, 1992; Durham, 1991; Hirschfeld and Gelman, 1994; Lumsden and Wilson, 1981, 1983; Steele and Shenan, 1996; Tattersall *et al.*, 1988; Trinkaus, 1989). Our archetypal propensities (which evolutionary psychologists call 'modules' or 'evolved psychological mechanisms') determine the kinds of cultures we form, and these in turn influence the reproductive strategies adopted by individuals living in them (Ridley, 1994). As a consequence, cultures impact on genes as surely as genes influence cultures, the psyche acting as an intermediary between them.

Richard Dawkins has introduced the term 'meme' as a cultural equivalent of the gene. A meme is a cultural unit, such as an idea, a motif, or a symbol, which survives in the memories of successive generations. Memes are transmitted by teaching, initiation, imitation, and learning, and, provided they achieve wide enough dissemination, do not die out when local populations become extinct. In this manner they constitute a 'meme pool' which, at the cultural level, corresponds to the gene pool at the DNA level.

Not everyone is happy with the term 'meme', however. As the cognitive scientist Dan Sperber (1996a) has pointed out, memes are less stable than genes. Unlike genes, memes (ideas and symbols) are not true replicators, because they tend to undergo some degree of change every time they are transmitted. Whenever a folk tale is recounted it is somewhat modified in the telling. Nevertheless, like folk tales, many ideas retain their essence and prove resistant to the erosion of transmission, despite dissemination through one generation after another. What is it, Sperber asks, that makes some ideas more resilient and more contagious than others?

When it comes to folk botanical and zoological concepts, Sperber has no doubt that we possess 'an innate disposition to categorize plants and animals' and that this explains why such classifications are remarkably consistent across cultures. Yet ideas concerning the supernatural are unconstrained by everyday verification. Nevertheless, 'throughout the world's cultures, the same kinds of gods, dragons, devils and ghosts recur again and again'. Ideas of the supernatural may vary more from culture to culture than do ideas about plants and animals, but, insists Sperber, 'they vary in directions which are predicted by commonalities of the human mind' (1996b). It is with the symbolic consequence of these 'commonalities' that this Thesaurus is primarily concerned.

That the progressive complexity of human cultures from Stone Age times to the present has been associated with parallel developments in the complexity of human consciousness seems a likely proposition, though it is not easy to state with any degree of certainty what these developments may have been. One approach to the problem which has attracted many adherents is to examine the contents of myths in the context of history and to relate them to the archaeological record. Most influential among these researchers have been Lucien Lévy-Bruhl, J. J. Bachofen, C. G. Jung, Ernst Cassirer, Mircea Eliade, Jean Gebser, Julian Jaynes, Erich Neumann, and Ken Wilber, whose relevant works are cited in the Bibliography. One of the most recent contributors to this field of informed speculation is Steven Mithen (1996) who adopts what he calls a 'cognitive archaeological' approach to the developmental prehistory of mind and of culture, using the symbolism of light and the theatre to present his argument.

COGNITIVE ARCHAEOLOGY

The drama of mental development occurs, according to Mithen, in four acts, the first beginning in darkness (to symbolize relative unconsciousness), the last ending in brilliant light (symbolizing the consciousness of the post-industrial computer age).

Act 1 begins in Africa 6 million years ago with the ancestor we share with our nearest relative, the chimpanzee. Unfortunately, this common ancestor, or 'missing link', has left no trace.

Act 2, Scene 1 begins 4½ million years ago with the appearance in Africa of *Australopithecus ramidus*, followed 300,000 years later by *Australopithecus amanensis*. Both australopithecines (literally, southern apes) lived in woodlands and were primarily vegetarians. Three and a half million years ago, 'Lucy' (*Australopithecus afarensis*) arrived on the scene, a descendant of *A. ramidus* or *A. amanensis*, with a brain size of 400–500cc. She was adept at both climbing trees and walking upright on two feet. The stage is lit during this scene by a single flickering candle. With Act 2, Scene 2 the lighting gets somewhat brighter with the arrival on the stage 2½ million years ago of *Australopithecus africanus*, and half a million years later the lighting gets a little brighter still with the entrance of *Homo habilis* ('handy man'), whose brain size is 500–800cc, and who is capable of using stone tools, and catching and butchering animals.

Act 3, Scene 1 opens at the very beginning of the Pleistocene, the Lower Palaeolithic, 1.8 million years ago. The stage lighting is still poor, but there is a noticeable improvement in Scene 2. In Scene 1 *Homo erectus*, a descendant of *Homo habilis*, appears in East Africa, China, and Java, and by 500,000 years ago he has moved into Europe. His brain size is 750–1,250cc, and he makes use of symmetrical pear-shaped stone tools, known as handaxes. Act 3, Scene 2 marks the beginning of the Middle Palaeolithic 200,000 years ago, and the development of tools made of carefully shaped and pointed stone flakes designed for specific purposes. Neanderthal man emerges 150,000 years ago. He has a brain between 1,200 and 1,750cc and is adapted to living in glacial environments. He still uses tools made of stone or wood, although he begins to use unmodified pieces of bone.

Act 4 opens 100,000 years ago and consists of three action-packed scenes. Our own species *Homo sapiens sapiens* (brain size 1,200–1,700cc) is already on stage in Scene 1, having evolved during the previous 50,000 years. He is first seen in South Africa and the Near East and the stage lighting becomes markedly brighter as the action proceeds. This anatomically modern human not only buries his dead but adds animal carcasses as grave goods – presumably to feed the departed spirit on its journey to the other world. He also uses red ochre, possibly for bodily adornment, and makes beautifully shaped harpoons by grinding pieces of bone. Act 4, Scene 2 begins 60,000 years ago in South East Asia, where *Homo sapiens sapiens* builds boats enabling him to make the crossing to Australia. By 40,000 years ago he has arrived in Europe, and the Upper Palaeolithic (Late Stone Age) begins. He fashions tools and weapons out of bone and ivory; builds dwellings, using stones, branches, and mammoth bones; develops ceramic technology for making clay figurines and pots; makes needles for sewing clothes; and paints sophisticated representations of animals on cave walls (Leroi-Gourhan, 1982; Marshack, 1972). About 35,000 years ago Neanderthal man disappears and *Homo sapiens sapiens* remains alone on stage. Towards the end of this scene recurrent influxes to the Americas occur across the now submerged landmass of Beringia between Siberia and Alaska. The stage lighting is now very much brighter. Act 4, Scene 3 begins 10,000 years ago with people in the Near East planting crops and domesticating animals, and the light intensity goes on increasing up to the present.

THE MENTAL CATHEDRAL

Mithen's account of mental development draws heavily on the work of the evolutionary psychologists Leda Cosmides and John Tooby, who compare the mind to a Swiss Army knife, with its specialized tools and blades, which they liken to the 'multiple mental modules' that make up the human mind-brain (see p. 335). These 'modules' equip all young children with *intuitive* knowledge about the world in at least four domains, which Mithen calls 'intuitive psychology', 'intuitive physics', 'intuitive biology', and 'intuitive language', each of which evolved in the context of our ancestral hunter-gatherer existence.

In addition, Mithen endorses Sperber's assertion that the mind has evolved a special, overriding module concerned with forming 'concepts of concepts' and involved in generalized linguistic capacities, self-consciousness, and the use of symbols (Sperber, 1975, 1996a).

All these Mithen draws together in the symbolic image of a cathedral, the nave consisting of general intelligence (which is involved in general-purpose learning and decision making) and the numerous side chapels representing the 'multiple mental modules' concerned with their own specific intuitive domains. This cathedral represents the basic mental equipment of *Homo sapiens sapiens* as he appeared on the scene 100,000 years ago. Then between 60,000 and 40,000 years ago, the cultural revolution coincided with a major change in mental functioning: it was as if doors and windows had been inserted in the chapel walls, or as if a new 'superchapel' had been constructed to incorporate them all, thus enabling the different cognitive domains to interact and influence each other. This greater mental flexibility, which Mithen calls 'cognitive fluidity', made it possible for our ancestors to go much further than the mere interpretation of 'natural symbols' (such as hoof prints or the parallel marks in sandy soil made by a recently passing snake) to create images possessing symbolic meanings (as in the practice of the arts).

Although Mithen presents a persuasive case, it must be acknowledged that it is in the nature of a theoretical fantasy. There is no evidence to suggest that any fundamental change occurred in the neuroanatomy of the brain 60,000 to 40,000 years ago. The brains we have now are probably identical with those possessed by our ancestors 100,000 years ago. What has happened is a progressive improvement in our cultural means of storing information and of transmitting it from generation to generation. The development of 'cognitive fluidity' was not a neurophysiological 'big bang' as Mithen implies but a consequence of making better use of the cognitive faculties which we already possessed by virtue of being members of *Homo sapiens sapiens*.

MYTHICAL COGNITION

Being an archaeologist, Mithen makes little use of the mythological material presented by the authorities mentioned above, but this material nevertheless fits reasonably well into the framework that Mithen has provided. Thus Wilber, following Gebser, distinguishes four structural stages in the development of consciousness and culture:

(1) the pleromatic-uroboric (6 million to 200,000 years ago)

(2) the magical-typhonic (200,000 years ago to 10,000 BC)

(3) the mythical-membership (10,000–2,500 BC)

(4) the mental-egoic (2,500 BC to the present).

These stages are themselves interpretive fantasies which the authors have projected on to the mythological material, but as imaginative constructs they are persuasive. We shall examine each of them briefly:

(1) **the pleromatic-uroboric** The Gnostic term 'pleroma' roughly equates with the Hindu *prakriti*: it signifies the dynamic potential out of which all things were created. The uroboros, the primordial symbol of the snake eating its tail, signifies the self-sustaining processes basic to organic life. It is seen as representing the 'biblical paradisical primal state' when 'the soul still sleeps', and at this stage, according to Gebser (1966), there prevails 'a complete lack of separation or distinction between the individual and the whole'. This is in complete agreement with the views of Cassirer (1953–7) and Neumann (1954). As Neumann puts it: 'The original situation which is represented mythologically as the uroboros corresponds to the psychological stage in man's pre-history when the individual and the group, the ego and unconscious, man and the world, were so indissolubly bound up with one another that the law of *participation mystique*, of unconscious identity, prevailed between them.' This was also the view of Lucien Lévy-Bruhl and C. G. Jung. While this may indeed describe the conscious condition of the ancestor we share in common with the other apes, who lived 6 million years ago, the probability is that by 200,000 years ago *Homo erectus* had developed a much sharper awareness of his situation than Wilber's schema would allow.

(2) **the magical-typhonic** The logical, verbal, conceptual capacities

of mind have not yet developed by this stage, nor are body and self clearly differentiated. This stage represents the consciousness of early *Homo sapiens*, and would be roughly equivalent to the emotional and sexual chakras of kundalini yoga. Wilber chooses 'typhon' as the appropriate symbol for this stage because in this mythic figure both man and animal, human and uroborus, are still intertwined: R-complex and limbic system (the reptilian and mammalian components of the triune brain) are still not subject to overriding neocortical control (*see* Figure 7, p. 334).

A better symbol than typhon would perhaps be the 'Sorcerer of Trois Frères', the figure, probably of a shaman, etched into the wall of a Palaeolithic cave at Trois Frères in France. Joseph Campbell (1959), describes it as follows: 'The pricked ears are those of a stag; the round eyes suggest an owl; the full beard descending to the deep animal chest is that of a man, as are likewise the dancing legs; the apparition has the bushy tale of a wolf or wild horse, and the position of the prominent sexual organ, placed beneath the tail, is that of the feline species – perhaps a lion. The hands are the paws of a bear.' But, according to Wilber's definition, 'any figure that is structurally half animal and half man is a typhonic figure'. In this Thesaurus such a figure is classified as a 'monster' or 'fabulous beast'.

Wilber cites the **totem** as the 'perfect example of magic-typhonicism', because through totemism man is 'still structurally linked to animal ancestors'. Our mental apparatus was still subject to the powerful influences of the R-complex and limbic system and, as a result, subject and object, psyche and world, were not yet well differentiated. 'Magic' is appropriate to this pre-differentiated stage: it provides a vital emotional-instinctive nexus, not a logical-objective nexus, which was to come later. We still find ourselves reverting to the magical, pre-differentiated, emotional-instinctive nexus in our dreams.

(3) **the mythical-membership** The tenth millennium BC marked the most important transformation in the history of the world. For it was then that humanity took up farming. This coincided with a mutation in consciousness from the magico-typhonic (Stage 2) to the mythical-membership (Stage 3), when humanity, finding itself in fertile locations, ceased to live in hunter-gatherer groups of about sixty individuals

and settled in villages of 200–400 people, then towns of 3,000–5,000, and finally cities of 50,000 or more. This concentration of large numbers of people in one confined area was something entirely new and it demanded the development of both inner psychic and outer social controls. The result was a strengthening of superego admonitions, imperatives, and prohibitions within the psychic apparatus, and the inauguration of a hierarchically structured society within the city state or nation, with monarchs, nobles, and high priests at the top, and peasants, serfs, and slaves at the bottom. It was within this context that the mythical-membership structure of consciousness emerged. The hierarchy was extended upwards to include the gods, and the superego became, in the minds of susceptible individuals (prophets, gurus, charismatics, shamans), the (hallucinated) 'voice of God'. In this way, civilized states, with their tightly integrated myths and religions, were formed.

Farming brought with it the capacity to conceive of extended time and the ability to make preparations for the future harvest. People had to learn how to postpone gratification. This could never have occurred without language or symbols, both of which provide the means to deal with the non-present world, the past, and the future. Farming inaugurated the stage of mythical cognition – which is intermediate between magical emotional-instinctive ('limbic') consciousness and the logical, rational, conceptual ('left-hemispheric') consciousness – and it coincided with the world's greatest, most enduring mythologies, religions, and civilizations: the Sumerian, Babylonian, Egyptian, Aztec-Mayan, Chinese, Indian, Mycenaean, and early Grecian.

A major preoccupation clearly afflicted humanity at this stage: the problem of death. Dawning awareness of the self as an individual presence holding membership in a group went along with the knowledge that life is finite: it ends in death. Confronted by this tragic fate it is inevitable that people should wish to circumvent it. A major impulse behind the religions which now emerged was the need to find magico-ritual means of compensating for death fears and transcending them. The problem of death afflicts us as much as it did our early farming ancestors, but where they found a solution in religious practices, we tend to find a solution in repression and denial. The symbolism of life, death, and rebirth is, however, as alive for us as it was for them.

(4) **the mental-egoic** By the beginning of the modern era all the essentials of civilized urban life were present: farming, the state, organized religion, hierarchy and rank, money, warfare, kingship, mathematics, writing, the calendar, and the beginning of self-consciousness as individual members of a group. The period 2,500–500 BC saw the gradual emergence of philosophy and politics culminating in sixth-century BC Greece with such towering intellects as Anaximander, Pythagoras, Solon, and Thales, whose thinking we can appreciate without difficulty.

During this period an entirely new kind of myth begins to emerge. In place of the old Great Mother myths, in which the individual is an entirely dependent appendage or victim to be castrated, mutilated, or sacrificed, we have the revolutionary development of the hero myths, in which the individual frees himself from the Great Mother, defeats her, and triumphs over her. Wilber identifies the hero with 'the new egoic structure of consciousness', which coincides with the recurrent myths and legends of the hero's triumph over the Great Mother or one of her consorts, such as the old serpent–dragon–uroboros or the Medusa, or one of her offspring, such as Typhon. According to this view, the treasure hard to attain, which the serpent-monster protects, is the new ego structure itself – the personal, willing consciousness of man with a say in his own destiny.

To accept Wilber's argument is not to agree with Julian Jaynes's (1976) extraordinary assertion that prior to the second millennium BC man 'did not have any ego whatsoever'; a more reasonable supposition is that the ego, already present, became more aware of the power it could now exert over nature, over the plant and animal kingdom, and over his fellow man – and woman.

REFLECTIVE CONSCIOUSNESS

Whether or not one goes along with Wilber's terminology and time scales, it seems highly probable that the symbolic canons of myth and religion began when people started to reflect on their circumstances in the natural world instead of blindly existing through them, and it is clear that something of great importance occurred to us about 60,000 years ago – the time when our astrobiological preoccupations began in earnest. It is as if, through the evolution of human consciousness, the cosmos finally became aware of its own existence. The human psyche provided the mirror in which Nature could see her face reflected.

Since 'magical-typhonic' times our cultures would seem to have passed through animistic, totemistic, megalithic, lunar, and solar stages, and much later, when principles of agriculture and animal husbandry were formulated, there emerged the idea that the heavenly bodies, numbers, plants, and animals, all obeyed certain laws, predictable regularities, and recurring rhythms that could be known, studied, and recorded for the benefit of future generations. These advances coincided with the development of polytheism, monotheism, and, eventually, alchemy, moral philosophy, and natural science. From the Neolithic era has come clear evidence of ideas of space, number, life, death, and rebirth, which have preserved the same symbolic forms through subsequent millennia. It is these forms which will be considered in this section.

i Religion and the Sacred

A number of anthropologists and behavioural scientists are coming round to the view, propounded by C. G. Jung earlier this century, that religious beliefs and practices, which are universally characteristic of human communities, are archetypally determined (Stevens, 1986). As Jung put it: 'The idea of the moral order and of God belong to the ineradicable substrate of the human soul' (*CW*8, para. 528). Shortly before his death the distinguished American anthropologist Victor Turner (1983) declared his agreement with this view. Sociobiologists also share it, regarding religions as essentially biological phenomena which contribute to the 'inclusive fitness' of those who subscribe to them. 'It is certain,' writes Walter Burkert (1996), 'that the basic religious structures had evolved before humans reached America [over 24,000 years ago], for despite thousands of years of isolation, the religions of American aborigines remained comparable and similar to their Old World counterparts in many respects.'

Religious behaviour may thus be considered a species-specific characteristic of humankind (Boyer, 1994). That the implications of this realization have hitherto been left out of consideration has been due to the insistence of behavioural scientists that each culture should be studied as an autonomous system entirely peculiar to itself. Although this approach has added to our understanding of individual religions in the social context in which they developed, it does not tell us how or why religions emerged in the first place or why religious practices should be so persistent and ubiquitous.

The psychosocial importance of religion for the development and stability of human community life is very apparent. Not only does it provide a mythic explanation of how things began and how a special relationship was formed between the community and its gods, but it ensures group cohesion by granting absolute validity to the moral code on which society is based; its rituals rejuvenate the beliefs and values of the collective and its rites of passage assist and sometimes propel individuals through the crucial stages of the life-cycle. Most important of all, religion provides a transcendent context for human experience promoting awareness of a higher purpose over and beyond the mundane preoccupations of everyday life.

As with symbolism generally, a particular religion is not directly inscribed in the human genome any more than a particular language. But the propensity for religious beliefs and behaviour is innately 'prepared for', like the propensity for speech. The particular set of religious beliefs and rites practised in a given society has to be learned by each generation in the same way as its language. But the idea that there will be a religious system and a language which will have to be learned appears to exist in all growing individuals as an *a priori* assumption.

Precisely how our religious propensities emerged in the evolutionary history of our species is still a matter of speculation, but the human tendency to project psychic contents into the unknown must have played a role in the development of religious doctrine as it did in the creation of alchemy and astrology. The capacity for this kind of animistic projection is evident in children from a very early age. One example is given by Brant Wenegrat (1990). A little boy of two lay in bed listening to a story read to him by his mother. Suddenly, the house was shaken by an earthquake: the windows rattled deafeningly and the building creaked and groaned. Scooping the boy up in her arms, the mother ran with him to the nearest doorway, where they would be safe from falling debris. As soon as the shaking stopped, the child remarked with evident relief that the Earthquake had gone away. It was not immediately apparent that he had personified this frightening phenomenon, but later he described it as a being who had come to the house and shaken all the windows. Gently, his mother explained that no one had come to do it but that the ground had moved of its own accord. But when his father came home later in the day, he was informed by his son that the house had been visited by the Earthquake who had rattled the windows and then gone down beneath the ground. Although his father repeated the information already imparted by his mother to the effect that earthquakes are not people but spontaneous movements of the ground, the child persisted in his personification. The event had obviously scared him and he was apprehensive that it might recur: for some weeks afterwards he would go to the window and cry, 'Go away, Earthquake! Don't come here any more!'

In this episode we see the spontaneous emergence of a mythic being akin to the Greek god Poseidon. As Wenegrat comments, the most salient feature is the rapid and fixed personification of an anxiety-provoking event: 'in trying to understand what had happened, the boy invented a nature god and a rudimentary liturgy' (ibid., p. 85).

ii Gods, Goddesses, and Demons

The array of gods, goddesses, and demons created by human beings since the beginning of time is so vast as to defy description, as is the variety of symbolic representations to which they have given rise. The pantheons of Sumerian, Egyptian, Greek, and Semitic peoples are well accounted for, as are some of those of indigenous Americans, Africans, and Asians, but these deities make up only a tiny fraction of all the supernatural beings that have been set up, sacrificed to, and worshipped since our species began to behave in this way. The anthropologist Anthony Wallace (1966) has estimated that we have in the course of our evolution produced somewhere in the region of 100,000 religions of one sort or another. All we can do here is present the more common and ubiquitous of these divine motifs and symbols which have been recorded and which still emerge from time to time in our dreams.

As in the case of the little boy who spontaneously created Poseidon, or something very like him, the earliest religions probably arose through the attribution of deity to natural forces and phenomena, such as the sun, moon, sky, earth, earthquakes, thunder, the rain, and the wind. On the whole, deities linked to the sun, sky, thunder, fire, and wind tend to be masculine, while those linked to the moon, earth, water, crops, and plant life tend to be feminine.

Essentially, gods and goddesses are personifications of archetypal potential. They evoke feelings, ideas, and images which are experienced as familiar because their stories, powers, and personalities embody the projected facets of human nature. It requires a degree of objectivity and psychological sophistication to understand this, for, deprived of such 'superior' insight, people actually *believe* in their gods and goddesses as existing and real. This sophistication is achieved at a price, however, for a culture that no longer believes in its gods is spiritually adrift and in danger of disintegration. Commenting on our collective loss of myth and religion in Western society, Jung wrote: 'Only an unparalleled impoverishment of symbolism could enable us to rediscover the gods as psychic factors, that is, as archetypes of the unconscious . . . Since the stars have fallen from heaven and our highest symbols have paled . . . heaven has become for us the cosmic space of the physicists, and the divine empyrean a fair memory of things that once were' (*CW*9i, para. 50).

In the majority of creation myths, the cosmos is brought into existence by a primordial figure experienced as remote and indifferent to the fate of human beings. However, this aloof creator proceeds to generate more personable gods and goddesses, culture heroes and heroines, whose adventures begin to approximate to the archetypal patterns of human existence. In particular they stress the qualities necessary for survival – sexual union and procreation, the provision of vital resources, the conquest of monsters and enemies, the establishment of rites and rituals to govern the relationship between humanity and supernatural forces, and to guarantee the perpetuation of the group (and, *inter alia*, the species).

In the creation of all myths and religions, the parental archetypes perform a central role. The FATHER ARCHETYPE personifies as the Elder, the King, the Father in Heaven. As lawgiver he speaks with the voice of collective authority, and is the living embodiment of the Logos principle: his word is law. He is the guardian of the *status quo* and a bastion against all enemies. His symbols are Heaven and the sun, thunder, lightning and the wind, the phallus, the weapon, and the bull. While the sky symbolizes the spiritual aspirations of the masculine principle, of which the Father is the prime carrier, it is not always the realm of universal good: it is also the source of natural disasters and catastrophes. Heaven is the primordial patriarch's throne room from which he passes judgement, punishes with thunderbolts, and rewards with boons, freely exercising his powers of life and death over his wives and children. For like the Mother, the Father has a terrible aspect: as with Zeus, Jahweh, Jehovah, and the Hindu god, Shiva, he is both nurturing and destructive. He is Kronos who prevents his sons from replacing him by eating them alive.

As with the archetypal Father, the MOTHER ARCHETYPE is not an innate image but a dynamic complex of the phylogenetic psyche. The symbolic canon to which the Mother archetype gives rise is very extensive, as may be discovered by consulting Erich Neumann's *The Great Mother: An Analysis of the Archetype* (1955). A universally encountered manifestation of the archetype is as Mother Nature or Earth Mother, goddess of fertility and dispenser of nourishment; as water or sea she represents the origins of life as well as personifying the unconscious, the fount of all psychic creativity; as moon goddess she exemplifies the essential periodicity of womanhood. She also takes the form of divine animals: the bear (jealous guardian of her children) and the celestial cow, who nourishes the earth with milky rain.

The Great Mother is the very nucleus of the feminine archetype. The epithet 'Great' indicates her timelessness and her numinous superiority over everything mundane and merely human. Like all archetypes, the Great Mother possesses both positive and negative attributes: she who gives also withholds; she who grants life may also take it away. Thus, where the Good Mother's symbols are the flowing breast, the abundant cornucopia, the fruitful womb, the Terrible Mother is the bloodstained goddess of death and destruction. She is Kali dancing on the hapless form of Shiva; she is 'dark, all-devouring time, the bone-wreathed lady of the place of skulls' (Neumann, 1955), the Mayan goddess Ixchel, with deadly snake on head, animal claws, and crossed bones on her mantle – the emblem of death; she is Rangda who steals children; and the Gorgon with writhing snakes round her head, at whom men have merely to glance to be instantly turned to stone. The animal forms which she most characteristically adopts are the dragon and the devouring sea serpent, with whom the heroes of countless mythologies have done battle down the aeons of man-made time.

Separation of the 'good' from the 'terrible' aspects of the parental archetypes is formalized in religions which allocate good and evil functions to different deities. The Christian separation of the godhead into all-good, all-powerful God and His evil adversary, Satan, made it possible for the faithful to hate the Devil while professing unambivalent love for the Almighty. Freudian analysts have suggested that what the Devil is to the father-figure the witch is to the mother, but this formulation fails to acknowledge an additional component which becomes active in the second half of the first year of human life – the archetype of the stranger/predator/evil intruder (Jung's 'SHADOW' ARCHETYPE), which features not only in the demonologies of the great majority of religions round the world but also in the nightmares and night terrors of childhood. Christian iconography identifies the Devil with the dragon and with the serpent, which, like its prototype in the Garden of Eden, tempts man to sin. The evil woman, Lilith, with her serpentine associations, adopts her natural role as Satan's wife, giving birth to phantom creatures in the wilderness, suckling little children with poisoned milk, and sending them horrible dreams.

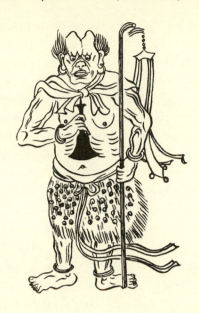

To the Greeks, however, who readily accepted that their gods and goddesses were capable of terrible as well as admirable deeds, demons – *daimones* – were also morally ambivalent. Greek demons could be protective as well as malign and acted as intermediaries between mortals and immortals. They were identified with a person's 'genius', and with the special gifts and intuitive powers responsible for determining one's fate. But in the majority of demonic manifestations throughout the world, the shadow archetype is clearly at work.

Sky gods Ethnography has established the existence of a virtually universal belief in a sky deity, endowed with infinite knowledge and wisdom, who is said to have created the universe, decreed the laws on which it should be run, and guaranteed the fecundity of the earth through the regular provision of rain. This universal hierophany of the sky is due to its ubiquitous presence as a celestial arch of seemingly infinite height. The invincible power of the sky god is attributed to him through the perception that, seated on his heavenly throne, he is at the very peak of the social hierarchy – the ultimate expression of the RANK ARCHETYPE, whose symbols are the mountain, the pyramid, the ziggurat, the tree. From the exalted heights of the Empyrean, this Supreme Being sees everything, and must, therefore, know everything,

177

and through the infinite powers at his disposal is in a position to govern, to judge, and to punish. Zeus, Jupiter, and Thor are typical and well-known examples. But there are many more.

The Sumerian *me* means man, male; it also means sky. Moreover, the Sumerian ideogram for divinity was also the same as that for sky, and it was pronounced *ana* or *anu*. *An* also means rainy sky. This complex of meanings was personified in the Sumerian sky god Anu, who subsequently became the Supreme God of the Babylonians. His temple at Uruk was called *E-an-na*, Sky House. He sat on a throne in the sky, bedecked with the trappings of sovereignty: sceptre, diadem, headdress, and staff. He was both Father and King of the Gods. The principal feast of Anu was held at the New Year when the creation of the world was ritually commemorated. With the passage of time, however, the New Year feast was to become consecrated to Marduk, a younger god, who became important about 2150 BC, at a time when the storm god Enlil-Bel was replacing Anu as the Supreme God of Babylon.

Mircea Eliade has demonstrated that in the historical development of religions there is a tendency for the original Supreme Being of the sky to give way to divine figures more directly involved in the daily events of human life, so that they provide protection against adverse powers as well as guaranteeing such crucial resources as rain, fertility, success in warfare and the hunt. Thus the sky god is demoted, or, as in the case of the Greeks, actually castrated, eventually to be replaced by gods, goddesses, and demons who satisfy deeper, demiurgic needs and regulate more immediate economic realities.

This development is often generational, as in a family, though the timescale greatly exceeds that of human generations. The history of that difficult and incestuous family at home on the peak of Mount Olympus is a case in point. As this generational progression continues, the original sky god is differentiated into other gods, often his sons and grandsons, whose specialized functions emphasize different elements of the Father archetype, such as his sovereign power, his hierogamic duties as the spouse of the Great Mother, and his responsibilities as storm god assuring rain and fecundity.

Some authorities have postulated the existence of an original sky god, Dieus, common to all Indo-European tribes, from which later sky gods evolved. However, a prototypical sky god is not a necessary postulate in view of the readiness with which the magnificence of heaven can evoke the hierophantic experience. The Indian god Dyaus, the Greek Zeus, the Roman Jupiter, and the Germanic Tyr-zio are all expressions of the same archetype projected on to the celestial vault. Their very names reveal their consanguinity: the Greek genitive of Zeus is *Dios*, which at once links him to the Indo-European Dyaus. The Sanskrit *Dyaus-Pitar* (Zeus Pater, Father Zeus) is the origin of Jupiter, the sky god of the Romans. Like Dyaus, Zeus bears the connotations: day, brightness, sky; the Cretan *dia* = day; Latin *dies* = day; Sanskrit *divus, devos* = god, shine, day, and is the root of divinity. The Germanic Tyr-Zio (*Tiwaz*) corresponds again to the Sanskrit *deivos*. With the passage of time, Dyaus loses his sacred power and is replaced by another deity Varuna. In the Vedas and in post-Vedic writings Dyaus scarcely appears, except as a common name for sky or day, as in *dyavi dyavi*, from day to day. Gods, like the symbols they give rise to, evidently have a life-cycle of their own.

Whereas Dyaus incorporates all elements of the Father archetype, Varuna emphasizes sovereignty and power. He *binds* his subjects in thrall to him and is invariably represented with a rope in his hand. Again, this power is implicit in the etymology of his name: the Sanskrit *varatra* = rope, strap. The faithful dedicated to Varuna call themselves his bond slaves. Although primarily a sovereign, Varuna nevertheless remains a sky god: from his starry home he sees and knows everything; he notices every sin and punishes all who break his laws by binding them, so preserving the universal order. Varuna's nets are feared as much as his ropes because they are bonds that trap, paralyse, and exhaust. The etymology *var vrnoti* = to cover, to close in, emphasizes Varuna's celestial as well as his binding or netting qualities (Eliade, 1958).

Ouranos, the original sky god of the Greeks, is known to us only from the myth recorded by Hesiod. Ouranos and Gaia constituted the primordial Sky–Earth Pair, from whom the first gods, the Cyclops, giants, Hecatoncheires, and other monstrous creatures were born. The unpopularity of Ouranos with his wife and children was due to his practice of binding his progeny and hiding them in Gaia's body, which caused her agonizing pains. His rule was ended by Kronos, his youngest son, who, prompted by his mother, lay in wait for Ouranos to come to earth, as he always did at nightfall, and, cutting off his father's genitals, threw them into the sea (an act which, incidentally, led to the birth of Aphrodite out of the bloody foam).

Kronos proved to be little better than his father, exercising similar tyrannical powers, eating all his children, and binding his adversaries in chains. Zeus, who was preserved by his mother Rhea from his father's voracious appetite, also exercised sovereignty through bondage, as did his brother, Hephaestos, on catching his wife, Aphrodite, in adultery with Mars, and trapping them under a net of iron for all the gods to see.

By historical times Ouranos and Kronos had disappeared, to be replaced by Zeus as ruler of the elements and of the lives of the gods and men. The tripartite division, common to all mythologies, between the three cosmic levels of Heaven, Earth, and Underworld, applied no less to the pantheon of the Greeks. Zeus (Sky and Upper Air) ruled with the aid of a cabinet composed of his family – his brothers Poseidon (Sea and Earthquakes), Hades (Underworld and the Dead); his sisters Demeter (Agriculture), Hestia (Home Affairs); his wife Hera (Marriage and the Family); his sons Apollo (Health), Hermes (Communications), Ares (War), Dionysus (Wine and Ecstasy), Hephaestos (Crafts, Inventions, and Heavy Industry); and his daughter Persephone (Seasons and the Underworld) – the whole family mafia having been started, by common knowledge, by Ouranos lying on top of Gaia, and, prior to their separation, copulating without cease.

The idea of dominance and control through BONDAGE is not only ubiquitous in the symbolism of sky gods but in the contemporary ritual practices of sado-masochists, where the dominance–submission and sexual archetypal systems have become fused (Stevens and Price, 1996). Eliade (1958) provides numerous examples of religious bondage, in addition to those already mentioned. The Akkadian god Adapta, supremely wise instrument of progress and civilization, who was worshipped about 3000 BC, was particularly celebrated for his obedience, bound hand and foot to his master Ea. Marduk, whose chief weapon is the net, the gift of his father Anu, does battle with the monster Tiamat, binds him, chains him up, and kills him. The binding of Isaac is the central Jewish icon of man's faith in God. Judaism is and always has been a father–son religion which strictly forbade the worship of goddesses. As a result it emphasizes obedience rather than love.

However, the god who binds also liberates. Odin, or Wotan, Germanic god of war and divination, wins in battle through use of magic, paralysing his adversaries with fear, and binding them. Odin lived on mead and wine and, as a consequence, was a god of trance and frenzy, capable of liberating uncontrollable forces, as in the *Furor Teutonicus*, which seized Nordic or Germanic warriors in battle. Odin was also 'the great shaman' of his people, his qualities betraying his links with the shamanic practices of Northern Asia: he could evoke the *Furor Religiosus* as well as the *Furor Teutonicus*.

Storm gods These emphasize those aspects of the Father archetype that have to do with rain-provision and fertility; they are commonly identified with the **bull**, the nurturant earth being symbolized by the **cow**. For example, Enlil, son of Anu (supreme sky god of the Sumerians), was 'Lord of the Violent Wind', who governed the waters as well as the rains and was responsible for the Flood; he was also a bull god. In this he resembles Min, consort of the Egyptian cow goddess Hathor, and prototype of the god Ammon. Enlil also has close affinity with his Phoenician successor Ba'al or Hadad, and with Zeus, the Thunderer, who, disguised as a bull, carried off Europa on his back. The link between storm gods and the bull is further emphasized by the use of the 'bull-roarer' in initiation rites – the bellowing of the bull being likened to thunder. The bull is also associated with the moon, which controls tides, rains, and fertility, the horns of the bull being symbols of the crescent moon.

Storm gods embody the violence and unleash the powers on which the vitality of the cosmos depends. Indra, the Indian storm god, is Master of the Plough, the Bull of the World, and his sexual powers over fields, animals, and women are positively Gargantuan. The principal Hindu god Shiva, who together with Brahma and Vishnu makes up the divine trinity of Hinduism, is Creator, Preserver, and Destroyer, as well as 'Lord of Creatures'; his animal companion is the bull Nandi, and his temples are full of bulls.

The universal symbol of Shiva is the LINGAM, the erect phallus, thus exhibiting beyond all doubt his male generative powers. Such ithyphallic deities are found all over the world. Examples are Hermes, the Norse god Freyr, the Egyptian gods Min and Osiris, the Japanese Dosijin, and the Australian Djanggawul. These deities are associated with territory, the land, agriculture, the Underworld, procreation, and with domesticated animals such as the bull, boar, goat, and horse.

All these gods of storm and fertility are symbolical products of an historical process set in motion by the discovery of agriculture and animal husbandry over 10,000 years ago. As the original supreme sky god gives way to them by a process of differentiation and specialization, his absolute sovereignty is diluted and he declines into the more 'human' role of consort of the Great Mother. His union with her, as is the case of all such divine pairs (e.g. Freyr with his sister Freyja, Osiris with his sister Isis), represents the *hieros gamos* (sacred marriage) necessary for renewal of the life-giving powers of the earth. With his demotion, the sky god may even yield precedence to the Great Mother goddess and her 'son', who invariably turns out to be a vegetation god, who dies and rises again, guaranteeing the regenerative life of the crops as well as the eternal life of the soul.

Dionysus (son of Zeus), Osiris (son of the Egyptian sky goddess), Aleion (son of the Phoenician Ba'al) – all were associated with suffering, death, resurrection, and initiation. The son of the sky god invariably shares the lot of humanity, and, through the provision of initiation rites into his sacred mysteries, assures redemption and eternal life. It was against the storm gods of fertility that the Semitic people produced their monotheistic, Messianic revolution. The triumph of Jahweh over Ba'al represented the reassertion of 'heavenly' values over the 'earthly' preoccupations with mere fecundity. Nevertheless, Jesus (son of God) conforms to the same historic tradition of those other sons of the sky god who underwent suffering, death, and resurrection to guarantee the eternal continuance of the cycle of life.

Sun gods and **the sun** As the exalted rank of the sky god declined, so, it appears, the self-esteem and confidence of the new agriculturalists was rising. Just as sky divinities were gradually transformed from supreme beings into gods of storm and fertility, so, in Egypt, early Europe, Asia, Peru, and Mexico, they were also turned into divinities of the sun. Sometimes this history can be traced in the divine career of a single god. Mithras, for example, began life as a sky god, was transformed into a sun god, and later became a hero-saviour (*sol invictus*), while at the same time ensuring the continuance of life by slaying the bull from which all plants and grains originated.

Early in the development of Egyptian religion, which more than any other is dominated by sun worship, sky deities were 'solarized' into such figures as Min-Ra, Ammon-Ra, etc. This process reached its zenith during the fifth dynasty, when an interesting rivalry became apparent between Ra, the sun god, and Osiris, the corn god, both guarantors of immortality. In this rivalry the rank archetype performed a crucial role, the sun's sovereignty being confirmed by its association with the aristocratic elite, those of royal blood being guaranteed life in the beyond as an automatic perquisite of their birth. Osiris, on the other hand, was part of the 'human' evolution of the sky god in the direction of adopting a more 'democratic' participation in life on earth, providing immortality to anyone capable of emerging victorious from the initiatory trial or ordeal (originally the struggle with a bull).

The notion that the sun is the eye of the sky god is an evident stage in his solarization. It is found not only in Egypt but among the San Bushmen of the Kalahari Desert, the Semang Pygmies, and the inhabitants of Tierra del Fuego, encountered by Charles Darwin on his voyage in HMS *Beagle*. A later stage is marked by the emergence of the sun as the earth's consort, as in Timor, where the Lord Sun, *Usi-Neno*, marries Lady Earth, *Usi-Afu*, and the whole world is the result of their union. Timor chieftains claim to be 'children of the sun', tracing their ancestry directly to the sun god.

As in the career of Mithras, the solarization of the sky god causes his decline to the semi-human status of the solar hero, who, having been swallowed up in the Underworld in the West, emerges triumphant next morning in the East as *sol invictus*. This motif is linked to initiation rites, such as those practised in Australasia, through which the initiate becomes identified with the solar hero, and, in the process, himself becomes the son of the sky god. The initiation is, like all other initiations, a death and rebirth experience, whereby the symbolism of the setting and rising of the sun is symbolically repeated and ritualized.

Although sun-worship has never been as widespread as was once thought, the sun is nevertheless the origin of heat and light and its resurrection every morning as well as its return after the winter solstice are matters of primary concern to every human being who has ever existed. It is not surprising, therefore, that sun symbolism, unlike sun-worship, is ubiquitous. One obvious example is the DISC which carries the additional meaning of completeness, wholeness, and perfection. Frequently the disc has wings or is represented as the solar eagle or hawk to explain how it flies on its daily passage across the sky.

One of the oldest and most complex of all solar symbols is the SWASTIKA. It has been found in virtually all parts of the world, including pre-Columbian America. Its form suggests rotation about a central axis, and there are in fact two kinds of swastika: the right-handed *swastika*, and the left-handed *swavastika*. These have been variously interpreted as male and female, solar and lunar, clockwise and anti-clockwise movement, the rising vernal sun and the descending autumnal sun, and so on. That the reversed swastika is indeed feminine is suggested by its association with the vulva in representations of Artemis and Astarte. In China the two swastikas depict the Yin and Yang forces. The swastika has also been associated with the winged solar disc and with the Pole and the revolution of the stars round it. Both the Pole and the Zenith coincide with the mystic Centre and the *axis mundi*. The implied fourfold movement of the swastika suggests the circling of the square and the squaring of the circle apparent in mandala symbolism.

Another ubiquitous symbol which combines the implications of the disc with the idea of movement is the **wheel**. The radial arrangement of its spokes further emphasizes the wheel's solar associations. The number of spokes varies with geography: in the Far East there tend to be eight, linking them to the eight petals of the lotus flower, the eight chakras of kundalini yoga, and the eight trigrams of the *I Ching*; in the Near East there are more likely to be twelve, associating them with the twelve signs of the zodiac, twelve months of the year, etc.; sometimes both eightfold and twelvefold symbolisms are combined. At Konarak ('Place of the Sun') on the East coast of India there is a temple dedicated to the Vedic sun god, Surya. The temple was designed to resemble a huge chariot to be drawn by seven enormous horses, for like the Greek sun god Helios, Surya requires a horse-drawn chariot to pull him across the sky. Along each side of the temple are twelve stone wheels, each nearly ten feet high and each having eight spokes (Moon, 1991).

The very first wheels were solid and may have been more readily associated with the moon than with the sun: the wheel's solar implications became more apparent when spokes came into use. This is reflected in the history of the zodiac, which was originally a lunar wheel of solid wood – 'Ishtar's Girdle' the pre-Islamic Arabs called it; to the Babylonians it was the 'House of the Moon'. The simplest form of solar wheel had four spokes, representing the cardinal points and four seasons, as well as the four phases of the moon. The introduction of six, eight, or twelve spokes further strengthened its solar implications and weakened its identity with the moon. To both Hindus and Celts, however, the wheel was much more than a solar symbol, it was a cosmic symbol, the hub being the still centre of the world.

That the centre of the hub remains still while the spokes and rim circle round it, further enhances the symbolic possibilities of the wheel. To the Taoists this resembled the sage, who could cause movement without himself being moved (the *wu-wei*, 'action through non-action'); to the Aristotelian it similarly represented the 'unmoved mover'; to the alchemist it resembled the contrast between the volatile and the fixed; to the Buddhists the hub is the place where celestial power is concentrated: the Buddha, the Ruler, the Universal Man resides there and is the only being in the universe who remains unchanging in a world of ceaseless transformation.

The mandala form of the wheel, which the oriental psyche likens to the lotus, suggests the rose to the Western mind: the *oculi* of Romanesque churches, as well as the rose windows of Gothic cathedrals, make aesthetic use of this associative configuration. The inexorable forward movement of the wheel once momentum has been established makes it emblematic of fate and the 'Wheel of Fortune', the tenth enigma of the Tarot pack, which symbolizes the cycle of life, the inexorable alternation of good fortune with ill, and of one life with another.

As a symbol of solar energy, the WHEEL OF FIRE is found in many parts of the world: it comes into its own at times of solstice, blazing wheels being bowled through the narrow streets of medieval Europe, or, more specifically, carried to hilltops at the summer solstice and rolled down hillsides at the winter solstice. The Celtic wheel of fire revolved alternately in both directions, suggesting the symbolism of the double spiral, namely, evolution and involution, birth, death, and rebirth. In Northern latitudes, the winter solstice inevitably gives rise to fears that the sun may continue on its journey South and never return. Rituals involving the wheel of fire are designed to ensure that this disaster will not occur.

The HALO, nimbus, or aureole, is a symbol of solar radiance which has been assimilated to the radiance of sanctity, holiness, and divinity. If the spoked wheel represents the sun's beams, then the halo stands for the transcendental, supernatural light emanating from the head (the noblest part) of a saintly or holy personage. When extended to the whole body, the halo becomes the almond-shape aureole, the 'mystic almond' or MANDORLA; the linking of the two sides representing the *coincidentia oppositorum*, the union of opposites. In Christian iconography Christ is represented with a cruciform halo, while in Hindu paintings Shiva is depicted with a halo of flames. Not surprisingly, sun gods such as Apollo, Phoebus, and Mithras were commonly represented with haloes, as were Roman Emperors who had been deified.

Sun gods are often depicted with RAYS issuing from their heads or

shoulders. Straight rays represent the light of the sun while undulating rays represent its heat. The CORONA RADIATA is the hair of the sun god, as in the golden rays of Helios. **Gold**, the sun's colour, symbolizes incorruptibility, durability, eternity. To the Aztecs gold was the 'excrescence of God' and to the Egyptians 'the flesh of the gods'. The association of gold with sun gods such as Apollo is considered under **Colours** pp. 146–9.

Earth goddesses   Of all goddesses, the most impressive and most ancient is the GREAT MOTHER: it seems that she has always been with us. The Maternal-as-Archetype may well have been the first transpersonal principle to be the object of religious awe and veneration, just as the mother-as-person is the first object of our love to this day. Not only is the goddess still widely revered as the Virgin Mary but her cult has been revived in the biologically regenerated Gaia, Goddess of the Earth.

The primordial notion of the Earth as Mother of all Creation is found, in one form or another, all over the world. In the Mediterranean region she was *Terra Mater*, who gave birth to all living things. To the Amerindians she provided the womb deep in the earth where human beings grew like embryos until they emerged on the Earth's surface. In Greece, Gaia or Ge (in Modern Greek 'earth' is feminine and still called γη) herself gave birth to her primordial partner, Ouranos, before beginning to populate the world with his grudging assistance.

Everywhere the Great Good Mother occurs as the source of life and abundance; she is the nutrient earth, the cornucopia, the ever-fruitful womb. Whether she manifests as Isis, Hathor, Cybele, Ishtar, Lakshmi, Parvati, Tara, Kwan-yin, Demeter, Sophia, or Mary, she is invariably beneficent, nourishing, and creative. Her symbols are legion, and include all that is protective and enclosing – the cave, wall, earth hut, house, church, temple, city; all containers or vessels of nourishment – the cup, cauldron, basket, horn of plenty, vase, yoni; all waters and all that comes from them – shells, fishes, pearls, the dolphin; all food-producing animals – the cow, sow, goat, deer. Among birds her attributes are the dove, swan, goose, swallow, partridge; among plants and flowers, the lily, rose, lotus, and fruit trees.

The hierophantic assimilation of the earth to the mother archetype is as readily understandable, therefore, as the hierophantic identification of the father archetype with the sky. Territorial attachment to the soil from which one sprang is a bond which modern men and women can form as strongly as their ancestors, though it may not be felt with the same mystic intensity. This too is understandable, for, to begin with, the human infant appears to make little distinction between his mother and the world. For him she *is* the world. Only later, with differentiating consciousness, does he begin to make a distinction between the two. But even then, it is as if he experiences the world as an extension of his mother, and, as a result, he extends his investment of love for the mother to an investment of love in his immediate environment. Gradually, the world begins to rival the mother as a source of numinous enticement.

So exploration begins, with the mother functioning as a 'secure base' to and from which the infant crawls in the course of his first adventurous excursions. This recurrent to-ing and fro-ing is a paradigm of all subsequent development, a rhythmic cycle of separation and reunion, progress and regression. It helps to explain the nostalgia which many experience for their native soil, which can call them back again and again, not least when the time comes to die. *Hic natus, hic situs est*, says a Roman sepulchral inscription (Here he was born, here he is laid); *Hic quo natus fuerat, optans erat illo reverti*, says another (Here where he was born, he desired to return). For many peoples this is, and always has been, a wholly natural desire to 'go home' to the maternal earth-womb from which one was born. Hence the neolithic practice of burying the dead in the foetal position – a necessary preparation if one is to be born again.

In all places, at all times right up to the present century, the mother has been identified with the landscape – the hills forming her breasts, buttocks, and hips; the grass and vegetation her hair; the rocks her bones; the gorge or valley her vagina; the cave her womb, and so on. This identity inspired the sculpture of Henry Moore and informed the Gaia hypothesis of James Lovelock (1987), that the earth and the ecosystem form a living being like Mother Earth and that we must revere and protect her if we are not to murder her with our rapaciousness. This was beautifully expressed in the 1890s by the Amerindian prophet Smohalla of the Umatilla tribe, who refused to till the soil when his people were deprived of their hunting range. 'It is a sin,' he said, 'to wound or cut, to tear or scratch our common mother by working at agriculture . . . you ask me to dig in the earth? Am I to take a knife and plunge it into the breast of my mother? But then, when I die, she will not gather me again into her bosom. You tell me to dig up and to take away the stones. Must I mutilate her flesh so as to get to her bones? Then I can never again enter into her body and be born again. You ask me to cut the grass and the corn and sell them, to get rich like the white man. But how dare I crop the hair of my mother?' (Eliade, 1960).

Terrible Mother As we have already seen, the Great Mother is never experienced as wholly beneficent: she has a savage, bloody aspect and possesses powers of sorcery and witchcraft. As the ensnaring and death-dealing Terrible Mother, she is Astarte, Kali, Durga, Lilith,

Hecate, Circe, the Gorgon or Medusa with serpent-hair and hideous appearance. She is goddess of the chase, war, and death, as well as goddess of fertility. Everywhere her rites have been bloody and orgiastic: slaughter and dismemberment, sacrificial offerings of blood, are demanded by her if she is to guarantee earthly fertility. The archaic connection between blood and fertility is probably due to the observation that menstruation ceases during pregnancy and to the deduction that embryos must be formed out of the stored blood. Thus, it follows, by this primitive logic, that the earth must drink blood if it is to be fertile.

That goddesses, like gods, evolve out of one another is nowhere more evident than in Hinduism, the oldest religion in the world (possibly as much as 10,000 years old), where multiple manifestations of the same divinity are the rule rather than the exception. According to one tradition, all Hindu goddesses are transformations of a single female deity, DEVI. Devi's positive aspect manifests in Parvati, consort of Shiva (their union being symbolized by the conjoined lingam and yoni), and also in Shakti (feminine creative energy); while Devi's fierce, terrible aspect is apparent in Durga, a goddess whose numerous arms brandish weapons of war as she rides on the back of a lion.

Durga was created out of the combined masculine energies of the gods in order to conquer demons who could only be destroyed by a female deity with quasi-masculine powers. Durga also appears as KALI, the dark goddess adorned with parts of the human body. Kali is the familiar of cremation grounds who accepts blood offerings, and who, as Camunda, assumes her most terrible form – an emaciated devourer of the dead, adorned with snakes, scorpions, and skulls, filling the world with hideous cries as she seeks to satisfy her insatiable, agonizing hunger for human corpses. Camunda's name is derived from Canda and Munda, two demon chiefs whom she decapitated.

Kali bears a resemblance to the Greek goddess Athena (the Roman goddess Minerva) in that both are warriors and both are born out of the head of a parent deity: Athena from the head of Zeus (Jupiter), Kali from the head of the goddess Ambika, yet another manifestation of Devi. But whereas Athena is associated with masculine solar values (e.g. reason and justice), Kali owes her origins to the feminine earth and the underworld. Thus, both Kali and Camunda are examples of the Terrible Mother, who devours life, clawing it back into her mawlike womb.

That the Terrible Mother is not confined to India, Asia, or Europe is demonstrated by the existence of the Aztec earth goddess Coatlicue, whose head and hands were made of rattlesnakes, her feet of jaguar claws, her bodice adorned with human hands and hearts, and, from beneath her skirt, which is woven from snakes, there flows a serpent of blood. Like the uroborus she embodies the inexorable dynamic of life and death (eat and be eaten) that sustains the cosmic process.

Goddesses appear to have an affinity for the COSMIC TREE and the serpent. Eve is but one consequence of this archetypal association which got her and her partner Adam into such grave trouble with the jealous, patriarchal Jehovah, who would have no other gods (and certainly no goddesses) before him. Listening to the snake (giving attention to her own unconscious instincts) results for Eve in instant punishment: banishment from the Garden of Eden (itself a symbol of the all-containing womb of the Great Mother goddess). Sap-filled trees were venerated throughout Africa as representatives of divine motherhood: the sycamore goddess, an embodiment of Hathor, the mother goddess of ancient Egypt, is an example. In the pre-Aryan civilization of the Indus Valley a nude goddess was represented standing next to a sacred tree: this Cosmic Tree, at the centre of the world, source of life and endless regeneration, associated with a nubile figure, is an evocative celebration of youth and fertility.

Throughout the Mediterranean region and the Near East the affiliation between the Great Mother and the **serpent** is everywhere apparent. In addition to its regenerative, numinous powers, the serpent is an intimate denizen of the earth and a symbol of the ever-fertilizing phallus. Moreover, its association with chthonic goddesses of the Underworld makes the snake a familiar of spirits of the ancestors in the kingdom of the dead. In the lowest layers of excavations at Ur and Erech statuettes were found which represent the mother goddess and her child, both having the head of a snake. Neumann (1954) attributes this symbolism to a development from one of the oldest manifestations of the Great Mother – the uroboros, the Chaos Serpent, Leviathan girdling the earth.

APHRODITE, goddess of love, beauty, and fertility, has origins which predate Indo-European culture and connect her with Mesopotamian goddesses of love and war. In ancient Sumer she was called Inanna (Lady of the Sky); to the Semites, who conquered Sumer, she was Ishtar; to the Canaanites, Astarte; and only latterly did she become Aphrodite for the Greeks. In the course of this succession, Aphrodite lost her warlike aspect, which was carried for her by her lover Mars, god of war. HERA, goddess of marriage and family life, long-suffering wife of constantly philandering Zeus, also has origins in pre-Hellenic myth.

As these lineages demonstrate, with the passage of time earth goddesses all go in for specialization of different aspects of the Mother archetype in ways which parallel the progressive differentiation of the Father archetype in the historical development of gods of the sky.

Moon goddesses So completely accustomed have we become to the use of artificial light that it is difficult for us to conceive how important the moon was to hunter-gatherer communities: the light of the moon extends or deputizes for the hours of daylight, and this fact alone provided the hunter with an invaluable resource. In a hot climate, such as that in which we evolved, prey animals often sleep during the day and are difficult to find, but at night they seek water and food and can be hunted more successfully by the light of the tropical moon.

Fear of the dark, a universal human characteristic which could militate against nocturnal hunting, is minimized when there is a good moon. Hence, it is not surprising that goddesses of the hunt, like Artemis (Diana), are moon goddesses. But Artemis, like Demeter, goddess of the grain, and her daughter, Persephone, Queen of the Underworld, probably derives from a primordial earth goddess. For Great Mother goddesses share as much in the sacred nature of the moon as of the earth.

Unlike the sun, which is always the same, the moon waxes and wanes, it disappears ('dies') and reappears (is 'reborn'): it is thus profoundly implicated in the recurring cycles of life and death; the tides of the sea; the menstruation of women; the sowing, growth, and gathering of the crops; the fertility of fields, animals, and women; the timing and conduct of ceremonies of initiation. As a result, the moon is experienced as not merely measuring these events but as controlling them; and it is therefore natural that the moon should be perceived as a numinous manifestation of divinity.

For three nights every month the sky is dark: there is no moon. But on the fourth night it reappears. 'As the moon dieth and cometh to life again,' say the Juan Capistrano Indians of California, 'so we, also having to die, will again rise.' This symbolism is apparent in all initiation rites, which consist of a ritual 'death' and 'rebirth', the initiate 'dying' to his old identity and being 'reborn' into the new. The characteristic disappearance and regeneration of the moon link its symbolism to that of the **snake**, which is cunning at concealing itself and which regularly casts off and renews its skin. Being tellurian, the snake is also closely associated with the fertility of the earth. Moreover, to many tribes, the snake is endowed with 'moon force' and is responsible for the menstruation and the fecundity of women. Another animal linking divinities of the earth and moon is the **cow**, whose horns are emblematic of great goddesses of fertility and at the same time represent the two crescents (waxing and waning) of the moon. The cow is both celestial and chthonic. Also associated with the moon is the **spider**, probably because the rhythms of the moon weave together with weblike threads the existence of humanity with the regular pulses of all living phenomena. Like the spider, lunar goddesses are seen as 'weaving' the cosmic veil, which enmeshes human destiny in its threads. Moon goddesses are therefore arachnoid in the sense that they are spinners and weavers of fate. (Spiders, incidentally, got their scientific name after Athena turned Arachne into a spider for daring to rival her.)

iii Creation Myths

The crucial questions to which all human communities have attempted to find answers are: Where did we come from? How did the cosmos begin? Only recently have these answers been framed in scientific terms. For the great span of human existence they have been stated in the pre-scientific terminology of myths and symbols. When all these mythic and scientific explanations are compared, a profoundly interesting fact emerges; they often overlap in such a way as to suggest that the primordial mind and the modern mind have been working along similar lines.

For example, the Big Bang of modern cosmology was anticipated, as we have already seen (p. 74), by the Buddhist belief that the universe grew from a centre when the Buddha entered a timeless moment just before the world was created. The modern idea that the universe, which is at present expanding, will at some moment start contracting to a central point, and that the whole process may be repeated again and again, is paralleled by the Hindu view of cosmic creation as an endless cycle of creation → expansion → contraction → destruction → quiescence → creation → etc. The notion that all life originally emerged from the sea is common to a great many mythic cosmologies, as is the idea that the world originally belonged to the animals before humans came on the scene. Tara, supreme goddess of Mahayana Buddhism, known as the Great Saviourness, has a male counterpart Avalokitesvara, the Saviour of Mankind. Together they give birth to monkeys, which gradually develop into humans (they turn out to be Tibetans) – thus crudely anticipating the ideas of Charles Darwin by thousands of years. The physical laws relating to the conservation of energy are compatible with the ancient Vedic view that the world was created and continues to exist through a sacrificial renewal of divine powers – i.e. something that exists cannot cease to exist in physical reality; it can only be transformed. A large number of peoples hold the belief that the moon and the earth were originally of the same substance. The Upanishads expressed the conviction that all that apparently exists is but a transitory manifestation of a profounder dimension of reality – a truth which the modern mind sees as related to the elementary particles and quantum mechanics of field theory, which enshrines the basic laws of physics.

These fascinating parallels are hints that archetypal processes are links between physical and psychic realities – that the laws on which the universe proceeds may also help shape our mental attitudes to them and the hypotheses we formulate to comprehend them.

The ultimate koan (Zen riddle) posed to all would-be cosmologists is how something can come out of nothing. When there was no time, no space, and nothing in existence, what was there? And then, what miraculous change occurred to set the great cosmic experiment in motion? To assert that suprahuman deities were involved is only a partial answer because it does not explain who or what created *them*. The solutions which the more imaginative members of our species have played with have inevitably been expressed in symbols, the most ubiquitous relating to some primal deity, who is sufficient unto him or herself, and whose attributes are represented by the circle, the mandala, the sphere, the COSMIC EGG, the ANTHROPOS, and, most dynamic and primitive of all, the **uroboros**. 'Therefore the demiurge made the world in the shape of a sphere,' declared Plato, 'giving it that figure which of all is the most perfect and the most equal to itself' (*Timaeus*).

Timeless and eternal, without beginning and without end, the sphere is entirely self-contained. It is the philosophical world egg, the nucleus of the beginning in a state of perfect repose. Within its substance all opposites are united and no conflicts exist, for the world has yet to begin. It is the Chinese *T'ai Chi* containing white and black, day and night, heaven and earth, male and female. It is the primordial HERMAPHRODITE containing the World Parents, locked together in their timeless erotic embrace. It is the Gnostic PLEROMA, the Father–Mother source of all being. It is Plato's androgynous Original Man and the Hindu *Purusha*, who was Soul (*ātman*), alone at the beginning of the world: 'Looking around he saw nothing else than himself. He said first: "I am" . . . He was, indeed, as large as a woman and a man closely embraced. He caused that self to fall (*pat*) into two pieces. Therefrom arose a husband (*pati*) and a wife (*patni*)' (*Brihadaran-yaka Upanishad*, 1.4 1–3).

The idea of self-sufficiency, self-containment, and self-completion is beautifully expressed by the primordial dragon or serpent with its tail in its mouth, the self-nourishing, self-begetting uroboros. In *The Origins and History of Consciousness* (1954) Erich Neumann collects together an impressive number of examples (many of them illustrated) of this, the 'most ancient deity of the prehistoric world': a Babylonian *mappa mundi* with the uroboric ocean ringing the world, a Mesopotamian bowl and a Mexican calendar stone, an Indian representation of Maya, the eternal spinner, encircled by a serpent, Navajo Indian sand paintings, and gypsy amulets.

The human psyche has given rise to all these symbols in its attempt to grapple with the as yet unsolved mystery of the primal cause, and, comments Neumann, they are as alive today as they ever were: 'They have their place not only in art and religion, but in the living processes of the individual psyche, in dreams and fantasies. And so long as man shall exist, perfection will continue to appear as the circle, sphere, and the round; and the Primal Deity who is sufficient unto himself, and the self who has gone beyond the opposites, will reappear in the image of the round, the mandala.'

Many mythic cosmologies begin their account of creation at a later stage than the original round or Cosmic Egg. In some, Father Sky, as Supreme Being, does it alone, like God in Genesis who first creates the world, then Adam, and, finally, as something of an afterthought, Eve. In others, the Great Mother is primary and she gives birth to Father Sky, like Gaia giving birth to Ouranos. But in all these instances the implication is that the original creator must be androgynous in the sense that she/he contains within her/himself the seeds of both masculine and feminine possibilities.

In numerous myths the cosmos is not created *ex nihilo*, but is brought into existence as the result of the sacrifice of a god (e.g. Prajapati), a primal monster (Tiamat or the giant Ymir), a superman (Purusha), or a primeval animal (the bull Ekadath of the Iranians). Creation through sacrifice is recounted in myths originating from a very large number of different peoples and traditions, and it expresses the notion that matter can neither be made to exist nor cease to exist but only transformed. That sacrifice is necessary for transformation to occur is at the heart of the symbolism of initiation and its rituals, which characteristically re-enact the original sacrifice of creation as it was performed *in illo tempore*.

Jung and his followers (e.g. Neumann, 1954; Edinger, 1992) have linked the symbolism of the sphere, the world egg, and the uroborus to the phenomenology of the primal Self as it slumbers in the womb and in early infancy. At this stage, the ego is a mere germ of conscious potential: it 'swims about in the round like a tadpole', says Neumann; it sleeps within the circling coil of the uroborus, waiting for the 'coming of light', the dawning of consciousness. In mythology, this stage is symbolized by the separation of the world parents by the hero; in young children it coincides with conscious recognition of themselves and their parents as separate personalities in their own right. Through the medium of symbolism and the symbolic story (myth), ontogeny and phylogeny interact and give rise to parallel psychic epiphanies. This is not to repeat the Haeckelian fallacy, as do both Neumann and Eliade, that 'ontogeny repeats phylogeny', or that 'every infant in its pre-natal state is re-living the life of primordial humanity' (Eliade, 1958), but that, in attempting to *formulate* the pre-natal state and the life of primordial humanity, the psyche makes use of the same symbolism.

As the source of human awareness of existence, the primal Self is also represented in the symbolism of the Anthropos, the COSMIC MAN, from whom the whole universe comes into being. One example, already mentioned, is Ymir in the Germanic Edda ('from Ymir's flesh the earth was formed, from his bones the mountains'). In China he is P'an Ku, who became the cosmos. According to Von Franz (1975), P'an means eggshell and 'to make firm', while Ku means underdeveloped, unlightened, or embryonic: 'When P'an Ku cried the Yellow River and Yang-Tse-Kiang came into being, when he breathed the wind sprang up, when he spoke thunder arose, when he looked around lightning flashed. When he died the four holy mountains of China (with the Sung-mountain as fifth in the middle) came from his body. His eyes became the sun and the moon – much later he reincarnated through a virgin, "the holy mother of the first cause", and became a cultural hero.'

With the symbolism of the Cosmic Man we return to the equivalence of the macrocosm and the microcosm. At the opposite pole from the macrocosmic man we find the idea of man as microcosm embodying

all the potential of the universe in miniature. His smallest version is found in the pre-scientific belief that the male sperm was a man or woman in miniature, a homunculus, who grew into a baby in the mother's womb.

Once the world egg has hatched, the cosmos is set in motion. The uroborus differentiates into masculine and feminine halves, the World Parents separate, and, with this schism in the original unity, the opposites are constellated, and conflict enters the world. Creator gods give rise to other gods and these give rise to heroes, whose ordeals, trials, battles, adventures, loves, and exploits define the archetypal modes of human existence.

iv Paradise and the Fall

The idea of an original paradise, where man lived in bliss amid plenty, from which he was eventually excluded and to which he longs to return, is extremely widespread. The Genesis story of the Garden of Eden and the Fall of Adam is but one of many examples.

Paradise is derived from Persian words meaning the walled garden of a king. As the Biblical description makes clear, the Garden of Eden is laid out as a perfect **mandala** (p. 117): from the roots of its central Tree of Life a spring or fountain feeds the Four Rivers of Paradise, which flow to the four cardinal points, forming the vertical and horizontal arms of a cross. Here time stands still. Nothing and no one ages. The Garden is full of bird-song, succulent fruits, and sweetly scented flowers. Humanity, animals, plants, and God all live together in perfect accord. There is no misery, conflict, suffering, or privation; everything one could possibly want in life is there.

Medieval maps, such as the *mappa mundi*, place Paradise on the very edge of the inhabited world to the East, the source of the rising sun. The Greeks, however, placed their Garden of the Hesperides – the Sisters of Evening, who, according to some, were the daughters of Nyx (Night) or Erebus (Darkness) – on the edge of the world to the West, on the slopes of the Atlas range. As in the Zoroastrian Paradise, the 'Abode of Song', the main delight of the Hesperides was to sing as they, together with the serpent Ladon, guarded the Golden Apples. The recurrent association of woman, garden, apple, and snake is too obvious to require comment.

The Chinese located their Paradise in Central Asia. It was inhabited by Dragons of Wisdom (the snake again) and also had four rivers arising from a common source, the Lake of Dragons. As with the Sumerian Paradise Dilmun, and the Egyptian Aalu, this Chinese Paradise was evidently well watered and plentifully supplied with crops.

Both Hesiod and Ovid tell us that the creation of the world was followed by four ages of history – the Golden, Silver, Bronze, and Iron. The Golden Age coincided with paradise on earth: Saturn ruled and people lived to a great age in a garden of beauty and plenty, free of all legal restraints and the necessity to work. When the Golden Age gave way to the Silver, this blissful state was dissolved for ever: men had to learn to build dwellings against the cold and to labour in the fields for their bread. They now learned the difference between right and wrong; and the figure of Justice, with her scales, hovered over the landscape, while men toiled below. Then the Iron Age followed, according to Hesiod, 'to the hurt of man', and the horrors of organized warfare became an ever-present possibility.

In Iranian mythology, the Golden Age was ruled over by Yima, the King of Men. At this time the land was so beautiful and rich that men and their flocks multiplied till there was no longer room to accommodate them. Three times Yima stretched the earth to make room for them in a vain attempt to keep pace with the ever-increasing population. Eventually, Ahura Mazda (the supreme deity of the Iranians, whose name literally means Lord of Wisdom) instructed Yima to make an enclosure and place within it the best men, women, animals, and plants to protect them from the bitter winters which were to come and destroy all the evil on the earth (the Flood motif).

In these, and many other examples, Paradise is invariably an enclosed place, surrounded by a wall, or, as in St Brendan's Isle or the Greek Isles of the Blessed, by the sea, ensuring its separation from the profane world of conflict, suffering, trade, and warfare. When Paradise is lost, harmony disintegrates into discord, and humanity is plunged into time, labour, suffering, and death. It means the dispersal of humanity from the divine centre of the cosmos and a persistent longing to return.

What is this universal and recurrent symbolism about?

Paradise Lost

John Milton's great epic poem, published in 1667, tells the story

> Of Man's first disobedience and the fruit
> Of that forbidden tree whose mortal taste
> Brought death into the World, and all our woe,
> With loss of Eden.

This 'loss of Eden' can be understood on at least five symbolic levels: the migration of our early ancestors from forest to savannah; the transition from the hunter-gatherer existence to pastoral and farming life, and the emergence of civilization; the expulsion of the baby from the womb; the differentiation of the ego from the Self; and the development of human consciousness.

(1) **Early migration from the forest** The early ancestral transition from the primeval forest to the open savannah entailed the abandonment of a predominantly vegetarian diet of gathered fruit and the adoption of a more carnivorous diet of hunted meat. Elaine Morgan (1990) has argued persuasively that our ancestors also went through a long period of seashore living with a diet consisting mostly of seafood. Necessity drove us from one place to another and we have had to adapt to differing environments, climatic conditions, and diets, and this has gone along with the development of larger brains and a greater capacity for consciousness (Stringer and McKie, 1996).

The vegetarian life of the primeval forest is echoed in the Genesis story. In Eden, God says: 'Of every tree of the garden thou mayest freely eat' (Genesis 2:16). There is no mention of meat. All that Adam and Eve required for their nourishment literally grew on trees. No bloodshed was required, just browsing – no hunting, no danger, no labour, no tears.

(2) **The hunter-gatherer becomes agriculturalist** This very recent transition, which began only about 10,000 years ago, meant giving up dependency on 'what the Lord provided' in favour of producing for ourselves what we needed to feed much larger populations. Hunting gave way to herding, and the domestication and breeding of farm animals; while gathering was at first replaced by tending natural gardens and later by sowing seeds and cultivating crops. That the Fall is about the end of hunter-gathering and the beginning of farming is suggested by the occupations of Adam's first sons, Cain and Abel, a ploughman and a shepherd respectively. God tells Adam that he must now feed off the land: 'in sorrow shalt thou eat of it all the days of thy life; Thorns also and thistles shall it bring forth to thee; and thou shalt eat the herb of the field; In the sweat of thy face shalt thou eat bread, till thou return unto the ground' (Genesis 3:17–19).

(3) **An allegory of birth** The first nine months of human existence are spent in a gynaecological paradise bounded by the containing wall of the maternal womb. It is a life devoid of tensions and effort, in which everything that is required for the development and continuation of life is provided by the all-giving placenta through the physiological 'Tree of Life', the umbilical cord. Trouble starts when the contractions begin and one is forcefully expelled from this warm and tranquil Eden to the 'booming, buzzing confusion' that awaits in the world outside. The unity of the original uroboric state is disrupted, the opposites are constellated, and all the tribulations of mundane existence are set in train.

(4) **The ego emerges from the Self** Physically, the expulsion from the Garden represents the birth of the child from the womb. Psychologically, it represents the birth of ego-consciousness from the previously unconscious 'uroboric' state. The mandala garden with its central fountain and four rivers radiating from it is an image of the primal self, still incorporating the ego's original oneness with nature and the divine. At first the ego exists only *in potentia* as a component of the Self. Then, as maturation proceeds, the ego gradually differentiates itself out from the Self: 'It is the initial, unconscious, animal state of being at one with one's Self. It is paradisical because consciousness has not yet appeared and hence there is no conflict. The ego is contained in the womb of the Self' (Edinger, 1992).

As with Adam and Eve, the first set of opposites to assail the consciousness of the growing infant is that of good and bad. Consciousness brings with it awareness of one's instinctive animality – nakedness and sex. The demands of society, mediated by the parents, set up a conflict between the social call to adjust and the physical call of the flesh. The price of consciousness is duality, inner division, dissociation, guilt. One is now excluded from the wholeness, completeness, possession of all that is desirable and necessary, compressed within the womb-like wall encircling the Garden. Understandably, the dream of regaining Paradise is one that has obsessed the imagination of humanity: it is the dream of healing all these divisions and being whole again.

(5) **The development of human consciousness** The snake tells Adam and Eve that if they eat of the fruit, their eyes will be opened (they will become conscious) and they *will be like God*. 'There is deep doctrine in the legend of the Fall,' wrote Jung; 'it is the expression of a dim presentiment that the emancipation of ego-consciousness was a Luciferian deed. Man's whole history consists from the very beginning in a conflict between his feeling of inferiority and his arrogance' (CW9i, para. 420). To be conscious is to become aware of creation, like the God who created it, and to know it for what it is. Humanity is no longer passively subservient to Nature but well on the way to mastering it.

The 'demiurge' that created Eden would have kept humanity in ignorance (unconsciousness): 'But of the tree of the knowledge of good and evil, thou shalt not eat of it; for in the day that thou eatest thereof thou shalt surely die' (Genesis 2:17). Adam's disobedience to God, like Prometheus's theft of fire, is a *felix culpa*, a happy sin, for it advances the cause of human consciousness. Accordingly, the Orphites, a Gnostic sect of the second century AD, celebrated the serpent as the principle of *gnosis* – of knowledge and emerging awareness. The serpent, like Prometheus, initiates development at the price of suffering, for consciousness brings with it knowledge of the tragic fate of every human life – the inevitability of death. Pain, suffering, and death exist in the absence of consciousness, it is true, but if there is no consciousness to experience them, then they do not exist *psychologically*. Without consciousness, life is a state of anaesthesia. Accordingly, Prometheus suffers the eagle's visits to gnaw at his liver during the daytime (consciousness), and the wound heals up at night (unconsciousness). During the night we all return to that original unconscious wholeness out of which we (and the ego) were born. In this way the ills and traumas of the day are healed by the sleep that 'knits up the ravell'd sleeve of care'.

As described in the sections on the hero (p. 208) and the monster (p. 367), the development of consciousness demands mastery over the beast and enslaving the two-million-year-old human in ourselves in the name of civilized order and commerce: it represents the apotheosis of the left pre-frontal cortex over the rest of the brain. The development of cities, armies, and empires would never have been possible without such self-discipline: 'the city, once conceived as a representation of Heaven, took on many of the features of a military camp,' wrote Lewis Mumford (1966), 'a place of confinement, daily drill, punishment. To be chained, day after day, year after year, to a single occupation, a single workshop, even finally to a single manual operation . . . that was the worker's lot.' This was the triumphant outcome of the hero's recurrent victory over the monster. A hollow victory indeed! And, not surprisingly, it set off dreams of regaining Paradise.

Paradise Regained

Awareness of loss of Paradise has resulted in profound nostalgia for it, intense fantasies of having it restored in Heaven, and in attempts to find or recreate Paradise on earth.

Nostalgia for the womb, for the Golden Age, for the life of Rousseau's Noble Savage, represents a desire to put the clock back to a more innocent, unpolluted past, to live in harmony with nature. As described on p. 100, this longing may well be associated with innate preferences for the type of landscape in which our ancestors evolved.

The hope that virtue in this life may be rewarded by a return to Paradise in the next is not only enshrined in the Christian tradition, but in the Elysian Fields and Isles of the Blessed of the Greeks; the Iranian House of Yima, where no fights ever occur; the Egyptian Aalu; the Norse Valhalla; the Celtic Avalon, the apple-tree Paradise to which King Arthur is carried when mortally wounded; the Irish Paradise Emain Abhlach ('Emain of the Apple Trees'); and the Moslem Paradise, where everyone wears green silk, lies on couches with silver vessels of delicious drinks, and with grapes always within easy reach – unlike the Greek Underworld, where Tantalus is parched and starving, and the succulent fruits set before him are always beyond his grasp.

Just as the opposite of Paradise is Hell, so the Isles of the Blessed have an opposite – the Accursed Island, full of infernal apparitions, tortures, and dangers. Heaven and Hell represent absolute opposites: the celestial versus the infernal. Paradise, invariably celestial, is consequently related to the passage of the sun. The Isles of the Blessed, for example, are situated neither to the East like Eden nor to the West like the Garden of the Hesperides, but in the centre of the zodiac, the individual signs being conceived as an encircling archipelago of twelve islands. According to medieval legend, St Brendan visited such an island: a huge tree grew near a fountain and its branches were full of birds. Two rivers flowed across the island, the River of Youth and the River of Death, from East to West in accordance with the flight of the sun. The celestial Jerusalem, with its great wall and twelve gates, the River of Life proceeding out of the central Throne of God and of the Lamb, the Tree of Life bearing twelve different fruits (one for each month of the year, its leaves capable of healing nations), represented a vision of Paradise translocated from pastoral woodland to the city. The emphasis on twelve again relates to the zodiac.

For centuries, travellers have attempted to seek out the actual site of the Garden of Eden, usually in remote places like the South Sea Islands, where the climate is clement, the soil good, and the food abundant. Thus, the early settlers thought they had found Eden in Virginia, and at first the Indian Adam proved hospitable. But they soon gave him smallpox, whisky, and guns, then shot him, and dispossessed his children of their lands. EL DORADO, a fabulous city of enormous wealth ruled by the legendary gold-skinned King of Manoa, was thought to be situated on the Amazon, but neither of Sir Walter Raleigh's expeditions succeeded in finding it. In the absence of actual Edens, fantasies of Utopias, Erewhons, and New Atlantises abounded. UTOPIA, Sir Thomas More's imaginary island (Greek *ou* = not; *topos* = a place), was created in accordance with the ideals of the English humanists, so that poverty, crime, and injustice did not exist. ARCADIA, an area of the Peloponnese celebrated by Virgil, was to become a symbol of the simple, rustic life of idyllic tranquillity far from the civilized vice of cities. Celebrated paintings of the scene by Guercino and by Poussin show a shepherd's tomb, however, which bears the inscription *Et in Arcadia ego* ('Even in Arcadia am I'), indicating that death is still present in the most ideal earthly life.

Since the publication of *Robinson Crusoe* in 1719, people have entertained fantasies of the perfect DESERT ISLAND as a refuge from the conflicts and responsibilities of the world. A place of peace and sanctuary, it is protected from enemies and predatory beasts as well as from the raging seas (the passions and the unconscious). The island is a hermitage, a place of solitude and isolation, a temenos for contemplation, and, ultimately, a Land of the Dead. It is also a place of sexual freedom and erotic fantasy, such as CALYPSO'S ISLAND of Ogygia, where Calypso lived alone. She fell in love with Odysseus when he called there on his way home from Troy and promised to make him immortal if he would stay and live with her for ever. She kept him all to herself for seven years, but he yearned for Ithaca and Penelope, and Zeus eventually persuaded Calypso to let him go.

The awful truth is that after a while Paradise becomes a bit of a bore; for over against the human desire for beauty, peace, and tranquillity must be set the urge for danger, conflict, and excitement. Hence the need to maintain a wall or moat around Paradise to protect its precious integrity and keep those who long for adventure outside. Once they have left, they are not readmitted – even if they can find it again (the story of Alain-Fournier's *Le Grand Meaulnes*). The great Italian and English traditions of garden creation are evident manifestations of the desire, shared with the Persian kings, of creating Paradise on earth.

v Heroes and Heroines

These figures are of great importance because they provide the sacred paradigms for a culture and its values. They exemplify its mores, customs, and beliefs; they teach the arts of hunting, fishing, cultivation, childbirth, and healing; they destroy the monsters that threaten the community; they instruct their people in the use of fire and language, lead them to their promised land, designate sacred groves, and devise the rituals that must be practised in them.

Heroes are the products of archetypal propensities and historical events. When hunter-gatherer groups split, and disaffected members migrate to new territories, charismatic leaders are commonly thrown up, who, like the majority of successful shamans, are 'borderline personalities' (Stevens and Price, 1996): they have more ready access than most to unconscious data, which makes them impressive orators, who claim, as often as not, to speak with the authority of the ancestors or the gods. This attracts followers, who perceive them as gurus, worthy of veneration. If they succeed in leading their people to new territories, with adequate resources for survival, then legendary achievements are attributed to them, which, through repetition from generation to generation, become inflated to suprahuman dimensions.

Many have discerned an historical development in the mythologies of the Middle East and India (e.g. Campbell, Jaynes, Jung, Neumann, Wilber; *see* pp. 162–70). From being a dependent appendage (and often victim) of the Great Mother, man breaks free from her and becomes the hero. This seems to have occurred between the end of the Bronze Age (*c.* 2500 BC) and the beginning of the Iron Age (*c.* 1250 BC), when hero myths replaced those centring on the Great Mother and ushered in the patriarchal mythologies of the mountain-living, thunderbolt-hurling sky gods. This shift coincided with the social, economic, technological, and cultural transformations which followed from the discovery of agriculture and the establishment of city states, armies, and empires.

At this period of cultural transformation, the uroboros, eternally locked in its own embrace, uncoils to meet the hero as he advances, iron spear or club in hand: Zeus joins battle with Typhon (the youngest child of Gaia) and wins, and the patriarchal order is established on Mount Olympus; Indra destroys the cosmic serpent Vritra and becomes King of the Vedic pantheon. With these heroic triumphs, the cyclic time of primordial subsistence gives place to the linear time of the civilized world; and traditional 'cool' societies are transformed into the newly emerging 'hot' societies, which now enter the maelstrom of history.

Hero myths have a great deal in common. In accounts gathered from all over the world, the hero is singled out from the beginning by having one divine and one human parent. His mother is either a Mother Goddess herself, or a mortal betrothed to a god. The mother of Gilgamesh is the goddess Ninsun; Romulus and Remus are the sons of Mars (who raped their mortal mother Rhea Silvia); while Herakles is the son of Zeus by Alcmene, wife of Amphitryon. If not of divine parentage, then the hero is taken up by a deity, as was Odysseus by Athena, or he attains divinity as a result of his gifts or achievements, as does Orpheus. Usually his mother is a VIRGIN, which means that she belongs to no man and is therefore available for the god to impregnate. The story of the virgin birth predates the Christian myth by a very long time: it probably owes its origins to that epoch of human emergence when the significance of male semen was unappreciated. The woman was thought to be entirely responsible for the child's creation, its conception being attributed to the *numinosum* – the divine wind or the spirit of the ancestors. If the phallus played a part, it was merely as a means to 'open the way' for the generative spirit to enter the womb and cause the accumulation of blood to be miraculously transformed into a child.

Despite his auspicious parentage, however, the hero is typically abandoned at birth and is adopted by some well-disposed personage or animal. He grows up in a commonplace home where he eventually receives the call to adventure. Usually, he crosses some kind of threshold, and is then subjected to a series of ordeals, which are designed to test his power, ingenuity, and manhood. The feats demanded of him are far greater than any mortal man could hope to accomplish without some form of supernatural assistance, and this is invariably forthcoming from helpful animals, friends, or divinities. Psychologically, these can be understood as representing hitherto unrecognized and unused potential in the Self.

Eventually, the hero undergoes the 'supreme ordeal' – THE FIGHT WITH THE DRAGON, the encounter with the sea-monster, the descent into the Underworld, etc. – and his triumph is rewarded with the treasure hard to attain (e.g. the release of the captive princess, the award of her hand in marriage, and the ascent to the throne of the kingdom). Though born mortal, the hero is ultimately deified and ascends into heaven to live with the gods in eternal bliss.

As may be readily appreciated, hero myths express in symbolic form the experience and ambitions of Everyman: to embark on the adventure of life, he has to free himself from his parents' tutelage and win a place for himself in the world (the throne of the kingdom); if he is to win a mate (the princess) he must undergo a second birth from his mother (a final breaking of the psychic umbilical cord) to free himself and become available for a woman of his own age. Victory over the dragon-mother commonly involves entry into her to permit a symbolical transformation through which the hero 'dies' as his mother's son and is 'reborn' as a man worthy of the princess and the kingdom. Failure to acquit himself through the ordeals and overcome the monster signifies a failure to get free of the mother. The hero will then languish in her belly for ever, leaving the damsel (his anima) in the monster's clutches (i.e. engulfed by the mother complex, she is trapped in perpetuity in the unconscious).

While all heroes embody within themselves both divine and human elements, not all of them are dragon-slayers. An alternative kind of hero emerges whose struggle is fought entirely on the spiritual plane. He is the DIVINE MAN, the prophet, the saviour, the sacred king, the messiah; he is Elijah, Moses, Christ, Mohammed. Generally, these figures are represented with a halo, the divine light betokening a state of blessedness. But dragon-slayers are much more common. In Christendom, St George is the most celebrated example. As usual, a town is being terrorized by a dragon. Having fed it all their sheep, the people are reduced to offering it their children (chosen by lot) to satisfy its insatiable hunger. When St George arrives, the lot has fallen to the king's daughter, who has just been sent out to meet her doom. St George rides after her, transfixes the dragon with his lance, and rescues her. This story may well have been derived from the Greek legend of Perseus, who rescued Andromeda from the sea-monster; and the Greek story may, in turn, have come from the Egyptian tales of Horus, who was depicted riding a horse and piercing a crocodile with his lance.

The prime example of this type of hero in Western cultural history is HERAKLES/HERCULES, whose mortal mother, Alcmene, was married to Amphitryon, grandson of Perseus. One night, while Amphitryon was away avenging the death of Alcmene's brothers, he is impersonated by Zeus who sleeps with Alcmene. The result of their union is twins, of which Alcaeüs (Herakles) was one. From the start, Hera hates him as being yet another example of her husband's infidelity. When the twins are but ten months old, Hera sends two snakes to kill them, but the infant Herakles strangles them with his bare hands.

In the course of his life, Herakles slaughters a vast array of creatures, to say nothing of the especially dangerous beast he destroys in the course of the ten or twelve labours imposed on him by King Eurystheus. The labours are performed by Herakles in expiation of the sin of killing his own and his nephew's children in a fit of madness induced by Hera's implacable hostility. When he has successfully completed the labours, so the Delphic Oracle assures him, he will gain immortality.

The labours involve the destruction of (1) the Nemean lion, monstrous offspring of Echidna with either Orthrus or Typhon, and (2) the Hydra, hideous, many-headed half-sister of the Nemean lion; the capture of (3) the Cerynitian hind, sacred to Artemis, and (4) the Erymanthian boar; (5) the cleaning out of the Augean stables; (6) the removal of the man-eating Stymphalian birds; the capture of (7) the Cretan bull, father of the Minotaur; (8) the man-eating Mares of Diomedes; (9) the belt of Hippolyta, Queen of the Amazons (after which he rescues Hesione by killing the sea-monster sent by Poseidon), and (10) the cattle of Geryon guarded by Eurytion and Orthrus, the two-headed sons of Typhon and Echidna; (11) the acquisition of the golden apples of the Hesperides, guarded by the hundred-headed snake Ladon, whom he kills, and (12) the descent into the Underworld to capture Cerberus, the monstrous guardian of Hades.

Eventually, after many other adventures, Herakles achieves the immortality promised him. He ascends to Olympus, where he becomes reconciled to Hera, who, some say, adopts him. He marries her daughter Hebe and lives for ever among the gods.

It will be seen that, with the exception of clearing out the Augean stables, and acquiring the belt of Hippolyta and the apples of the Hesperides, each of the labours involves establishing mastery over a variety of highly dangerous reptilian, mammalian, avian, and monstrous beasts. In his eventual triumph, Herakles displays himself as the truly archetypal hero.

The symbolic functions of the hero may be summarized under five headings: developmental, exemplary, neurophysiological, biological, and cultural.

(1) **Developmental** The universal appearance of the hero/heroine in myths, religions, folk tales, and legends reveals it to be an archetype which becomes salient at the adolescent stage of development. At this time in our lives we all have to accomplish a number of 'heroic' tasks: if one is to leave home, support oneself in the world, attract and keep a sexual partner, and eventually start a family of one's own, then the bonds to the parents must be loosened, a job prepared for and found, sexual development completed, an appropriate social persona acquired, and enough confidence and self-esteem achieved to be able to play a useful role in society.

Both boys and girls have to overcome their dependency on the parents and prove that they are not 'free-riders' but mature members of their sex, worthy of social status and a mate. This is a period of struggle for both sexes, but wherever initiation rites have been practised, they have, with few exceptions, been harsher for the male. His masculinity is put to the test: he has to demonstrate his readiness to do battle and expose himself to the danger that the **dragon** symbolizes. Though myths demonstrate the Terrible Mother qualities of the dragon, they also reveal that it has masculine attributes as well – the phallic snakes and tusks of the Gorgon, and Hecate's attributes (the key, whip, snake, dagger, and torch). The monster who would have consumed Andromeda, had not Perseus rescued her, was sent by Poseidon from the depths of the ocean, the domain of the Great Mother. Moreover, it is not merely his fear of the Terrible Mother that the hero has to overcome, but of the devouring father as well. For her part, the captive waits for the hero to liberate her, and then marries him. Such is the essential outcome of dragon fights the world over. It celebrates the culmination of developments proceeding in the adolescent male and female psyche.

(2) **Exemplary** Heroes and heroines perform an exemplary function. They are role models for what it takes to be an initiated adult member of the society concerned. Listening to accounts of the exploits of the heroes and heroines recorded in the myths and folk tales of the tribe provides boys and girls with the 'mental set' to survive the terrors of initiation. To the boy, the hero displays what it is to possess the masculine strength, determination, dedication, and will-power to get through the rites to come. By identifying with the hero, he excites within himself the heroic spirit necessary to be judged worthy of initiation into the hunter-warrior brotherhood of men.

For girls, heroines exemplify the feminine virtues which are most prized by their community: these are commonly those of chastity, loyalty, maternity, piety, and devotion. One such heroine is Susanna, celebrated in the Jewish literature of the Babylonian captivity. Susanna, whose name in Hebrew means lily (a symbol of purity), is propositioned by two elders, who spy on her bathing in her husband's garden. They threaten to say they saw her committing adultery (for which the punishment is death) if she will not submit to their desires. Susanna defies them, saying she would rather die than sin in the eyes of God. When the elders carry out their threat and bring her to court, she is rescued by Daniel, a messenger from God, who proves they are lying. Susanna is exonerated and the elders sentenced to death.

The heroine may also be the saviour of her people. One such is

Judith, the Jewish patriot from Bethulia, who saved her people from the victorious Assyrian army by gaining entry to the enemy camp and pretending to seduce their general, Holofernes. Thrilled at the prospect before him, Holofernes gets drunk, and, before he has even touched her, Judith cuts off his head, returning with it in a sack to Bethulia. The Assyrians are completely demoralized by this catastrophe and flee when the Jews attack. Viewed in a context of world mythology, Judith displays her spiritual kinship with those goddesses of love and war in India and the Middle East described above. Similar heroines are Hippolyta, Joan of Arc, and Boudicca. The kind of heroine who actually fights for her man is exemplified by Psyche, and her story is told in *Eros and Psyche* pp. 220–35.

(3) **Neurophysiological** The conflict between the hero and the reptilian monster resulting in the triumph of the hero may be seen as an allegory of the control exerted by the pre-frontal cortex and the dominant hemisphere of the brain over the R-complex – the ancient reptilian component of the brainstem. This intriguing possibility is examined on p. 368.

(4) **Biological** The hero's biological antecedents are very ancient indeed. The responsibility assumed by the hero to seek a priceless item, find the Holy Grail, kill the monster, rescue the captive damsel, realize special powers, are all mythic elaborations of biologically essential patterns of behaviour – the quest for food, for territory, for status, for a mate. In practically every fundamental, the hazards encountered by the hero in folk tales and myths have been experienced by animals for the last three hundred million years. It is little wonder, therefore, that the hero continues to exercise a powerful symbolic influence in our inner and outer lives.

(5) **Cultural** At the cultural-historical level, the Terrible Mother symbolizes that aspect of the natural world that humanity has always been intimidated by. The hero fulfils our longing to escape our helpless vulnerability to Nature's whims. This is why the hero is such a crucial figure in folk tales and myths throughout the world. His triumph is our triumph over the evil predators and sinister powers that might otherwise destroy us. He is our champion, our defender, our liberator and saviour. Moreover, not content with defeating the monster and disinfecting the kingdom of fear, he goes on to show us how nature

may be exploited, and, with the wealth generated by agriculture, how cities and temples can be built and new civilizations created. This stage sees an explosive increase in practical know-how and a dramatic expansion in the capacity for consciousness: everywhere the hero is cast as the 'bringer of light'. And, like Prometheus who steals the gods' fire, and Adam who dares to eat of the Tree of Knowledge, he encourages us to stand up to the jealous, devouring father as well as the terrible, vindictive mother. The World Parents separated, the hero shows how they can be transcended and humanity set free.

Inevitably, there is also a negative side to the story. The ruthless determination that makes it possible for the hero to destroy the dragon, also spurs him to over-reach himself and provoke retaliation from the gods. Prometheus is bound to a rock, his liver daily consumed by an eagle; Adam is banished from the Garden to labour for his lifetime and face death at the end. Icarus flies too close to the sun and crashes into the sea. Nemesis is the consequence of hubris: when the hero disturbs the natural order of things, the homeostatic balance is disrupted. Gilgamesh not only slaughters the monster Tiamet, but destroys the great cedar forests as well. This is the tragic element of the hero's history. He not only transcended the Great Mother, he 'killed' her; and he has been feeding his children off her corpse ever since. The reverent worship of Mother Nature, propitiating her with sacrifices, rituals, and blood, gave way to her destruction through technological assault and the establishment of masculine patriarchal supremacy throughout the civilized world. At the psychological level, the heroic conquest of Mother Nature coincided with two critically important consequences: the repression of the feminine potential in

the male psyche; and the dissociation of the spirit from matter, of the intellect from the body, which was endorsed by Christianity and formalized by philosophy as the Cartesian split.

vi Initiation, Male and Female

The gruelling tests of masculinity undergone by the hero find their personal equivalents in the rites of initiation traditionally imposed by numerous societies on boys at puberty. But rites of passage were by no means confined to puberty: they existed to mark the typical life crises which occur as individuals move from one stage of the life-cycle to the next. From an extensive analysis of such ceremonies, Arnold van Gennep (1960) concluded that they all proceed through three stages: separation, transition, and incorporation. Baptismal initiation, for example, proceeds through the stages of baptism, chrism, and communion; and these correspond to the three degrees of mystic life: purification, illumination, and union. The stages are commonly symbolized by three concentric rings, the outer ring representing the rite of purification or lustration, the middle ring the ordeals and sacrifice, and the inner ring the arrival at full initiation into the next stage.

Virtually all initiations incorporate rites of death and rebirth: the individual 'dies' to his or her previous circumstances (separation) and is 'born again' into the new role or situation (incorporation). While they are actually passing through the rite, initiates are held to be sacred, whereas those who do not participate in the rite remain profane. Once they have passed through the transitional state and have been incorporated into the new status, the initiates return to the profane realities of life.

That so many human beings in different parts of the world have regarded such rites as indispensable is not hard to understand: they enable both individual and society to cope with major transitions through life without undue disturbance, and they provide public recognition of the fact that the transition has occurred. At the psychic level, the realm of the sacred corresponds to the archetypal realm of the collective unconscious, while the profane corresponds to that of the personal psyche. The symbolic and ritual elements of the rites possess intense sacred numinosity because powerful archetypes are constellated. The function of the ritual is to permit these previously unactivated archetypes to be experienced and integrated within the personal psyche, thus enabling the individual to accept and live up to his or her new role or status.

Rites of initiation, therefore, are culturally evolved means of facilitating the primary imperative built into the Self for incarnation in the phenomenal world – that is to say, to be actualized in consciousness, in personality, and in action or behaviour. The demand is repeated again and again in the course of the life-cycle (Mahdi, 1987, 1996). Comparison of rites from all over the world suggests that initiation rituals themselves possess an archetypal structure, for the same symbolism, the same underlying patterns and procedures, are universally apparent. Although the superficial details of male puberty initiations vary in different cultures, there are, nevertheless, a number of standard elements:

1 Initiation is primarily an all-male concern.

2 The young initiates are removed from all contact with females.

3 They are subjected to ordeals and trials of endurance by the older males: they are hazed, harassed, and physically mutilated, usually in the genital region (e.g. circumcision or subincision), but sometimes by tattooing or by knocking out teeth.

4 They are instructed in tribal lore, myths, and traditions.

5 They are ritually slain, dismembered, and brought back to life.

6 Everything is done in the name of tradition, hallowed by the tribal gods.

Precisely why male initiation rites should conform to this pattern is a subject which has long been disputed. Orthodox psychoanalysis saw the rites purely as a means of reinforcing the incest taboo: the elders inflicted painful mutilation on the genitals of the young initiates so as to heighten their 'castration anxiety' and so make them leave their mothers alone (i.e. to their fathers). Bruno Bettelheim (1955), on the other hand, argued that puberty initiation rites not only reduced castration anxiety but minimized envy of the opposite sex by inducing a symbolic form of 'male menstruation'. In this way men could ritually emulate women's miraculous childbearing capacities. But formulations such as these, ingenious though they may be, miss the main point of initiation rites – that of bringing an end to one phase of the life-cycle and activating the next phase of the archetypal sequence. The function of initiation ceremonies is to initiate.

At the same time they guarantee the stability of the social order. All successful societies in the history of our species have had to develop means of disciplining their young men and coercing their aggressive and sexual energies into the service of the group. By devising initiation rites, human societies developed a highly effective means of brainwashing potential delinquents into brave hunters and defenders of the tribe. In the process, initiates loosened their ties to the parents, 'died' as their mothers' sons, and through ritual dismemberment and reassembly were 'reborn' as men among men.

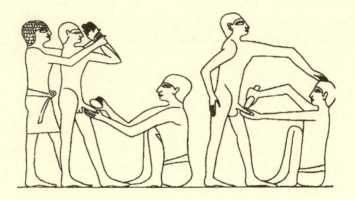

The physical mutilations to which initiates are ritually subjected are not just a test of courage: they symbolize total *dismemberment* – a necessary disintegration of the old state before the new can be refashioned out of the pieces. Thus, Daramulum, the Supreme Being of the Yuin tribe of Australia, is believed to cut young initiates into pieces, burn them, then restore them to life as men, but each with a tooth missing (which a medicine man knocks out in the course of the ritual). The physical ordeal is a technique for heightening the psychic ordeal so as to accentuate the intensity of the initiatory drama and ensure its efficiency as a means of transformation.

Female initiation at puberty is a less common practice than male initiation, and, with the exception of the appalling practice of female circumcision, is usually less traumatic and less public. It generally consists of rites which grant recognition that menstruation has begun and that the young woman has entered the reproductive phase of her life. In many cultures the transition is marked by no rites at all, and it is left to the initiated male to bring about her awareness of herself as a woman. This would explain why the heroine in so many myths, legends, and fairy tales lies sleeping until a prince comes to awaken her. She is the Sleeping Beauty, the lady of Tubber Tintye, Snow White, and Brünnhilde, who slumbers within a circle of fire placed round her by Wotan till Siegfried comes to release her. As the captive damsel in thrall to the monster, or locked up in her father's tower, she is the goal of the hero's quest. In the male psyche, she is the anima who waits patiently in the unconscious for the son to win his liberation from the mother.

Analysis of these tales, such as that conducted by Vladimir Propp (1968), reveals at least five characteristic stages in the development of the plot:

1 Something happens to make the heroine leave home, separating her from childhood, parents, and family.

2 A period of seclusion ensues, an idyllic hiatus spent either in a house or temple, or in a forest remote from human habitation.

3 The idyll is disrupted by some catastrophe – usually the arrival of a special male (a demon, hero, or god), who violates the girl and leaves her pregnant.

4 A period of tribulation follows, when she is subjected to sore trials, punished, or imprisoned.

5 Finally she is rescued, is married, and gives birth to a child, generally a son, who, in Greece, turns out to be a hero (e.g. Danaë gives birth to Perseus, Antiope to the Boetian Dioscures, and Kallisto to Arkas).

Other well-known stories which follow this pattern are those of Persephone, Psyche, and Rapunzel. As with hero tales, the maiden's tale follows the natural biological progression from childhood to adulthood. Five dramatically important events mark this transition: menarche, leaving home, mating (intercourse), pregnancy, and childbirth. How a girl deals with this transition psychologically is of crucial significance for her individuation. To illustrate this, the story of Psyche is told in *Eros and Psyche* pp. 220–35.

Female rites of passage emphasize the same stages as the maiden's tale. The rites usually begin with the first menstruation and commonly involve separation from family and seclusion in an isolated place or hut. The initiatory process is intensified by the rites attendant upon betrothal, marriage, pregnancy, and birth of the first child. The unconscious biological programme is symbolically translated into a series of conscious rites which evidently carry the social purpose of guaranteeing the programme will unfold in the normal manner.

vii Eros and Psyche

The narrative of the maiden's tale provides a rich symbolic tapestry woven out of threads from the psychology of feminine experience, the biology of the life-cycle, and the teleological process of individuation. This fascinating work of psychosynthesis can be best understood from the examination of a story such as that of Psyche, which tells of her love affair with Eros, her failure to trust and obey him, and the trouble she gets into with her future mother-in-law Aphrodite. It is a tale which amply displays the advanced psychological understanding which had been attained by classical times.

The account we have is the romance told by Apuleius in the second century AD in his *Metamorphoses or the Golden Ass*, but it is a much older story with parallels in myths and tales from Egypt, China, and India, as well as from Greece, which probably provided Apuleius with his source. We shall, therefore, use the Greek rather than the Latin names for the characters involved.

Psyche, the youngest of three daughters of a certain king, was so fair that speech was too inept to describe her beauty. Men were struck dumb by her loveliness and worshipped her as though she were Aphrodite herself. When Aphrodite got to hear of this she was not pleased, and resolved at once that the upstart should be made to suffer for her presumptuous beauty. Summoning her son Eros, Aphrodite implored him, by all the bonds of love that bound him to her, to avenge his mother's slight by causing the maid to become enamoured of one who was 'the vilest of men': 'So spoke she, and with parted lips kissed her son long and fervently.'

Meanwhile, Psyche had no joy of her loveliness. All men gazed upon her but none came forward to claim her hand. Her father, fearing the wrath of the gods, went to the most ancient oracle, and with prayers and burnt offerings besought Apollo to send a husband to wed the maid whom none had wooed.

Apollo replied with the following doom-laden words:

> *On some high crag, O king, set forth the maid,*
> *In all the pomp of funeral robes arrayed.*
> *Hope for no bridegroom born of mortal seed,*
> *But fierce and wild and of the dragon breed.*

Stricken by this terrible oracle, the king returned to his queen, and they wept and lamented for many days. But the commands of heaven had to be obeyed and Psyche must prepare to meet her doom. In deepest grief the bridal procession forms up and moves off to the appointed place. But Psyche is brave and tries to comfort her parents: 'Lead me on and set me on the crag that fate has appointed. I hasten to meet that blest union, I hasten to behold the noble husband that awaits me.' Sorrowfully they climb a lofty mountain and come to the crag at its peak. There they place Psyche and all depart from her. Trembling and afraid, she sits upon the very summit of the crag and weeps. Suddenly, the West Wind blows and, raising her up, bears her gently down the mountainside to a grove beside a gliding stream where stands a gorgeous palace, 'built by no human hands but by the cunning of a god'.

She enters to discover that the walls are made of gold ingots, the floors paved with precious stones, and a lofty chamber is filled with treasure. 'Nothing may be found in all the world that was not there.' Unseen servants attend her, giving her delicious things to eat, and invisible musicians enchant her with their heavenly strains.

When she has had her fill of these delights, Psyche retires to bed. In the darkness of the night her unknown husband comes to her and makes her his bride. He departs in haste before dawn. Henceforth, he comes to her each night in the same way, and they make love. So, for a long time, her life passes in this idyllic state, though she is never allowed to see her lover.

Eventually, Psyche begins to fret at being kept captive in her luxurious prison and longs to see her sisters and to reassure her parents that she is happy and well. Although Eros warns her not to, she eventually prevails upon him, and he agrees. But he orders her never to tell her sisters what her husband is like. If she yields to their curiosity, he says, she will lose him for ever. She promises: 'Sooner would I die a hundred deaths than be robbed of your sweet love,' she says. 'For whoever you are, I love you and adore you passionately.'

The West Wind collects her sisters and delivers them to the palace, where Psyche shows them all her treasures and lavishes hospitality upon them. Understandably, they are stupefied by her great good fortune, and begin to grow envious. They grill her as to who the lord of these celestial marvels could be. Psyche tries to heed her lover's warnings, but, on the spur of the moment, she finds herself telling a white lie: he is a beautiful young man, she says, who spends his days out hunting.

Having laden them with golden gifts and jewelled necklaces, Psyche summons the West Wind and sends her sisters home. There the gall of envy consumes them and they plan to wreck their sister's happiness. That night Eros warns Psyche of her peril. 'Those false she-wolves are weaving some deep plot of sin against you,' he says, 'whose purpose is this: to persuade you to seek to know my face, which, as I have told you, if once you see, you will see no more.' He admonishes her, 'Neither give ear nor utterance to anything concerning your husband. For soon we shall have issue, and even now your womb, a child's as yet, bears a child like you. If you keep my secret in silence, he shall be a god; if you divulge it, a mortal.'

Psyche rejoices that she should be blessed with a divine child; she exults in the glory of the babe to be and is proud that she is to become a mother. But when her sisters come on their next visit, they again interrogate her about her husband. This time, Psyche, forgetting the details of her previous lie, lets slip that he is a rich, middle-aged, businessman. From this, the cunning sisters deduce that Psyche has no idea what he looks like and decide to scare her into finding out. They say they know the truth about his identity and that it is very terrible indeed: 'He that lies secretly by your side each night,' they say, 'is a huge serpent with a thousand tangled coils; blood and deadly poison drip from his throat and from the cavernous horror of his gaping maw. Remember Apollo's oracle, how it proclaimed that you should be the bride of some fierce beast.' They affect great distress, and warn Psyche: 'So soon as your time has come, he will devour you with the ripe fruit in your womb.'

Poor Psyche, who is a gentle soul, is seized with terror at this melancholy news. Despite herself, she fears her sisters could be right: 'You say well that he is some strange beast, and I accept your words. For ever with stern speech he terrifies me from seeking to have sight of him, and threatens great woe to me should I strive curiously to look upon his face.'

The sisters advise her that there is only one course for her to adopt: that night, she must wait until her husband is sleeping, light a lamp, and cut his head off with a sharp knife. 'As soon as you have won safety by his death,' say the sisters, 'we will hasten eagerly to your side, join hands with yours to bear away all your treasure.'

In great perplexity of soul, Psyche resolves to do their bidding. But as soon as the lamplight reveals the secrets of her couch, she sees the kindest and sweetest of all wild beasts, Eros himself, fairest of the gods. So handsome is he that even the flame of the lamp, when it beholds him, burns brighter. Enraptured, Psyche gazes again and again upon the beauty of his divine face and her soul grows in strength and joy. 'But even as her swooning spirit wavered in the ecstasy of such bliss,' Apuleius tells us, 'the lamp, whether foul falseness or guilty envy moved it, or whether it longed itself to touch and kiss so fair a body, sputtered forth from the top of its flame a drop of burning oil, which fell upon the god's right shoulder. Ah! rash over-bold lamp!'

Badly burned, Eros leaps from the couch, and, seeing that his secret has been betrayed, tears himself from the kisses and embraces of his bride and flies away without a word.

Deranged with grief, Psyche flings herself into the river which flows hard by, but the kindly stream catches her in his current and lays her unhurt upon the bank. It happens that at that moment Pan should be sitting there with Echo in his arms, teaching her to make melodious answer to sounds of every kind. He diagnoses Psyche's condition and advises her to lay aside her sorrow and rather address Eros, the mightiest of gods, with fervent prayer and win him by tender submission, 'For he is an amorous and soft-hearted youth.'

Psyche accepts Pan's advice, but first she gets even with her sisters. Going to each of them in turn, she says that her husband proved to be no monster but the divine Eros himself. She tells each sister that, at the moment of discovery, Eros cried: 'In atonement for the foul crime you have purposed, begone from my couch and take with you what is yours. I will marry your sister [mentioning her name] with all due ritual.' Intoxicated by these words, the sisters ascend the mountain, one by one, and throw themselves from the crag; but no West Wind supports them, and they crash to their deaths.

Meanwhile, the injured Eros has flown home to his mother and lies in her chamber groaning from the pain of his wound. When Aphrodite learns what has happened she flies into a towering rage: 'Truly your behaviour is most honourable and worthy of your birth and your good name!' she screams at him. 'First to trample your mother's, or rather your queen's, bidding underfoot, to refuse to torment my enemy with base desires, and then actually to take her to your own wanton embraces, mere boy as you are, so that I must endure my enemy as my daughter-in-law! Oh! You seducer, you worthless boy, you matricidal wretch!'

Mad with fury, Aphrodite rampages about the world determined to find Psyche and visit the most frightful punishments on her. Psyche begs Demeter and Hera for their protection, but both decline, fearful of provoking their sister even more. Realizing that there can be no escape, Psyche decides to give herself up.

No sooner has the goddess beheld her than she bursts into wild laughter, such as men will utter when mad with wrath: 'So, at length you have thought fit to come and greet your mother-in-law! Or have you come to visit your husband, who is in danger of his life, thanks to the wound you gave him? But you need not be frightened! I will give you such a welcome as a good daughter-in-law deserves. Where,' she cries, 'are my handmaidens Trouble and Sorrow?' They are summoned and Psyche is given into their charge.

Aphrodite has her beaten and tortured and declares that her child will be born a bastard. Then having satisfactorily vented her wrath, she subjects Psyche to a protracted series of impossible labours. Each ordeal sets tasks so far beyond her capacity that she despairs – until some well-disposed helper comes to her aid.

First she is shown a great heap of mixed seeds – corn, barley, millet, poppy, chickpeas, lentils – and told to put them into separate piles. 'I cannot conceive that any serving-wench as hideous as yourself could find any means to attract lovers save by making herself their drudge,' comments Aphrodite. Ants come to Psyche's rescue and by nightfall the task is done.

Next Psyche is commanded to collect a wisp of the fleece from golden sheep which are dangerously mad and can give venomous bites. Knowing this to be beyond her, Psyche plans to cast herself down a cliff. But a green reed by the river whispers to her that the sheep are only maddened by the hot sun and that she must wait till evening when their fury will have abated. Then she may collect the golden wool which has snagged on the lower twigs of a plane tree. True to the reed's bidding, Psyche collects the soft golden wisps and returns to Aphrodite with her bosom full of them.

Aphrodite remarks bitterly that her wayward son must be in some way responsible for the help Psyche is evidently receiving. So she decides on an impossible trial to discover whether Psyche has 'a stout heart and prudence beyond the prudence of a woman'. She gives Psyche a small crystal urn and tells her to go to a lofty mountain peak and collect water from the icy waterfall of the Styx. To touch this water is death, even to the gods, and the source is inaccessibly high up, protected by fierce dragons. This time the eagle of Zeus comes to her assistance and, poised on the vast expanse of his beating pinions, swiftly oars his way past the dragons and returns with the urn full of water, which Psyche delivers to Aphrodite.

With a baleful smile upon her lips, Aphrodite says: 'In truth, I believe you are some great and potent sorceress, so nimbly have you obeyed my hard commands! But you must do me yet this one service, sweetheart. Take this casket and straightway descend to the world below and the ghastly hall of Hades himself. There present the casket to Persephone and say, "Aphrodite begs of thee to send her a small portion of thy beauty, such at least as may suffice for the space of a brief day. For all her beauty is worn and perished through watching over her sick son." '

Knowing that she is finished, Psyche goes to a high tower that she might throw herself headlong from it. But the tower informs her that she can accomplish this final task if only she will follow its instructions. She must take with her cakes kneaded of pearl barley and mead to feed Cerberus, and two coins for the ferryman's toll. On no account must she listen to the entreaties of afflicted souls she encounters on the way, and she must decline the rich feast Persephone will offer her. When she has received the casket containing the beauty ointment Aphrodite has requested, the tower solemnly warns Psyche that she must on no account attempt to open it or try to see what is concealed within.

Following this advice, Psyche accomplishes her terrifying mission. But having returned from the Underworld, she succumbs to an impulse to steal some of the ointment so as to win once more the grace of her fair lover. She unclasps the casket: 'But there was no beauty therein, nor anything at all save a hellish and truly Stygian sleep.' She falls to the ground and lies motionless, no better than a sleeping corpse.

At this point, Eros, who has recovered from his wound and is unable to bear the separation from his beloved a moment longer, slips through the high window of his bedchamber and, with strong, well-rested wings, flies swiftly to Psyche's side. He wipes the sleep from her, puts it back in the casket, and wakes her with a harmless prick from one of his arrows. 'My poor child,' he says, 'your curiosity almost brought you to destruction yet a second time.' Bidding her take Persephone's gift to his mother, Eros soars up to heaven's farthest height and tells Zeus the story of his and Psyche's love.

Zeus decides the time has come for decisive action. Summoning all the gods whose names are written in the Muse's register, he declares his opinion that Eros must have some curb placed upon the wild passions of his youthful prime. He there and then decrees that the wanton spirit of Eros's boyhood shall be enchained in the fetters of wedlock. Turning to Aphrodite, Zeus reassures her that she need have no fear that her son's marriage will shame her lofty rank and lineage, and he sends Hermes to catch up Psyche and to bring her to heaven. Once there, Zeus gives her ambrosia to drink and renders her immortal.

A great wedding feast is prepared and all Olympus rejoices. 'Thus did Psyche with all solemnity become Eros's bride, and soon a daughter was born to them: in the language of mortals she is called Pleasure.'

Commentary on the story of Eros and Psyche

This charming tale, so beautifully told by Apuleius, is about the psychic maturation to young adulthood of both a boy and a girl, told primarily from the girl's point of view. It has been subjected to detailed analysis by such authorities as Erich Neumann (1956) and Marie-Louise von Franz (1970), and my own commentary is heavily indebted to their work. It is a variation on the theme of the monstrous bridegroom, the demon lover, Beauty and the Beast, containing the classic details of the mysterious lover, the jealous sisters, the enchanted castle, invisible servants, the ordeals which helpful creatures enable the heroine to overcome, and the eventual transformation of the animal bridegroom into a handsome, princely husband. It is, as Marina Warner (1994) has said, a kind of Pilgrim's Progress which has to do with the institution of exogamy and a young woman's natural fears of 'marrying out' – going to a neighbouring tribe or village to marry an unknown husband by arrangement, and live in the mother-in-law's house – which has been the lot of most brides in patrilocal societies till recent times.

The plot is set in motion by the conflict between the older and the younger woman over the issues of beauty and male attention. Aphrodite is losing her power to Psyche, the beautiful usurper. This conflict develops into a more bitter rivalry between the possessive mother and the prospective daughter-in-law, who wishes to capture the love of a handsome son. Later it becomes a struggle between the tyrannical mother-in-law, who treats her son's wife as a skivvy, demanding that she earns approval through drudgery, yet never granting it however diligently she labours. Eventually the conflict is resolved through the power of masculine consciousness, authority, and love, rewarding the maiden who has won through to woman's status, and the lysis is marked by a celebration of the *hieros gamos* in heaven.

From the cultural standpoint, Psyche is born at a crucial moment in history, when the forlorn cry 'Great Pan is Dead' heralded the end of classical antiquity. Humanity's dependency on the gods is giving way to greater confidence in itself. Men no longer pay worship to a goddess, but to a beautiful young woman.

Psychologically, the story is about the feminine experience of exogamy as it is enshrined in the Greek myth of the mother–daughter partnership of Demeter and Kore being shattered by Hades, the ravishing, subterranean aspect of the male. For every mother–daughter bond, exogamy means a tearing apart, a rape of their tenderest emotions, the death of all they have held dear. Marriage demands 'the death of the maiden', the encounter with the fearful unknown male, and the ritual affirmation of the fertile wife. 'From this point of view,' comments Neumann, 'every marriage is an exposure on the mountain's summit in mortal loneliness, and a waiting for the male monster, to whom the bride is surrendered.'

Apuleius's tale conforms to the hope inherent in all folk tales about animal bridegrooms – that although the father has delivered the daughter into the power of the alien beast, the monster will be transformed into a handsome, tender lover. All convey to the unmarried maid the conviction that this fearful initiation is unavoidable and that she had best approach the fate in store for her with the same brave resignation as the heroine, in the faith that the miraculous transformation will occur. Thus, Psyche prepares herself for the craggy encounter with her bridegroom of the dragon breed with the incongruous words, 'Lead me on and set me on the crag that fate has appointed. I hasten to meet that blest union, I hasten to behold the noble husband that awaits me.'

Her faith is justified, for in place of the predicted horror she finds herself in the paradise of Eros's love. Death in the fangs of a hideous monster becomes erotic ecstasy at the hands of a loving husband. The fact that he is unseen and unidentified does not disturb her: she is content enough to live in bliss.

What destroys this paradise is the introduction of the familiar fairy-tale motif of the jealous sisters, with their no less familiar suggestion that a taboo must be broken to throw light on a hidden secret. The fantasy they communicate to Psyche – that nightly she is submitting to the 'embraces of a foul and venomous snake' – is a regression to the monster theme, a recrudescence of the sexual disgust of the exogamously afflicted female. This, together with their suggestion that Psyche must rebel against her lover's insistence on his anonymity and see him for herself, Neumann interprets as the projection of Psyche's own unconscious tendencies. The sisters are Psyche's 'shadow' and their murderous, anti-masculine agitation represents a valid resistance of feminine nature to Psyche's imprisoned status and passive attitude – 'the beginning of a higher feminine consciousness'. Through their prompting, she breaks the taboo that Eros has imposed on her and in so doing builds the foundation for her own psychological development. In this the sisters function in a similar manner to the snake in the Garden of Eden which encourages Adam and Eve to break the taboo imposed by Jehovah. Expulsion from Paradise results in contact with the real world and a development in consciousness. Disobeying Bluebeard's command, his errant wife enters the forbidden chamber and discovers his guilty secret. Disobedience is about defying the dominant male, refusing to be subordinate, and coming to selfhood. It is a necessary step on the path to individuation, the realization in consciousness of one's full Self-potential.

Lighting the lamp, sharp knife in hand, in the dark bedchamber, Psyche resembles the solar hero lighting a fire in the belly of the whale and cutting his way out of the darkness. When she sees her sleeping lover and examines his accoutrements, Psyche accidentally pricks herself with one of his arrows and thus 'falls in love with Love'. She emerges from the unconscious paradise, where each is the other's unseen *machine à plaisir*, and at last recognizes the true nature of her love in living reality.

When Eros also wakes to consciousness, realizing that the taboo has been broken, and that he has been seen, he behaves like Eurydice in similar circumstances: he vanishes. Then Psyche, like Orpheus, becomes aware of the magnitude of her loss. Eros is now put on the spot: hitherto he has lived a double life – as his mother's son and his mistress's lover. This psychic dissociation must now be healed, like the burn in his flesh, if he too is to achieve his own psychic wholeness.

Before his encounter with Psyche, Eros is the son-lover of his own Great Mother, who kisses him with parted lips long and fervently. His love for Psyche presents him with the challenge to stand up to his jealous, domineering mother, and insist that he is now a man who will love and marry whom he wishes. Instead, he merely deceives Aphrodite, slipping away in the darkness to keep a series of nightly trysts. Not only does he keep his mistress in the dark but his mother too. The light which Psyche throws on the situation, by contrast, makes everyone conscious of what has been going on and creates the central crisis for the protagonists which now has to be resolved. The separation and sufferings which ensue are necessary stages on the way to an authentic maturity and a higher, more developed consciousness.

It is time, too, for Aphrodite to grow up, 'be her age', and develop a modicum of objectivity and wisdom; and when she rails to Demeter and Hera against her son's behaviour, they tell her as much: 'Who among gods and men', they ask her, 'will permit you to sow passions broadcast among the peoples of the earth, when you forbid your own household the charms of love, and debar them from all enjoyment of woman's foibles, an enjoyment that is open to all the world?'

At first, Psyche, like Orpheus when he loses his lover, is filled with suicidal despair; but she is comforted by Pan, the voice of Nature, who encourages her to remain true to her love, seek Eros out, and be reconciled to him. Her eventual decision to stop running away from Aphrodite and instead to suffer the worst that the jealous mother goddess can do to her is an act of courage made necessary by Eros's spinelessness. Since he has shirked the trials and ordeals necessary to become a man, she will have to undergo them for his sake, and, as women will, she does it out of love.

The labours imposed by Aphrodite on Psyche seem meaningless until one penetrates the symbolism wrapped up in them. It is quickly apparent that all four labours are about *pairs of opposites* as constellated between the nature of each ordeal and the nature of the helper that comes to Psyche's assistance. The labours are the seeds and the ants; the golden fleece and the reed; the River Styx and the eagle; and the Underworld and the tower.

(1) **The seeds and the ants** Sorting out a mound of seeds into separate piles is a familiar fairy-tale motif. It is about imposing conscious order on natural profusion and chaos. The ants represent the capacity for orderly discipline which must be organized for this task to be performed. It is a parable of humanity's conquest of Nature

and woman's part in it: sorting out the life-growing principles of vegetation, so that they can be tabulated, stored, and knowingly sown, irrigated, tended, and harvested when the appropriate seasons occur. It is not coincidental that the only other species that cultivates gardens is a species of ant.

(2) **The golden fleece and the reed** The golden wool that Psyche has to collect from the venomous sheep is a clear reference to the quest of Jason and the Argonauts for the Golden Fleece protected by a venomous dragon in Iolchus. That fleece, too, Jason collects from a tree, not at nightfall but when the dragon is sleeping off the effects of a drug donated by Jason's helper, the witch Medea. The Golden Fleece comes from the **ram** on which Zeus mounted to the sky, and it possesses solar connotations. Like the Holy Grail and the treasure hard to attain, it represents the peak of spiritual achievement, the goal of individuation realized. The tree on which the fleece is hung in Iolchus is the Tree of Life.

The reed, through which the wind, like Pan, plays sweet music, is rooted, as is the lotus, in the earth beneath the water (female 'elements'), while the Golden Fleece of the ram relates to the fiery heat of the sun in the firmament (the masculine realm). The ram is the zodiacal sign of springtime, the time of rutting, aggressive male impulsiveness. At the height of noon these masculine and feminine principles are furthest apart and the tension between them is at its greatest. Then the rams are at their most dangerous and Psyche is most vulnerable to their aggression. But at nightfall, the situation is transformed, for then the solar masculine spirit returns to the feminine depths.

In many fairy tales reeds are the carriers of secret knowledge which they convey to the hero or heroine when the wind blows through them or when they are cut by a shepherd and turned into a pipe. In this tale, the reed is Psyche's intuitive inspiration and it warns her, in its vegetative wisdom, not to confront the rams under the broiling sun but to wait until evening, when they will be more tranquil and approachable. Then, fruitful contact between masculine and feminine opposites becomes possible.

(3) **The River Styx and the eagle** Here the opposites of height and lowness, ascent and descent, are constellated. From the plain below,

Psyche looks up to the highest crag of the huge mountain from which a spring, guarded by dragons, feeds water into the Rivers Styx and Cocytus which pass into the Underworld. Again we have another symbol of the Goal of the Quest: the Water of Life, Death, and Rebirth. The vessel which Aphrodite scornfully gives Psyche to accomplish this evidently impossible task is, as Neumann suggests, the vessel of individuation, a feminine 'mandala-urn'. The extraordinary, numinous quality of the spring derives from its symbolic evocation of the cycle of life through generation after generation, for its motion is circular – 'uroboric', Neumann says; it 'feeds the depths of the Underworld and rises up again to issue from the highest crag of the "huge mountain"'. Thus it unites within itself the symbolism of the highest and the lowest, of ascent and descent.

To accomplish this task of feminine individuation Psyche requires masculine help, and it appears in the form of the eagle – an attribute of Zeus, the masculine spirit whose element is the air; the eagle is king of the sky, companion of the sun. Effortlessly, he soars past the dragons with Psyche's urn, fills it with the awesome water, and returns it to her.

(4) **The Underworld and the tower**   The symbolism of levels is stressed yet again. In the third labour the treasure hard to attain was on the highest mountain peak; in the fourth and final labour it is in the lowest depths. Moreover, before Psyche makes her descent she climbs to the top of the 'far-seeing tower', intending to throw herself off – this being the most direct route to the Underworld and out of her misery. But the tower comes to her aid. Whereas the ant, the reed, and the eagle are 'natural' symbols, representing components of Psyche's own unconscious, the tower is a 'cultural' symbol, a man-made product of conscious, architectural endeavour. It gives her sound, practical advice about how the task can be accomplished. But this time Psyche has to achieve it herself, no helper will do it for her.

This is the moment of her initiation. By relying on her own strength, determination, and will-power, she can triumph as a human individual against the deadly alliance of goddesses above and below the ground. The factor critical for her success is that she must on no account grant assistance to those lost souls in the Underworld who ask her for help. In other words, she must demonstrate the 'ego stability' demanded of all who are to be initiated. Whereas male initiates have to show indifference to physical pain and demonstrate their ability to fight and kill, the female has to establish her capacity *to resist pity*. The ego must concentrate its attention single-mindedly on the goal and must not allow itself to be deflected. In these circumstances the greatest danger for the female is that she will be distracted by her genius for relationship. This, Psyche must at all costs resist.

The beauty cream which Psyche obtains from Persephone and carries back in the casket is 'death cream'. Aphrodite is like the wicked witch who gives Snow White the poisoned apple which puts her into a deathlike sleep and a glass coffin. This is another of Aphrodite's dirty tricks. She knows that no mortal woman could resist the temptation to open the casket and use the divine beauty cream of a goddess. Her design is to return Psyche to the unawakened, childlike state she was in before she met Eros and keep her there in perpetuity. It is inevitable anyway that Psyche will disobey the tower's injunction not to open the box, just as she disobeyed Eros's injunctions not to talk to her sisters and not to try to see him, because it is always thus in fairy tales. As soon as characters are forbidden to do something, you know perfectly well they will go straight off and do it. It is the *felix culpa* that results in greater consciousness. But when Psyche opens the box, and the sleeping death takes hold, it is as if she returns to Persephone in Hades – like Eurydice when Orpheus turned to look at her. Psyche's advantage is that she is above ground and falls into that sleeping state which heroes find irresistible. As with Brünnhilde and Snow White, her prince will come, and at the critical moment he does. It is as if this final crisis, after all Psyche has gone through on account of him, gives Eros the power to break free of his mother complex and come to Psyche's rescue.

Although much the stronger and more determined of the two, Psyche has to indulge in a paradoxical failure at the height of her achievement to get Eros to live up to his responsibilities and be a man. Just as becoming conscious drove him away, Psyche has to become unconscious again to bring him back; but it is an unconsciousness from which *he* now awakens *her*, and the relationship moves into its final phase in which all differences are reconciled and their union is blessed in heaven.

As the story of Eros and Psyche illustrates in its deliciously ironical way, individuation is about differentiating opposites in full consciousness, bearing the tension and suffering the conflict between them, and then, by mobilizing all one's psychic resources, endeavouring to transcend them in the quest for wholeness. Psyche's original union with Eros, lived out anonymously in the dark, symbolizes the archetype of relationship between man and woman existing as unconscious potential as yet unactualized in conscious reality. 'The embrace of Eros and Psyche in the darkness represents the elementary but unconscious attraction of opposites,' says Neumann. By throwing light on the situation, Psyche constellates these opposites in consciousness and they become separated – the first step on the way to turning their physical passion into psychic love. The truth which the story enshrines is that feminine individuation and the spiritual development of the feminine are readily effected through love. Although Psyche needs masculine help to perform her labours – and she develops her own masculine strength (her animus) as she does so – she remains true to

her own womanhood to the end, something that it appears increasingly difficult for the modern heroine to do.

viii Individuation and Transcendence

Symbols relating to the notions of individuation and transcendence are grouped together in this subsection, since many of them incorporate elements common to both ideas.

Individuation is the term used by Jung to designate the process of personality development which leads to the fullest possible actualization of the Self, (the central nucleus of the personality which contains all the archetypal potential with which an individual is innately endowed) (*see* p. 63).

The transcendent refers to ideas, images, and symbols which lie beyond ordinary mundane experience. It is as if the psyche is subject to a transcendent imperative which enables it to deal successfully with the opposing or conflicting tendencies of which life is full. Through this *transcendent function* of the psyche, thesis and antithesis encounter one another on equal terms and achieve a symbolic synthesis which transcends them both. This is a factor of great psychological significance because it enables one to move beyond conflicts which would otherwise prove sterile, and avoid narrow one-sided modes of adjustment. Its action is powerfully enhanced when one attends to dreams and if one assumes conscious responsibility for the transcendent symbols arising from them. This is essential if one is to become committed to the goal of individuation and self-completion.

In all religions, and in the subjective experience of most of us, there is a sense that the psyche is supraordinate to nature, that it enables us to transcend the finite limits of physical life on this planet. In imagination one can find oneself in distant places or participating in scenes from ancient history; in dreams we fly, hold conversations with animals, and listen to the voice of God. One very old and recurrent idea is that the soul is a visitor, a stranger on earth, that it has descended from On-High, where there is neither time nor space, and now finds itself enmeshed in the corporeal status of a human being. According to many esoteric traditions, the soul is unaware of its extraterrestrial origins for most of the time, but some gifted individuals are thought to possess the capacity to remember them, while others, it is believed, can be trained to recall them through meditation. Then a new awareness is experienced, at once liberating and enlightening, which goes beyond the corporeal and induces a feeling of oneness with the origin of all things: this is the experience of transcendence.

As described in **Landscape** pp. 99–115, the path to individuation is represented by the **journey** and the QUEST, which symbolize the ego's task throughout the passage of life to actualize the full potential of the Self. At birth the Self is all, the ego existing only *in potentia*, a SEED waiting to germinate within the matrix of the Self. An archetypal image of the Self at this pre-ego stage is the **uroboros**, while the most impressive expression of the individuated, consciously realized Self is the universal symbol of the **mandala**.

The mandala is a transcendent symbol *par excellence*; it represents the achievement of the goal: the opposites are reconciled in a state of dynamic balance. Other transcendent symbols occurring at earlier stages of the journey incorporate the idea of rotation about a centre: the Buddhist WHEEL OF TRANSFORMATION, the SWASTIKA, the **spiral**, the WHEEL OF FORTUNE, and the ZODIACAL CYCLE. The **omphalos** represents the central origin of all things, while the **labyrinth**, the PILGRIMAGE to the Holy Land, the quest for the **Holy Grail**, and the **alchemical** *opus* for the *lapis philosophorum*, all symbolize the goal of existence as a centre, a NEW JERUSALEM, the mystic centre of the universe towards which the individuation principle is ultimately striving. Religion, myth, and alchemy have all sought to guide the pilgrim on this journey. With their demise, the quest for the centre has become the dual responsibility of depth psychology and natural science, the former finding it in the psychodynamics of the Self, the latter in that minute point of finite concentration which was the originator of the Big Bang.

Throughout the East, mandalas have been used as an aid to meditation, assisting the spirit to move along its evolutionary course from the lower realm of the corporeal and mundane to the higher realm of the spiritual and sacred. The mandala configuration is not only built into temples and cathedrals but can be danced and processed or ritually followed by walking through a labyrinth such as that marked out on the floor of Chartres Cathedral. The mandala is a symbol which combines both the journey and its destination, the ideas of differentiation and the oneness of all things, the *unus mundus*. Examples still persist from Palaeolithic times as, for instance, in Rhodesian rock engravings. Such images, when they occur in modern dreams, are thus spontaneous re-creations of the most basic religious symbol known to humanity.

These and other symbols of individuation and transcendence are described in alphabetical order below. Some of them appear in other subsections, where additional aspects of their meaning are described. The route to their discovery is, as always, via the Symbol Index.

Alchemical *opus* Jung realized that the stages of the alchemical *opus* granted rich insights into the individuation process. Originally four stages were distinguished according to the colour changes characteristic of each stage. These were described by Heraclitus as *melanosis* (blackening), *leukosis* (whitening), *xanthosis* (yellowing), and *iosis* (reddening). In the fifteenth century the colours were reduced to three, the yellowing stage being omitted, and their Latin names came into general use: *nigredo* (blackening), *albedo* (whitening), and *rubedo* (reddening). Alchemy continued to deal with four elements, however, and four qualities (hot, cold, dry, and moist). The change from three to four stages cannot have been for experimental reasons because the process never led to the desired practical goal, so it must be attributed, as Jung says, to 'the symbolical significance of the quaternity and the trinity; in other words, it is due to inner psychological reasons' (CW 12, para. 333).

The blackness of the *nigredo* (the first stage) is associated with the separation (*separatio, solutio*) of the elements in the *prima materia* which are then grouped into male and female opposites. These are brought together in a union (*coniunctio, coitus*). The product of their union then dies (*mortificatio, putrefactio, calcinatio*) to produce the blackening characteristic of this stage. Jung identified the *prima materia* with the primal Self, which contains all the archetypal potential and all the dynamic oppositions necessary to achieve the goal both of the *opus* and of individuation. The black aspect symbolizes the depression, the *melancholia* which commonly begins the process of self-examination and brings people into analysis. The encounter with negative aspects of the self (which Jung called the shadow personality) is experienced as a *mortificatio* since these humiliating parts of oneself have to be confronted and integrated, and the associated feelings of guilt and worthlessness have to be suffered, taken on, and worked through (Edinger, 1985). The idea of 'working through' is expressed in the alchemical concept of the *circulatio*, which, like the rotating wheel of Indian solar mythology, represents the continuous cycle of ascent and descent indispensable to all processes of transformation.

According to some alchemical traditions, the *nigredo* constitutes the 'death' of the *prima materia*, which corresponds, in analysis, to a dying to the old neurotic way of life, and to the emotional dependencies of childhood. The *albedo*, the second stage of the *opus*, results from the washing (*ablutio, baptisma*) of the products of the *nigredo*. The soul (*anima*) which 'died' in the *nigredo* is released, refined, and then reunited with the revitalized *materia* to produce the glorious stage of many colours, the 'peacock's tail' (*cauda pavonis*), which then transforms into white (*albedo*), which contains all colours, like white light. This is associated with the symbolism of sunrise and leads on to the final stage, the *rubedo*. In this stage, the white becomes united with the red through raising the heat of the fire. The white is associated with the queen and the red with the king, who now arise and perform their *coniunctio oppositorum*, the union of all opposites as symbolized by the conjunction of the archetypal masculine and feminine in the 'chymical marriage', the *hieros gamos*. This results in the grand climax, the achievement of the goal, the *lapis philosophorum*, the hermaphrodite embodying the united king and queen, the *filius micro-cosmi*, 'a figure we can only compare with the Gnostic Anthropos, the divine original man' (*CW*10, para. 335).

The king and queen perform their *coniunctio* and melt into a single being with two heads. But their son, the *filius philosophorum*, is 'not born of the queen, but queen and king are themselves transformed into the new birth' (*CW*16, para. 473). Jung translated this mystery into the language of psychology: 'The union of the conscious mind or ego-personality with the unconscious personified as anima produces a new personality compounded of both . . . Not that the new personality is a third thing midway between conscious and unconscious, it is both together. Since it transcends consciousness it can no longer be called "ego" but must be given the name of "self" . . . the self too is both ego and non-ego, subjective and objective, individual and collective. It is the "uniting symbol" which epitomizes the total union of opposites.' In other words, 'The one born of the two represents the metamorphosis of both.' This can only be expressed by means of symbols, which occur in dreams and fantasies and find objective form in mandalas like the Golden Flower – 'an image born of nature's own workings, a natural symbol far removed from all conscious intention' (CW16, paras 474 and 475).

Arabesque Type of ornamentation incorporating the idea of repetition, of movement turning back on itself in a labyrinthine, sinuous manner.

Caduceus The staff with two opposing serpents coiled about it, surmounted by wings or a winged helmet, is a widely distributed symbol of great antiquity. To the Mesopotamians 2,600 years before Christ, it was the symbol of a healing god. In the Far East the snakes refer to the **kundalini** and the staff to the *axis mundi*, up and down which all messenger gods travel between Heaven and Earth, between gods and men. It has come down to us through the myth of Hermes/ Mercury who intervened in a fight between two snakes which promptly curled themselves about his wand. In addition to Hermes, the caduceus has been carried by Anubis, Ba'al, Isis, and Ishtar. The two snakes have variously been taken to symbolize healing and sickness, good and evil, ascent and descent, fire and water; the staff to represent earth; and the wings air. Also the wings represent the life of the spirit, the snakes the life of instinct. Everywhere the caduceus has come to represent the idea of dynamic balance between equal and opposing forces aspiring to unite in a higher form.

Child In dreams, myths, and folk tales, the child appears as a symbol of the nascent Self: 'The child motif represents the preconscious, childhood aspect of the psyche', says Jung (CW9i, para. 273). Commonly it appears as the DIVINE CHILD, born in extraordinary circumstances, yet at once exposed to adversity (e.g. abandonment or persecution) which underlines the vulnerability of each life that seeks its own fulfilment. 'It is a striking paradox in all child myths that the "child" is on the one hand delivered helpless into the power of terrible enemies and in continual danger of extinction, while on the other he possesses powers far exceeding those of ordinary humanity. This is closely related to the psychological fact that though the child may be "insignificant", unknown, "a mere child", he is also divine . . . The "child" is endowed with superior powers and, despite all dangers, will unexpectedly pull through . . . It is a personification of vital forces quite outside the limited range of our conscious mind . . . It represents the strongest, most ineluctable urge in every being, namely the urge to realize itself. It is, as it were, an incarnation of *the inability* to do otherwise . . . The urge and compulsion to self-realization is a law of nature and thus of invincible power, even though its effect, at the start, is insignificant and improbable. Its power is revealed in the miraculous deeds of the child hero, and later in the *athla* (works) of the bondsman or thrall (of the Herakles type), where, although the hero has outgrown the impotence of the "child", he is still in a menial position. The figure of the thrall generally leads up to the real epiphany of the semi-divine hero' (CW9i. para. 289).

The symbolic implications of the child motif for the individuation process are evident in all its manifestations: 'Sometimes the child appears in a cup or a flower, or out of a golden egg, or as the centre of a mandala. In dreams it often appears as the dreamer's son or daughter or as a boy, youth, or young girl; occasionally it seems to be of exotic origin, Indian or Chinese, with a dusky skin, or, appearing more cosmically, surrounded by stars or with a starry coronet; or as the king's son or as the witch's child with daemonic attributes. Seen as a special instance of "the treasure hard to attain" motif, the child motif is extremely variable and assumes all manner of shapes, such as the jewel, the pearl, the flower, the chalice, the golden egg, the quaternity, the golden ball, and so on' (CW9i, para. 270).

Always the child points to the future and carries within itself the seeds of its own maturity and completion. Symbols of potential wholeness frequently emerge at the beginning of the individuation process, as in the dreams and drawings (often in mandala form) of early childhood. It is, comments Jung, as if 'something already existent were being put together' (*CW*9i, para. 278).

Circumambulation Literally means 'walking round about'. It is a universal ritual practice, which heightens the sacred importance of what lies at the centre, whether it be an altar, a throne, a cathedral, or a city. Its symbolism bears unmistakable cosmic connotations. Most circumambulating processions move in a clockwise direction, following the apparent movement of the sun in the northern hemisphere. Occasionally the movement is anti-clockwise in sympathetic imitation of the revolution of the stars round the Pole. When the Emperor of China ritually circumambulated the Forbidden City, he halted at each of the twelve gates, corresponding to the twelve signs of the zodiac. Muslims going in procession round the *Ka'aba* at Mecca make seven circuits in accordance with the number of the celestial spheres. This is, in fact, a continuation of what was a pre-Islamic rite. The ancient purpose of the circumambulatory ritual was presumably to guarantee the maintenance of cosmic order, ensuring that the microcosm proceeded in harmony with the macrocosm.

City A symbol of the Self, for all life is there. The city of one's birth, the Holy City, or the capital city of one's country particularly carries this meaning. 'The man who is tired of London is tired of life', said Dr Johnson. The city is the great cultural achievement of the agriculturalist; it marks the end of the nomadic or hunter-gatherer existence. While nomads typically arranged their tents in a circle, cities were invariably built in a square, a symbol of fixity, stability, and settled purpose. The four main gates are situated at the cardinal points; opposite gates being joined by two main streets at right angles to one another crossing at the centre, where is situated a building or monument of central importance to the culture – a cathedral, temple, or holy mountain. The city thus obeys the configuration of the mandala and it has similar symbolic implications.

Column(s) The column or pillar takes its origin, and consequently much of its symbolism, from the tree. Like the *axis mundi*, the megalithic menhir, and the ladder, it links the three cosmic levels –

particularly Heaven and Earth. God guides the Children of Israel across the wilderness, leading them with a pillar of cloud by day and pillar of fire by night. Where a pillar served as a sacrificial altar, the animal was sacrificed at its top, the heavenward part. The centre-pole of the shaman's tent is the pillar he ascends on his flights to heaven. The column is a symbol of social as well as spiritual ascent: it is the way to 'higher things'. Trajan's Column celebrates that Emperor's victories in 115 episodes depicted in relief images which ascend in a spiral from its base to its summit. The single column is also unmistakably phallic, as in the Djed Pillar of Osiris, the Lingam of Shiva, and the Herm, representing both the generative masculine principle as well as the notion of life everlasting. Two columns, like the two serpents of the caduceus, represent the balanced tensions of opposing forces, male and female, good and evil, life and death, mercy and severity, etc. In Masonic symbolism, for example, two columns face the Blazing Delta. One is marked J for Jachin and the other B for Boaz. Column J is identified with the sun and is painted red to represent its active, male, fiery qualities, while column B is associated with the moon and painted white to represent passive, female, airy virtues. Columns also mark boundaries or limits, as with the Pillars of Hercules/Herakles which mark the end of this hero's Eastward expedition to slaughter the dragon guarding the Garden of the Hesperides and obtain the Golden Apples. One of the pillars was Mount Calpe (Gibraltar) in Europe, and the other Jebel Zatout (above Ceuta) in Africa. The line between them marked the threshold between the Mediterranean and Atlantic, beyond which it was not permitted to go.

Cross A universal symbol of immense antiquity long predating the life of Christ. The fundamental role played by this configuration in permitting conscious orientation in space and time is considered in **The Psychic Compass** (pp. 116–23). It represents the QUINCUNX, the four directions and the four elements of the world united at the fifth point, the centre, the *quinta essentia* of the alchemists. The vertical member of the cross, like the *axis mundi*, has to do with the symbolism of levels (ascent and descent): it is experienced as active, masculine, and celestial; it bears connotations of religious, social, and intellectual aspiration and of the transcendent world of spiritual evolution. The horizontal member relates to the tension between opposites of equal valency and is felt to be passive, feminine, and earthly; it carries connotations of relationship and reconciliation, the *coincidentia oppositorum*. As a total configuration the cross integrates these vertical and horizontal implications as a symbol of wholeness, the realization of the full potential of the Self and of life. The Celtic cross accentuates this meaning by encapsulating the cross within a circle. The Egyptian looped cross, the *crus ansata* or ankh, the key of life, combines male and female symbols as well as those of Heaven and Hell, life and eternal life in death. The loop, having no beginning and no end, stands for the soul which is eternal. The cross, therefore, is the very essence of reconciling antagonisms and of transcendence.

The symbolism of the cross has been richly augmented by two millennia of Christendom, and the implications of this symbolism for the individuation process were extensively examined by Jung. It is significant that medieval icons commonly depict Christ as crucified between paired opposites, placed on opposing sides of the picture – e.g. between the sun and the moon, the good and bad thief, the lance and the chalice, male and female (the Virgin and St John), Heaven and Earth, with the Holy Spirit placed at the top and Adam's skull at the bottom. In terms of Jungian metapsychology, Christ as both man and God represents both ego and Self, and bridges both personal and archetypal realms. For the Christian to adopt the way of individuation is to follow symbolically in the path of Christ: it means the **sacrifice** of inflated ego-importance and assertiveness and the suffering of crucifixion between the opposites in order to transcend them. That individuation demands the sacrifice of ego-centred arrogance is implied by Christ in his teaching: 'If you would be perfect [*teleios* = complete, full grown],' he tells the rich youth, 'go, sell what you possess and give it to the poor, and you will have treasure in heaven; it is easier for a camel to pass through the eye of a needle than for a rich [i.e., ego-inflated] man to enter the Kingdom of Heaven [the full realization of the Self].'

Crossroads A meeting of the ways: a place of choice, decision, fate. Oedipus, escaping from his fate, meets his father Laius at the crossroads and kills him there, thus sealing his own fate. All over the world and at different times in history, shrines are erected at cross-roads, for crossroads are critical places of transition from one stage of life – or one state of mind – to another. The crossroad is a place to pause and meditate, to offer up a prayer or make a sacrifice, to cross oneself, and rededicate oneself to the next stage of the journey in the hope, or faith, that one has taken the right road (Mahdi, 1996).

Garden An allegory of the Self. The Garden of Eden is an image of the uroboric, pre-conscious paradise of the womb, while the Heavenly Paradise is a mandala image of the goal of life fully and properly lived. The garden is thus a symbol of the Self-as-potential and the Self realized as a work of conscious individuation. The first gardens were created in the homelands of agriculture and they represent the triumph of civilization over raw nature: they are the results of horticulture placed at the service of art, and are among the highest achievements of human culture. The Persian word for paradise, *jannit*, means 'a garden full of fruit trees, sweetly scented plants, and streams of running water'. Classical Persian gardens were based on the same ground plan as ancient cities, which is to say they were square or rectangular in shape, surrounded by a wall, with four pathways meeting at right angles, with a palace or 'mountain' at the centre. The Garden of Eden is characteristically represented in a form which precisely follows the same plan: a fountain with the Four Rivers of Paradise radiating at right angles from the centre, with the Tree of Life and Tree of Knowledge hard by. The mandala symbolism is again unmistakable.

Gate or **Door** Typically set in walls of cities, temples, churches, and gardens at the four points of the compass, gateways mark the threshold between the inside and the outside, between the sacred and the profane. They are both a barrier and an invitation to proceed. When open, they lead to the centre (the centre of the world, the Holy of Holies, the presence of God, etc.). They are usually protected by guardians whose function is to exclude the unworthy and admit the elect. They are thus linked to the symbolism of initiation (entrance) and transition from one state to another.

The Grail The most sacred of holy objects, the quest for which represents the desire to attain the highest state of beatitude, or the sense of inner completion that is the goal of individuation. According to legend, the Grail was the vessel used by Jesus at the Last Supper and later by Joseph of Arimathea to collect and preserve the Saviour's blood after the Crucifixion. The theme of the miraculous vessel is much older than Christianity, however: it is a feminine symbol representing the womb in which a miraculous, life-giving transformation occurs. The vessel or *vas* was central to the alchemical tradition which began in ancient China and reached Northern Europe in the twelfth century. The Gnostics believed that one of the original gods had made a gift to humanity of a *krater*, a mixing vessel, in which those who sought spiritual transformation were immersed. This Gnostic tradition seems to have entered European alchemy through the influence of Zosimos of Panopolis, one of the earliest and most influential alchemists, a man much given to visions. The medieval mystics adopted the vessel as a symbol of the soul, which exists to be filled and replenished endlessly by Divine Grace. It is thus thematically related to the cornucopia.

The association of the Grail legend with England and King Arthur's Knights of the ROUND TABLE came through the figure of Merlin, the great magician, shaman, and bard of Celtic mythology. Merlin was born of an illicit union between the devil and an innocent virgin and thus emerged as a counter-balance to the figure of Christ. Early in his career, Merlin presides over a dragon fight which results in the deposition of the old usurper King Vertigier and his replacement by King Uter, to whom Merlin confides the secret of the Grail, instructing Uter to set up a Third Table. The First Table was that of the Last Supper; the Second was the Table on which Joseph of Arimathea kept the Grail, and it was square; the Third Table, which King Uter provides, is round. This rounding of the square is, as we have already noted, the very essence of the mandala configuration and symbolizes the achievement of wholeness, the complete realization of the Self. The quest for the Holy Grail is, therefore, the individuation quest undertaken *sub specie aeternitatis*.

Inversion Related to the symbolism of opposites. Common symbols of inversion are the hourglass, the double triangle (Solomon's Seal), the double spiral, the inverted tree, the letter X, and the man hanged upside-down in the Tarot. All such images represent the *coincidentia oppositorum* and the universal tendency for all things to go over to their opposite: the principle of *enantiodromia*.

Key Closely linked with the symbolism of the gate or door, it possesses the power of opening and closing. In our culture it is associated with the symbolism of Janus, the god who looks in two directions, the 'inventor of locks', and the god of initiation. The key is the emblem of St Peter, the guardian of the Gate of Heaven.

The Knight The great tradition of medieval knighthood was an institutionalized attempt to produce the complete, superior, most worthy man – strong, dedicated, moral, capable of incredible feats of bravery and endurance, never counting the cost to himself, only desiring to serve his God, his King, and his mistress. As supreme horseman, he was the epitome of soul in control of instinct, spirit commanding matter, Logos prevailing over chaos. Cirlot draws an interesting parallel between the rising scale of colours in the alchemical *opus* (black → white → red) with the Black, White, and Red Knights of chivalric tradition. The Green Knight is the 'pre-knight', the squire, the apprentice sworn to knighthood. Knighthood, says Cirlot, should be understood as a superior kind of pedagogy, helping to bring about the transformation of natural (steedless) man into spiritual man. He sees the wandering or ERRANT KNIGHT as being intermediate between the 'saved knight' and the accursed hunter: unlike the accursed hunter, the knight errant is not trapped in the pursuit of his desires but is striving to master them. He has to become the Black Knight and suffer withdrawal, penitence, and sacrifice before he can aspire to the higher stages of true knighthood. In the purely psychological context, there-fore, knighthood can be understood as a coherent symbolic expression of the individuating ego.

Kundalini Symbolized by the serpent which lies coiled up at the base of the spine in the lowest CHAKRA known as the *muladhara*, it represents latent energy, unawakened being, the primordial *shakti*, which lies sleeping until activated by yogic exercises. Then, say the yogis, it begins to ascend through the chakras (wheels of life), mobilizing increasing energy, until it reaches the highest chakra, the sacred centre of enlightenment, situated in the forehead (Shiva's third eye). Kundalini yoga thus conceives of the spinal column as a kind of sacred *axis mundi*, and it provides yet another metaphor of the individuation process.

A striking parallel exists between kundalini yoga and the 'hierarchy of needs' postulated by Abraham Maslow (1968). According to Maslow there are five levels of need, starting with the basic physiological needs for water, food, and warmth. When these are met, the next needs to emerge are concerned with security and protection. Then comes the need for love and attachment. Satisfaction on this level leads to the emergence of the need for status and self-esteem. Finally, at the top of the hierarchy, comes the need which demands fulfilment when all the 'lower' needs have been met: the need for self-actualization – 'to become everything that one is capable of becoming'.

Maslow's first, third, and fourth levels correspond to the first three chakras of kundalini yoga, which, in ascending order, have to do with food, sex, and power. There are also evident parallels with the main theoretical orientation of the major schools of psychoanalysis – love and attachment (Freud and Bowlby), status (Adler), and self-actualization (Jung and the individuation principle).

Labyrinth A complicated system of passages through which it is difficult to find one's way and from which it is impossible to escape without completing the journey. It is, therefore, a perfect symbol of the individuation quest. Labyrinths are of two kinds: unicursal, a single route taking the traveller into the centre and out again, covering the total area without treading the same ground twice; and multicursal, containing blind paths and requiring many excursions to reach the centre by trial and error and then to escape again. Knowledge of the mystery of the way may be granted by initiation into a secret society or mystic cult and is felt to be an inestimable boon for successful passage through the labyrinth (through life and into death). It is this knowledge in symbolic form that all religions, esoteric disciplines, and psychologies aspire to provide.

Ladder or **staircase** Relating to the symbolism of levels and the hierarchy archetype, which fundamentally influences all notions of social and religious organization (pp. 59–61). The ladder is the 'mystic ladder' – the means of climbing from Earth to Heaven. It is thus thematically related to the Cosmic Tree, *axis mundi*, mountain, ziggurat, etc. Ladders are the instruments of spiritual ascension from a base to a higher state. They symbolize the path to individuation through transcendence since all realization of potential is conceived by the human imagination as an ascent, an elevation of the spirit. Examples abound in the religions, myths, and legends of the world: Jacob's ladder, Ra's ladder linking Earth and Heaven, the *mi'raj* of the Prophet Mohammed, the seven-notched birch tree of the Siberian shaman, Buddha's staircase of seven colours, the ladder of Mithraic initiation with seven metal rungs, the brazen ladder of St Perpetua's vision received during her martyrdom, the seven-runged ladder set against a fig tree down which the Sun-Lord descends annually to copulate with Earth Mother in East Timor, the seven steps of the alchemical *opus* leading up to the water bath in which the King and Queen perform their *coniunctio*, the creative union of the masculine and feminine archetypal principles, and so on. The 'dialectic of verticality', *ascensus* versus *descensus*, whereby opposites compensate one another and *les extrêmes se touchent*, is emphasized by the top of the ladder being placed directly above its base. 'What is most high in unfathomable godhead,' wrote Meister Eckhart, 'corresponds with what is most low in the depths of humility.' 'All things from Almighty God down to the foulest slime,' said Macrobius, 'are one and are linked mutually by bonds which can never be broken' (*In Somnium Scipionis* 1 14,15). The ancient symbol of the double ladder or double staircase further stresses this vertical dialectic. The Freudian equation of ascending and descending a ladder with sexual intercourse seems trivial in comparison with these ultimate considerations but derives support from the Greek word for ladder: *climax*.

Lamp Pertaining to the symbolism of light and darkness (p. 141). The single lamp represents the consciousness of the individual. There is no such general entity as human consciousness, only the consciousness of individuals: each of us carries a single lamp for humanity. When our lamp gutters it makes little difference to the general illumination, as there are many others to sustain it. But each lamp throws light on (makes conscious) the small part of the cosmos we inhabit, and through our personal awareness that part of creation is *known*. God, say the Buddhists, understands himself through the eyes of the many. The continuously burning lamp represents the cycle of rebirth: Nirvana is blowing out the lamp.

Lost object The search for the lost object, a common theme in folk tales, is analogous to the Grail quest and the alchemical *opus* for the *lapis*. It is the search for enlightenment, the 'pearl of great price' for individuation.

Lotus The flower mandala with petals arranged in perfect symmetry is celebrated in the East as the lotus and in the West as the lily and the rose. The lotus is the Flower of Light, created by the generative fire of the sun quickening the lunar fecundity of the waters, thus uniting masculine with feminine, and spirit (fire) with matter (earth and water). Since it opens in the morning and closes at night, the lotus lives in harmony with the diurnal course of the sun, echoing the quintessential solar symbolism of death and rebirth, eternal regeneration and immortality. The lotus is the epitome of spiritual aspiration, development of the soul, and the individuation of the psyche, since it is rooted in the life-giving mud, grows upward through the opaque, nurturant water, and flowers in the warm light of the sun. Since it bears buds, flowers, and seeds all at the same time, the lotus also epitomizes time – past, present, and future. In creation myths, gods arising from the lotus signify life evolving from the primal waters of the chaos.

Mandala Sanskrit word for magic circle, a geometric figure incorporating both a circle and a square, divided up into four (or multiples of four) segments radiating from the centre. It stands as a symbol for the wholeness of the Self, the deity, and the cosmos. 'Most mandalas take the form of a flower, cross, or wheel, and show a distinct tendency towards a quaternary structure reminiscent of the Pythagorean *tetraktys*, the basic number. Mandalas of this sort also occur in sand paintings in the religious ceremonies of the Pueblo and Navaho Indians. But the most beautiful mandalas are, of course, those of the East, especially the ones found in Tibetan Buddhism . . . mandala drawings are also produced by the mentally ill, among them persons who certainly did not have the least idea of the connections we have discussed' (Jung, CW13, para, 31). Christian mandalas show Christ at the centre with the four evangelists, or their symbols, at the cardinal points. Jung comments: 'this conception must be a very ancient one, because Horus and his four sons were represented in the same way by the Egyptians' (ibid.).

Mirror As a symbol of self-discovery, self-knowledge, contemplation, and reflection, it is one of the Eight Precious Things of Chinese Buddhism. The earliest mirror known to man was water, in the surface of which he saw his soul reflected. Like consciousness itself, the mirror possesses the capacity to reflect the actuality of the visible world. The cosmos can be conceived as a huge Narcissus regarding his own reflection in human consciousness. The mirror is also related to moon symbolism on account of its reflecting and passive characteristics; for it receives images and reflects them in the same way as the moon receives and reflects the light of the sun. Like the echo, the mirror is related to twin symbolism, and to the thesis and antithesis of logical and psychological progression. In fairy tales, mirrors are commonly magical and have the same capacity as the human psyche to store up remembrance of things past. The mirror can be taken as the symbolic token of Socrates's injunction to Know Thyself.

New Jerusalem The symbol of the goal as achieved. Inevitably, the Holy City is visualized as a mandala, the walls of the city being arranged in a square with twelve gates, corresponding to the Twelve Tribes, the Twelve Apostles, the signs of the zodiac, and so on. Each gate is guarded by an angel and the Tree of Life is situated at the centre, bearing fruits: there are twelve of them – one for each month of the year.

Omphalos The cosmic centre where all conflicts originate and all are resolved, the navel of the world, the centre from which the universe originated and is nourished. There is a sense in which every sacred or consecrated place is an omphalos. In our civilization, Delphi is the prime example. It is the quintessential symbol of the Great Mother, representing the Earth and the birth of all things.

Paradise Like the omphalos and the uroborus, paradise is a womb symbol of earliest beginnings, before conflicts arose, when humanity lived at oneness with God and in total harmony with Nature. The notion of paradise as a lost Golden Age is found in the legends and symbolic traditions of peoples all over the world. THE FALL represents the loss of this uroboric state, the polarization of all things into their opposites, and conscious realization of the conflict between them. The path through life to the New Jerusalem of Paradise Regained is symbolized by the labyrinth and other symbols of the individuation journey. Paradise is another symbol of the cosmic centre, where time stands still, the Great Time which Aboriginal Australians call the Dreaming Time. Paradise is thus a symbol of the collective unconscious at the moment of birth, the sum total of humanity's archetypal potential, the primordial Self (*see also* **Paradise and the Fall**, pp. 200–208).

Passage A symbol of the way of transcendence, from the profane to the sacred, to higher states of consciousness transcending the pairs of opposites, the path to Paradise Regained. The path is necessarily difficult and strewn with hazards, represented by such symbols as the Strait Gate, the eye of the needle, the razor's edge, the passage between clashing rocks, between Scylla and Charybdis, or the ring in the jaws of the monster. Implicit in all this symbolism is the understanding that the way cannot be negotiated physically but only spiritually by the transcendent function of the psyche. The 'Way' of Taoism, Hinduism and Buddhism, the 'Strait Gate' of Christianity, and the *tariquah* of Islam are all descriptive symbols of the passage through life to the ultimate goal of individuation. RITES OF PASSAGE symbolize both the ordeals and the necessary means to realization of this goal.

Rainbow As described (p. 144), the rainbow, like other natural phenomena occurring without human intervention, has an emotional impact which generates a symbolism of rich complexity. Obviously an expression of heavenly glory, the rainbow is the throne of the sky gods and, like the ladder and the Cosmic Tree, it is a bridge between Heaven and Earth. Its different colours represent different states of consciousness, as well as the seven planetary gods, or four basic elements, depending on how many colours the rainbow is thought to contain. In Buddhism the rainbow is the highest *samsara* state attainable before the 'clear light' of Nirvana, and in Hinduism the 'rainbow body' is the highest *samsara* state of all to be obtained by yogic practice. In numerous mythologies, the rainbow is the celestial serpent that quenches its thirst in the sea – a kind of hemi-uroboros, in fact.

Rebis An alchemical term for the *lapis* or the Philosopher's Stone, it represents the reconciliation of all the opposites which were originally differentiated out of the *prima materia* (sun and moon, male and female, king and queen, sulphur and quicksilver). The rebis thus symbolizes the attainment of unity and wholeness, achievement of the centre, the perfecting of the Hermaphrodite, and arrival at the supreme moment of true enlightenment.

Spiral An extremely ancient, complex, and ubiquitous symbol representing the creative power of the universe emanating from the navel, centre, or omphalos, it shares in the symbolism of the labyrinth. The double spiral represents evolution and involution, the basic rhythms of nature, Yin and Yang, feminine and masculine, yoni and lingam, shakta and shakti. It resembles the caduceus.

Temple The habitation of God(s), the temple contains within itself all the symbolism of physical and spiritual orientation, the notions of origin and finality, of depth and aspiration, of union between Heaven and Earth, and between divine powers and humanity. The location of the temple – on the top of mountains, in plains, or underground – emphasizes its function as *imago mundi*, its incorporation of the three worlds in one: Heaven, Earth, and Underworld. Cave temples represent the womb of human origins, the beginning of all things, realm of the uroborus, the primordial Self, the Great Mother, and the unconscious. The ground plan of virtually all temples keeps to a mandala configuration, constructed round a central altar or pillar, the *axis mundi* or Cosmic Tree. The horizontal dimension represents the ontological plane of human existence on earth, while the vertical dimension represents the stages of human aspiration to the divine, the ultramondane, the transcendent.

Thule The mythic Peerless Land, the land of the Hyperboreans, which marked the northernmost limit of the known classical world. It has variously been identified with Unst, the most northerly of the Shetland Islands, the polar region, the White Mountain, the Isles of the Blessed, the Island of Jewels, Avalon, Paradise, and so on. The white symbolism is important. The Latin *albus* (white) corresponds to the Hebrew *lebanah*. Albania and Albion (as in the white cliffs of Dover) stress this symbolism of the special or promised land. The island, like the mountain, is a refuge or temenos of permanence and eternity, rising above the conflicting energies, the tides, and temporal fluxes which rage about it.

Tree The general symbolism of the tree is considered on pp. 379–81, where its status as one of the most profound and universal symbols is established. In his essay 'The Philosophical Tree', Jung publishes a series of pictures produced by patients in analysis. Commenting on these, Jung says, 'it is evident that authors of such pictures were trying to portray an inner process of development independent of their consciousness and will. The process usually consists in the union of two pairs of opposites, the lower (water, blackness, animal, snake, etc.), with an upper (bird, light, head, etc.), and a left (feminine) with a right (masculine). The union of opposites, which plays such a great and indeed decisive role in alchemy, is of equal significance in the psychic process initiated by the confrontation of the unconscious, so the occurrence of similar or even identical symbols is not surprising' (CW13, para. 462). In a preceding passage Jung says: 'If a mandala may be described as a symbol of the Self seen in cross section, then the tree would represent a profile of it: the Self depicted as a process of growth' (CW13, para. 304).

Summing up his reflections on the tree in relation to the individuation process, Jung comments: 'The whole process, which today we understand as psychological development, was designated the "philosophical tree", a "poetic" comparison that draws an apt analogy to the natural growth of the psyche and that of a plant . . . merely intellectual understanding is not sufficient. It supplies us only with a verbal concept, but it does not give us their true content, which is to be found in the living experience of the process as applied to ourselves . . . no understanding by means of words and no imitation can replace actual experience' (CW13, para. 482).

Unus mundus An image of one world, expressing the unity of all things in the cosmos, a vision of all entities and forces existing and interacting within a unitary whole.

Wheel A symbol of the individuating Self, whose solar implications are considered on pp. 185–7. In terms of Jungian metapsychology, the hub represents the primal Self, the collective unconscious or phylogenetic psyche, the sum total of the archetypal potential with which one is endowed at birth: it is the nucleus of the personality. The rim represents the actualized potential of the Self in the personal or ontogenetic psyche in which consciousness orbits like an electron round its nucleus. Ego-consciousness at any given moment occurs at the point where the revolving wheel hits the ground (outer reality). The spokes represent the two-way channels between ego-consciousness and Self, along which information flows in both directions, from the centre to the circumference and from the circumference to the centre. The forward movement of the wheel represents progression through the life-cycle, on which the individuation process is contingent (*see also* p. 78).

Zodiac One of the most ancient of symbols despite its complexity. Its existence in pre-Columbian America (the Inca zodiac) as well as in China, India, Mesopotamia, Egypt, Greece, and Northern Europe is a clear demonstration of man's archetypal propensity to orientate himself via the circle divided into four, eight, or twelve segments making three quaternaries (or four ternaries corresponding to the four seasons and four cardinal points) in relation to the heavenly bodies. Our name for this primordial configuration comes from the Greek words *zoë* (life) and *diakos* (wheel), and this ubiquitous 'wheel of life' bears a close resemblance to the uroboros, the never-ending cycle of involution and evolution.

Here again the archetypal opposition of conflicting yet complementary forces arises out of an original unity, the first six signs of the zodiac (Aries to Virgo) representing involution, and the second six signs (Libra to Pisces) evolution. This applies to all phenomena: individuals, the nation, periods of history, the cosmos itself.

Moreover, Ptolemy described alternating signs as masculine and feminine, 'as the day is followed by the night, and as the male is coupled with the female' (Cooper, 1978). The masculine signs are Aries, Gemini, Leo, Libra, Sagittarius, Aquarius, and the feminine are Taurus, Cancer, Virgo, Scorpio, Capricorn and Pisces.

Evidence for the great antiquity of zodiac symbolism is derived from Neolithic rock paintings in Spain and Portugal. The earliest

systematic knowledge of astrology has been traced to King Sargon of Agade who lived about 2750 BC. That animals have been used to identify signs suggests that they were originally of totemic origin – which is going back very far indeed in the evolutionary history of human cultural life.

'In the symbolism of the zodiac one can sense the resolve to create, as in the Tarot pack, an all-embracing archetypal pattern – a kind of figurative model to serve as a comprehensive definition of each and every existential possibility in the macrocosm and the microcosm. As is the case with other symbolic forms, zodiacal symbolism is the product of the *serial* intellection of the universe, arising out of the belief that all things occupy positions and situations in space-time which are limited and typical, and implying, not determinism, but belief in the "system of destinies", that is to say, the theory that certain antecedents must cause certain consequences and that any given situation must have ramifications that are neither replaceable nor arbitrary' (Cirlot, 1971).

ix Death and Rebirth

We are probably the only animal with any clear idea of what it is to be alive, and to have systematized our conjectures about what it means to die. Whatever we may think about it, death is a constant with which we have to live: 'In the midst of life we are in death.' From this fact comes a major impetus to the religious belief that a non-physical part of us can survive after death and that ritual actions performed before or at the time of death can ensure that this survival will occur. The perception that death is unavoidable has consequently given rise to the religious imperative to prepare for it, to meet it, and to overcome it. This has generated the symbolism of suffering, death, and resurrection as embodied in the stories of Osiris, Dionysus, and Christ, as well as the *opus* of the alchemists and their quest for the elixir of life, the Philosopher's Stone.

The Ark A symbol of preservation, salvation, and renewal. It expresses the idea that the essence of all life can be extracted and contained within a small vessel until the time is propitious for its regeneration in the world. It thus shares in the symbolism of the alchemical retort, semen, the seed, and the womb. That the ark is crescent-shaped and floats on the waters emphasizes its feminine connotations as the preserver and re-creator of life and its association with the moon and cyclicity. The mythology of the ark and the flood is extremely widespread: Hinduism tells how an ark was built by Satyavrata at the command of Manu and that it carried seeds; the Old Testament account tells how Noah built his ark at Jahweh's order and that it carried the Noah family and animals. In all instances, the ark is the means for the conservation, purification, and regeneration of life (Cohn, 1996).

Dying gods Symbolize cyclic death and rebirth both on the human and vegetative plane. Examples are Osiris, Zagreus, Dionysus, Tammuz, Attis, the Dictean Zeus, Orpheus, Mithras, Ba'al, Baldur, Adonis, Wotan/Odin, and Christ. Dying gods share common characteristics: their birth is often announced by a star, they are born of a virgin in a cave, they are sometimes visited by wise men, as children they teach their instructors, they commonly predict their own death and second coming, they die on trees, descend into the earth for three days (corresponding to the three days when the moon is not visible from the earth), and they are resurrected. They never attain full maturity, and are always identified with their divine father. The initiatory symbolism of dying gods is very apparent, therefore, and it is usual for initiates to identify with them as they pass through the ritual.

Elixir A miraculous liquid which, when consumed, ensures immortality. The Indian *soma* and the Iranian *hoama* are beverages of divine origin which confer immortality on those who drink them. Ambrosia and nectar, the food and drink of the Olympian gods, became the food and wine of the Eucharist, the body and blood of Christ, the stuff of immortality. The identification of alcohol with spirit is a piece of projection induced by the experience that it 'liberates the spirit' and alters one's mode of consciousness; it is but a brief step to equate it with the essence of the god. Sometimes alcohol is a gift of the gods, sometimes it is stolen from them, like Prometheus's theft of fire. Odin stole sacred MEAD, the source of poetic inspiration, from the giants. The mead was made from the blood of the god Kvasir, the all-wise, by dwarfs who killed him and mixed his blood with honey. Odin changed himself into a serpent to steal it and then into an eagle to fly home with it to Asgardr, the fortress of the Aesir gods. He put it in three urns at the entrance, spilling a portion outside the walls, where it fell into the world so that men could drink it. Mead was also sacred as the blood of the gods in Crete, and was initially associated with Dionysus on the Greek mainland before he became celebrated as the god of WINE. In the worship of Odin and Dionysus, mead or wine was consumed to induce frenzy, a state of altered consciousness in which one attained superhuman insight and strength and became as a god.

The elixir of life belongs to the widespread symbolic canon which includes remote mountain passes, like Shangri-la, and inaccessible islands inhabited by those who have discovered the secret of immortality: these are all fantasies evidently generated by knowledge of the certainty of death and by compensatory longings for life everlasting.

CINNABAR, red sulphide of mercury, was regarded by Chinese alchemists as 'liquid gold' – the elixir of life. The combination of sulphur (Yin) and mercury (Yang) represented but one stage of the alchemical *opus*: the objective was to achieve pure Yang through successive calcinations and the progressive freeing of mercury; the alternation between cinnabar and mercury being symbolic of life, death, and rebirth in a process of perpetual regeneration. That cinnabar is red means that it also participates in the symbolism of blood.

Since SPERM constitutes the immortality of the species, Taoist alchemists also believed it might be possible to generate cinnabar in the body through the distillation of SEMEN and its concentration in 'the fields of cinnabar' within the cavities of the body and the brain. This could be achieved by various exercises, such as hanging upside-down, with the objective of encouraging semen to gather in the cerebral vesicles, where the embryo of immortality might be alchemically prepared. One name for the cinnabar fields is *K'un Lun*, which signifies both the Mountain of the Western Sea (the sojourn of the Immortals) and the secret nuptial chamber of the brain (where Nirvana resides). Such is the ingenuity of the human imagination.

Feathers Because of their relative weightlessness and their links with the air and flight, they are associated with the spirits of the dead and with the capacity possessed by special individuals (e.g. priests and shamans) to visit them. In the story of Gilgamesh, the dead have birds' feathers; Assyrian priests wore them, as do Siberian shamans, symbolizing their capacity to fly to the other world. Virgil compared the ghosts of the dead to thronging birds.

Flood or **deluge** Associated with the symbolism of the ark: fallible, sinful humanity is overwhelmed, a few chosen individuals are saved in the ark, and a new era is inaugurated when the floodwaters recede, leaving the world cleansed of wickedness. Deluge symbolism is not only comparable to baptism but also to the *solve et coagula* principle of alchemy. Submersion does not mean total destruction, but 'a temporary reintegration into the formless, which will be followed by a new creation, a new life or a new man, depending on whether the reintegration in question is cosmic, biological or redemptive' (Eliade, 1958). As described on p. 131, the floods which feature in the myths of many diverse peoples may have their basis in historical fact.

Incest Occurs between gods, sovereigns, and pharaohs as a means of preserving closed societies and perpetuating their exclusive supremacy. Thus, Isis married her brother Osiris and bore four children to her son Horus. Jung interpreted incest as symbolizing a longing for union with the essence of one's own Self and, consequently, for individuation. He also saw incestuous longing for the mother not merely as a regression but as *reculer pour mieux sauter*, as a necessary *regressus ad uterum*, before rebirth – a stage symbolized by the solar hero being temporarily engulfed in the belly of the whale.

Phoenix A widely distributed symbol of resurrection and immortality, of death and rebirth by fire; a fabulous bird which dies by self-immolation. It remains dead for three days (the period of the dark or absent moon), and rises again from its own ashes on the third day.

Rhizome Symbol of the human genotype and the notion of constancy underlying perpetual flux. Writing of the rhizome, Jung (1963) commented that its true life is invisible, hidden beneath the ground: 'The part that appears above the ground lasts only a single summer. Then it withers away: an ephemeral apparition. When we think of the unending growth and decay of life and civilizations, we cannot escape the impression of absolute nullity. Yet I have never lost a sense of something that lives and endures beneath the eternal flux. What we see is the blossom, which passes, the rhizome remains.'

Sacrifice A form of reciprocal altruism and gift exchange between humanity and the gods; a means of keeping the gods on our side by constant expressions of gratitude and gestures of goodwill. Regular offerings, accompanied by hymns of praise, are designed to keep them well-disposed, to propitiate their wrath, and to prevent natural disasters from occurring. Such behaviour is often conceived as man's highest duty, for on it preservation of the group, tribe, or nation will depend, as well as the spiritual peace and psychological well-being of its members. Gods everywhere, it seems, like to receive the attention which is their due and get furious if they are ignored – like all high-ranking individuals.

The sense of reciprocal obligation between humanity and the gods depends on the realization, which must have occurred fairly early in our first religious formulations, that in this world there is no such thing as a free lunch. Not only do we make sacrifices for the benefit of the gods but they make sacrifices for the benefit of humankind – sometimes the supreme sacrifice. From numerous planting cultures come myths of divine beings who died or who were slain and dismembered, and whose remains provided the origins of the staple crops on which the life of the community depends. This original divine sacrifice is then repeated in an annual ritual sacrifice of a human or animal victim to guarantee that each year the crops will be re-created and that the community will again escape starvation. Frazer's *The Golden Bough* is full of such examples from Africa, Asia, Europe, and the Pacific littoral. The very cycle of the agricultural year, whose maintenance is the responsibility of the gods, is a cycle of gift exchange – life for life – a biological economy based on the homeostatic principle of reciprocity.

Serpent The capacity of this reptile to shed its skin and, leaving its old corporeal remains behind like a corpse, to go cheerfully off about its business makes it an obvious symbol of the cycle of death and rebirth.

Sickle or **scythe** An attribute of Kronos/Saturn and of various figures representing the Reaper and Death. It also represents rebirth because of its connection with the harvest and therefore with gods of vegetation.

Tree Mythic examples of the tree in relation to the symbolism of life, death, and resurrection are given on p. 380. The tree is frequently associated with the snake, not only in the myth of Adam and Eve: the tree corresponds to the passive, vegetative principle; the snake to the active, animal principle. While the tree symbolizes earthbound corporeality, the snake represents the emotions, vital instincts, and the immortal soul. 'Without the soul,' comments Jung, 'the body is dead, and without the body the soul is unreal. The union of the two ... would mean the animation of the body and the materialization of the soul. Similarly, the tree of paradise is an earnest of the real life which awaits the first parents when they emerge from their initial childlike (i.e. pleromatic) state' (CW13, para. 316).

Uroboros The snake, or dragon, biting its own tale, symbolizes the inexorability of time and the continuity of life. In the *Codex Marcianus* it is referred to as 'the One, the All' (Figure 3, p. 142. The body is represented as half light and half dark, alluding to the counterbalance of opposing principles as in the Chinese Yin and Yang symbol. It has active (evolutionary) and passive (involutionary) halves and represents not only the life-cycle of the individual but of the universe itself, together with the dependence of each animal in the food chain on other organic life. It is thus symbolic of self-sufficient nature, the eternal processes of creation and destruction, the never-ending cycle of death and renewal.

Wheat The basic foodstuff, whose annual cycle is the quintessence of the resurrection principle on which all agriculture, and all life, depends. During the Eleusinian Mysteries celebrating the marriage of Zeus and Demeter, a grain of wheat was displayed like the Host in a monstrance, and worshipped in silence. So great was the mystery that nothing could be said about it.

x Morality

As we saw in Chapter 4, 'How Do Symbols Work?', all societies possess a moral code, and their continuity depends upon the ability of new members to assimilate the code. Were this not so, the alternative would be anarchy and a collective incapacity for competition or defence. We also encountered the neo-Darwinian proposal that our capacity to cooperate, to act decently to one another, and to detect and ostracize 'free-riders' is due to our need to form alliances so as to compete for food and sex and get our genes into the next generation. In organizing this complex social behaviour, the neo-Darwinists believe, our genes are the prime movers: we do their bidding for *their* sake while operating under the illusion that we do it for our own. However, what is of advantage to our genes is also of advantage to ourselves and so we are honest and decent to one another because it pays off: in other words, our altruism is a form of enlightened self-interest. Our survival and reproductive success depend on it (Ridley, 1996; Wright, 1995).

This 'selfish gene' theory of human virtue is backed up by evidence from computer simulations of the 'prisoner's dilemma' type and by detailed examination of altruistic behaviour among members of human and other animal species. Computer models are relevant because genes are as mindless and as blindly programmed as computers. They can be used to test 'game theory' predictions as to how self-interested individuals will cooperate or cheat in different situations. In the 'prisoner's dilemma' situation, so much beloved of game theorists, two 'prisoners' are put in separate cells and each offered lenient treatment if he will grass on the other. Clearly, it is to the advantage of both prisoners to remain silent if they are to avoid heavy sentences. But if one is prepared to grass on the other he can be sure of getting off lightly while the other goes down for a long time. In these circumstances, how can one prisoner be sure that the other will not grass? Or to change the situation, if I get you to build my house by promising to help you build yours, what is to stop me reneging once mine is built? The best strategy to adopt in such situations, so the game theorists find, is incorporated in the programme called 'tit-for-tat' (Axelrod, 1984): the highest pay-off comes through adopting a strategy of cooperating with cooperators and retaliating against defectors. Such a strategy not only makes good sense but it corresponds closely to how we feel we want to behave in such situations. Moreover, this strategy is enshrined in the moral code of the great majority of human groups.

However, what neo-Darwinists usually fail to take into account is the role that consciousness can play in modifying human behaviour: they seem unaware of the fact that biological imperatives can be overruled by Kant's 'categorical imperative' to do as we would be done by – not out of a desire for our own self-aggrandizement or genetic advantage, but out of an ethical choice to treat people as ends in themselves rather than as means to achieving our own reproductive success. Selfish genes operate at the unconscious level to influence our choice and behaviour, to be sure, but we can become conscious of these promptings and exercise conscious decision over whether or not to obey them. This is what saints and philosophers have always told us. Were they wrong?

By leaving the psyche out of their reckoning, as if it were an irrelevance, biologists neglect the essential link between genes and culture. As sentient beings who have to live with the selfish demands of our genes, our psychological experiences involved in mediating these demands must always be primary. If psychological experience and conscious choice were unimportant, and if all behaviour were determined by the imperative to get one's genes into the next generation, men would have no time to engage in cultural activities since they would all be too busy seducing sexual partners for one-night stands and queuing up outside sperm banks.

Because of its fundamental importance for the survival of any human community, the moral code has everywhere been accorded the dignity of divine sanction. Through parental tutelage, the child acquires its own version of the moral code and builds it into an intrapsychic moral complex. Freud called this complex the SUPEREGO, and thought that it emerged during the Oedipal phase of libidinal development in response to a fear of being castrated as a punishment for forbidden incestuous desires. A more plausible explanation is that the superego possesses an innate basis in the neurophysiological system, since the universally apparent phenomenon of GUILT would otherwise be incomprehensible. Had the superego no foundation in phylogeny, we should be condemned to live in psychopathic amorality, 'free-riders' all, incapable of mutual toleration or trust, and it is likely that our species could never have come into existence or, indeed, survived.

That the moral complex formed by members of different communities should show culture-related peculiarities is not surprising: the critical factor is the way in which members of all human communities learn rapidly to distinguish between 'right' and 'wrong', and display an impressive degree of agreement on the kinds of behaviour to be included in each category. The TEN COMMANDMENTS not only describe the main features of the Judaeo-Christian superego but are, when broadly interpreted, a pretty good approximation to the archetypal moral sensibility of humankind. The incest taboo, for example, is, for good genetic reasons, a universal phenomenon in human communities, as are ideas that there is a fundamental distinction between murdering a member of one's own community (who may well share a proportion of one's genes) and killing an enemy in warfare (who almost certainly does not); that parents are obligated to their children (who carry 50 per cent of their genes) and children to their parents; that it is wrong to seize your neighbour's property or his wife (in the name of good order and social reciprocity), and so on.

The researches of Bowlby and his followers have made it clear that individual motivation for superego development is not, as Freud believed, fear of being castrated by the father but rather fear of being abandoned by the mother and ostracized by the community for being unacceptable. The fearful prospect of being rejected because of some revelation of the Self is at the bottom of all feelings of guilt, all desire for punishment, and all longings for atonement and reconciliation.

As a defence against the catastrophe of ABANDONMENT, the superego is established as an inner watch-dog whose function is to monitor our behaviour so as to ensure relative conformity to the values of society. Those aspects of the Self that we fear will prove 'unacceptable' are kept hidden or repressed in the personal unconscious, where they form a complex which Jung called the SHADOW. Jung's terminology is in line with the finding that in dreams moral issues are commonly represented by the symbolism of light and darkness, day and night, right and left. The archetypal battle between Good and Evil is also represented by pairs of warring TWINS, such as Osiris and Set. Cain and Abel, Jacob and Esau, are also brothers at enmity with each other and they take on the symbolism of the conflicting twins. Frequently, as described on p. 142, the twins are represented as being one light and one dark, stressing their links with day and night, good and evil. The struggle between Apollo and Python is also linked to this symbolism, as is the battle between the eagle and the snake. This conflict is paralleled by the Christian splitting of the godhead into All-Good Almighty God and All-Evil Satan, the Prince of Darkness.

Responsibility for ensuring that taboos are not broken and the Divine Commandments obeyed is shared by the individual (through the superego), the community, the priests, and the elders (through the moral code), and, ultimately, by the gods (through divine rewards and punishments). Religious rituals, particularly those of praise and sacrifice, are designed to sustain the cosmic as well as the social order through the maintenance of harmonious relations between the gods and humanity. These relations are conceived as hierarchical ('In the eyes of God,' said Evelyn Waugh, 'we are all working class') and based on the principle of RECIPROCITY.

Reciprocity is indispensable to harmonious social functioning because it makes cooperation possible. A basic commandment implicit in most moral codes is 'Thou shalt not cheat' or 'Thou shalt not bear false witness', because, in the long run, as the game theorists have demonstrated, honesty really is the best policy. The pay-offs from long-term trading based on giving and getting value for money are greater than those from cheating or stealing on a one-off basis. 'Free-riders', who make a practice of cheating, only get away with it as long as they are plausible, highly mobile, and keep moving on. Most societies exercise powerful sanctions against them. The principle of reciprocity is thus an indispensable feature of the moral code, and it is expressed in the symbolism of the gift, money, oath-taking, sacrifice, the scapegoat, theft, and the trickster, as well as the Greek concepts of hubris and nemesis.

Gift A symbol of good intentions which carries an inevitable subtext – an implicit invitation to reciprocate. A basic form of reciprocation is the giving and receiving of food – a pattern at the basis of human family life: man (the hunter) providing the meat, and woman (the gatherer) providing the fruit and veg. Food-sharing is observed among chimpanzees as well as among hunter-gatherers, but systematic gift-exchange and trading is a uniquely human accomplishment. Since human beings invariably use the same social skills to relate to their gods as they use to relate to each other, gift-exchange is ritualized in the religious practices of sacrifice and prayer – i.e. giving associated with begging. **Paradise** is the dream of escaping the treadmill of reciprocal obligation and enjoying a limitless abundance of all the good things of life absolutely free of charge – a return to the enormously privileged status of the baby in the womb or at the breast.

In societies where men are indisputably in control, arranged marriages are the rule: the female assumes the status of a gift or tradeable commodity capable of being given to a suitor by her father in return for a dowry or some contractual obligation. Sex can thus be turned into a tradeable item, either in marriage (long term) or prostitution (short term).

A negative form of reciprocal giving is retributive punishment: an eye for an eye, a tooth for a tooth; measure for measure. The culprit receives his due for the offence he has given; the punishment fits the crime.

Ultimately, reciprocity is implicit in the universe, with its homeostatic balances and counter-balances based on mathematical equations; religion has sanctified this universal principle and institutionalized it for the good of society (and, of course, the priests).

Hubris and **nemesis**   The Greeks originally used the term hubris to refer to passion or violence arising from pride and arrogance which drove men to usurp the privileges of the gods. It is the crime of getting above oneself, of trying to ascend too far – the crime of Icarus and Tantalus. In the Greek view, a man should have *aidos* (reverence) for the gods and for the limits they set to human presumption. Those who are too well off or reared in luxury are particularly prone to this sin: the result is nemesis (retribution).

Nemesis was the goddess responsible for visiting retribution on those who committed crimes with apparent impunity or who received inordinate good fortune. Excessive or repeated strokes of good luck make people superstitiously anxious, as if they fear that the gods (and other people) may grow envious. Psychologically, this refers to the danger of ego-inflation, of losing touch with homeostatic balances inherent in the Self: 'pride goeth before a fall'. This was a central moral concern of the Greeks and there are impressive examples in their mythology and history: Polycrates, the triumphantly successful ruler of Samos, whose sacrifice was rejected by the gods, and who ended up being crucified by rebels; Ixion, who attempted to seduce Hera, for which Zeus bound him to a wheel of fire; Prometheus, who stole fire from the gods, and who consequently had his liver eaten on a daily basis by Zeus's eagle; and then there was the cautionary tale of Phaeton.

Phaeton believed himself to be the natural son of the sun god Helios (or Apollo, according to Ovid, by whose time Apollo had taken over the duties of Helios). Stung by taunts about his parentage, Phaeton travelled through Persia and India to the fabulous palace of the sun god in the East, where the sun rises each morning, and begged his father to give him proof of his paternity. Helios acknowledges Phaeton as his son and offers to grant him any boon he wishes. The rash youth asks permission to drive the sun chariot across the sky for one day. Helios at once regrets his promise, but, because Phaeton clamorously persists in his demand, reluctantly consents.

Elated, Phaeton sets off, but once in the sky he panics. The four horses drawing the sun chariot sense an amateur at the reins and bolt – first upwards to scorch the sky (the result is the Milky Way) and then down towards the earth, scorching the people of equatorial Africa black, drying up the lakes and rivers, and setting the world on fire. According to one source, Zeus quenches the flames by releasing Deucalion's flood upon the earth; according to others, he kills Phaeton with a thunderbolt. But whatever the exact nature of the outcome, hubris was punished by nemesis.

Money A symbol of value, which permits a more impersonal form of gift-exchange than barter. Minting coins and introducing them into the economy is an illustration of the intrinsic process of symbol formation whereby the act of investing an object with value turns it into a symbol. Money affords an excellent demonstration of the truth that symbolism enables us to deal effectively with the non-present world. With the invention of money we were able to represent an equivalent amount of goods (e.g. grain, olive oil, flour) without having to cart them about with us. The money rendered these goods symbolically present. In this way money makes possible the measurement of credit, debt, and reciprocal obligation: credit anticipates a future return on past generosity.

The value of a coin is expressed by its size, its material substance, and its beauty. To counterfeit or debase the coinage is a knavish piece of trickery because it undermines the good faith on which all mercantile transactions are based.

In China, the *cash* was a round coin (symbolizing Heaven), with a square hole (Earth) in the middle; the space in between bore the superscription of the Emperor, son of Heaven and Earth, representative of Universal Man.

So potent a symbol is money that it can seem supremely important in its own right. In a secular society it can take the place of the sacred or holy and become the symbol of ultimate bliss, the possession of which is the highest objective of life. We are all affected by this symbolism. Money is mana. If you doubt it, see if you can set fire to a £10 or $20 note; it is, after all, merely a piece of paper. Its value is purely symbolical.

Oaths Lying, fraud, and trickery are endemic in nature, as in death-feigning, various forms of mimicry, camouflage, etc. Such dishonesty is particularly apparent in human communities, and is exemplified in tales of robbers, bandits, and tricksters (free-riders). Even chimpanzees, taught to use sign language, are alert to the possibilities this provides for tricking their trainers with lies. Humans have endeavoured to control this propensity through religion, not only by stigmatizing deceit as displeasing to the gods (Thou shalt not bear false witness), but through invoking the presence of the gods to witness the swearing of a solemn oath ('I swear by Almighty God, that the evidence I shall give . . .'). This is a further reason why gods are necessary for the satisfactory conduct of human affairs: 'Without gods', writes Burkert (1996), 'there would be no oaths, and hence no basis for trust and cooperation, for legal action, or for business . . . No contract, no treaty, no administration of justice proceeds without an oath.'

The symbolism of oath-taking commonly involves the spilling of blood, the life-substance. Having sacrificed oxen and read the Covenant to the people of Israel, 'Moses took the blood, and sprinkled it on the people, and said, Behold the blood of the Covenant, which the Lord hath made with you concerning all these words' (Exodus 24:8). Swearing an oath in the *Iliad*, Agamemnon cuts the throats of sacrificial sheep and all present pour wine from their goblets on the ground, saying: 'Whoever does wrong against the oath, his brain shall flow to the ground as does this wine . . .' Blood, wine, and brain are equated in one symbolic act to make the oath absolute.

Sacrifice The role of sacrifice in the maintenance of fertility and the cycles of nature is examined on p. 260. Here we will consider sacrifice as a form of ritual gift-giving in anticipation of celestial reciprocation.

On the face of it, giving to the gods is an irrational activity, for there is no guarantee that one's bounty will be noticed, acknowledged, or rewarded. Moreover, it is not possible to hand over one's gifts directly, for the recipient is both invisible and intangible, and his presence (if present he is) is purely symbolical. Consequently, the gifts have to be symbolically given. This is done in a number of ways: (1) the gift is removed from the sphere of human consumption and conspicuously wasted or destroyed – it is poured away (a libation), consumed by fire (a burnt offering), or cast into the sea; or (2) it is dedicated to the god and then ritually consumed by the faithful – as in a feast or ritual meal, like the Eucharist; or (3) it is presented to the deity and then kept as a sacred object in his temple or church.

The ritual feast, at which the sacrificial beast is consumed by the faithful and a part (usually inedible) reserved for the gods, probably derives from the well-attested custom of hunters apologizing to the animal they have hunted and killed. The religious feast is thus a ritual extension of the food-sharing which followed the kill.

Ritual sacrifice of beasts, or parts thereof, is a widespread and ancient custom. Nowhere was it more assiduously practised than in Greece: 'We cannot begin to understand the culture and literature of ancient Greece,' wrote G. S. Kirk (1974), 'if we overlook the ubiquitous altars reeking with fresh blood, the constant throat-slitting of bulls, cows, sheep, goats, pigs, and occasionally dogs. Greek cities had no abattoirs; the slaughtering was done mainly in front of the temples. Priests were butchers, hacking up animal corpses, tearing out thigh-bones and wrapping them in fat to be burned for the god, dabbling in entrails, jointing the rest of the carcase and selling parts of it to the worshippers, keeping back specified portions for themselves. Zeus' most hallowed place at Olympia was a great heap of ashes, the ashes of burnt offerings, and in the precincts of Apollo at Delphi and Delos there towered piles of horns, a concrete record of piety by slaughter.'

Whether or not the gods gave just returns for all these massacres was never subjected to statistical analysis. Had it been, it could well have led to the blasphemous conclusion that the gods were cheating. If they were, they were not alone in their trickery. For the Greeks invariably offered up the inedible thighbones to the gods; the rest they kept for themselves. On one famous occasion, however, Zeus caught

Prometheus doing just this, and as a punishment withdrew fire from men, so that henceforth they would have to eat raw meat. It was when Prometheus stole fire back for humanity that Zeus finally chained him to a rock and sent an eagle to feed nightly on his liver. HOLOCAUST – the burning of whole animals – represented the much more serious sacrificial intent of Semitic peoples at the Temple of Jerusalem.

The principle underlying the practice of sacrifice is the understanding that one can never hope to get something for nothing; and this applied to the gods themselves as well as to humanity. In Scandinavian mythology, for example, it is common for gods to sacrifice parts of themselves in order to acquire a particular quality or gift that they desire. This is usually done on the basis of losing a little of what one hopes to gain in abundance. Thus, Tyr sacrifices a hand in order to possess great strength; Heimdallr forfeits an ear to acquire superb hearing; and Odin gives one of his eyes to Mymir to gain access to the well of wisdom at the base of Yggdrasil, the World Tree, so as to become master of divination and prophecy.

This is the principle of sacrificing *pars pro toto*, the part for the whole. It is an ancient biological trick which animals play on predators and humans play on their gods, secure in the knowledge that they will be taken in by it. Examples are the lizard relinquishing its tail to a predator's grasp, a spider sacrificing a leg, and the 'terror moult' of birds leaving their attackers with a mouthful of feathers. It is what Burkert calls 'the trick of abandoning what can be spared'.

In folk tales and fairy tales from many parts of the world, a hero escapes from a monster or a demon by cutting off or biting off a finger: he saves his whole body by sacrificing a part. In the same way, an animal whose foot is caught in a cruel snare will bite it off in order to escape. Ritual FINGER SACRIFICE has been practised in many different societies (examples come from Oceania, India, Africa, and Ancient Greece, as well as from a Palaeolithic cave dating from 20,000 years ago). Coins thrown into fountains, pools, and sacred streams, relate to the same function – a bribe or a ransom, a sustainable loss for an incalculable gain. To surrender your money to a mugger to avoid getting stabbed is a contemporary example of sacrifice of the part for the whole.

Finally, the most widespread and fundamental use of sacrifice is to propitiate the gods so as to avert some feared disaster, to atone for some serious transgression, to expiate one's sin, and to escape retribution from the gods by appeasing their wrath. This mechanism is further discussed in **Sickness and Healing,** pp. 274–9.

Scapegoat Scapegoating is the ego-defence mechanism whereby one evades the guilt of acknowledging one's own shadow and disowns it by projecting it on to someone or something else. This is a universally applied psychological technique. The first example recorded in our own culture is that described in Leviticus, when two goats were chosen by lot, one to be sacrificed to God in the usual way, the other to be laden with the sins of the people and driven out into the wilderness as an offering to Azazel (the Demon of the Wilderness). Religious scapegoating thus involves the abandonment or sacrifice of a single individual to ensure the safety of the group – in the same way as finger sacrifice permits the whole body to be saved through abandonment of a part.

In this sense, Christ was a scapegoat for humanity: 'He was wounded for our transgressions, He was bruised for our iniquities: the chastisement of our peace was upon Him; and with His stripes we are healed' (Isaiah, 53:5).

What biological antecedent may be deduced for this behaviour? To Burkert (1996), it resembles the reaction of a herd of zebra threatened by a carnivore. When one is attacked and killed by lions, the other members of the herd cease to exhibit alarm: 'The instinctive program seems to command: take another one, not me. This ancient program is still at work in humans, still fleeing from devouring dangers and making sacrifices to assuage and triumph over anxiety.'

Theft Theft from the gods Jung interpreted as the *opus contra naturam* necessary for the development of consciousness. The theft of fire by Prometheus (for which he was severely punished by Zeus) represents a human appropriation of a fundamental secret of nature: 'With this theft [Prometheus] appropriated something precious and offended against the gods. Anyone who knows of the primitive's fear of innovations and their unforeseen consequences can imagine the uncertainty and uneasy conscience which such a discovery would

arouse. This primordial experience finds an echo in the widespread
motif of robbery (sun-cattle of Geryon, apples of the Hesperides, herb
of immortality)' (*CW*5, para. 250). It is also related to the motif of
disobeying an injunction – Adam and Eve eat the apple, Psyche shines
a lamp on Eros and opens the coffer of beauty, Bluebeard's wife enters
the forbidden room, etc. – the *felix culpa* is committed and it results
in conflict, development, and the growth of consciousness.

The Trickster If the neo-Darwinists are right and 'free-riders' are
prone to occur in all human groups, then one would expect them to
feature in myth, legend, and folk tale. They do. They appear in the
form of a negative hero figure known as 'the trickster', who manages
through pranks, knavery, and rank stupidity to achieve what the true
hero accomplishes through courage, strength, and determination. In
many ways he resembles an undisciplined and uninitiated adolescent

boy, and bears a strong similarity to MERCURIUS, the protean spirit of alchemy, who is capable of transforming himself into many different forms as the situation demands. On the one hand Mercurius is sly, evil, and smelly, on the other hand divine: Jung saw him as a personification of the *coniunctio*, providing 'the third party in the alliance' between opposites (*CW*16, para. 384).

Because of his spontaneity and unfettered liveliness, the trickster becomes of creative importance when the conscious personality has become too one-sided and rigid in its ways. The trickster then appears wiser than the ego − like the Fool in relation to King Lear − and promotes the compensatory function of unconscious processes in accordance with the principle of *enantiodromia* (which states that everything has a tendency to go over to its opposite). When the trickster gets out of hand and remains unconfronted by the ethical standards of the ego or the community, the individual is in danger of adopting a 'free-rider' strategy and being classified as a ne'er-do-well or psychopath. The trickster thus stands as an executive of the shadow personality: one cannot get rid of him and it is unwise to repress him. But confronted responsibly by consciousness he can make a vital contribution to the individuation process. The trickster can be a necessary corrective to the *status quo*.

xi Sickness and Healing

The symbolism of healing is very ancient indeed, probably as old as the species. Evidence of healing behaviour has been observed in primates other than human beings, especially chimpanzees (e.g. the application of certain leaves to heal wounds; Rosen, 1992). Our own species evolved in circumstances of great vulnerability, threatened by the elements, by predators, hostile neighbours, and malevolent forces bringing disease and death. In such conditions it is not surprising that healers and healing practices should emerge.

The function of healing symbols and rituals is to mobilize and channel powerful propensities which are as old as evolution itself. Successful healers are those who have the knack of perceiving what is needed and knowing how to manipulate conditions so as to make it possible for the organism to heal itself.

The essence of the healer–patient relationship is expressed by the archetypal symbol of the WOUNDED HEALER. The Greek god of healing, Asklepios, was himself taught the art of healing by Chiron, a centaur, who suffered from an incurable wound. A slightly later version of the wounded healer is offered by the symbol of the crucified Christ. The successful healer, it appears, is one capable of acknowledging his own woundedness. This implies that in every healer there is a patient and in every patient a healer. When two people enter into a therapeutic relationship this archetypal field is constellated between them. An essential part of the training analysis through which all potential analysts have to go is the bringing to consciousness of their own woundedness and their own experience of being healed.

Like all archetypes, the healer, once it has been activated, *personates* in the ontogenetic psyche – sometimes as a man, sometimes as a woman, and sometimes as an animal or object possessing symbolic healing potential. Not only does the healer archetype appear in dreams and in active imagination but it is often experienced as a numinous presence in the transference (Stevens, 1993). When projected on to the person of the analyst it confers on him or her great therapeutic – and occasionally great destructive – power. The most commonly projected archetypal images are the magician, shaman, witch doctor, quack, charlatan, saviour, alchemist, and wise old man or woman. Activation of these archetypal figures seems to be a crucial part of the healing process and it would help to explain why it is that the charisma of the healer plays so important a part in his or her success.

Cross-cultural parallels reveal a remarkable degree of agreement about ideas of disease causation (aetiology) as well as the symbolism of sickness and its cure (Leff, 1981). Essentially, sickness is seen as due to a deficiency, to an intrusion, and to a transgression. The deficiency is usually attributed to 'loss of soul', the intrusion to something evil, and the transgression to breaking of a taboo.

Loss of soul The idea that the soul can leave the body is extremely ancient and widespread. Many peoples accept this idea as an explanation of death as well as of dreams, believing that our souls actually go off and do the things we dream about once we are asleep. There are many theoretical explanations as to how the soul can be lost and cause sickness but most are agreed that the night is a particularly dangerous time. One might, for example, be woken up suddenly from a dream while one's soul is wandering in a far off place, so that its passage of return is forgotten, or it may be captured by evil spirits. Successful treatment then depends on locating the soul and returning it to its rightful owner. In our own culture depression is subjectively experienced as a 'loss of soul', as it is in many other cultures. The notion of loss of soul also occurs in alchemy in the departure and return of the anima spirit during the stage of the alchemical *opus* known as the *mortificatio*. In *Modern Man in Search of a Soul* (1933), Jung diagnosed our whole culture as suffering loss of soul. He cured the condition in himself, and sought to cure it in his patients, through working with dreams and using the imagination in accordance with the therapeutic procedures employed by analytical psychologists all over the world.

Evil The most dreaded force, widely believed to have the capacity for invading a patient and causing disease, especially mental disease, is the force of evil. The theory of demonic possession and the practice of exorcism are the primordial roots from which dynamic psychiatry and psychoanalysis have sprouted. At the basis of this aetiological conception lies the archetype of the predator, the quintessence of malevolent hostility – that is to say, it is widely believed that a patient has become sick because an evil external force or object has intruded into his body. It is the healer's task to diagnose what has got into the patient and to remove it. In Nepal, for example, the healer sucks the illness from the patient and spits out something (which on subsequent examination proves to be a piece of animal or vegetable tissue) on to a brass plate. In the Philippines, so called 'psychic surgeons' carry out 'operations' without the use of instruments. With their bare hands they appear to remove tissues from the abdomen which have the appearance of bloody internal organs. When these 'extracted' tissues are analysed, however, they again prove to be of animal origin.

Transgression The idea that illness is due to possession by evil spirits is linked to the parallel concept of illness as due to sin – namely, that the patient has brought the illness on himself through his own evil-doing. The healer treats these conditions by hearing the patient's confession, granting absolution, and performing rituals for the propitiation of the gods. Modern psychiatry, like analysis, has replaced the idea of sin by the notion of guilt. There is little doubt that confession in the consulting room plays a fundamental role in psychotherapeutic success.

Healing techniques In our culture the archetype of the healer is embodied in the figure of Jesus Christ. Christ's healing technique was similar to that used by native healers throughout the world when dealing with mental illness (Leff, 1981). The healer commands the devil to leave the possessed sufferer, transfers the evil spirit to the bodies of animals, and the animals are subsequently killed. There is the additional element of water which is used to wash away the spirits. For example, Jesus treated one psychotic ('My name is Legion: for we are many') by commanding the 'unclean spirits' to leave him and enter a herd of swine: 'And the herd ran violently down a steep place into the sea.' Numerous parallels to this can be found in the ethnographic literature. For example, Yoruba healers stand their mental patients in a swiftly flowing river. They use three doves as living sponges to wash the evil away from the patient. The doves are then killed and their bodies flung downstream, and the evil is carried away by the river. Such symbolism is still apparent in the dreams of contemporary patients in analysis. It is the function of the analyst to enable the patient to participate as fully as possible in the psychic drama as it is played out, and in doing this the analyst performs the same role as the traditional healer.

Sanctuaries of healing The symbols of water and animals, particularly SNAKES, are much in evidence in the sanctuaries of healing like those dedicated to Asklepios in ancient Greece. The healing ritual began with PURIFICATION rites: patients' clothing was removed, they drank and bathed in sacred waters, and then put on clean clothing. They were then led into the *abaton*, the sacred abode of the god. There a sleeping draught was administered and they were left to sleep – on the ground in earliest times (*incubation* means lying on the ground) but later on a couch called the *kline* (the forerunner of the Freudian analytic couch and the doctor's examination couch in his clinic). Asklepios customarily appeared to patients in a dream, conveying a message of healing which could itself be instrumental in producing a cure. Snakes were often present both in actuality and in the dream. The dream required no interpretation: the experience was itself the cure.

Conventional and alternative modes of healing The influence of Asklepios began to decline after the time of Hippocrates, who died in Larissa at a great age in 356 BC. Modern physicians and psychiatrists are the heirs of Hippocrates, while 'alternative' therapists and analysts are the heirs of Asklepios. With our modern understanding of cerebral lateralization and the different functions of the two sides of the brain, we can see that in being more rational and rejecting the use of magic and ritual, therapeutic medicine is the product of the left cerebral hemisphere with its sequential, verbal, digital modes of functioning. Analysis, on the other hand, like other alternative therapies, makes great use of the feeling, symbolic, and intuitive functions, operating more in the realm of the right cerebral hemisphere (holistic, non-verbal, and analogical), and the old mammalian brain, with its archetypal modes of response.

The modern, Hippocratic approach has been termed ALLOPATHIC or SANISTIC (from *sanare* to make healthy), while the traditional Asklepian approach has been termed HOMEOPATHIC or MORBISTIC (relating directly to the 'morbid' quality of disease). Sanistic therapies are full of solar symbolism and the gods who rule over them are sun gods (Apollo, Herakles, and Helios). The symbolism of the morbistic approach, on the other hand, is underworldly (Ziegler, 1988).

The triumph of the sanistic over the morbistic approaches in modern society is prefigured in Greek mythology by the triumph of Apollo over his absolute 'other', the monstrous Python which inhabited the swamp near Delphi and threatened to destroy all humanity. This symbolizes the apotheosis of the dominant left cerebral hemisphere and its triumph over the world through the use of reason, discipline, and self-control.

In Jungian terms, sanistic therapies mobilize the energies of the conscious ego while morbistic therapies are designed to mobilize the Self. Analysis does not, however, favour Python at the expense of Apollo: it gives due weight to both sides of the struggle. The way to healing is to bring the two sides together – in other words, to activate that psychic function which Jung called transcendent.

Charlatanism Although by the standards of contemporary medical practice many traditional healers are charlatans, there can be no doubt that their ministrations often prove therapeutically effective. Evidently the object 'extracted' by psychic surgeons and their like serves as a *symbol* of the disease. The secret of the healer's power is that his personality and his actions excite the patient's belief that the disease has been accurately diagnosed and treated. The healer convinces him that he is no longer ill but well. This is in effect what hypnosis achieves and it would explain why so many traditional healers make use of trance. The patient's conviction that he has been cured is also the cause of the PLACEBO EFFECT.

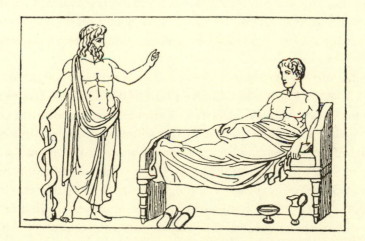

xii Tools, Weapons, Utensils, and Musical Instruments

One of the most extraordinary events in nature has been the rapid development in size of the hominid brain in the remarkably short time of two to three million years. The impressive genetic changes necessary to achieve this development could only have occurred in response to powerful and unremitting selective pressures that penalized humans with small brains and favoured those with larger ones. Evidently what was being selected were those faculties that large cerebral hemispheres impart − intelligence, speech, the capacity for social organization, strategic planning, tool and weapon making, and a more differentiated conscious awareness that enabled these early people to respond creatively to changes in their circumstances − all of which are invaluable in collaborative hunting and warfare. Those with larger brains could therefore be expected to do better in the competitive struggle for existence than their smaller-brained contemporaries. More favoured individuals would be more likely to survive and breed and to pass on selectively advantageous genes to their offspring.

Making things and taking pains to make them as well and as beautifully as one can is one of the great pleasures of life, whether the object is a garment, a necklace, a pot, a ploughshare, or a weapon. There has never been a time when tools and weapons and their manufacture have not been a source of fascination and delight to men. Stone cleavers, knives, and lanceheads of flint, quartz, and serpentine have been collected from Palaeolithic sites all over the world, as have knives made from bone and, in northern Europe, from reindeer horn.

Making tools, tending fires, and hunting for meat were indispensable activities for the cultural revolution which occurred between 60,000 and 40,000 years ago, but they go back much further than that. Crudely flaked pebble implements date from about 3 million years ago, while Acheulian hand-axes were devised by *Homo erectus* about 1.4 million years ago and appear in Eurasia about 400,000 years later. The Neanderthalers were more sophisticated tool users than *Homo erectus* and a great variety of tool shapes began to emerge; with the evolution of modern humans this variety radically increased, while hand-axes disappeared altogether. These developments went along with the emergence of logistic big game hunting, cooking, systems of notation, religious ritual, music, dance, art, and the establishment of a cultural way of life in its modern, symbolic form about 45,000 years ago (Knight, 1996).

Since the manufacture of these items has been a human activity for so long, it is not surprising that they should feature very often in our dreams. In addition to their normal utilitarian function, they are loaded with symbolical meanings.

Tools

Axe An attribute of sky gods as well as an implement of woodmen. The attribution may have derived from the impressive way in which a single flash of lightning can split a tree in two. As a result, thunderbolts were equated with axes, and attributed to the storm gods of Mesopotamia, Crete, and Scandinavia, and to the Greek gods Zeus and Apollo. Single and double axes assumed sacred ritual significance, and, since they symbolized divine powers of punishment and retribution, axes became symbols of justice and the law – as in the *fasces* (a bundle of rods with an axe) carried in procession by lictors before Roman magistrates. Axes were, of course, also used in warfare as battleaxes.

Chisel Like all sharp-edged tools, the chisel represents the active male principle which penetrates and changes passive female matter (wood or stone).

Compasses A cultural symbol of the refined consciousness and intelligence that civilization has made possible. Compasses are emblematic of the exact and applied sciences, in particular mathematics, geometry, astronomy, geography, and architecture. They introduce the notion of measure, regulation, and moderation in all things, and as a result have traditionally been associated with the virtues of prudence, justice, temperance, and truth. Because of the two legs and their function in describing a circle, compasses provide a symbol of duality and its transcendence, one leg remaining stationary at the centre while the other moves round to return to its point of departure. Compasses thus represent an image of the Self: 'The Self is not only the centre but also the whole circumference which embraces both conscious and unconscious,' wrote Jung; 'it is the centre of this totality, just as the ego is the centre of the conscious mind' (CW12, para. 44). In China, the image of compasses combined with the T-square represented Heaven and Earth, and similar imagery occurs in Masonic rituals, where compasses represent, among other things, the balance between mind and matter. So indispensable did compasses become to all creative endeavour that they were attributed to the Great Architect himself, *Deus Artifex*, who is depicted holding a pair of compasses.

Hammer An indispensable tool in all kinds of craft and manual work, it has come to symbolize work itself, as well as the political ambitions of the working class – as in the Communist symbol of the hammer (industrial work) and sickle (agricultural work). As a symbol of power and strength it has been especially identified with the blacksmith and the magic of working white-hot iron. So highly prized have the skills of ironwork been in the past that smiths were deified, as in the case of Hephaestos (Vulcan) and Thor. When angry, Thor used his hammer as a weapon and wherever he flung it, lightning struck. Smith-like qualities were also attributed to Jehovah: 'Is not my word like as fire?' He asks Jeremiah, 'and like a hammer that breaketh the rocks in pieces?' The fall of the hammer signals a decisive moment as in an auction or at a public meeting (the gavel).

Knife From the earliest flint knives used by our hominid ancestors right up to the present, the knife has been indispensable to hunters, fishermen, tanners, shoemakers, furriers, butchers, gardeners, warriors, and priests making sacrifices. As with many other cutting or hitting implements, the knife carries unmistakable masculine connotations, not only because it is used in so many activities traditionally the preserve of men, but because it works on passive 'feminine' matter. The knife is also a symbol of consciousness in its separating, differentiating, analytical, or dissecting functions. It is also a symbol of circumcision.

Pestle A phallic symbol whose grinding or pounding motion in relation to the contents of the **mortar** is symbolic of sexual intercourse.

Plough A phallic symbol of fertility; its effect on the earth is compared in agrarian cultures with man's impregnation of woman, and this symbolic notion has found widespread ritual application.

Sickle and **scythe** Symbols of the harvest which recurs each year; and by association symbols of time and of death. The days of the corn are numbered and when it ripens its life is cut short, it is reaped: hence the image of Father Time, originally with a sickle and later with a scythe. The image of Father Time originated with the Greek god Kronos, who personified time, although he was originally a god of the harvest. This is one reason why Kronos was commonly depicted with a sickle; the other reason is that he used a sickle to castrate his father Ouranos. In Roman myth Kronos became Saturn, and with his rediscovery at the Renaissance, his sickle was replaced with the more sophisticated modern implement, the scythe. Kronos/Saturn became the allegorical figure, Tempus, at first represented as an old man, later as a skeleton; because of his scythe and his link with harvesting he was known as the Great Reaper. In view of its shape, the sickle is also associated with the crescent moon, particularly that which precedes the full harvest moon. This is a more hopeful image, bringing with it the promise of new life and a good harvest.

Spindle and **distaff** Because of its shape and regular motion, the spindle is a phallic symbol, as well as a symbol of fate and of eternal recurrence. A forerunner of the spinning wheel, the spindle was traditionally used to wind thread from a distaff of wool, and is associated with the symbolism of the spider's web (p. 351). Together, the spindle and distaff form an image universally representative of womanhood, as characteristic of the feminine (creativity and the continuance of life) as is the sword of the masculine (warlikeness and flirting bravely with death). In Greek mythology, the distaff is an attribute of Clotho, youngest of the Three Fates: Clotho prepares the thread of life which Lachesis spins and Atropos cuts off.

Weapons

In theory, war could be waged and animals could be hunted without the use of weapons, but in practice it is unlikely that they ever have been. Naked men are poorly equipped for the activities of attack and defence. In comparison with most other predators – the great cats, for example – man's teeth and jaws, his toenails and fingernails, and his capacity for sudden, murderous bursts of energy are not impressive. Lacking the physical structures necessary to wound and kill, man has, as a consequence, had to use his intelligence to compensate for his anatomical deficiencies by developing weapons and the use of collaborative strategies and tactics. To protect himself from carnivores and compete with them for prey, he had to make himself as deadly as they. Human survival and later mastery of the planet has depended upon male cooperation in the use of weapons.

Inevitably the development of offensive weapons was balanced by the development of weapons of defence, the earliest of which (probably made of leather, wood, or fibre) have disappeared from the archaeological record. But numerous defensive weapons have survived from the Bronze Age – bronze helmets, cuirasses, arm guards, fingerstalls, and bronze shields. Later use of iron permitted further improvements in the manufacture of all weapons, and warfare began to take on the lethally destructive quality characteristic of modern times.

As offensive weapons increased their range and destructive power, so defensive weapons were created to counteract them – and vice versa. These developments occurred cyclically and were an early version of the modern arms race. They were also a cultural superimposition on an ancient biological process, which underlies the whole story of evolution. The arms race began very early in the history of this planet: over 500 million years ago, primitive fish started covering themselves with small bony scales of calcium phosphate to protect themselves from aggressive scorpion-like creatures which preyed on them.

Since man was a hunter before he became a warrior, his original weapons, strategies, and tactics were based on those of his competitors – the lion, tiger, and wolf – who were so much better equipped than he by nature. As a result, his weapons were improvised claws, horns, and tusks, and his tactics were mainly those of surprise from ambush or darkness, followed up by pounce and retreat. Only much later, with the arrival of civilization and professional armies, did complicated tactics involving mass charges and battles of manoeuvre become feasible and elaborate fortifications get built. Then fighting groups increased in size, discipline improved, engagements were prolonged and more determined, more destruction occurred, and more people were killed.

All this, of course, required enormous ingenuity and inventiveness, and since weapons have played such a crucial role in our evolution and success as a species they have become heavily endowed with symbolic meanings.

Arrow Before the invention of gunpowder, canons, and bullets, an arrow shot from a bow was the fastest and most devastatingly effective weapon known to man. It was also silent and could strike down its victim suddenly and without warning. Its phallic symbolism is unmistakable, hence its link with Eros, god of love: falling in love is often experienced with the unanticipated suddenness of an arrowshot. In the Middle Ages the arrow became the symbol of sudden death, as when people were struck down in the prime of life by some contagion such as the plague. Apollo, who sent plagues and also cured them, had an arrow as one of his attributes, but since he was a sun god his arrows probably represented the rays of the sun. In pre-Columbian America arrows also symbolized the sun's rays.

Bow Carries both masculine and feminine connotations: masculine in the sense that it is the power behind the arrow; feminine in its resemblance to the crescent moon. Thus bows and arrows are the attributes of Apollo, Eros, Artemis, and Diana. They also appear as the weapons of Ishtar and Inanna as war goddesses.

Lance A phallic symbol carrying the connotations of warfare, bravery, and aggressive masculine power. The lance of Longinus (the lance that the Roman soldier thrust into Christ's chest to determine that he was dead) became important in medieval Christian iconography and appears as the bleeding lance in the Grail legend. The malaise of the Fisher King and his land is symbolized by his broken lance (impaired potency), which is restored when the Questor Knight asks the right question. The lance is held upright over the Grail, dripping Christ's blood into it. Sir Galahad heals the Fisher King by anointing his 'legs' (a euphemism for genitals) with the blood. Together, the lance and the Grail represent the masculine and feminine principles. The lance was developed from the SPEAR, one of the earliest weapons, originally little more than a sharpened stick, later tipped with flint, bone, or metal. The HARPOON was an early modification used for fishing. All such weapons bear unmistakable phallic implications.

Shield A defensive weapon on which a warrior's life depended. It was either decorated with scenes and images of everything that makes life worth living (all that is at stake in battle) or with a face so terrifying as to petrify the enemy. As a religious symbol it is the 'shield of faith' capable of warding off evil and guarding against the temptations of the world, the flesh, and the Devil. In this, the shield participates in the symbolism of other defensive weaponry – armour, helmet, breastplate, etc. 'Put on the whole armour of God, that ye may be able to stand against the wiles of the devil,' says St Paul in his Epistle to the Ephesians. '. . . Stand therefore, having your loins girt about with truth, and having on the breastplate of righteousness. And your feet shod with the preparation of the gospel of peace; Above all, taking the shield of faith, wherewith ye shall be able to quench all the fiery darts of the wicked. And take the helmet of salvation, and the sword of the Spirit, which is the word of God' (Ephesians 6:11–17).

Sword A highly prized weapon of great symbolic significance; it is not only phallic in relation to the feminine sheath, but a symbol of honour, strength, and courage, of the highest achievement of knightly chivalry, of royal prerogative and power, of marshal vigilance, and of intellectual discrimination. Gods of war and storm commonly have a sword as one of their attributes, and the sword consequently becomes a symbol of divine justice, dividing good from evil, as in the 'flaming sword' that drove Adam and Eve out of Paradise. As with the hammer and the axe, the sword is associated with lightning: for example, the sword of Vedic priests is called 'the lightning of Indra'. The sword in its sheath is a symbol of restraint, temperance, and prudence.

Utensils

Utensils owe their symbolic meaning to their womb-like nature. The alchemical *vas*, the hermetic vase in which the *prima materia* is transformed into gold, inheres in the life-giving power of the womb capable of generating the *filius philosophorum*. The sealed and transformative capacity of the *vas* makes it a symbol of the analytic relationship proceeding within the therapeutic matrix of the consulting room, with its confidentiality under the seal of Hippocrates and its awakening of new unconscious potential. The CAULDRON used for making stews or witches potions is also a horn of plenty, a source of life regeneration, a limitless provider of nourishment and of wisdom. The CHALICE or **Grail** contains the draught of immortality and is homologous with the VESSEL, the ship and the ark, holding the precious seeds of cyclical rebirth. The Grail is both the receptacle of Christ's blood (the guarantee of resurrection and immortality) and the realization of the inner wholeness for which humanity is ever questing (the goal of individuation). JARS, URNS, and AMPHORAE are the attributes of river gods from which water gushes in an everlasting flow; urns are also repositories for dead children, as in ancient Crete, ensuring for them the protection and the prospect of new life in the 'mother's womb'.

Being porous, the SIEVE provides different, discriminatory symbolism, that of sifting, selecting, differentiating, especially of distinguishing what is valuable from what is worthless and what is good from what is bad. It has consequently found use as a symbol of divine justice at the Last Judgement.

Musical Instruments

Music is auditory symbolism: it communicates directly with the imagination and the emotions. It is universally distributed and very old: no culture has been found that lacks it. Palaeolithic cave paintings depict dancing figures, and the bone flutes found in these caves suggest that they danced to music. The rhythmical power of music has the effect of coordinating the movements in a group in such activities as marching and repetitive manual work, as well as the dance. It has the added advantage of relieving boredom and reducing fatigue.

Music induces all the symptoms of AROUSAL (p. 63) and thus provides ready access to the *numinosum*, hence its importance in religious rites, dances, and rituals. Music draws people together and produces in them a common mood. The essential aim of music, said Igor Stravinsky, 'is to promote a communion, a union of man with his fellow man and with the Supreme Being' (*Poetics of Music*, 1947). The powerful influence of music on the emotions was clearly recognized by the Greeks, who classified it in three modes: the Dorian (warlike), the Phrygian (ecstatic), and the Lydian (mournful). 'Rhythm and harmony,' said Plato, 'find their way into the inward places of the soul.'

Drum Warlike affect has probably always been induced by music and war dances: the steady, inexorable beat of the drum, with braying trumpets and blaring horns, instils valour in the attackers and fear in the enemy. War-drums have been associated with storm gods and sky gods from Ares to Indra, while magic drums are used by Siberian shamans to induce trance and magic flights of healing. In China, the drum beats the sun across the sky and comes into its own with the winter solstice, which marks the start of the sun's ascensional phase and the beginning of the growth of Yang.

Flute Thought to be of Phrygian origin and used in the service of Cybele, the flute did not find favour in Greece, where the lyre was the most favoured of instruments. The flute was an attribute of Dionysus, however, long, hard, and phallic in shape; sweet, soft, and feminine in sound. It was played at fertility rites, betrothals, weddings, and initiations.

Harp The first truly recognizable harp is depicted on the tomb of Rameses II (*c.* 1220 BC). Later it appears in various places round the Mediterranean, except in Greece and Rome, where the lyre and the cithera were favoured. The Irish developed their own harp with a large sounding box. Since it is an instrument of wind deities (e.g. the Aeolian harp), it came to be associated with angels and Heaven. Druids believed that the strains of the harp released the soul from the dead body and conveyed it heavenwards.

Lyre Invented by Hermes who presented it to Apollo in return for being allowed to keep the oxen he had stolen. Because of its importance for Greek song and dance, the lyre was an attribute of both Orpheus and Terpsichore. Its power to charm was so great that in Orpheus's hands it could tame wild animals and move trees. Like the harp in other cultures, the lyre was an instrument of the winds linking Heaven and Earth.

Pipe Pan fell in love with the nymph Syrinx. One day he chased her to the banks of a river and she called out to the naiads to save her. Just as Pan seized hold of her, the naiads turned Syrinx into a bed of reeds thus rescuing her from his clutches. Pan gave a deep sigh of vexation and the reeds responded with a strain of music under his breath. Comforted by the sound, Pan cut seven reeds of different length and bound them together into the instrument the Greeks called the syrinx. Henceforth, whenever Pan played on his pipe he possessed Syrinx symbolically, and the music expressed his passion.

Although Pan invented it, he was tricked out of the pipe by Hermes, who then sold it to Apollo. As a wind instrument made of reeds growing out of the earth by the waterside, the pipe is inevitably implicated in linking Earth with Heaven. A natural instrument of the shepherd, it possesses the magic power of allurement, causing hearers to follow the piper like sheep. The pipe's sweet, warbling note is redolent of pastoral peace, in contrast to the warlike rhythms of the fife and drum.

Tabor A small drum, played with a single stick, possessing a more sprightly tone than the ponderous drum; used on joyous, carefree occasions. Bacchantes involved in Dionysiac orgies are depicted with tabors and rattles in their hands.

Violin A stringed instrument capable of inducing the deepest passions, it is a symbol of erotic delight, the male bow exciting the strings of the feminine-shaped instrument to induce ecstasy.

xiii Transport

Nowadays, journeys are seldom made on foot; in dreams the dreamer is usually using some form of transport, whether it be private or public, by road, rail, sea, or air. The kind of transport used, and how effectively it copes with the journey, can say much about the dreamer's subjective sense of attractiveness, self-esteem, social status, personality integration, and mode of adjustment to life. Such dreams provide insight into the dreamer's progress along the path of individuation.

Some forms of transport – the horse, cart, chariot, and ship – have a much longer history than others, such as the car, aeroplane, submarine, and space ship. In dreams and myths, however, we have always been capable of flying, either under our own power, like Icarus, or on an eagle, like King Etna, or a winged horse, like Bellerophon on Pegasus.

Aeroplane Aircraft assimilate much of the symbolism of ascent, air, and birds. We have always been fascinated by birds, envying their ability to fly up to the heavens, and identifying with them in fantasy. For less than a century we have been able to emulate them in practice, and this long-dreamed-of miracle is now taken entirely for granted. In dreams, however, we still experience the exhilaration of freeing ourselves from the force of gravity and soaring in the realm of ideas, thoughts, and fantasies. The aeroplane supplements the symbolic attributes of the car, with the added factors of ascension and greater freedom of route, direction, and speed. A plane crash in a dream carries meanings similar to the fall of Icarus – a lack of judgement, overweening ambition, or one-sided intellectual development at the expense of a more grounded, more balanced sense of being earthed in one's feelings and in reality.

Fear of flying is a phobic state made up of much older constituent fears which possessed adaptive functions in the ancestral environment – the fear of being shut into a confined space with no means of escape, of loud noise, of being high up, and of not being in personal control of one's destiny (inasmuch as one ever is).

Suffering an aerial bombardment is feeling under attack from the father complex, as if Zeus were casting thunderbolts in one's direction.

Bicycle A very private, personal mode of progression (unless it is a tandem), which owes its movement entirely to the will and physical effort of the rider. Progress has to continue if balance is to be maintained. One steers one's own course without being beholden to anyone else. Bicycle riding, therefore, is about developing independence and autonomy. However, should dreams persist in which the bicycle is the sole means of transport, this could point to excessive introversion, social isolation, or schizoid withdrawal. The bicycle also relates to the symbolism of the **wheel** (p. 185).

Boat or **Ship** A symbol of the body carrying the soul on its voyage through life and beyond into the Underworld. Rich in feminine symbolism, the ship or vessel, always referred to as 'she', is a womb that contains, preserves, and delivers life. It enables the ego to navigate the waters of the unconscious and to encounter the denizens of the Underworld in dreams. The funerary symbolism of the ship is apparent in all civilizations known to history. Germanic graves were boat-shaped and the dead were buried in ships in Oceania as well as Scandinavia. The dead Baldur was cremated in his own ship as it sailed out to sea. The notion of 'crossing the bar' is apparent in numerous contemporary death dreams.

Egyptian iconography, concerned more with the dead than the living, depicts the departed soul sailing through the twelve regions of the Underworld, past serpents, demons, and evil spirits with long knives. The huge serpent Apophis, a terrible incarnation of Set, tries to capsize the boat in which stands the sun god Ra, with the dead person kneeling before him, Isis at the bow, and Nephthys at the stern, pointing the way ahead and holding aloft the *ankh*, symbol of eternal life. Sometimes a pig is on board: this is the Devourer, a prefiguration of the Devil, who waits to take the damned – those who have been weighed in the balance and found wanting – to eternal torment in Hell. If all goes well on this perilous voyage, the sacred vessel sails out into the light of the rising sun, to be welcomed by Khepri, the golden scarab beetle, into the bliss of eternal life.

Similarly, the sun makes its diurnal journey through the Underworld in the Boat of the Sun from its evening disappearance below ground, passing through the intestines of Apophis, to emerge triumphant with the dawn. The sun thus needed two ships: a day ship (*Me'enzet*) and a night ship (*Semektet*).

The symbolism of the ship is further enhanced by that of its constituent parts – the anchor, figurehead, hull, mast, rudder, and sails.

The ANCHOR is a symbol of firmness, stability, and salvation in times of peril. From the psychological standpoint, it represents one's sense of security.

A FIGUREHEAD is the personification of the soul of the ship. Its origins probably go back to the worship of Isis, who is sometimes depicted with a ship headdress, and even further back. Eyes painted on the prow to assist the vessel to find its way similarly go back at least as far as the sacred ship of the Egyptian sun god Ra.

The HULL symbolizes the womb of the ship, carrying the passengers and sailors, as well as the nourishment necessary to complete the voyage to its point of termination. It also relates the ship to the symbolism of the **ark** (p. 256).

The phallic aspect of the feminine ship is represented by the MAST. The mast is related to the Tree of Life, and, accordingly, is sometimes represented with a serpent coiled round it.

The means of steering the ship on the course chosen by the captain is the RUDDER: at the subjective level it is the means of navigating through life, at the public level the government's ability to steer the 'ship of state'. A rudderless ship is one adrift at the mercy of winds, tides, and rocky shoals. Without a rudder a ship becomes flotsam:

> Time drives these lives which do not live,
> As tides push rotten stuff along the shore.
>
> Stephen Spender

SAILS are the means of capturing and transforming the wind into energy providing the motive power of the ship. When the sails fill with wind, the ship is quickened with the 'breath of life'. The billowing sail, inspired by the masculine wind, is also a symbol of fertility: 'we have laughed to see the sails conceive/And grow big-bellied with the wanton wind' (*A Midsummer Night's Dream*, II. i).

Car Cars have become such an indispensable part of contemporary life that we experience them as extensions of our own personality: we identify with them, cherish them, and project our fantasies into them.

For this reason, car dreams can tell us a great deal about the dreamer's self-concept and unconscious psychodynamics. Considerations such as the make of car, the state of its paint work and upholstery, the power of its engine, the efficiency of its brakes, all carry important symbolic implications. One major question to ponder is who is driving. Is it the dreamer? If so, how well, reliably, or safely? If someone else, who may it be? Could it represent a complex which is controlling the dreamer's ego rather than the other way about? Is the car overloaded or running out of fuel? To ask such questions may yield revealing answers.

Gestalt psychology examines not only how the driver feels but how the car feels as well. This can be a useful exercise, because the car itself symbolizes important information about unconscious psychic and physical processes. For example, the driver may be eager to get to an appointment on time but the car's engine is labouring and keeps back-firing; the more impatient the driver becomes, the more poorly the engine performs, until eventually it seizes up altogether. Such dreams can provide a salutary warning about how the dreamer is living his or her life.

Chariot The first chariots were heavy, cumbersome things with solid wheels and pulled by oxen. But by 1800 BC Syrian tribes had developed light, mobile chariots with spoked wheels: they were pulled by horses and could be driven at considerable speed. This important use of the wheel, together with its solar symbolism, gave rise to the mythical idea that the sun was driven across the sky by a sun god in a chariot drawn by white or golden horses. The human charioteer was to become a hero-figure, like the modern racing driver, and the tripartite image of chariot, horses, and charioteer became a symbol of the human body, life-force, and guiding intelligence. Eventually, many gods and goddesses came to have their chariots pulled by creatures which symbolized their qualities: Ares (Mars) drives a chariot drawn by war-horses or wolves, Cybele's is drawn by lions, Poseidon's by Tritons blowing conch shells, Aphrodite's by doves, Apollo's by golden horses or swans, Juno's by peacocks, Zeus's by eagles, Dionysus's by goats or leopards, Hades's by black horses, Shiva's by lunar gazelles, Thor's by solar rams, and Freyja's by lunar cats.

Motor-bike A symbol of masculine power and heroic risk-taking with powerful initiatory overtones. This symbolism is accentuated by the leather jackets, trousers, caps, helmets, boots, tattoos, and hairstyles adopted by 'bikers', and the like-minded gangs to which they belong.

Space craft Being round, spherical, or disc-like, unidentified flying objects (UFOs) are symbols of the Self, and, since they are projected into the heavens, symbols of deity, reminiscent of the solar divinities of Sumerian and Egyptian times. In *Flying Saucers: A Modern Myth of Things Seen in the Skies* (1959) Jung argued that they provided an example of how a myth can arise which is appropriate to the times in which it emerges. The decline of Judaeo-Christianity in the Western world had coincided with the division of that world into two bitterly hostile camps capable of annihilating each other with nuclear weapons. The divine imago, previously carried by the Judaeo-Christian god, had fallen into the unconscious to be reprojected on to the 'alien intelligence' thought to be watching over us, sending ministering angels in the form of flying saucers to keep on station, in case the need should arise for their active intervention to redeem and save humanity from itself. Since publication of Jung's book, the myth has spread and taken root in certain quarters with the intensity of a religious conviction, many actual 'sightings' being reported, together with circumstantial accounts of people having been abducted and experimented upon by these visitors from outer space.

Psychologically, these experiences represent 'close encounters' with the Self – that is to say, they represent a spontaneous eruption of unlived or unactualized unconscious potential which may compensate for an otherwise limited or too literal mode of conscious adjustment. In these circumstances, a UFO, whether in a dream, a fantasy, or a hallucination, functions as a transcendent symbol. However, its contribution to the individuation process will depend on its meaning being experienced symbolically rather than concretized.

Capsules in which human beings fly to the moon or to the planets also assume the quasi-religious power of numinous symbolism, representing a means of transcending the mundane human condition and reaching out into the timeless infinity of space.

Train As with other forms of public transport, train dreams relate one's journey through life to its social context. Since a railway is a highly organized network with trains running on fixed LINES in accordance with a strict timetable, it reflects the regulated patterns of social life which demand a modicum of conformity if one wishes to get by without too much difficulty. The railway STATION is a place of arrival, waiting, and departure, a locus of transition from one stage or direction to another. Being late or missing a train is a common dream situation, as is losing one's LUGGAGE. Such dreams express feelings of not being in control of one's life and can be a warning on the part of the unconscious that one needs to put conscious effort into 'getting one's act together'. The CARRIAGE represents the immediate social and physical conditions impinging on one's daily existence. Travelling without a TICKET or in a class higher than one is entitled to indicates 'free-riding' tendencies, while travelling in a lower class may indicate feelings of low self-esteem. Derailment is an indication that one is living inappropriately or that one is not progressing on the right lines.

The ENGINE, especially the steam engine, has functioned as a powerfully compelling symbol of libido, energy, and motive power ever since its invention. If the car assimilates the symbolism of the chariot, the motor-bike of the horse, the aeroplane of the bird, then the steam engine incorporates the symbolism of the monster-dragon, with fire in its belly, steam pouring from its nostrils, as it charges inexorably across the landscape, plunging in and out of cavernous tunnels with a deafening roar. Like the ubiquitous dragons of China, the steam engine combines all four basic 'elements' in its structure and function: earth (coal), air (steam), fire, and water. Its great thrusting pistons and ejaculating smoke stack give it unmistakably phallic connotations, as does the fireman as he rhythmically shovels heaps of coal through the open furnace door.

xiv Performance and Ritual

As noted (p. 21), dreams in which the dreamer makes repeated attempts at performing a task are among the commonest dreams recorded. Such dreams reflect the never-ending preoccupation of all human beings with the need to master environmental vicissitudes, physical skills, rituals of various kinds, social customs, etc., as well as learning the various pieces of knowledge, myths, folk tales, and arcane wisdom which form the cultural resources of all societies. In dreams one may find oneself undergoing any kind of test or ordeal, making a speech, telling a story, acting a role, playing a game, singing a song, writing an examination, participating in a rite of passage, trying to catch a train, and so on. Very often a certain amount of anxiety is involved and one feels inadequately prepared – the 'actor's nightmare' kind of dream, which is common to the practitioners of all professions and crafts. The purpose of such dreams seems to be to keep the dreamer up to the mark. The contribution that such dreams make to survival in the biological sense is self-evident.

To work with dreams, and the symbols arising from them, is to understand that we are moved by energies and influenced by structures that we do not control. To recognize this is to take an essentially *religious* understanding of reality. Such energies and structures are experienced as 'divine' because they come from the biological ground of all being: we do not create them, they create us. Rituals, whether public (rites) or private (dreams), canalize these energies and activate these structure: in a ritual something transcendent to the intentions of the individual takes over, and personal will is sacrificed to the will of the collective: the ego becomes to the Self, in Jung's phrase, as the moved to the mover.

Anthropology attests the ubiquity and power of ritual practices, which invariably centre on the use of symbols, as in the rituals of clan-gathering or corroboree and of hunting. Corroborees serve to preserve the integrity of the clan, to celebrate its shared beliefs and kinship patterns, and to dispel the danger of disintegration. These events can result in a form of collective frenzy which is generated in the name of the gods and ancestors, and is focused on some symbolic representation of the essence of the clan, such as a **totem** or a **flag**. Equivalent modern behaviour is observed among dedicated supporters of a football team, with their special song or chant, uniform of team colours, mascot, etc. Ritual displays of this kind generate powerful feelings of unity, commitment to a common cause, and aggressiveness directed against a shared 'enemy'. Team games are essentially ritual wars. When too much frenzy is generated, the result is the kind of pitched battle that has become all too familiar.

Pre-hunting rituals, such as those considered by some commentators to have accompanied the painting of hunting scenes in Palaeolithic art, were practised, it has been suggested, out of the belief that ritual killing of a stag in effigy would heighten the probability that the stag would actually be killed on the hunt. If this was so, Neumann (1954) has argued, then it probably worked not because of the effect the ritual had on the stag but because of the state of readiness it induced in the hunter. Neumann's point is that religious rites work by acting on the person who performs them. The outcome, whether it be in hunting or in warfare, is objectively dependent on the powerful subjective effect the ritual has on the performer. The result is precisely what participants in such rituals all the world over have always anticipated – actual success on the hunt or in the battle. However, the effect proceeds via the subject (the hunter/warrior) not via the object (the hunted/enemy). The outcome is, comments Neumann, in the highest degree objectively dependent on the effect of the ritual.

Since virtually all symbols can be put to ritual purposes there are few specifically ritual-related symbols listed in this subsection.

Flag Viewed objectively, a flag is nothing but a piece of dyed cloth with a design woven into it; yet it can mobilize emotions of great power and trigger actions of collective significance. This paradox was noted by Thomas Carlyle: 'Have I not myself known 500 living soldiers sabred into crows' meat, for a piece of glazed cotton which they called their *Flag*, which had you sold it at any market-cross, would not have brought above three *groschen*?' (*Sartor Resartus*). Like flags, national anthems, postage stamps, seals, and coins also stand as national symbols. To burn a national flag as part of a political protest can carry very powerful emotional overtones: it is seen as an attack on the entire ethos of the nation that the flag represents.

In the West, flags were preceded historically by insignia of various kinds, such as the eagle standard carried before Roman legions. Modern cloth flags were derived from the East and probably trans-mitted to Europe by the Saracens. While national flags function as powerful *symbols*, signalling flags function as *signs*. The latter convey information through their inherent design and by moving them about in various ways agreed by convention (e.g. dipping slowly and raising smartly in salute, flying at half-mast as a sign of mourning, flying upside-down as a sign of distress, and so on). This affords a further demonstration of the difference between symbols and signs: while symbols express complexes of ideas and emotions, signs communicate information or facts.

Totem A term derived from the Algonquin *ndodem* meaning guardian spirit or family emblem. Totemic features have existed among most preliterate peoples from North America to Africa and Australia. The totem is usually an animal or plant which acts as guardian, guide, and ancestor, with whom all members of the same totem group claim kinship. It possesses superhuman power. Totemism probably owes its origins to the mystical connection (*participation mystique*) experi-enced by hunter-gatherers to the animals and plants in their environ-ment. Loyalty to one's totem involved absolute duties and taboos. For example, it was forbidden to marry within the totem group, or to touch, eat, or kill the totem animal. Advantages of this arrangement were to demarcate communities into exogamous groups, and to protect and provide food for other totem groups.

SECTION 3

PEOPLE, ANIMALS, AND PLANTS

3

People, Animals, and Plants

Symbols relating to people, animals, and plants are presented here in the same section because the unconscious psyche (as manifested in contemporary adult dreams), like the conscious psyche of hunter-gatherers and young Western children, functions in a manner both animistic and anthropomorphic. The anthropologist Tim Ingold (1992) reports that for modern hunter-gatherers 'there are not two worlds of persons (society) and things (nature), but one world – one environment – saturated with powers and embracing both human beings, the animals and plants on which they depend, and the landscape in which they live and move'. The Inuit of the Canadian Arctic, for example, 'typically view their world as imbued with human qualities of will and purpose' (Riddington, 1982). 'Modern hunter-gatherers do not live in landscapes composed merely of animals, plants, rocks, and caves,' writes Steven Mithen (1996). 'Their landscapes are socially constructed.'

As argued in the first part of this book, the two major archetypal complexes which determine the way human social constructs are made and symbolized have to do with (1) sex, gender, bonding, and child-rearing, and (2) power, rank, discipline, law and order.

The first of these is represented by the horizontal axis (affiliation versus detachment) in Figure 1, p. 58, while the second is represented by the vertical axis (dominance versus submission). Since both archetypal complexes are active (and *interactive*) in everyone, the reader is asked to bear this orthogonal schema in mind while considering the symbolism discussed in the next two subsections, as well as in the subsections dealing with animals, monsters, and plants.

i Sex, Gender, Bonding, and Child-rearing

One of the oldest and most sophisticated attempts to conceptualize the nature and function of masculine and feminine principles is that of the ancient Chinese Taoists with their concepts of YANG and YIN, those fundamental forces held to permeate all reality and to be present and active in both males and females.

The basic teaching of Taoism centres on the eternal law which underlies all states of becoming: 'the principle of the one in the many' as Wilhelm (1951) put it. 'Everything flows on and on like this river,' said Confucius, 'without pause, day and night.' The source of the river is the 'great primal beginning'; *T'ai Chi* had a still earlier beginning, *Wu Chi*. *Wu Chi* was traditionally represented by a circle; *T'ai Chi* by a circle divided into interlocking elements of light and dark, Yang and Yin, whose distinctive characteristics persist as omnipresent polarities underlying all changes and all transitions.

The Yang principle is characterized as energetic and assertive; its attributes are heat and light (symbolized by the sun and its rays); its realms are heaven and the spirit; in its phallic, penetrating aspect it arouses, fructifies, and creates; in its aggressive form it combats and destroys: its orientation is essentially extraverted; it is positive and impulsive, but also disciplined and ascetic.

Whereas Yang is assertive and initiating, the Yin principle is passive and containing (symbolized by the moon and the cave); its realms are

Figure 4. T'ai Chi

earth, nature, and the womb, for it is essentially concerned with gestation, giving form to the energy of Yang, and bringing light out of the darkness; its movement is essentially introverted.

Our culture is not alone in regarding assertiveness, physical aggression, and destructiveness as male attributes and gestation, nurturance, and life-enhancement as female ones. These are universally apparent distinctions, and their very universality betrays their archetypal origins. The largely artificial distinction between sex and gender, fashionable in the 1960s and 1970s, which saw sex as strictly biological and gender as a wholly social construct, has been examined – and rejected – elsewhere (Ridley, 1994; Stevens, 1991; Stevens and Price, 1996; Wilson, 1989). Instead, we shall go along with the view accepted by practically all human cultures is that gender is the psychic recognition and social expression of the sex to which nature has assigned us. This is justified, for the sexual dimorphism apparent in the great majority of societies, where child-rearing is almost invariably the responsibility of women, and hunting and warfare the responsibility of men, has a biological basis which long predates the emergence of *Homo sapiens sapiens*. Though it is true that social stereotypes peculiar to a given culture play a part in shaping 'acceptable' forms of masculine and feminine behaviour, these forms are but local variations on universal archetypal themes. When it comes to gender differences, stereotype to a very large extent reflects archetype.

The genetic and cultural influences on the development of gender-related behaviour, which equipped males and females to survive and reproduce in the ancestral environment, have been well documented and their consequences summarized (Stevens and Price, 1996). These archaic patterns continue to influence the behaviour, needs, desires, and symbolic lives of modern men and women to a greater extent than fashionable contemporary assumptions would allow.

Masculine behaviour The greater strength, size, and aggressiveness of males equipped them to compete with each other for rank and female partners, to patrol and hunt over a large territorial range, and to vie with neighbouring groups for environmental resources. Highly developed spatial abilities enabled males to explore the physical environment and to maintain an accurate sense of orientation when away on the hunt, while their efficient coordination of large muscle groups permitted them to use weapons and throw projectiles effectively. The widespread occurrence of male puberty initiation rites served to test and validate masculine hunting and warrior skills, to cement bonds between males of the same cadre, and to eliminate 'free-riders' from the group. Lastly, the evolved sexual strategies for males prompts them to be lustful, novelty-seeking, susceptible to visually arousing erotic stimuli, and prone to seize sexual opportunities when they present themselves.

Feminine behaviour The extended family configuration of small human groups developed the qualities of nurturance, loyalty, and devotion in females so that they functioned effectively as mothers, educating their offspring, and protecting them up to the age of puberty. Highly developed communication skills (language, feelings, intuitions) equipped females to maintain close attachment bonds with their children, husbands, and kin. Female puberty initiation rites, where they occurred, affirmed a female's status in the community as a mature woman capable of fulfilling her reproductive functions. The evolved sexual strategies for females prompt them still to be selective and to seek to confine sexual relations to the context of a secure and lasting relationship.

Differentiation of Yang and Yin symbolic principles into two poles – dynamic at one pole and static at the other – is in accordance with these archetypal masculine and feminine behavioural manifestations. DYNAMIC YANG is aggressive, combative, phallic, striving for dominance and self-assertion, and is represented in classical mythology by gods such as Zeus, Ares (Mars), and Dionysus, and heroes such as

Herakles and Perseus. STATIC YANG is rational, reflective, discerning, respectful of law and order, justice, discipline, abstraction, and objectivity. This Apollonian pole corresponds to what Jung called the Logos principle. DYNAMIC YIN expresses itself in the need to become involved with individuals rather than things or abstract ideas: it is intensely subjective and personal, and corresponds to Jung's Eros principle. STATIC YIN is the gestating, womb-like aspect of Yin: it is unconscious and instinctive as in nature (*physis*) where it finds expression in the unending cycle of life and death in all living things. This is what Whitmont (1969) calls the 'gestative motherly pole of Yin' and is ruled by the Great Mother archetype.

Jungian analysts have attempted a further differentiation of these archetypal elements. Taking **the archetypal feminine** as the starting point, Toni Wolff (1956) agreed that one set of polarities existed between the Great Mother and Love Goddess figures, but believed these to be transected by another set of polarities which she termed Amazon and Medium. Once again this provides four basic types:

(1) **The Mother** This aspect tends to be impersonal or collective in the sense of being instinctive and conventional in its concern with gestation, nurturance, child-rearing, and home-making. This pole is represented in mythology by Great Mother figures such as Gaia and Demeter, and in modern history by Queen Victoria.

(2) **The Love Goddess** or **Hetaira** This aspect, exemplified by Persephone, Psyche, and the younger Aphrodite, stands at the opposite pole to the Mother. She is primarily concerned with her love life, relating to her man at the intensely personal level rather than taking on the social responsibilities implicit in becoming a wife and a mother. A woman who is too closely identified with this pole remains the eternal daughter or sister, the *puella aeterna*; she eschews commitment in favour of flirtation and living the provisional life. Marilyn Monroe is one of many modern examples of this kind of 'love goddess'.

(3) **The Amazon** This type tends to be independent and self-sufficient; in modern life she is the ambitious woman who puts career before home and children. She functions more as a comrade or competitor with men than as a wife or mother. Her orientation is not towards individuals but rather tends to be impersonal and objective. It is hard to distinguish this aspect of the archetypal feminine from the animus,

since it has evident masculine overtones. When integrated with the conscious personality it can enable a woman to achieve her goals in life and further her own individuation; however, should she become unconsciously identified with it, the result can be a demonic 'organization' woman, who tyrannizes and manipulates her underlings so as to implement her will. It is not hard to think of contemporary examples.

(4) **The Medium** This type lives in close relationship with the collective unconscious: she is immersed in her subjective experience and speaks with the conviction of an oracle, as if she had access to knowledge denied to most of us. The Pythoness at Delphi was a classic example of this type; modern examples are Madame Blavatsky and Jung's mother.

These four aspects of the archetypal feminine are schematically represented in Figure 5. Examples of 'pure' types are put at opposite ends of the coordinates with intermediate types placed between them.

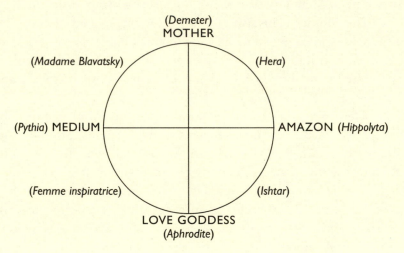

Figure 5. *Polar aspects of the archetypal feminine*

A similar analysis has been performed for **the archetypal masculine** by Edward Whitmont (1969). The types are as follows:

(1) **The Father** This is the patriarch, the upholder of law and order, the voice of collective authority: he knows only children and subjects, not individuals or equals. Examples are Jehovah, Zeus, Indra,

Abraham, and Moses. Examples from history are Tamburlaine (or Tamerlane) the Great, Genghis Khan, Kaiser Wilhelm II, and Joseph Stalin.

(2) **The Son** Like the Hetaira type of female, he is preoccupied with his personal concerns and love affairs and cares little for his social responsibilities: he is thus inevitably at loggerheads with the opposite pole, the Father. He is the *puer aeternus* who is tempted to adopt a 'free-rider' attitude to life, seizing erotic and economic opportunities as they arise, exploiting them, and then cheerfully moving on. The last thing he wants is to be tied down or committed – either to a job or a woman. Characteristically, this kind of man has lacked a salient father-figure with whom he could identify in childhood. As a consequence of contemporary single-parent trends, the incidence of men like him is greatly on the increase. Examples are Eros, Don Juan, Peter Pan, and Adonis.

(3) **The Hero** This figure stands at the dynamic, out-going pole of the Yang principle. Like the father, he too is orientated to collective values. As soldier, ambitious professional, or thrusting businessman, he strives for prestige within the social context. When he attains his goals it is through courage, determination, aggression, and the assertion of will. The hero archetype inspires the hunter and politician as much as the warrior and knight. Examples are Herakles, Nimrod, Dionysus-Zagreus, Sir Galahad, Siegfried, Nelson, Napoleon, and Winston Churchill.

(4) **The Wise Man** This type is more concerned with meanings and ideas than with actions and people. He is the scholar, teacher, sage, prophet, shaman, hermit, saint. Examples are Elijah, Aristotle, St Peter, St Augustine, Mohammed, Erasmus, Wittgenstein, Schweitzer, Jung.

These aspects of the archetypal masculine are schematized in Figure 6.

Freudian symbolism The fundamental and ubiquitous nature of these Yang and Yin principles inevitably gives rise to symbolism of the richest complexity. Accordingly, Freud (1900) felt justified in reducing a vast number of objects to their masculine or feminine *sexual implications*: 'All elongated objects, such as sticks, tree-trunks and umbrellas

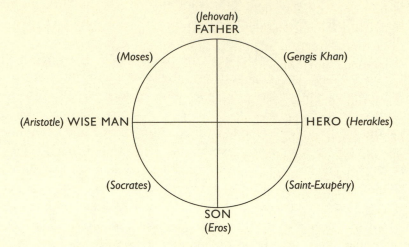

Figure 6. Polar aspects of the archetypal masculine

(the opening of these last being comparable to an erection) may stand for the male organ – as well as all long, sharp weapons, such as knives, daggers and pikes. Another frequent though not entirely intelligible symbol of the same thing is a nail-file – possibly on account of the rubbing up and down. Boxes, cases, chests, cupboards and ovens represent the uterus, and also hollow objects, ships, and vessels of all kinds. Rooms in dreams are usually women; if the various ways in and out of them are represented, this interpretation is scarcely open to doubt . . . A dream of going through a suite of rooms is a brothel or harem dream . . . Steps, ladders or staircases, or, as the case may be, walking up or down them, are representations of the sexual act.

'In men's dreams a necktie often appears as a symbol for the penis . . . nor is there any doubt that all weapons and tools are used as symbols for the male organ: e.g., ploughs, hammers, rifles, revolvers, daggers, sabres, etc.' (*The Interpretation of Dreams*, pp. 470–73)

All these objects can indeed represent the human genitals, but usually after they have represented a lot of other things besides. The trouble with the reductiveness of Freud's interpretations is that it robs these symbols of all their other implications. The PHALLUS, for example, is a symbol of power and fertility as well as male sexuality:

as Jung once quipped, the penis is itself a phallic symbol. It would seem that nature intended it this way, for the human penis is proportionately three times larger, in relation to body size, than in any other primate (Diamond, 1991). Eugene Monick (1987) has coined the term 'phallic resurrection' for the recurrent cycles of tumescence after detumescence: 'Each time phallos explodes in orgasm, it dies', but it returns to life again and again. Phallos, he says, has a mind of its own; it will not be dictated to by the ego. It behaves in a way that tangibly manifests the autonomy of unconscious forces. An erection cannot be manufactured by a conscious act of will: it either happens or it doesn't, as the circumstances dictate. As a consequence, an erection can be experienced as an epiphany.

Phallic worship has been widespread and could be crudely sexual (Priapus), spiritual (the Lingam of Shiva), regenerative (the maypole), and resurrective (the Djed Pillar). Shiva says: 'Wherever there is an upright male organ, I, myself, am present, even if there is no other representation of me.' The LINGAM is unmistakably apposite as a symbol of generativity: it is the channel through which the seed of the species is introduced into the next generation and therefore a direct expression of the creative force of divine nature. The lingam is the ithyphallic image of God: it represents mastery of the world. Vishnu and Brahma argued about this, but, as they did so, a luminous penis appeared, so enormous that neither its peak nor its base could be seen (it became assimilated to the *axis mundi*). Brahma turned into a boar to grub about in the earth to discover its base while Vishnu changed into a goose to fly up into the sky and find its peak, but both were unsuccessful. Then Shiva dramatically emerged through the lingam, which was cleft into a lozenge, and Vishnu and Brahma were forced to acknowledge Shiva's (and the lingam's) supremacy. The phallus is much more than a mere sign for the male organ.

Similarly, the VULVA is more than the female sexual organ: it is the gateway of life as well as the entrance to Paradise and the house of temptation. The ubiquitous symbolism of the *vagina dentata* equates the vulva with the mouth which greedily swallows the penis and semen and regurgitates life in the form of blood and a child.

Attraction of opposites The symbolism of coitus (literally a going or coming together, from the Latin *coitio* and French *co* + *ire* [*go*]), like the symbolism of the sexual organs (the lingam and yoni), reaches far beyond the facts of sexual intercourse. Indeed, sexual union can itself be a symbol of the *coniunctio oppositorum* or *hieros gamos* which was both the central preoccupation and the goal of alchemical aspiration, as well as the basis of ancient fertility rites. The *coniunctio* represents the marrying of opposites as a psychic process. Similarly, the child that the union produces is a symbolic child which recombines the opposing natures which were involved in the union, and the result is a new constellation which occurs within the psyche.

The transcendent reconciliation of opposites is an archetypal configuration which finds symbolic fruition through a variety of conjunctions: the King and Queen in the alchemical water bath, a man and a woman in bed, the sun and the moon in the heavens, or a bull and a cow in a field – in every instance the same mystery is being celebrated.

The longing for union with the opposite is not merely for a member of the opposite sex: it is for what is perceived as opposite and needed if one is to be whole. The desired opposite quality may well be carried by a member of one's own sex, by an animal, by a mythic creature or by anything which is felt to be lacking and necessary for one's completion. It was this central and recurrent desire that was addressed by Plato in his myth of the original round human being, divided by the gods into two halves, both of which are constantly seeking to be reunited with one another. The union of Heaven and Earth in early astrobiological religions, the marriage of the Prince and Princess in fairy tale, the union of *Sol* and *Luna* in alchemy are all examples of *coniunctio* symbolism whose substrate resides in the phylogenetic psyche.

The sacred marriage As with all constellations of an archetype, there is a compulsion to project them into matter, animals, and other people, as well as to experience them psychologically. Such projection is at the basis of religious fertility rituals in which a *hieros gamos* is enacted between a divine pair to guarantee renewal of the life-giving powers of nature. It is possible that all ritual enactments of the sacred marriage are essentially re-enactments of the original union of the

World Parents, Mother Earth and Father Sky, *in illo tempore*: the sunlight, the air, and the rain of Father Sky all quicken the soil of Mother Earth to engender the plant and animal life necessary for the continuance of human existence. The rainbow bears poetic witness to this union.

The union of brother and sister divinities, like the Egyptian Osiris and Isis, or the Norse Freyr and Freyja, are examples of this archetypal pattern. In ancient Sumer, the King would ritually assume the identity of Tammuz to enact a sacred marriage to the goddess Inanna (later known as Ishtar or Astarte), who was rendered symbolically present by the priestess who performed her role. As a result of this ritual, the sacred power of the goddess flowed through the King into the land over which he ruled.

Consummation of the sacred marriage, resulting in the birth of a hero-saviour, god or divine man, is a theme which occurs in numerous traditions other than the Christian and Greek stories so familiar to us. Zeus impregnates the woman of his fancy (usually by adopting some disguise, such as a bull, a swan, or a shower of gold), producing a hero of supernatural power, who triumphs over various torments and ordeals to be deified and rendered immortal. The Holy Spirit of God impregnates the Virgin Mary who brings forth Jesus who is crucified and ascends into heaven to sit at the right hand of his Divine Father. The Amerindian Skaoaga is impregnated by the bear god and gives birth to semi-divine bear twins, who become culture heroes of the Haida people of the Northwest Coast. Beowulf is another example of a 'bear son', who, among other heroic tasks, descends into the Underworld and does battle with a dragon.

The alchemical *coniunctio* performed by the King and the Queen in the water bath to produce the hermaphrodite or *filius philosophorum* is but a further example of the same archetypal constellation, as is the mystic union of a nun or female saint with God in the Sacrament of the Bridal Chamber. Saint Teresa expresses this in frankly erotic terms: 'It pleased our Lord that I should see the following vision a number of times. I saw an angel near me, on the left side, in bodily form . . . He was not tall, but short, marvellously beautiful, with a face which shone as though he were one of the highest of the angels, who seemed to be all of fire: they must be those whom we call Seraphim

. . . I saw in his hands a long golden spear, and at the point of the iron there seemed to be a little fire. This I thought that he thrust several times into my heart, and that it penetrated to my entrails. When he drew out the spear he seemed to be drawing them with it, leaving me all on fire with a wondrous love for God. The pain was so great that it caused me to utter several moans; and yet so exceeding sweet is this greatest of pains that it is impossible to desire to be rid of it, or for the soul to be content with less than God.' (Peers, 1927; quoted in Moon, 1991)

Saint Teresa's ecstasy can be interpreted either as the erotic fantasy of a sexually frustrated woman or as an expression of the soul's longing for union with the Divine. It could, of course, be both. Carvings of loving couples which occur on the walls of Hindu temples are both highly erotic and intensely spiritual: they symbolize the union of complementary opposites to compose the Absolute. The union of the sexes in the Vedas, Dyaus (Heaven) with Prthivi (Earth), is represented in later Hinduism by the union of Shiva with Shakti, or Vishnu with Lakshmi, and, as in so many other places, their sacred marriage was linked to the liturgical life of the agricultural year.

Bonding The archetypal systems involved in bonding between sexual partners and between parents and children form the crucial group of archetypes which govern the life of human beings and guarantee the survival of the species. Dreams centred on these themes are among the most common of all dreams, and, far from being disguised or bowdlerized in the way that Freud described, their meaning is usually explicit. As a result, such dreams can have a soap opera feel about them, and their frank nature means that they usually portray their intentions in straightforward images without resorting to unduly complicated symbolism. That the sexual dreams of contemporary people should not on the whole need to have recourse to all the running up and down stairs, putting swords in sheaths, and generally thrusting long, straight objects into round, receptive holes, as insisted on by Freud, may have something to do with his liberating influence on our sexual attitudes. However, symbols of bonding still prevail: these include the cord, the knot, and the ring.

The CORD or ROPE is a symbol of individual life. Fortune is depicted holding a rope because at any moment she can bring life to an end by cutting the thread on which it hangs – like the sword of Damocles. But the main symbolism of interest here is that of BONDAGE, both in the sense of tying equal partners together through loving commitment and mutual consent, and tying unequal individuals in a relationship based on dominance and submission, as in the status of 'bondsman' or 'bond slave'. Usually, these two forms of bondage are clearly differentiated. In sado-masochistic sexual relationships, however, they may be combined – as they can in worshipful submission to a deity, the 'god who binds' (p. 179). In Greek legend, Ocnos is everlastingly occupied in Hades plaiting a rope which is eaten by a she-ass as quickly as he plaits it – an eternal symbol of the hard-working man who marries an extravagant wife.

The KNOT is another symbol of uniting, bonding, or tying together, as in a betrothal or marriage, a business partnership, or a covenant with God. Varuna, the god who binds and releases, is styled by his devotees 'the tier and untier of knots'. The knot thus shares in the symbolism of the net, the noose, and the lasso, as a means of controlling, dominating, and tying down. The Gordian Knot, which, in its tangled complexity resembles a labyrinth, was simply cut by Alexander the Great, who preferred the short, direct approach to all problems. The same Alexandrian tactic is increasingly employed in the contemporary world on the knots of holy wedlock.

As a closed circle, the RING is a symbol of continuity, wholeness, completion, and the union of opposites. As such it is a powerful symbol of marriage. The all-inclusive nature of the ring has clear cosmic connotations as in the ring of flame round the dancing form of Shiva, representing the cosmic cycle of creation and destruction. The ring is also a symbol of initiation, of having passed through a rite of passage and become united with one's new status, as with a fraternity ring, symbol of entry into a brotherhood of peers. A ring held in the jaws of a monster standing guardian at an entrance, or placed on a door as a knocker, or on the keystone of an arch, similarly marks a passageway from one status to another. This again stresses its power as a symbol of marriage in the act of exchanging rings. It is an act of union symbolizing a coming together in wholeness for eternity.

The Child As a symbol, the child represents the ontogenetic potential of the phylogenetic psyche – in Jungian terms, the Self. The programme for personal development encoded in the Self, which insists that a child must become firmly attached to a mother or mother-substitute from early infancy, is just as insistent that this bond must be loosened at puberty. Initiation rites evolved, at least in part, to facilitate this loosening – a second parting of the umbilical cord. The child symbol, says Jung, essentially means 'evolving towards independence. This it cannot do without detaching itself from its origins' (CW9i, para. 287). Hence the themes of abandonment and danger, the trials and ordeals, suffered by all child gods and young heroes. However, the child is particularly prone to emerge in the dreams of adults when they have become cut off from their past, their roots, their own instinctive and emotional childhood state. To experience such dreams is not necessarily a regression but often a corrective, a therapeutic dynamic annexed by the individuation process – a *reculer pour mieux sauter*. The significance of the child motif for the individuation process is dealt with in **Individuation and Transcendence**, pp. 235–56).

The Hunter Hunting has been man's primary activity for 99 per cent of our existence as a species. The hunter is therefore an archetypal symbol of great power and significance. Hunting, shooting, and fishing can become male obsessions, as can the life of the warrior, and civilization has been a process of disciplining and sublimating these archetypal propensities and harnessing them to the service of Church and State. With the emergence of civilization, the hunter/warrior has been relegated to the shadow complex of the personality and is only allowed to re-emerge in the rituals of the countryside and of state-sanctioned war. As a result, the hunter is demonized in many traditions, as indeed he is by the anti-field-sports lobby in our own society. The demon hunter loses sight of what really matters by indulging himself in the ecstatic pursuit of the quarry rather than improving himself in the eyes of God and society. Thus, Hindu religion sees the hunter bound to the 'wheel of incarnations' and Lao Tsu taught that hunting maddens the passions and reveals desire as an enemy to be conquered. The ACCURSED HUNTER is a recurrent figure in myth and folklore – the priest who abandons the Holy Sacrament to go after his dogs in pursuit of prey and, as a punishment, is condemned to run headlong after his baying hounds forever.

King The supreme symbol of temporal masculine power, the representative of God on earth: hence the 'divine right of kings'. The King unites with the Queen to be living embodiments of the *hieros gamos* on earth, the conjunction of the masculine and feminine halves of creation in a perfect whole. In many cultures the vitality of the King has been held responsible for the health of his people and the fertility of the earth, and when his powers begin to wane he has to be replaced.

Masculine and feminine: from duality to quaternity The ancient Greek pantheon was a projection of the Self on to the peak of Mount Olympus, incorporating gods and goddesses who represented different aspects of the archetypal masculine and feminine, and exemplified the idea of wholeness. The great monotheistic religions which replaced the Greek – Judaism, Christianity, and Islam – were very different. Being the products of nomadic tribesmen, they were exclusively masculine and patriarchal: they rigorously excluded the feminine and maternal. In place of the polytheistic exuberance of Greece we find monotheistic repression by the jealous God of the Jews: 'Thou shalt have no other gods before me' (Exodus 20:2).

The story of our culture starts with Adam and Eve. But our beginning was other peoples' ending, for the morality tale of our Primal Parents in the Paradise Garden is full of more ancient religious components. The association of a naked or partially clothed young goddess with a snake and the Cosmic Tree recurs throughout the Near East, Africa, and pre-Aryan India long before the advent of Judaism. The nubile figure indicates youth and fertility, the Cosmic Tree at 'the centre of the world' symbolizes life and endless regeneration, while the snake stands for the chthonic creative power of the Earth Mother. By listening to the serpent (i.e. giving attention to her own feminine instinct), Eve is prompted to lead Adam into direct disobedience of God's exclusive command. The result is instant punishment: banishment from the Garden of Eden, itself a symbol of the all-containing womb of the Great Mother Goddess.

This, the core myth of Judaeo-Christendom, has proved a mixed blessing: on the one hand, ejection from Paradise is necessary if ego-consciousness is to separate itself from the unconscious and from a childish dependence on the parents in order to establish individual autonomy. But, on the other hand, the Genesis story has been responsible for promoting the patriarchal arrogance so characteristic of Western Judaeo-Christian and Islamic social history, with its associated repression of feminine values. The demand of the patriarchal God for strict submission to His will, and His commandment that there shall be 'no other gods' (or goddesses) before Him, has effectively inhibited the human psyche's potential for wholeness. If Eve is alienated from her serpent powers, then Adam is alienated both from Eve (his anima) and from the serpent energy in himself. No longer in relation to Mother Earth, Adam rampages over her Holy Body, seeking his own fulfilment at her expense. The result is the ecological disaster that his efforts are creating.

The picture was modified by the coming of Christ and the prestige this conferred on his mother. To the vertical (dominance/submission) relationship between Jahweh and his people, Christ's anima introduced the horizontal dimension of love, compassion, and intimacy (Figure 1, p. 58). Though Christ respected the patriarchal order and wished to do nothing to change it ('Render unto Caesar the things which are Caesar's, and unto God the things that are God's'), maintaining that the essential changes were those occurring in men's hearts, He was opposed, nevertheless, to the masculine struggle for dominance and status – something that His disciples did not quite understand: 'He asked them, What was it that ye disputed among yourselves by the way? But they held their peace: for by the way they had disputed among themselves, who should be the greatest. And He sat down, and called the twelve, and saith unto them, If any man desire to be the first, the same shall be last, and servant of all. And He took a child and set him in the midst of them: and when He had taken him in His arms, He said unto them, Whosoever shall receive one of such children in my name, receiveth me: and whosoever shall receive me, receiveth me not, but Him that sent me' (Mark 9: 33–7).

These are the words of a man whose Logos and Eros are in splendid harmony, and Christ's intervention, together with the Christian doctrine of the TRINITY, went some way towards restoring the possibility of psychic wholeness: for, according to St Augustine, the Holy Spirit provides the love which binds God the Father to God the Son and to all humanity. The Catholic Church carried the process further through its institutional devotion to the Virgin Mary and the female saints, much to the fury of the Protestants, who remained rigidly patriarchal and viewed such popish practices as a violation of the doctrines of 'no other gods' and 'no graven images'. The Catholic movement to reinstate the feminine aspect of the godhead culminated in the promulgation of the Dogma of the Assumption of the Blessed Virgin Mary, which Jung viewed as 'the most important symbological event since the Reformation'. This was a momentous step, for in effect the Holy Trinity became a QUATERNITY, the Four in One.

In its most creative manifestations, the feminist movement has sought to repair the split in the Judaeo-Christian psyche which occurred with Eve's 'temptation' of Adam and their joint banishment from the Garden, their aim being to reinstate Eve, her serpent, and their joint feminine chthonic energies to the pantheon of the Self. Practical consequences of this mythic progression are not only the improved social position of women but a growing ecological awareness (e.g. the Gaia hypothesis), a holistic approach to health, and a transcultural commitment to the notion of a global village.

One early attempt to anticipate these changes was the Gnostic heresy that arose in the second century AD. The Gnostics saw beyond and behind Jahweh to what they termed the PLEROMA, the ultimate source of all being, of which Jahweh was but an emanation, 'Yaldaboath'. Sophia, a figure who features in the Hebrew Wisdom Literature (whom Jung diagnosed as Jahweh's forgotten and repressed femininity – His anima so to speak), the Gnostics were inclined to see as Jahweh's mother. But both Jahweh and Sophia originated from the primordial pleroma, the Father–Mother of all things.

Reviewing these events in a brilliant essay 'The Dream of Wholeness', Murray Stein (1994), wrote: 'Three is a number of masculine dynamism, unfolding and expanding, and it was this energy that converted a minor sect of a minor Near Eastern religion into a global force, Christianity. Christianity enlisted politics, economics, and military force and harnessed them all to its ends of converting the entire world. It produced an energetic and restless religion, not a peaceful one, and the latter day representatives of this tradition – the explorers, inventors, the empire builders – exemplify this kind of expansive energy. The movement from Three to Four transforms this restless expansiveness into quiet emptiness and repose, features that are more characteristic of eastern, oriental, religions.'

Maypole A phallic pole with a feminine discus as the top; a fertility symbol erected to celebrate spring, sexual union, and the renewal of life. Originally the Sacred Pine of Attis, ritually erected in the temple of Cybele. Much later it reappears in the Roman Hilaria (the Spring Festival) and most recently in the May Day celebrations of the May Queen and the Green Man. The seven ribbons held by the dancers as they gyrate round the pole represent the seven colours of the rainbow, the seven planets, etc.

Nymph The nurturant, protective aspect of the feminine: since ancient times, mountains, springs, groves, and fountains have had nymphs as their guardian spirits.

Prince and **Princess** Potential sovereignty, a stage on the initiatory progress to adult status and the assumption of full masculine and feminine power and authority.

Queen The archetypal feminine as regal authority, Great Mother, Queen of Heaven. In alchemy she is quicksilver to the King's sulphur, and in cosmology she is lunar silver to the King's solar gold. Together they consummate the *hieros gamos*, the union of the masculine and feminine, representing the union of all opposites in the *coniunctio oppositorum*.

ii Power: Dominance and Submission

Although we are capable of altruism, love, and compassion, our genetic make-up ensures that we are also committed to a quest for our own personal advantage: in particular we all share, in some degree, the predisposition to ascend the social hierarchy. This is what Joseph Lopreato (1984) calls the climbing manoeuvre: 'a tendency whereby an individual, perhaps a social class, or any type of aggregate, maximizes its chances of moving up from a lower social position to a higher one'. It is this predisposition that Freud excluded from his theory but exemplified in his life and for which he expelled Alfred Adler from the psychoanalytic movement when he made good the deficiency. 'Whatever name we give it,' wrote Adler (1932), 'we shall always find in human beings this great line of activity – the struggle to rise from an inferior position to a superior position, from defeat to victory, from *below* to *above*. It begins in our earliest childhood; it continues to the end of our lives.' Others have made the same observation before him and since: Nietzsche called it the 'will to power', Auguste Comte the 'instinct to dominate', and modern behavioural biologists the 'motivation to increase Resource Holding Potential'.

Power-seeking is a drive or capacity that depends for its satisfaction on the existence of a dominance hierarchy, for power is a meaningless concept when considered in isolation from a hierarchically structured social order. In sociobiological terms, power is less an instinct than the measure of a resource – an index of the degree to which an individual or group enjoys access to relatively scarce goods and services (which are distributed via a dominance order) and has the capacity to deny them to others. Power is thus a measure of 'Resource Holding Potential'.

Competition for a dominant status is apparent between members of the same reptile species and governs relations of social mammals and birds where a hierarchical social structure (or 'pecking order') is in evidence. In virtually all such species, dominance is indicated by erect posture, breadth and height; subdominance or submission by bowed posture, narrowness of form, and 'lowliness'. Power-seeking and attempts to ascend the social scale involve tournaments (ritual agonistic behaviour) which, once decided, result in the establishment of a dominance hierarchy which persists relatively undisturbed. This makes for social cohesion and cooperation and contributes to the competitive efficiency and survival of the group.

Dominant and submissive behaviour patterns are associated with characteristic complexes of emotions, ideas, and symbols, and contribute to the psychopathology of manic-depressive disorder as well as sado-machochism. SYMBOLS OF DOMINANCE, therefore, are those of ascent, height, and grandeur (ladders, towers, high places, thrones, palaces, sumptuous clothes, the orb, sceptre, and crown, and all the pomp and panoply of power), as well as instruments of force and coercion (chains, bonds, shackles, ropes, the staff, whip, yoke, sword, etc.). SYMBOLS OF SUBMISSION, on the other hand, are those of descent, lowliness, and poverty (hovels, the gutter, rags, livery, etc.) and gestures of abasement (uncovering the head, bowing, prostration, nodding, etc.).

Ascent within the dominance hierarchy is probably the symbolic model for aspiration to all 'higher' things, whether they be wealth, truth, beauty, consciousness, or God. Common linguistic usage makes use of this symbolism: high and low (meaning rich and poor); high as a synonym for excitement or mania, and low for despondency or depression.

How does the 'climbing manoeuvre' relate to the individuation principle? Individuation is about much more than mere status-enhancement, though that is part of the programme for the first half of life, when one has to 'earn the right' to individuate by discharging one's biological (sexual, bonding, child-rearing) and socio-economic (professional, property-holding, money-making) obligations. Then individuation proper (in the Jungian sense of spiritual development and making a cultural contribution) begins: the quest for wholeness. Self-enhancement in the sociobiological sense relates to activation of only part of the archetypal endowment of the individual.

Aegis The fearful shield of Zeus, forged by the divine blacksmith Hephaestos, covered by the skin of the goat Amalthea (which suckled Dictean Zeus), fringed with snakes' heads, and embossed with the terrifying visage of the Gorgon; it was a symbol of supreme power and of intimidation, designed to inspire terror among mortals and make them submit to the will of the Supreme God.

Bellerophon Having won victory over the Chimera with the aid of his winged horse Pegasus, Bellerophon was so intoxicated with the lust for power that he attempted to seize the throne of Zeus. Bellerophon symbolizes the overweening power-hungry revolutionary who wants to overthrow the *status quo* to gratify his own selfish goals. He is defeated and sent to Hell to keep company with other ambitious villains like Ixion. Osiris's brother Set is another example of this type.

Bucephalus Symbol of the devoted servant, loyal to only one master, Bucephalus was Alexander the Great's beloved and untameable charger, who would allow only his master to ride him. He was frightened of his own shadow and would gallop only towards the sun (i.e. towards the East and towards India, the goal of Alexander's imperial ambitions). Bucephalus shared with deathless devotion in all Alexander's plans till eventually killed in battle. The grief-stricken Alexander built a city round his tomb.

Chair A symbol of authority: to remain seated while others stand is universally considered the prerogative of a high-ranking person; to offer someone a chair is an act of courtesy and respect. The term for a bishop's region of authority – his see – comes from the Latin *sedes*, meaning a chair; the cathedral (from the Greek *kathedra*, meaning chair) is where he sits. A professor's academic authority is vested in his Chair.

Class The notion of class emerged with agriculture and the establishment of cities and civilizations. In Indo-European societies these are commonly three in number. The Hindus concretized this tripartite division in the CASTE system, the highest caste being the priests (*Brahmans*), the second the warriors (*Kshatriyas*), and the third artisans (*Vaishyas*). In pre-Revolutionary France, these corresponded to the Clergy, Nobility, and the Third Estate, and in England to the Lords Spiritual, Lords Temporal, and Commons. None of these tripartite class divisions included the common peasantry, however, who were considered in the same category as domesticated animals and the land. Like the untouchables in India, they were thought too lowly to warrant any official status. Even in our modern egalitarian times, the symbolism of class is still everywhere apparent in the form of status symbolism, although, in comparison with previous ages, it is somewhat understated.

Psychologically, the symbolism of class has been introjected in the tripartite divisions made by Freud between the superego, the ego, and the id, and by mystics between the superconscious, conscious, and unconscious aspects of the personality. Jung's division between conscious, personal unconscious, and collective unconscious is a further example.

Crown Surmounting the head, the summit of the body, the crown relates to what is 'on High' or 'All Highest': a supreme achievement is a 'crowning achievement'. The circular form of the crown relates it to sun symbolism and the notions of wholeness, unity, and perfection. It unites the person who wears it with what is above and below, celestial and earthbound, pertaining to god and to subject. The crown is a symbol of sovereignty, legitimized by tradition, heredity, and the gods. The spikes pointing upwards from the rim like horns represent both supreme power and beams of light: they echo both the cobras' heads crowning Egyptian gods and pharaohs, as well as Christ's crown of thorns.

In ancient Greece and Rome the statues of gods were consecrated with crowns made of leaves from trees or plants sacred to them – oak for Zeus, wheat for Demeter (Ceres), myrtle for Aphrodite. The laurel crown, sacred to Apollo, was awarded to the victor at the Pythian Games; the parsley crown, sacred to Zeus, at the Nemean Games; the pine crown, sacred to Poseidon, at the Isthmian Games; and the crown of wild olives, sacred to Zeus, at the Olympic Games. Thus crowns not only distinguish divinity or royalty but also outstanding human beings – victorious athletes, generals, poets, philosophers, etc.

The symbolism of the crown is always the same – to emphasize the height of human powers and achievements, to celebrate the god-given greatness which places certain elevated individuals 'head and shoulders' above 'the rest'.

Crozier Symbol of pastoral jurisdiction and care, a richly fashioned ceremonial shepherd's crook, used for returning stray sheep to the fold.

Horseman One who has mastered the forces of nature and disciplined them in service to his will. For many centuries, possession of a horse was a supreme status symbol: it not only marked one off from the majority of humanity, but literally heightened one's stature as well as symbolizing one's superior social status. For this reason, statues of victorious heroes, generals, and kings are commonly equestrian. Such horsemen have been responsible for winning (and losing) battles and creating (and destroying) empires since wild horses were first tamed and broken (subjugated to man's sovereign will).

Kingship Combines the notions of sovereignty, height, and centrality.

The Chinese ideogram for king (*wang*) consists of three parallel horizontal strokes representing Heaven, Mankind, and Earth, linked centrally by a vertical stroke. This beautifully summarizes the meaning of kingship. The King, as representative of Heaven on Earth, rules from his throne at the centre of the kingdom, his royal prerogatives extending to the four cardinal points, from which homage and tribute is returned to him. Thus the *wang* is identical with the World Axis. Similarly, the Bayon at Angkor is built in the form of a mandala, an eight-spoked wheel, at the centre of which stood a statue of the Buddha as King.

The 'divine right of kings' is an extremely ancient concept: King Zimri-Lim of Mari (Syria), who ruled from 1779 to 1761 BC, is represented in a wall painting, now in the Louvre, receiving his royal insignia from the goddess Ishtar – the rod and the ring. The rod represents both the authority to rule and the *axis mundi*, connecting the realm of the gods (the archetypes projected into Heaven), the realm of humankind (consciousness), and the Underworld (the unconscious). The ring represents the King's sacred marriage to Ishtar, the unending cycle of life and death, and his mystic union with the feminine powers of procreation. Similar forms of sacred marriage were performed between Sumerian kings and Inanna, Ishtar's predecessor. In these instances, the King was not himself divine but received the divine powers of fertility and warlike aggression through ritual marriage to the goddess. Where the King did achieve divinity in his own right, however, it was often by dint of being the son of a god, goddess, or sacred animal. Then the monarchy became a sacred institution, responsible for implementing the divine order on earth.

Orb Symbolizes the totality of the cosmos; held in the hand of a sovereign, the orb represents the totality of absolute, limitless, and unchallenged power.

Puppet At its most superficial level, a symbol of the individual who lacks autonomy and allow himself to be manipulated by others; at a deeper level, the puppet symbolizes the insight that the extent to which we are able to control our own destiny is limited and that we are like puppets whose strings are in the hands of fate, the gods, and the collective unconscious: 'As flies to wanton boys, are we to the gods; They kill us for their sport.' Many spiritual traditions teach that wisdom lies in surrender to the puppet-master and in identifying our will with the will of the one who controls us. This is the Taoist doctrine of 'acting without action' taught by the *Bhagavad Gita*, and the Islamic and Christian submission to the Will of God.

Puppetry represents a fascinating and widely popular form of theatre possessing a long history, testifying to our ready ability to project archetypal fantasies into dolls. Puppets are used not only to represent the primary dramas and emotions of human life, but in traditional or repressive societies they can do and say things which would otherwise be unthinkable and reprehensible. Puppets may therefore be the heroes and heroines of secret desires and hidden thoughts.

Sceptre A miniature *axis mundi*, an extension of the arm, symbolizing sovereignty; it is related to the club, phallus, thunderbolt, magic wand, Thor's hammer, mace, field-marshal's baton, and the staff. It may terminate in a *fleur-de-lys*, symbol of light and purity and a sign that the rod has 'blossomed', like Aaron's rod, and that the sovereign is thus chosen by God.

Staff First and foremost the staff is a weapon, like a club. When a stranger is walking through a forest with a hefty stick in his hand it is both a support (the pilgrim's staff) and an insurance against attack (a visible demonstration of the fact that he has the ability and the will to defend himself). The staff has thus come to symbolize power – the power to defend, to retaliate, to attack, and to punish. As its Greek name *skeptron* (sceptre) implies, the staff is a symbol of authority and the mandate to rule, an attribute of kings, judges, magistrates, bishops, constables, healers, magicians, and royal messengers. When an official is deprived of his power his staff is broken.

Since monarchs, like gods, cannot be in more than one place at the same time, they require emissaries to implement their will throughout their territories – hence the herald's or messenger's staff (the guarantee of respectful treatment), the field-marshal's baton, the caduceus of Hermes (Mercury), and the staff of Asklepios. The rods of Aaron and Moses were to become the conjurer's wand and the witch's broomstick.

The magic formula 'hocus pocus' incanted by magicians is a corruption of the Latin *Hoc est corpus* ('This is the body') spoken by the priest in consecration of the bread and wine in the Eucharist.

Because of its origin from the three and its symbolic attributes of central power, both divine and temporal, the staff is identified with the *axis mundi*.

Tantalus Symbolizes the man with ideas above his station. Having been invited to dine with the gods, Tantalus made the mistake of thinking himself their equal. Not only had he the audacity to return the invitation but he endeavoured to surpass the wonderful dishes the gods had given him. When he served up his own children, however, his divine guests considered he had gone too far and cast him into Hades, where the fruit and water he craved were kept just beyond his reach. The punishment thus parodied the crime, the human longing for elevated status reaches a point beyond which it cannot go: the wise man understands this and accepts his lot, for hubris results in nemesis (p. 267).

Throne The seat of spiritual and temporal sovereignty which shares in the most exalted connotations of the **chair**. The throne of God in Heaven is surrounded by four symbolic beasts and eight angels at the four and eight points of the compass respectively, representing the subordination of the entire universe to His rule. The throne is both the highest and the centremost place from which all rank and authority devolves. Its exalted position is emphasized by its majestic structure and its elevation upon a dais or pedestal or four pillars set at the cardinal points.

Tower An attempt to concretize the *axis mundi* – to build a human structure capable of reaching the realm of the gods; a symbol of aspiration, ambition, and prospective ascension. The tower particip- ates in the symbolism of the mountain, the cathedral spire, the pyramid, the ziggurat, and the ladder. The alchemists' furnace, the ATHENOR, was made in the shape of a tower to emphasize the transformative upward intention of the *opus*, to turn base matter into gold, instinct into spirit. THE TOWER OF BABEL is a symbol of human presumption, confounded by God (*Bll* means to confound). Because the builders spoke different languages they could not collaborate in their hubristic endeavour: the confusion of tongues split humanity into hostile factions, leaving God alone as the sovereign power. The story of the Tower of Babel comes at the end of the Old Testament account of human origins and marks the limits to human ingenuity which were becoming apparent at this first stage of history, for all its cultural achievements, its great cities, civilizations, and empires.

Wand Like the staff, the wand is a symbol of power and authority, but with magical connotations. It is thus an attribute of wizards, dowsers, seer, fairies, and magicians, who use it to cast spells, enchant spirits, trace circles, detect water or minerals, and transform people, animals, or objects from one state into another. The magic wand was probably derived from such sources as the healing staff of Asklepios, the caduceus of Hermes (Mercury), the rods of Aaron and Moses. The association of the staff with snakes, as in the wands of Asklepios and Hermes, clearly relates to the ancient tree cults and serpent worship of the Aegean area and the Middle East.

Yoke The bar of wood that enables oxen to be harnessed and controlled becomes, when applied to human beings, a symbol of oppression, enslavement, and toil. In ancient Rome vanquished enemies were made to crawl 'under the yoke' (the *jugum ignominiosum*, the 'yoke of shame'). The Latin *jugum* derives from the Indo-European root *yug*, from which comes the Sanskrit *yoga*, meaning the uniting or 'yoking' of everything together in the quest for oneness and wholeness.

Zenith Derives from an Arabic word meaning 'the way of the head', while **nadir** is similarly derived from an Arabic word meaning 'the opposite'. Zenith and nadir mark opposite ends of the *axis mundi*: the zenith is as high as one can climb, the nadir the furthest one can fall.

iii Animals

A crucial social capacity that young children develop by the time they are three is that of being able to attribute mental states to other people as a means to understanding their behaviour: in this way they begin to intuit the feelings, beliefs, and desires that cause people to do and say the things they do (Hirschfeld, 1996). At about the same time, children demonstrate an ability to grasp the essence of different types of things: this enables them to classify – and to enjoy classifying – animals, plants, and objects. These two types of capacity, which Mithen (1996) calls 'intuitive psychology' and 'intuitive biology' respectively, overlap in the ANTHROPOMORPHISM which children (and, for that matter, hunter-gatherers) employ to understand the mental states and predict the behaviour of animals by attributing human mentalities to them.

Apart from anything else, many millennia of hunting have taught us that we are made of the same flesh and blood as animals and this has resulted in bonds being formed between hunter and hunted based on intimate understanding. Such intimacy helps explain the ubiquitous existence of TOTEMISM, for just as hunter-gatherers credit animals with human characteristics, so they also conceive of humans as imbued with animal spirits; and their myths describe animal ancestors from whom members of a particular tribe or clan are descended.

The cave art of the Ice Age is a rich source for the study of animal symbolism: the bulls of Lascaux, the horses of Pech-Merle, the bison of Altamira. These are rich, detailed, boldly coloured images, but do they symbolize something more than the existence of such animals? Are they symbols or merely icons? We may never know, but they have certainly excited the symbol-forming capacities of the palaeontologists who have studied them. One idea that has found fairly general accept-ance is that the animals symbolized qualities and powers that Ice Age people felt the need to make actual in themselves. As Lévi-Strauss (1968) observed of the San Bushmen and the Australian Aborigines, certain animals were frequently depicted not because they were 'good to eat' but because they were 'good to think' (identify with). With animal symbolism we get down to the evolutionary bedrock. Jung argued that when we dream of snakes or wolves they are manifestations of the reptilian and mammalian components of the Self. 'Dreaming itself,' said Freud's colleague Sandor Ferenczi, 'is the workshop of evolution.'

Modern Western adults may like to think they are above the kind of anthropomorphic thinking indulged in by Aborigines, but one has only to hear them talking to or about their pets to realize that they are not. We still experience a form of kinship with animals: we understand their feelings, states of mind, and actions by making analogies with our own. This is particularly true of animals appearing in dreams. On the one hand they have the characteristics of the animal species they represent, but on the other they are our own mental inventions: they are composite figures which draw together human and animal qualities giving them a power, a meaning, and a dynamism all their own. This process of imaginative synthesis must be the source of all the fabulous beasts and monsters, part animal, part human, with which myths, folk tales, and legends are filled. It also explains why animal symbols retain their numinous fascination even for city-dwellers who have never encountered their prototypes in reality. The animals described in this section, therefore, all share these dual anthropomorphic and theriomorphic origins. As with all the other symbols, these have been selected on the criteria of their common occurrence in contemporary dreams and their prevalence in the ethnography of myth, religion, and folk tale, but this is not a complete bestiary.

As a species we tend to be self-congratulatory about our enormous cultural and intellectual achievements, and we too easily forget how much these depend on the brains of creatures that have gone before us. Each new stage of the evolutionary process not only transcends but encompasses and incorporates all the stages that have preceded it. Accordingly, our brains possess intact and active vestiges of our reptilian and mammalian past which still find frequent expression in our dreams and symbols.

As the American neuroscientist Paul MacLean has conceived of it, the human brain is not a unity but *three brains in one*, each with a different phylogenetic history, each with 'its own special intelligence, its own special memory, its own sense of time and space, and its own motor functions' (MacLean, 1976). MacLean's diagram of the three brains, which together make up what he calls the **triune brain**, is reproduced in Figure 7.

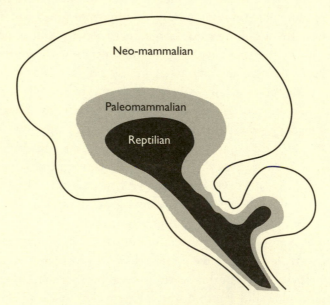

Figure 7. The triune brain

The **reptilian brain** is described on p. 340 in connection with the symbolism of reptiles. It is sometimes referred to as the R-complex. As Bailey (1987) puts it: 'Our drives, inner subjective feelings, fantasies and thoughts are thoroughly conditioned by emanations from the R-complex. The reptilian carry-overs provide the automatic, compulsive urgency to much of human behaviour, where free will steps aside and persons act as they have to act, often despising themselves in the process for their hatreds, prejudices, compulsions, conformity, deceptiveness and guile.'

The **palaeo-mammalian brain** is made up of those subcortical structures which comprise the limbic system. The limbic system is a homeostatic mechanism: it not only maintains a sensitive control of hormone levels but also balances hunger against satiation, sexual desire against gratification, thirst against fluid retention, sleep against wakefulness. It also plays an indispensable role in memory storage. By this evolutionary stage, the major emotions of fear and anger have emerged, as well as those of love and attachment, together with their associated behavioural response patterns, bonding and mating. MacLean (1985) particularly draws attention to three forms of behaviour that most clearly distinguish the evolutionary transition from reptiles to mammals. These are: nursing and maternal care, audiovocal communication for maintaining mother–offspring contact, and play.

Conscious awareness is more in evidence at this stage and behaviour is less rigidly determined by instincts, though these are still very apparent. In all mammals, including man, this part of the brain is a structure of the utmost complexity, controlling basic psychophysical responses and attitudes to the environment. An animal, deprived of its cerebral cortex, can still find its way about, eat, drink, and avoid painful stimuli, but it has difficulty in attributing meaning to things: a natural predator will be noticed, for example, but not apparently perceived as a threat.

The **neo-mammalian brain** constitutes the cerebral cortex. It is responsible for cognition and sophisticated perceptual processes as opposed to purely instinctive or affective behaviour.

Each of these components of the triune brain makes its contribution to symbol formation, but animal symbols, being of their very essence creatures of the imagination rather than biological entities, are not easy to classify along zoological lines. The imagination too readily crosses species boundaries to make associations which no biologist could tolerate. The scheme I have chosen to adopt is a compromise between cladistic rigour and imaginative expediency, and I apologize to those taxonomic purists who will be upset by it. In devising it I have allowed myself to be swayed by that archetypal division so beloved of the human psyche between water, earth, and air:

(1) **Water creatures**   These include **fish, amphibia, water-living mammals, crustaceans,** and other creature of the deep

(2) **Land creatures**   These include **reptiles, undomesticated animals,** and **domesticated animals**

(3) **Air creatures**   These include **birds, insects,** and mammals (namely, bats).

Water creatures

These were the first to evolve from the 'primal soup', and are thus extremely ancient. The **fish** symbols discussed here are the carp, perch, piranha, and salmon. In the general sense, fish are symbols of life and fertility because of their prolific powers of reproduction and the vast

numbers of eggs that they lay. As they are water creatures, they are gifts of the Great Mother as well as symbolical contents of the collective unconscious. In Christian symbolism Christ is identified both with fish and with the fisherman, while St Peter was called a 'fisher of men', rescuing souls for conversion like fish caught in a net.

Carp Because of its longevity, a symbol of long life and good fortune. In Eastern Asia a symbol of courage and endurance because it swims long distances upstream against a river's flow.

Perch The shape of fish and their mode of thrusting penetration through the feminine element, water, renders them evident phallic symbols. This is particularly true of the perch, which in the Far East is both a symbol of erotic desire and is consumed as an aphrodisiac.

Piranha This small Amazonian fish with razor-sharp teeth and a voracious appetite puts it in the same symbolic category as the crocodile, the shark, and the monster of the deep. The terrifying predator that attacks suddenly out of the darkness of opaque water resembles dangerous unconscious contents threatening to overwhelm the ego. It also represents the Great Mother in her terrible, devouring aspect.

Salmon A symbol of courage, determination, and self-sacrifice: it swims up rivers far inland, overcoming incredible obstacles without taking nourishment, and, after spawning, it dies. In Northern Europe the salmon is considered the King of the River Fish and is thought to be wise: like a hermit it hides in contemplative retirement and is consequently difficult to catch.

Among the **amphibia** the frog and the toad are most commonly attributed symbolic significance. Amphibia were the first creatures to sport four limbs and they bear a certain resemblance to human beings, especially when they swim. That they have to return to water to breed and produce aquatic larvae which undergo metamorphosis before becoming adults makes them a symbol of transformation through baptism or purification.

Frog It is an obvious symbol of transformation for not only does it change from tadpole to frog but it is as much at home in the water as it is on the land. It is a borderline or liminal case, hopping about on the threshold between consciousness and unconsciousness. Moreover, its human resemblance encourages the transformations so common in fairy tales whereby frogs turn into princes when kissed by a princess. The croaking of the frog which heralds the arrival of spring makes it a symbol of new life and fertility. However, its ceaseless and mindless repetition of this song makes the frog a metaphor for the boring conversationalist.

Toad Like the frog it is a lunar animal since it is associated with water and is prone to appear and disappear like the moon. While the frog is regarded as a symbol of resurrection and rebirth because of its metamorphosis, the toad is generally seen in a more negative light, its loathsome ugliness being associated with death and evil. Like the serpent, the toad can be equipped with a jewel in its head. In China, both creatures are representative of the lunar Yin principle: the three-legged toad actually lives on the moon, its three legs symbolizing the three lunar phases. The toad is particularly associated with the practices of witchcraft.

Water-living mammals are particularly attractive to us precisely because they are not cold-blooded fish. Being mammals, we can identify with their intelligence, their social life, their capacity to bond, and to be altruistic in their behaviour with one another.

Dolphin Always an animal of great fascination on account of its beauty, intelligence, friendliness, and legendary reputation for assisting drowning men. Sacred to Apollo, the dolphin gave Delphi its name. The legendary rescue of Orion on a dolphin's back provides one of many examples of the dolphin as saviour.

Otter Another water creature possessing lunar symbolism. Its capacity to live on land and plunge deep into the water to rise to the surface again makes it a psychopomp of shamanic significance. Consequently, otter skins are important attributes of shamans and play a significant role in shamanic initiation.

Seal A creature of the deep which, for good reason, shuns human society. It thus seemed a suitable form for the Nereid Psamathe to adopt when she tried to escape (unsuccessfully) the amorous attentions of Aeacus. As a result she gave birth to Phocus ('seal'). The seal can be seen as a symbol of a repressed psychic content: when it takes fright it slips into the unconscious (the sea).

Whale Like the crocodile, elephant, and tortoise, the whale is one of those animals responsible for holding up the world. As a huge monster of the deep it also possesses the capacity to swallow the sun at dusk, carry it under the world, and vomit it up again in the morning. It can readily perform the less indigestible task of swallowing and regurgitating solar heroes like Jonah, a process which has been symbolically related to Christ's death, burial, and resurrection.

Of the **crustaceans** the **crab** is most commonly attributed symbolic significance. A somewhat monstrous creature, armour-plated with large dangerous claws, it scuttles about on the body of the Great Mother in the ocean's depths. In cosmogonic myths the crab is one of those animals responsible for carrying the Earth on its back – like the crocodile, the elephant, and the tortoise. Because of their association with water and the tides, crabs are lunar creatures thought to possess rainmaking powers in times of drought.

Of the **other creatures of the deep**, the most symbolically important are the octopus and the oyster. The shapeless, tentacled **octopus**, with its suckers and hideous maw, appears particularly horrendous to the human imagination as a denizen of the Underworld and a symbol of all the manifold horrors of Hell. The octopus is a symbol of the Great Mother in her terrible, devouring aspect.

Although it is the lowest form of animal life, the **oyster** can also conceal an object of great prize, the **pearl**. It thus provides an allegory of humility as the true face of spiritual perfection.

Land creatures

These are divided into **reptiles, undomesticated animals,** and **domesticated animals.**

Reptiles The most primitive component of the human brain evolved in our reptilian ancestors about 300 million years ago. We share it with all other terrestrial vertebrates and it has remained remarkably unchanged by the march of evolution. It contains nuclei which are vital to the maintenance of life, such as those controlling the respiratory and cardiovascular systems. At the early evolutionary stage represented by the reptilian brain, emotions had not yet emerged, nor had cognitive appreciation of future or past events. Typical reptilian behaviours are territorial acquisition and defence, as well as dominance striving, ritual agonistic behaviour (RAB), and mating. In view of the continuing presence in our own brains of the nuclei mediating such behaviour our subjective fantasies and thoughts are conditioned by reptilian carry-overs which provide the basis of more primitive, atavistic, and compulsive forms of human behaviour, such as cold-blooded cruelty, heartless aggression, and sadism. It is not surprising, therefore, that reptiles feature as much in modern dreams as they did in the myths and legends of the past. The symbolic inferences of reptiles such as the crocodile and serpent are therefore enormous.

Crocodile In Western eyes, a monstrous, cold-blooded predator, archaic and totally without feeling for its victims; a symbol of evil malignancy, it bears a resemblance to prehistoric dinosaurs and legendary dragons.

The Egyptian crocodile Sobek is depicted waiting while souls are weighed: those found wanting he devours. Presumably because of this devouring aspect, the crocodile is associated with the Kingdom of the Dead in many Asian and pre-Columbian American cultures. It appears as a divinity of darkness and the moon whose greed demonstrates its kinship with monsters of the night which devour the sun at the end of the day.

Serpent The evolution of the serpent archetype is discussed on pp. 30–35, where it is suggested that a simple alarm system designed to protect our ancestors from dangerous reptiles came with time to be elaborated into a symbolic canon of great complexity and power. Snakes are as

ubiquitous in reality as they are in myths: some thrive in deserts, some hide in woods, others lurk near wells and springs; while aquatic serpents disport themselves in lakes, ponds, and estuaries. In the environment in which our ancestors evolved, they were plentiful, a constant source of fascination and danger, particularly at night. When encountered in reality, this awe-inspiring creature is experienced as numinous and sacred, inspiring reverence as well as dread. One is in the presence of something primeval, uncanny, and profoundly sinister. This cold-blooded, limbless, hairless, featherless creature, which 'crawls on its belly' about the world, its quick, darting movements and flicking tongue, its terrifying, unrelated stare with lidless eyes, makes it frighteningly unpredictable and the epitome of eternal vigilance and readiness to attack. From all points of view, it is the quintessence of 'lowness': cosmologically it is at the base of the world carrying the cosmos on its back; neurologically it dwells at the base of the brain; yogically it lies coiled up at the base of the spine; analytically it lurks in the lower levels of consciousness; and mythically it rules in the Underworld.

For the sake of clarity, the implications of serpent symbolism will be considered under four headings dealing with cosmology, death and the Underworld, sex and fertility, and sickness and healing:

(1) **Cosmology** The truly primeval quality of the snake is witnessed everywhere: like the Norse Midgardorm, he is 'older than the gods themselves' (*The Edda*). He is the Great Invisible Serpent, the Life-giver, the Great God of Darkness, the Old God at the beginning of

the cosmos. Midgardorm, like the Christian Leviathan, encircles the earth, and both owe their origins to the uroborus of first creation. In the creation myths, the primordial serpent is both male and female and self-generating, thus solving the problem of whether Sky Father or Earth Mother was born first: the World Serpent, out of its own substance, created them both. Moreover, it also hatches from an egg – the World Egg.

Ananta, the Naga, associate of Vishnu and Shiva, wraps its coils round the base of the *axis mundi* and is guardian of the nadir (in many myths the zenith is ruled by the eagle). Ananta carries the world on his back, and all those other world-supporting creatures – the crocodile, tortoise, elephant, bull – are but the Naga's deputies (in Sanskrit *naga* means both serpent and elephant). To prove the point, the world-supporting animals are commonly represented with their own heads but with a serpent's body.

The oldest creator god of the Mediterranean region is Atum, who, in the form of a serpent and through his own determination, emerged from the primal waters and masturbated the world into existence; at the end of time he will take the form of a mongoose and devour himself. The serpent is the symbol *par excellence* of primordial ocean from which all life derived and to which it must eventually return.

(2) **Death and the Underworld** As a lethal force of nature the serpent represents death and destruction. Just over halfway through its night voyage, so the Egyptian *The Book of the Dead* tells us, the sun encounters the enormous snake god Apophis, Lord of the Underworld, whose coils are 450 cubits long. Having successfully got past him, the sun-boat is dragged through the body of yet another monstrous serpent, this time 1,300 cubits long, to emerge from its mouth with the dawn. The notion of the engulfing belly and digestive tract must come from observations of the giant boa-constrictor ingesting its prey.

Not only in Egypt but all over the world the serpent is cast in the role of swallower and regurgitator of the sun, Lord of the Earth's Womb, Master Initiator and Regenerator, and it is the sun's great enemy with which it must do battle every night. The Huichol Cosmic Serpent, for example, has two heads with monstrous jaws: one swallows the sun at dusk, the other vomits it up at dawn. Psychologically, the sun hero represents the ego which descends into the womb of the unconscious every night to experience dreams in the Underworld.

The universal enmity between the sun hero and the monster of the deep is echoed in the conflict between the cortex of the forebrain and the R-complex which occurs with sleep and wakefulness. It is the battle between spirit and nature, between light and darkness, between Ra and Apophis, between Apollo and Python, between Zeus and Typhon, between the eagle and the snake. In doing battle with Typhon, Zeus relied on the support of Athena, daughter of his head, Reason. All the other Olympians took temporary flight to Egypt, where they became animal deities.

Culture takes sides in the battle. The sovereign crown of Egypt, the **Uraeus,** flaunted a golden cobra fashioned from the eye of God, but the splitting of the Judaeo-Christian godhead resulted in two millennia of repression and progressive demonization of the serpent, which became an attribute of Satan, the Prince of Darkness. The Enlightenment celebrated Apollo, while the Romantic Movement took the side of Python. The Victorians once more returned Python to her den, where Freud rediscovered her and set her free on the analytic couch. Python has been rampaging through the twentieth century every since. Her dynamism can never be extirpated: she has continued to haunt the dreams of Christians and non-Christians right down to the present day.

(3) **Sex and fertility** Another worldwide manifestation of the serpent is as Lord of Fertility. Here his phallic appearance must play a part. In many cultures it is, or was, believed that snakes can make women pregnant. In India, for example, an infertile woman who wanted a child would adopt a cobra. In many places the serpent is also held responsible for women's menstruation.

By renewing its skin, the serpent was believed to renew its vitality and youth, and this, together with its phallic power, makes it the symbol of regeneration. Its hermaphroditic implications are also apparent in palaeolithic depictions of the serpent with lozenges ('vulvae') down its back: this hints at its cosmogonic as well as its regenerative power. Medieval pictures represent the serpent in the Garden of Eden with a woman's head and breasts, stressing the seductive aspect of feminine sexuality as a source of temptation to the righteous man of God.

As Lord of Fertility, the serpent is the constant companion of the Great Earth Mother. Not only in Crete was the goddess depicted with a snake in each hand but, in Greece, Artemis, Hecate, and Persephone were similarly represented. These, together with the Great Mother goddesses – Isis (the royal cobra on her head, the gold Uraeus symbol of divine sovereignty, knowledge, life, and youth), Cybele, Demeter, and Eve – were all recycled by Christianity as Mary, Mother of God, who crushed the serpent's head and denied it audience. Under Christian condemnation, the serpent no longer symbolized fertility but lust.

Dionysus is richly implicated in the erotic symbolism of the serpent. According to Orphic tradition, Zeus fathered Dionysus by lying with Persephone in the form of a snake. As counterweight to Apollo (the sun god and upholder of law and order), Dionysus was on the side of the serpent, and so designated the 'Great Liberator' by the Greeks. The Romans called him Bacchus and identified him with their own god, Father Liber. The tension between Apollo, Dionysus, and the serpent was resolved through ritual excess; harmony being restored by the temporary madness of the Dionysiad. This corresponds to the wisdom of the Gnostics, who equated the snake with the spinal cord as early as 200 AD and venerated the serpent as the source of *gnosis*, knowledge through revelation. Through experience of the interaction of extremes, forebrain and R-complex re-establish a homeostatic balance in their mutual contribution to psychic adjustment. Christ understood this: 'Be ye therefore wise as serpents, and harmless as doves' (Matthew 10:16).

(4) **Sickness and healing** The shamanic links between healing, snakes, the unconscious, and the priesthood are reflected in the myth of Iamos, son of Apollo, sun god of healing, by a mortal woman, who is brought up by serpents and becomes the first in a famous line of priests. The healing potential of the snake was particularly celebrated in Greece, where the serpent was not only an attribute of Asklepios but of Hippocrates, Hermes, and Hygiena. The power of the snake as a symbol of healing lies in its ambivalence: it can both kill and cure. When God punishes the Israelites by sending them a plague of poisonous serpents, He provides Moses with the antidote, the Brazen Serpent, so that anyone who looked upon it would be saved. To Christians, the Brazen Serpent was a prefiguration of Christ. The staff

of Asklepios twined about by the snake symbolizes authority combined with 'the wisdom of the serpent', the World Tree encircled by the healing life force of nature.

Tortoise (**Turtle**) Because of its venerable disposition and undoubted antiquity, the tortoise receives cosmogonic projections. Its shell represents the cosmos, the dome of Heaven (curved upper part), superimposed upon the Earth (flat lower part). Its sturdy, stumpy legs and dogged determination, as well as its great age, make the tortoise a worthy supporter of the universe, and many cultures cast it in this role.

Both Chinese and Amerindian traditions adopt a Freudian view of the outward thrusting and inward retraction of its head, equating these movements with penile tumescence and detumescence, and with sexual intercourse.

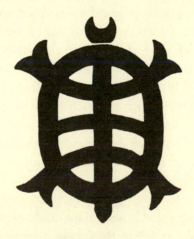

The **undomesticated animals** here listed have been important to us since hunter-gatherer times. Although we have never lived on such intimate terms with them as with those species we have domesticated, they all provided focal points for meticulous study by our ancestors, who made full use of the 'natural history intelligence with which hominid evolution endowed them' (Mithen, 1996). The condensed consequences of this intelligence are still with us in the symbolic meanings which these animals still evoke.

The complexity of the meanings surrounding each of these animal symbols is infinitely greater than can be encompassed in the space here allocated to them. What the following entries seek to achieve is a description of the core meaning of each symbol round which other related meanings cluster like petals round the stamen of a rose or piglets round a sow.

Bear Because it can walk on two legs, the bear is a ready target for anthropomorphic projections. Many peoples, particularly Eskimos, North American Indians, and Altaic peoples, regarded the bear as their ancestor. In Siberia there were graveyards for bears until quite recently. Being a powerful, dangerous animal, it symbolizes primal aggression and brutality. For the Celts the bear was the emblem of the warrior caste. The Celtic word for bear was *artos* which is directly related to the name of King Arthur (*Artoris*) and epitomizes his warlike spirit as well as that of his Knights of the Round Table. By contrast, when tamed and taught to dance, the bear's apparent simple-minded clumsiness identifies it with the symbolism of the buffoon.

As an intrepid defender of her cubs, the she-bear represents passionate and protective maternity, and she may well have been worshipped in palaeolithic times as an embodiment of the Great Mother goddess. Since the bear vanishes with the winter and returns with the spring after its period of hibernation, it participates in the symbolism of the moon which disappears for three nights every month. In Greek mythology the bear was an attribute of the moon goddess Artemis.

Boar A symbol of spiritual power. This could be because, like a holy hermit, it lives a solitary life in the forest, because it feeds on acorns, fruit of a sacred tree, the oak, and because it has the ability to find and uproot the much-prized truffle.

In view of its power and rashness, the boar, like the monster, offers a challenge to the hero: thus Herakles takes on the Erymanthian boar; and the Calydonian boar is hunted by Meleager, helped by Theseus and Atalanta. It was in the form of a boar that Vishnu raised the Earth to the surface of the primordial waters, and later rooted about in the earth at the foot of Shiva's Lingam in a futile effort to discover its base.

In Gaul the boar was represented on battle standards and on coins, but in most places the boar was an emblem of the priestly rather than the warrior caste.

Chameleon Because of its capacity to change colour in accordance with its immediate surroundings, the chameleon is a symbol of weakness of character, fickleness, untrustworthiness, and of taking the line of least resistance.

Fox Though he has seldom deigned to be domesticated, the fox lives in close proximity to human communities and owes his survival to has success in adopting a 'free-rider' strategy of waiting till the farmer's hens are plump, taking his pick, and then moving on. The fox thus symbolizes 'foxiness' – namely, sly cunning, craftiness, and guile. That he lives underground in an earth makes him a psychopomp, a familiar of the earth mother and of the dead.

Hare A lunar animal symbolical of fecundity on account of its nocturnal habit and copious progeny. Traditionally believed to sleep with its eyes open, it is a symbol of vigilance, and because of its formidable capacity for beating a hasty retreat it reminds us of the fleeting nature of life.

Hippopotamus Both revered as a fertility goddess (Egypt) and excoriated as a brute, Behemoth, whom only God can tame (Christianity).

Hyena A scavenger and voracious carrion-eater, the hyena is seen by some (e.g. Christians) as the epitome of coarseness and greed, and by others (e.g. African hunters) as an example of skill and craftiness.

Because the female is large and has a big clitoris, the hyena is wrongly considered androgynous.

Jackal Never a popular animal on account of its unpleasant howl, normally directed at the moon, and its hunger for corpses. Its connection with death makes it a suitable psychopomp for conducting souls to the next world. The jackal is identified with the Egyptian god, Anubis, the Pathfinder and Guardian of the Dead, though it seems that jackals were unknown in ancient Egypt, and Anubis may have been a wild dog with jackal-like features.

Jaguar Like the jackal, another chthonic, lunar custodian of the dead, particularly in pre-Columbian and Central South America, where it does battle with its opponent, the eagle. In line with this hostility to the eagle, a solar creature, it is the jaguar who swallows the sun at twilight.

Leopard A sleek, powerful, fast-moving animal of prey, it represents intrepid ferocity, and in classical times was associated with Artemis, Dionysus, and the maenads, as was the PANTHER.

Lion On account of its golden colour, its great strength, and its majestic, ray-like mane, he is the King of Beasts, the earthly representative of the sun. The belief that he never shuts his eyes makes this ferocious creature the ideal guardian of justice and the palaces of those in power. The young lion is equated with the rising sun, the old lion with the setting sun, while, in Egypt, two lions sitting back to back represent dawn and dusk. As a beast of prey, the lion is implicated in the symbolism of devouring and the fear of being overwhelmed or possessed by forces beyond one's control. The lion also represents our own violent, predatory aggression, available to us, as it is to the lion, in the limbic system of the old mammalian brain. The lion became the emblem of St Mark because his gospel stressed the royalty and majesty of Christ.

The **lioness** by contrast is a lunar creature, companion of the Great Mother, a symbol of fiercely protective maternity. Throughout the

Mediterranean region and as far as India and Tibet the lioness is found as the emblem of goddesses, particularly virgin war goddesses.

Mole Truly chthonian, a creature of the earth earthy. Asklepios, god of healing, was originally a mole god, and the underground labyrinth sacred to him at Epidaurus was probably based on the maze of underground tunnels which the mole inhabits. Possessing all the secrets of the earth and being in his element underground, the mole is an obvious guide to the Underworld.

Monkey As primates, monkeys and apes are our closest relatives. They fascinate us because we see ourselves caricatured by them. On the whole, we have adopted a superior, condescending attitude to them, dismissing them as skilled exponents of lewdity, deceptiveness, and guile. They appear in many mythologies as 'free-riding' tricksters, who invariably have an eye to the main chance, seizing every opportunity for self-gratification that may arise. In Greek antiquity, the Cercopes were merry brigands whose knavery so infuriated Zeus that he turned them into the monkeys that they were – and they are still to be found to this day in the long-tailed African monkey, *Cercopithecus*.

The Chinese, however, understood that there was more to the monkey than trickery: they saw him as cleverly concealing his intelligence and wisdom under a mask of buffoonery. In India, Hanuman, the royal monkey of the *Ramayana*, was celebrated for his quick-witted diplomacy and extraordinary powers of imagination. The dog-faced baboon Thoth was scribe to the Egyptian gods, recording the verdict of Anubis as he judged the souls of the dead. Although they appreciated the intelligence of monkeys, the Egyptians also understood and empathized with their passions – the hieroglyph representing the verb 'to be angry' was a baboon standing on all fours, teeth bared and tail arched in rage. To the Aztecs and Maya, monkeys were not so much crafty as craftsmen – hard-working potters, sculptors, and smiths – who possessed a cheerful and loving disposition. The monkey is thus a polyvalent symbol, carrying in important particulars the rudiments of many human capacities.

Rat Apart from their fecundity, rats seem to have very little positive to offer to humankind. Not only are they conveyers of disease, but they are inveterate pilferers, and are considered aggressive, filthy, and greedy. Mediterranean civilizations, however, attributed them with chthonian qualities and regarded them as carrying similar psychopompic propensities as serpents and moles.

Salamander This newt-like amphibian was believed in classical times to be capable of living harmlessly in fire; it could also extinguish fire through its extraordinary coldness. It was thought to be sexless and in medieval iconography it stood for chastity and the righteous soul who trusts in God, unconsumed by the fires of temptation.

Scarab (Dung Beetle) A symbol of the self-renewing sun and hence of resurrection. This symbolism arises from the scarab's practice of rolling pieces of dung into small balls in which the female deposits her eggs. That the scarab eventually emerges from these base bits of matter has impressed people from China to Central America with the same idea: that the scarab conceals within itself the secret of the eternal renewal of life.

To the Egyptians, the scarab was Khepri, god of the rising sun. Depicted with its legs outstretched, the scarab was the hieroglyph corresponding to the verb *khepr*, meaning 'to come into existence by assuming a given form' (Chevalier and Gheerbrant, 1996). The scarab, therefore, was an avatar, a metaphor for the principle of incarnation.

Scorpion Like the snake, the scorpion is both revered as a deity and feared as a force of evil. Its sting, permanently unsheathed and ready to deal death to anyone who comes into contact with it, serves as an instrument of divine retribution. When Orion, the great hunter, boasted to Artemis that he could kill all the animals of the earth, Gaia, Mother Earth, became alarmed and sent a great scorpion to sting his heel. The scorpion's reward is to be turned into a constellation which forever chases Orion across the night sky.

Snail Like all molluscs, the snail carries sexual implications, partly on account of the tumescence of its horns, and partly because of its motions and secretions as it extends itself and withdraws in its vulva-like shell. It is a lunar creature; its shell carries the spiral configuration which is everywhere associated with the eternal continuance and evolution of life.

Spider The spider as weaver of the web has always encouraged cosmogonic fantasies, especially as the web is made in the form of a mandala, with its creator sitting at the centre. The spider's life of weaving and killing, creating and destroying, is an allegory of the opposing forces on which the existence of the cosmos depends. A lunar animal, the spider presides like the moon over the cycles of life, and is a creature of fate, weaving the thread of destiny on which it hangs. It is also sinister, a dangerous, mindless beast of prey, sometimes possessing a lethal bite. Its inexorable mode of locomotion makes it an object of fear, in many instances amounting to frank phobia, which is probably phylogenetically induced.

Stag Because of its magnificent antlers, which regularly drop and grow again, the stag is linked to the Tree of Life, and symbolizes fertility, growth, and regeneration. Like the eagle and the lion, the stag is the natural enemy of the serpent, which puts him firmly on the side of the sky gods and the sun. The Gaulish god, Cernunnos, is depicted with the horns of a stag, which probably symbolize the rays of the sun as well as the branches of the Cosmic Tree. Surrounded by a profusion of different animals, Cernunnos sits in lotus-like posture, holding a torque in one hand and a serpent in the other: he is both God of Plenty and Lord of the Beasts. Medieval iconography depicts the stag with a cross between its horns, thus emphasizing its association with the Tree of Life on which Christ is crucified.

Tiger Particularly important in the mythology of China, India, and South East Asia. Like the lion, it has both solar and lunar character-istics, being both a creator and a destroyer. When locked in mortal combat with the serpent, the tiger is celestial, solar, and representative of the dynamic qualities of Yang; when in conflict with the dragon, it is chthonic, lunar, and representative of Yin. Its speed, strength, and aggressive savagery render it a symbol of the warrior caste. The 'Five Tigers', symbols of tenacious defence, were the guardians of the four cardinal points and of the centre.

In Hindu iconography, the tiger represents cosmic energy: it is ridden by Shakti; and Shiva is represented with a tiger skin.

Throughout South East Asia a mythic tiger ancestor exists as an initiatory grand master, who takes initiates into the jungle to dismember and reassemble them. Malaysian healers derive much of their therapeutic kudos from their ability to turn themselves into tigers.

Although the tiger lacks the dignity of the lion, it is no less beautiful and savage. In dreams, the tiger represents all these qualities: that they appear in animal form suggests that these aggressive, predatory instinctive forces have been activated in the limbic system of the old mammalian brain and have not yet been humanized – i.e. integrated with other mind-brain modalities, especially those subserved by the frontal lobes. It is clear that these primitive, mammalian components can take over and drive human consciousness, as when people are possessed by furious rage and commit bloody murder.

Wolf A complex symbol which like so many others carries both positive and negative connotations: it can be either solar or lunar, celestial or chthonic, nurturing or destructive, according to place, time, and tradition. As warrior hero, the blue wolf (symbolizing the light of Heaven) is the ancestor of Genghis Khan; as earth mother the she-wolf suckles Romulus and Remus. Anatolian and Altaic women call upon the wolf to make them pregnant when they are childless. But its dangerous, predatory urgency gives the wolf an infernal aspect in European folk tales like 'Little Red Riding Hood' and in myths like that of the Nordic wolf Fenris. Fenris can destroy iron chains and fetters and has to be imprisoned in the bowels of the earth, for the cosmic order can only be sustained if the powerful and chaotic forces of the universe are shackled. This will not be possible indefinitely, however, for come the twilight of the gods, the monstrous Fenris will once more break out of his prison and, devouring the sun, bring the whole cosmos to an end. The wolf's sharp teeth and large predatory mouth thus make it a devourer of the sun like the jaguar, the crocodile, and the monster of the deep. The wolf's association with the ideas of evil, death, and destruction is further apparent in Hades's cloak of wolf-skin, the wolf-ears of the Etruscan god of death, and the capacity of warlocks and evil men to turn themselves into wolves and were-wolves (lycanthropy).

Domesticated animals The long intimacy between humans and the animals we have tamed and domesticated has made us familiar with their ways and made them ready receptacles for our anthropomorphic projections. As a result, the symbolic implications of these creatures are extremely rich.

Ass (Donkey) A beast of burden generally thought to be stupid, obstinate, and lewd. Lucius in Apuleius's tale *Metamorphoses or the Golden Ass* is transformed into an ass as a punishment for his sensuality, while Apollo gives King Midas ass's ears as a punishment for preferring Pan's pipes to religious music in the temple at Delphi.

The ass is a sacred animal in some religions, however. It was sacred to Apollo and to Dionysus. Joseph put Mary and the Christ child on the back of a she-ass to escape Herod's edict, and it was on a she-ass that Christ made his triumphant entry into Jerusalem on Palm Sunday. The significance of the symbolism here is that the she-ass represents humility, self-abasement, patience, and courage.

Bull Because of its crucial importance to agriculturalists, the bull holds a supreme place in the complex symbolism of fertility and is closely identified with the sky gods, its irresistible strength and sexual vitality showering semen upon the fertile, receptive, and recumbent Mother Earth. As an emblem of the Sumerian sky god El, bronze figurines of the bull, precursors of the Golden Calf, were paraded on ceremonial standards. Examples have been found which date from the third millennium BC. In Greek mythology the bull is identified with Ouranos and Zeus; in India with Indra and Shiva.

Bulls were domesticated about 6,500 years ago from the great wild bulls which roamed the forests round the Mediterranean region. These were to survive in the forests of central Europe till the seventeenth century. They were enormous and extremely powerful, standing over six feet high at the shoulders and weighing about a ton. They were clearly of great interest to Stone Age hunters, who began to draw images of them about 35,000 years ago on cave walls in France and Spain. In the main chamber at Lascaux, for example, the ceiling is decorated with five colossal bulls, the biggest being seventeen feet in length.

The power and uncontrollable violence of the bull made it a ready subject for hierophantic reverence, and it is not surprising that it became the sacred embodiment of these qualities. Between 6,000 and 7,000 years ago, nomadic hunters began to settle in the lush grasslands of the Nile delta to become herdsmen. Each settlement adopted an animal as a totemic god, and this was most commonly a bull. When, much later, the kingdoms of Upper and Lower Egypt were united about 3,000 BC, a new capital was established at Memphis, where the creator god Ptah was worshipped in his incarnation as a bull – one bull being especially chosen from all the bulls of Egypt and, with great ceremony, ritually named Apis. Throughout his lifetime he was royally housed, being regularly anointed by his priests, participating in fertility rites, serving the cows that were brought to him, and accompanying the King on ceremonial occasions so as to renew the fertility of the fields. When, eventually, he died, he was renamed Osiris-Apis, and his body ritually embalmed and buried in the catacombs at Serais, where many immense granite bull sarcophagi were found in 1851.

In Greece, the bull was sacred to Poseidon, god of sea, storms, and earthquakes, and to Dionysus, god of wine and male fertility. Zeus took the form of a bull to seduce Europa, while Shiva tamed the bull Nandi to channel its physical energy into the service of the spirit and the practice of yoga. As a result, Nandi symbolizes justice as well as power.

The crucial event in the life of Mithras was the sacrifice of the primordial bull, the first living creature created by Ahura Mazda. Plant and animal life sprang up from the bull's blood, despite the efforts of the serpent and the scorpion (servants of Ahriman) to prevent them. Mithras, worshipped by legions throughout the Roman empire, is thus in the tradition of the hero-saviour who, through his god-like strength, prevails over the forces of evil. The BULL-RING still draws huge crowds as the *temenos* or sacred ground where the hero does battle with the monster. To win the Golden Fleece, Jason had to yoke a mighty pair of ferocious bulls which breathed fire and seemed untamable.

The BULL ROARER, a wooden musical instrument whirled round the head on a cord, produces a roaring sound suggestive of thunder as well as the bellowing of a bull. The sound summons up emotions associated with a complex of meanings extending from the fertility triad of thunder, lightning, and rain, to the primordial creative powers of the sky gods, to say nothing of their capacity for wrath and destruction.

Because of their pre-eminent significance as the embodiment of the fertility principle, bulls have in many places been linked to the moon

DE TAVRO.

and worship of the Great Mother. The bull is thus lunar in its association with fertility rites and solar through the fire of its blood and the copious trajectory of its semen. On a royal tomb in Ur there stood a bull with a golden head (symbolizing sun and fire) and with jaws of lapis lazuli (symbols of moon and water). In the second century AD, an initiation rite known as the 'taurobolium' was introduced into Italy, whereby an initiate was sprinkled with blood of a sacrificial bull and rendered *renatus in aeternum*, reborn to eternal life.

Camel Because of its capacity to travel long distances without water, enabling its rider to cross the desert, the camel is a symbol of endurance and sobriety, proceeding through the torments of life with hope and dogged determination. Not surprisingly, it also has a reputation for cussedness.

Cat On the one hand, the cat is graceful, gentle, and affectionate; on the other hand, it is predatory, sinister, a creature of the night. As a consequence, it can be a symbol of good or evil omen, depending on its colour (white = good; black = evil) or its geographical location. In ancient Egypt, the cat goddess Bastet was the guardian and benefactress of mankind, and decapitated the serpent Apophis, the Dragon of Darkness, responsible for trying to sink the boat carrying the sun on its journey through the Underworld. She represents the strength and agility necessary to overcome hidden enemies (Hannah, 1992). The Buddhist world, on the other hand, identifies cats with snakes as being the only creatures left unmoved by the death of the Buddha. Its aloof dignity makes it a model of independence and self-sufficiency.

Cow Among agricultural peoples a universal symbol of the Great Mother in her fecundating, nurturant aspect. Her association with the moon is emphasized through the association of her horns with the crescent moon. This symbolism links with that of the HORN OF PLENTY, the never-ending source of maternal bounty. The Egyptian cow goddess Hathor embodies all these qualities. In addition she is, in true Egyptian fashion, both wife and mother of the sun ('the Bull of his own Mother'). The power of this symbolism is apparent to this day in India, where the cow is worshipped and celebrated as the archetype of maternal fertility and nurturance.

Dog The rich and universal symbolism linked to the dog derives from its long history of domestic association with human communities. Its ready willingness to bond with human individuals when removed from its own pack makes it a symbol of loyal affection and faithfulness. At the same time, its reputation for carnivorous scavenging means that in practically all mythologies it is associated with death (Anubis in Egypt, Cerberus in Greece, Garm in ancient Germany, Xolotl in ancient Mexico, T'ien k'uan in ancient China). It is in his capacity as guard dog that he serves, like Cerberus, as guardian of the entrance to the Underworld. The dog's reputation as 'corpse-eater' has put him in bad odour with Moslems, but among the Celts his capacity for hunting and warfare was highly prized: to attribute hound-like qualities to a warrior-hero was to do him great honour (Serpell, 1995; Woley, 1990).

The pleasure all dogs display in lying close to a fire causes them to be cast in a Promethean role in a number of different myths as the dog-hero who stole fire from the gods.

Elephant Like bulls, tortoises, and crocodiles, elephants are animals which hold up the world and carry the universe on their backs, particularly in India and Tibet. Their size, power, and intelligence render them sovereign among animals and they are consequently ridden, especially on ceremonial occasions, by kings and emperors. The Hindu elephant god Ganesha symbolizes knowledge and intelligence.

Goat The lewd vitality and omnivorous appetite of the billy-goat make him the epitome of male lubricity and greed, and, as a consequence, he is cast in the role of **scapegoat** and looked down upon by Judaeo-Christianity as an attribute of Satan. The nanny-goat, on the other hand, has a more savoury reputation as representing maternal fecundity and nurturance. She is sacred to the Dictean Zeus, who as an infant was suckled by the goat Amalthea (her skin became the AEGIS, protector and preserver; and her horn the CORNUCOPIA, symbol of abundance and plenty). The wild goat is sacred to both Artemis and Dionysus, while Pan has the legs, horns, and beard of a goat. As often happens when one religion gives way to another, the gods sacred to the old religion are demonized and taken over by the new. Thus, the Christian Devil bears all the goat-like features of the Greek nature god Pan.

The association of the goat with the tragic art form (tragedy literally means 'goat song' in Greek) is probably due to the fact that all domestic goats must die prematurely to provide nourishment for their masters, and bleat plaintively as they are led off to slaughter.

Horse This splendid creature has been so crucial to the development of all civilizations, and to the conflicts generated between them, that it is not surprising it has come to be so loaded with anthropomorphic symbolism. Dazzling white horses have been particularly prized, both for monarchs to ride on and for gods in their chariots to drive before them across the skies. Not only kings and gods but messiahs and prophets are similarly mounted, and it is on a white horse that the Prophet Mohammed will ride at his second coming. On the pediment of the Parthenon, majestic horse draw the chariots of the sun and the moon.

Horse symbolism is not confined to the celestial realm, however: it extends to the Earth, the Underworld, and the sea. The horses that Poseidon lashes up out of the waves are the cosmic forces that surge out of the primordial chaos of the abyss. The taming and harnessing of these powers to man's will is an allegory of civilization itself – the triumph of disciplined intelligence and strength of purpose over the forces of nature. That heroic knights like St George ride a charger when they do battle with the dragon lends further stress to this allegorical implication. Similarly, the powerful steed who gallops across the countryside entirely subject to the horseman's guidance and will is a symbolic expression of the mastery that the ego (and the dominant left cerebral hemisphere) exerts over the instinctual energies of reptilian and mammalian components of the brain-mind in the service of cultural goals and objectives. In many parts of the ancient civilized world, HORSE SACRIFICE came to replace bull sacrifice as the most noble of all sacrifices.

Black horses herald death and are widely considered appropriate for funerals, carrying souls to the Underworld. Horses can thus have a sinister or catastrophic quality, as when the first of four seals of the Book of Revelation is broken and the four horsemen of the Apocalypse appear riding four horses symbolizing war, famine, pestilence, and death.

Lamb An enchanting manifestation of the regenerative power of spring, symbolizing innocence, purity, and new life. Because it is so prized, the lamb has been the main sacrificial victim throughout the monotheistic world. Performed at Easter, it represents the sacrificial death and resurrection of Christ. 'Behold the lamb of God, which taketh away the sins of the world,' exclaims St John the Baptist at first sight of Jesus (John 1:29).

The central importance of lamb symbolism in Christianity is apparent in the Book of Revelation where the Lamb stands in glory on Mount Zion in the centre of the Heavenly Jerusalem. The lamb is depicted on a hill with four streams, signifying the Church with the four Gospels and the four rivers of Paradise. The Apocalyptic lamb, carrying the book and seven seals, is Christ as Judge at the second coming: that it has seven horns and seven eyes denotes the seven gifts of the spirit. As the Good Shepherd, Christ cares for his flock and rescues the lost lamb that has gone astray. Such symbolism is particularly meaningful to a nomadic or agrarian people.

Ox Although sharing to some extent in the symbolism of the bull, the castrated status of the ox deprives it of the solar fertility symbolism and stresses its lunar implications as passive strength, natural power, and patient toil in the service of growth and regeneration. Throughout East Asia, the ox, and more especially the buffalo, are venerated as the most valuable assistants of man in his agricultural labours. On account of this value the ox is regarded in many places as sacred and is commonly offered as a sacrificial victim.

Pig The pig suffers a poor press all over the world as the epitome of selfish lust, uncleanliness, gluttony, and greed. The sow, however, on account of her fecundity, is associated with the Great Mother, and thus is a symbol of plenty.

Ram A symbol of masculine vigour and virility, associated with sun and sky gods (e.g. Zeus), and with the renewal of solar energy in spring – hence its place in the zodiac.

Reindeer To the people of the arctic regions of Eurasia, the reindeer carries much the same symbolism as does the horse among people living further south, especially in its funerary aspect as the psycho-pomp, carrying souls to the Underworld.

Sheep Unintelligent, passive, and gregarious, the sheep is a symbol of meekness and charity, the opposite of the wolf; it shares in the symbolism of the lamb, particularly its sacrificial value.

Air creatures

This subsection will examine the symbolism of birds, winged insects, and bats. The ability of **birds** to soar into the sky has made them a source of wonder and fascination to human beings since time immemorial. They are unmistakable messengers between Heaven and Earth and vehicles for the ascension of the immortal soul. As a consequence, angels have wings, as do shamans capable of 'spirit-flight', and cave paintings from Altamira and Lascaux showing bird-men may exemplify these. Their connection with heaven also makes birds a means of augury and divination through their appearance at certain times of day or certain seasons of the year, the direction of their flight, and on account of their song (the 'language of Heaven'). In ancient Egypt a dead person's soul was depicted by a bird with a man or woman's head, and *The Book of the Dead* describes the departed soul as a **falcon** on the wing.

On prehistoric monuments in both Europe and Asia, the Cosmic Tree is depicted with two birds in its branches. This is a common, indeed ubiquitous, symbol and it is known from surviving mythology that these birds represent human souls. Small birds represent the souls of children. By virtue of its inaccessibility at the top of trees, the BIRD'S NEST has been regarded as a symbol of Paradise which the soul can aspire to reach when it departs from the world and casts off the sins of the flesh.

Cock Associated with light, consciousness, and vigilance, because he watches for the first light of the dawn and because his crowing heralds the triumphant rebirth of the morning sun. Hence his station in the topmost branches of the Cosmic Tree, Yggdrasil (to warn the Norse gods when the giants are preparing to attack), and at the top of the weather vane surmounting church steeples (a symbol of the light and the resurrection of Christ).

Crane Because of its dramatic return in spring, a symbol of regeneration.

Cuckoo A popular bird on account of the welcome beauty of its song in spring, but its habit of depositing eggs in other birds' nests makes it a symbol of the 'free-rider', the lazy, parasitic trickster.

Dove Because of its billing and cooing, a symbol of love and conjugality. Its purity, simplicity, and whiteness make it a suitable vehicle for the Holy Spirit, and its delivery of the olive branch to Noah's Ark marks it as a bringer of peace and goodwill. The dove is also a symbol of the immortal soul ascending to Heaven.

Duck Ducks and drakes tend to keep together and swim in company, and consequently provide a symbol of marriage and conjugal felicity.

Eagle A symbol of ascension and spiritual aspiration. Its capacity for high flight and its affinity for mountain peaks makes it both the king of birds and a noble attribute of sky gods, Zeus being the primary example in our own cultural history. Its capacity to soar to the very highest place causes it to be a symbol of the zenith, the fifth cardinal point, and of the top of the World Axis. The Greeks told of eagles flying from the four corners of the earth to circle ceremoniously high above the omphalos at Delphi.

Its legendary opposition to the **serpent** represents the conflict between higher and lower, Heaven and Earth, light and darkness, good with evil. Its capacity to fly at all levels renders the eagle an obvious psychopomp capable of guiding the shaman's soul on its journeys up and down the Cosmic Tree. For this reason shamans in both Asia and America wear eagles' feathers.

The symbol of the double-headed eagle seems to have originated in the ancient civilizations of Asia Minor and to have spread to Europe via the crusades to be incorporated into the imperial arms of Austria and Russia. The doubling of a symbol has the effect of reinforcing its power. Although the double-headed eagle provides an example of how an ancient symbol can be transmitted from one culture to another to survive in modern times, it is nevertheless archetypally based: the universal, archetypal equation of the eagle with elevated status, power, and sovereignty persists across all ages and many geographical locations.

Falcon Like the eagle a symbol of ascension, the falcon is widely associated with the solar principle. An attribute of the Egyptian god Ra, the falcon symbolized the rising sun, while the falcon-headed god Horus had both lunar and solar connotations, one eye representing the sun and the other the moon. Generally, however, the falcon represents the triumph of the bright, male, solar principle over the dark, lunar, female principle.

Heron Like the eagle, ibis, and stork, the heron is a serpent-killer, and therefore committed to the battle between good and evil, light and darkness. The capacity of these birds to stand stock still for hours on one leg makes them the epitome of patient contemplation.

Ibis An incarnation of the Egyptian god Thoth, the patron of scribes, healers, and astronomers. It shares in the symbolism of the heron.

Kite A high-flyer with keen eyesight attributed with divinatory powers, the kite was sacred to Apollo and its flight was considered rich in omens.

Lark A symbol of ascent and descent and of passage from Earth to Heaven and from Heaven to Earth. On account of its delightful song, generally considered to be a happy bird of good omen.

Macaw Widely accepted as a symbol of fire and solar energy throughout equatorial and tropical America, presumably on account of its long red feathers.

Magpie Generally considered a gossip and a thief, it has been despised by Christians as doing the work of the Devil. According to legend, its black and white colouring is due to its refusal to go into mourning at the Crucifixion and because it declined to enter Noah's Ark. Magpies were sacrificed to Dionysus/Bacchus to assist wine in loosening tongues and promoting conviviality.

Owl A nocturnal bird, sacred to Athena and attributed with wisdom, the owl symbolizes introverted and reflective (lunar) consciousness in contrast to the eagle's extraverted and direct (solar) consciousness. In civilizations as far apart as Egypt and pre-Columbian America, the owl has been associated with darkness, coldness, and death.

Peacock Not surprisingly the symbolism of the peacock has all to do with the magnificence of its tail, which is by some attributed to vanity, but by others to the sun and to the heavens, its spread resembling a sun wheel and its 'eyes' the stars in the sky. It is thus an attribute of sun and sky gods (e.g. Zeus) and of royalty (the Kings of Burma).

Pelican A symbol of parental love and the charity of Christ on account of its legendary habit of feeding its young with blood pecked from its own breast. As a water bird it also represents the 'moist humour' which the ancients believed disappeared during the heat of summer to return with winter. This strengthened the identitification of the pelican with the body of Christ (*corpus Christi*) which spurted water and blood when pierced by the soldier's lance, and which disappeared from the tomb to return with the Resurrection.

Raven The raven enjoys a positive image in East Asia as a messenger of the gods, in Africa as a guardian spirit, in North America as a culture-hero, in Greece as an associate of Apollo, and it was a raven that fed Elijah in the desert. But in Europe and in India its reputation is entirely negative, being a messenger of ill-omen and death.

Stork Like all birds which stand patiently at the waterside, the stork is a symbol of contemplation and longevity. In addition, it affords an example of domestic peace and harmony, because it always returns to its nest at night, as well as exemplifying filial piety because it was believed to take care of its parents when they grew old. The striking mating dance of the stork marked it as a bird of fertility, capable of making women pregnant at a glance and of delivering babies.

Swallow Of all birds the one most linked with the cycle of the year and the coming of spring, fertility, and new life. Its restless industry, building its nest, feeding its insatiable young, represents diligence.

Swan Combining the elements of air and water, the swan has both solar and lunar implications. Sacred to Aphrodite and Apollo it is the form in which Zeus pursues and makes love to Leda, as well as to Nemesis when she has turned into a goose. In the Western tradition the swan thus indicates amorousness and the poetic celebration of love. In India, the swan is the divine bird that laid the Cosmic Egg on the primordial waters from which Brahma hatched. The tragic song of the swan on the brink of death is reminiscent of deathbed last words and of Christ's final exclamation on the Cross.

Vulture A scavenger and carrion-eater with a tactless tendency to wait about in close proximity to its next meal, willing it to die. It is, therefore, associated with death and disposal of the dying. Parsees place their dead on specially constructed towers for vultures to devour them, believing this facilitates rebirth. The Egyptians similarly conceived of the vulture as participating in the cycle of death and rebirth and considered it to be related to Mother Nature. Like the swan, kite, and raven, the vulture was sacred to Apollo and provided omens. Vultures indicated to Romulus and Remus the site on which to build Rome.

Woodpecker Its rhythmic drilling makes it a Freudian symbol of lust. It has the power to forecast the weather, as when announcing storms and summer rains in Greece by tapping the oak tree sacred to Zeus. It has maternal significance, building womb-like nests in tree trunks. It was a woodpecker that fed Romulus and Remus when their wolf foster-mother's milk was insufficient for their needs.

Of the **winged insects**, the most symbolically significant are the bee, butterfly, locust, mosquito, moth, and wasp.

Bee Like the ant, the bee is a symbol of self-discipline, social organization, and ceaseless toil But it is also productive: it collects nectar from sweet-scented flowers and converts it into honey, the immortal nourishment of the gods. The HIVE is a symbol of buzzing, well-organized, productive efficiency in which every individual performs his allocated task in selfless service of his queen. It is thus a symbol of a well-run, prosperous state, and the bee shares in the symbolism of the culture-hero who brings civilization and order through wisdom and example rather than force of arms.

Depicted on early Christian tombs bees were emblematic of everlasting life. This was presumably because they symbolized virtue rewarded and because during the three months of winter they disappear, like Christ who absented himself for three days after the Crucifixion. Their reappearance in spring is then equated with the Resurrection.

Butterfly A symbol of transformation and rebirth, the soul being freed from the body of its chrysalis. Having liberated itself to ascend in the air, it then lays its eggs, symbolizing the cycle of life, resurrection, and human reincarnation.

Locust A scourge laying bare vast tracts of land and, like the scorpion, an instrument of divine retribution: 'And there came out of the smoke locusts upon the earth: and unto them was given power, as the scorpions of the earth have power. And it was commanded them that they should not hurt the grass of the earth, neither any green thing, neither any tree; but only those men that have not the seal of God in their foreheads. And to them it was given that they should not kill them, but that they should be tormented five months: and their torment was as the torment of the scorpion, when he striketh a man. And in those days shall men seek death, and shall not find it; and shall desire to die, and death shall flee from them. And the shapes of the locusts were like unto horses prepared unto battle; and on their heads were as it were crowns like gold, and their faces were as the faces of men. And they had hair as the hair of women, and their teeth were as the teeth of lions. And they had breastplates, as it were breastplates of iron; and the sound of their wings was as the sound of chariots of many horses running to battle. And they had tails like unto scorpions, and there were stings in their tails: and their power was to hurt men five months.' (Revelation 9:3–10)

Mosquito A relentless predator that pursues its victims and sucks their blood, infecting them with fever. They breed from swamps and marshes, which are symbols of the unconscious, and the miasma that arose from them was thought to be as responsible as the mosquitoes for the plagues of malaria afflicting those who lived round them. The mosquito is thus a symbol of the feverish thoughts and painful emotions that may arise unheeded from the unconscious.

Moth In devotional literature, the moth fluttering round a lighted candle is a symbol of the soul seeking mystical union with the godhead, which is so powerfully numinous as to burn its wings.

Wasp Unlike the bee, the wasp carries negative connotations as a pest and an irritant. As an instrument of divine displeasure its role is minor in comparison with the scorpion or locust: 'hornets and wasps goad those sinners on the Dark Plain who had been neither good nor bad, and were outcasts of both Heaven and Hell', says Dante.

The only example of a **flying mammal** is the **bat**.

Bat A creature rich in symbolism on account of its biological peculiarities. Because it lives in caves – passageways to the Underworld – it is associated with death and immortality. Since it is both bird and mouse it carries the implications associated with monsters or fabulous beasts – as a winged dragon or devilish hermaphrodite. Its wings are worn by the denizens of Hell.

Because it can navigate accurately in the dark, it represents second sight, the capacity to 'see' with the 'third eye'. As it likes to hang upside-down, it takes an inverted view of the world, and is thus a symbol of sedition and wilful opposition to the *status quo*. Its enormous ears symbolize acuity of hearing and since it is the only flying creature to suckle its young it is a symbol of busy and diligent motherhood. Its rapid and unpredictable flight path makes it the embodiment of the uncertainty principle.

iv Monsters and Fabulous Beasts

Monsters are nightmare fossils still living in our minds. They relate us directly to our primeval origins, and they come out at night to threaten us in our dreams. They are hideous manifestations of the archetype of the huge-jawed, slavering, heavily clawed predator, capable of seeking us out wherever we hide. Their natural adversary, and our welcome ally, is the hero.

The story of a predatory dragon-serpent and its heroic destruction occurs in so many mythic traditions that it must have been one of the earliest dramas to excite the human imagination. Humbaba, the Babylonian monster, is slain by Gilgamesh and Enkidu; the Minotaur, who required a regular diet of seven youths and seven maidens, is destroyed by Theseus with the aid of Ariadne in the Labyrinth at Knossos; the great Python is overwhelmed by Apollo at Delphi; the

Medusa with her macabre coiffure of writhing serpents is killed by Perseus through divine assistance; while Cerberus, the guardian of Hades, a three-headed dog with snakes down his back, is indestructible and may only be placated with barley-mead cakes, yet Herakles manages to drag him away from the Gates of Hell.

How are we to understand these loathsome products of the human mind? Monsters may be conceived as evolutionary, neurological, and psychological constructs.

From the **evolutionary** standpoint, the struggle between the hero and the monster represents the actual struggle which occurred within the immensity of biological time between our ancestors and the dangerous predatory beasts with whom they were forced to compete for survival (Sagan, 1977). The evolution of intelligence and speech, together with our capacity to make and use weapons, provided us with the necessary 'magic powers' of the hero for our species to prevail.

From the **neurological** standpoint, monsters are a synthetic amalgam of the reptilian and palaeo-mammalian components of the brain. They are created through collusion between these ancient cerebral components and the powers of imaginative invention at work below the threshold of consciousness.

At the **psychological** level of analysis, the monster is the 'monster within' – the greedy, self-serving, destructive predator and rampant violator of innocents at the core of the shadow complex in Everyman. The Minotaur is the beast lurking in the labyrinth of men's minds, the symbolic precursor of the Freudian id which emerges in dreams: 'Then the Wild Beast in us,' wrote Plato in *The Republic*, 'full-fed with meat and drink, becomes rampant and shakes off sleep to go in quest of what will gratify its own instincts.' The monster is also a demonic personification of the terrible, destructive aspect of the Great Mother archetype, who devours her children and crunches up their bones rather than grant them freedom and independence. The hero's victory over the monster has to be accomplished anew in every generation, for this victory alone can guarantee the survival of civilization. The etymological derivation of the word monster is from the Latin *monstrum*, meaning a divine portent or warning, *monstro*, to show, *monstrator*, a teacher, and *demonstrator*, one who points things out.

The monster thus shows us our own destructive shadow and warns us how capable it is, given the opportunity, of devouring the finer aspects of the Self. It is a ghastly image of the vicious, unredeemed, and, perhaps unredeemable, part of the unconscious psyche.

Each culture and every generation breeds its own monsters and its own heroes to defeat them. In our culture it has been Christ's struggle with the Devil and his chthonic animal forms and familiars. Within this cultural context other monsters have emerged: Shakespeare's Caliban, the Marquis de Sade's debauchees in *The One Hundred and Twenty Days of Sodom*, Mary Shelley's monstrous creation in *Frankenstein*, Bram Stoker's *Dracula*, Hannibal Lecter in Thomas Harris's *The Silence of the Lambs* – all play on the archetypal keys of predation, fear, and heroic struggle, which are still as responsive in us as they were in our ancestors. Films like *Jurassic Park* and *Jaws* likewise play games with the monster-predator and his conquest.

It must not be forgotten, however, that there are positive fabulous beings as well as monsters – for example, Pegasus, the Griffin, and the Phoenix. These represent the *positive* shadow complex, that unlived, unconscious potential which can be highly creative for both the individual and the collective. Christianity, with its insistence on the importance of love, obedience, and the avoidance of sin, represented an attempt on the part of Western civilization to keep its collective shadow under control. Now that the Church has lost its moral authority, the danger becomes more acute that the monster in us will gain the upper

hand, and, with his post-nuclear apocalyptic powers, drive us to extinction. It therefore becomes a matter of psychological urgency to recognize and deal with the monsters in our minds, for this could be the critical issue for the survival of our species now and far into the future – always provided, of course, that the monster allows the future to occur (Cawson, 1995).

The creatures that follow are all powerfully disturbing examples of the kind of symbols humans can create out of their own atavistic propensities encoded in the reptilian and palaeo-mammalian components of their brains.

Basilisk A fabulous beast born of a yolkless egg laid by an aged cock (seven or fourteen years old) on a dung heap and hatched by a toad. Usually depicted as a cock with a three-pointed serpent's tail, a pointed head, gleaming eyes, and a three-pointed crown on its head, but sometimes represented merely as a serpent with cock's wings. An infernal creature, its threefold attributes are devilish inversions of the Holy Trinity. The basilisk is instantly fatal if one comes upon it suddenly and without warning, killing by the shock of its horrendous appearance or by means of its poisonous breath. It is thus symbolic of the terrible dangers that lurk in wait for the unwary and a warning to remain consciously alert when getting oneself into potentially damaging situations. As with the Gorgon, the only way to eliminate a basilisk is to use a mirror; the mere act of reflecting on its own nature is sufficient to destroy it. The basilisk is also an image of destructive unconscious potential, a reptilian psychosis waiting to strike its unwary victim.

Bucentaur Whereas a centaur is half man and half horse, a bucentaur is half man and half bull. Like the centaur he represents the dual nature of humanity – a mixture of culture and biology, reason and instinct, a mind in the body of an animal. The conflict between these spiritual and biological poles is reflected in the struggle between Theseus and the Minotaur.

Centaur Like the bucentaur, these fabulous creatures with human head, arms, and torso and the body and legs of a horse, display humanity's instinctive nature and animal origins. Centaurs liked to eat raw meat and were incapable of consuming wine without getting drunk. The males were apt to rape mortal women. With the exception of Chiron, healer and friend of Herakles, a noble example of the species, centaurs epitomized the human capacity for lust, violence, and brutality when not subject to self-disciplined control in service of a higher cultural purpose.

The knight or horseman is a culturally advanced expression of the same idea: for whereas centaurs are ruled by their passions and instincts, the horseman trains, disciplines, and guides the same elemental forces that the horse, in all its strength and vitality, represents.

Cerberus The hideous son of unspeakable parents (Echidna and Typhon), this three-headed dog with a serpent's tail and snakes hissing all over his back was the Guardian of Hades, barring entry to the living and denying exit to the dead. As with the basilisk, the threefold nature of Cerberus is, like the trident of Poseidon, an infernal inversion of the Holy Trinity. Cerberus was the embodiment of Hell and the dread of death. Only heroes could get past him: Orpheus charmed him with his lyre, Psyche delighted him with honey cakes, and Herakles characteristically carted him off by brute force.

Chimera Another hideous child of Echidna and Typhon. This one has a lion's head, goat's body, and dragon's tail. The Gorgons were its sisters, and, like them, it could not be fought face to face. The hero who eventually conquered it was Bellerophon, mounted on the fabulous horse Pegasus.

Dragon Dragons are fabulous beasts compounded of elements taken from various dangerously predatory animals such as serpents, crocodiles, lions, and prehistoric creatures, especially dinosaurs. The dragon is commonly attributed with keen eyesight and our word dragon may be associated with the Greek *derkein* (seeing). As lethal guardians of treasure, they have to be defeated if the treasure is to be won (Hoult, 1990).

In the East, however, the dragon's role is creative rather than demonic. As the uroboric dragon biting its tail, it represents

cosmogonic powers slumbering in primordial chaos. The dragon still embodies this power which existed before the world began and which will continue to threaten creation for all time. Here we can see our own psychic origins (the R-complex) identified with the origins of the cosmos. In Japan, four dragon species were distinguished: celestial, rain, aquatic, and chthonian. Chevalier and Gheerbrant (1996) argue that these are four aspects of a single cosmogonic principle – the life force, demiurge, or First Cause – and they cite the six strokes of the hexagram in the *I Ching* as representing six stages in the manifestation of the hidden dragon (imminent potentiality) as it develops into the visible flying dragon incarnated in reality. In their manifest form, dragons are at home in air, earth, fire, and water: they generate lightning, thunder, and rain, and ensure fertility, order, and prosperity.

Echidna The monstrous wife of Typhon, she had a woman's body with a serpent's tail, and bore him a brood of horrors such as Cerberus, the Gorgons, the Nemean Lion, the Chimera, etc. With one of her sons, Orthrus (a dog with one less head than his brother Cerberus),

Echidna had an incestuous union which produced the Sphinx. She was also the mother of the remorseless vulture which daily visited Prometheus, chained helplessly to his rock, to devour his liver.

Erinyes Known to Romans as the FURIES, these hideous goddesses of retribution sprang from the earth where drops of blood had fallen from the castrated penis of Ouranos. Their principal function was to avenge parents against their undutiful children. If a man failed to avenge the murder of a member of his family, for example, then the Erinyes avenged the murder on him. This put Orestes in an intolerable position, for his father had been murdered by his mother: if he failed to kill her, the Erinyes would be after him, but if he did kill her, he would be guilty of matricide, and they would be after him again. When, in fact, he did act to avenge his father, the Erinyes hounded him into insanity. Like Nemesis, the Erinyes owed their origin to the ancient Greek belief in divinely inspired retributive justice, and were not regarded as unduly malign, for their dedication to the principle of retribution protected those who went unavenged by man-made laws, and thus preserved the good order of society. As a result, in Athens, they were known by the euphemistic term, the EUMENIDES, the Kindly Ones. This ambivalent quality is not unusual among chthonian deities (e.g. Persephone).

Erymanthian Boar A giant boar that lived on Mount Erymanthus in Arcadia. As his fourth labour Herakles was required to bring it back alive to Tiryns. He succeeded by trapping it in deep snow.

Gargoyle These fabulous monsters, so beloved of medieval stone-masons, function as waterspouts round the eaves of churches and cathedrals. Their association with rainwater points to their origin as chthonic beasts of fertility, now enslaved by the servants of God to act as guardians and to remind heretics and non-believers of the inevitable horrors of Hell.

Gorgons The Gorgons (Medusa, Euryale, and Stheno) are the three monstrous daughters of equally monstrous parents, Typhon and Echidna. With hairdos of hissing, writhing snakes, boars' tusks for teeth, blood-red tongues lolling from their mouths, brass hands, and golden wings, they were not a pretty sight; and, indeed, to look at them directly was to risk instant death from the shock. Of the three, only Medusa was mortal, and she was killed by Perseus, who guided his hand, and saved his skin, by viewing her in a mirror.

Griffin The griffin, or gryphon (from the Greek *grypos* = hooked or curved, as of a beak), is a fabulous animal: eagle before, lion behind, with a serpent's tail. Probably of Indian origin, it spread to Western Asia, where it was a common symbol on seals, dating from about 1500 BC, and reached Greece about a century later. On the whole, a beneficent guardian of treasure, being made up of two solar creatures (the eagle and the lion) and only one chthonic or infernal (the snake). The latter was, however, sufficient to bring condemnation from Christians, who viewed the griffin as an attribute of the Devil.

Harpies Birdlike female monsters, to whom Homer refers as 'Snatchers' (the meaning of their name) and held responsible for sudden disappearances that could not otherwise be explained. Known as the 'Hounds of Zeus' they moved with the suddenness and swiftness of storm winds. Like the Erinyes, their principal concern was with vice, guilt, and punishment – though the Harpies, if anything, were more vicious than the Erinyes and took a delight in provoking sin as well as punishing it.

Hydra A monstrous serpent with seven or nine heads which lived in the swamps of Lerna, it presented a major challenge to heroes because as fast as they cut off one head another one grew in its place. Herakles solved the problem by cauterizing each severed neck with a fiery brand. Interpretations of the Hydra's endlessly regenerating heads vary from the incorrigible vices of mankind to the difficulties that continue to arise whenever one embarks on a deliberate course of action.

Lamia A beautiful woman whose traumatic history turned her into a monster of jealousy. She was beloved of Zeus, but Hera got to know of it and drove her away, killing all her children. Lamia, finding refuge in a cave and driven mad with despair and fury, gives vent to her jealousy of other mothers by stealing their children and devouring them. Since she is a chronic insomniac, Zeus takes pity on her, granting her the ability to remove and replace her eyes at will: as a result, she is able to sleep, preferably when drunk, when she has taken out her eyes. Lamia is a frightening symbol of the jealousy of the childless woman.

Leviathan A Phoenician monster of primeval chaos, Leviathan was adopted by Judaeo-Christianity as God's enemy, evil personified. Represented as a giant serpent or crocodile with huge jaws as the 'Gates of Hell', Leviathan cannot be captured or made useful and the Bible specifies that he should not be roused: to stir him into activity could reactivate the forces of chaos with the consequent destruction of the world. Rabbinical texts predict, however, that the Messiah will catch Leviathan at the end of time and divide him among the faithful as an immense store of food. Sometimes represented as a world-encircling uroborus, Leviathan shares much of the symbolism of the sea-monster and the whale.

Lilith Adam's first (earthly) wife, who left him because she would not submit to him. Her name is derived from the Babylonian *Lilit*, a demoness who seduced men in their sleep. She teamed up with her male counterpart *Lilu*, as a succubus and incubus pair. Like Lamia, she is a Terrible Mother figure, who haunts pregnant mothers and kidnaps their children. Her own demonic children, the *lilim*, have the haunches of asses.

Melusina Daughter of the fairy Pressine, she imprisoned her father in a mountain in retribution for the ill-treatment he had given her mother. For this, she was herself turned into a periodic hybrid: every Saturday she became a snake from the waist down. The only way she could obtain release from this fate was to marry a man who had never seen her in this semi-serpentine form. Eventually she finds one and makes him rich so as to prepare him to be her husband. But his curiosity is roused as to what she gets up to on Saturdays, and he looks at her (the motif of 'fatal looking' again) in her bath. As a result she flees from him in serpent form. Later, she appears as a sea-nymph, a siren luring sailors to their doom.

Minotaur The fabulous monster with a man's body and a bull's head imprisoned within the Cretan Labyrinth. He required the Athenians to provide him with a diet of seven youths and seven maidens to be served up every one, three, or seven years. This appalling meal was provided on only three occasions, as on the fourth, Theseus, helped by Ariadne with her luminous crown and golden thread, slew him.

Monsters with animal heads and human bodies are more primitive and more unconscious than those fashioned the other way round, like the bucentaur or centaur. The Minotaur emphasizes the monstrous element in man capable of devouring and destroying his decent, altruistic, idealistic, spiritual, and humane capacities. Female lubricity is also involved, however, since the Minotaur is the offspring of Pasiphae, wife of King Minos, who coupled with a bull. The Minotaur is thus a direct expression of her own unnatural lust and sexual guilt.

Phoenix A fabulous bird which has variously been likened to the stork, eagle, heron, falcon, and the peacock. Its peculiar qualities – which are celebrated in different mythologies from all over the world

– are its extreme longevity and its capacity, at the end of its life, for auto-combustion and self-regeneration from the ashes. The Turks called it *kerkés*, the Persians *simurgh*, and the Taoists the cinnabar bird. In Egypt it was called *benu*, and was sacred to the sun god Ra, and related to the regeneration of life which occurred with the annual flooding of the Nile. The phoenix is sometimes connected with the salamander, another fire creature, and is also known as the 'plumed serpent'. It symbolizes destruction and regeneration, eternal youth and immortality; and it represents the capacity for self-renewal possessed by the human psyche.

Scylla A monster who devoured sailors passing through the Strait of Messina. Once a beautiful virgin, the sea god Glaucus fell in love with her. But Circe, in one of her fits of jealousy, transformed Scylla into a monster with six heads on six long necks. Scylla lurked in a lair opposite the whirlpool **Charybdis** and seized sailors from their boats as they passed through the Strait between Sicily and the Italian mainland. In this manner she ate six of Odysseus's crew.

Siren Sirens were sea-monsters which in the Eastern Mediterranean region were said to have the heads and breasts of women together with the bodies of birds, and in Northern Europe to have the bodies of fish. They sang beautifully and had lovely faces but were as evil and as destructive as the Harpies; they lured sailors into the sea and then devoured them. On his homeward journey, Odysseus had himself lashed to the mainmast of his ship so that he could resist the seductive power of their call. They symbolize the peril that unbridled passion can lead a man into.

Sphinx In Egypt, a crouching lion with a benign and enigmatic human face. The most famous example is on the edge of the desert at Giza where it is placed so that it may contemplate the rising sun. It is thought to be a symbol of royal authority, protecting the good and punishing the rebellious. The Assyrians, Hittites, and the Phoenicians had sphinxes with the bodies of winged lions or steers, while among the Greeks the sphinx was a winged lioness with a cruel human face. The monster that ravaged the land around Thebes was a sphinx who asked riddles of passing wayfarers and ate them alive if they could not give the right answer. She is the embodiment of the Terrible Mother and represents the power that heartless authority and blind fate can exercise over human life.

Typhon Yet another hideous product of Hera's jealous rage. Because Zeus produced his beloved daughter Athena from the top of his head without any assistance from his wife, Hera decided to get her own back by spawning a monstrous opponent of Athena. The result of her efforts was Typhon, a gigantic horror, half human and half animal with wings, covered in vipers from the waist down, who possessed a hundred dragons' heads instead of fingers, and eyes which spat fire. When he attacked Olympus, the gods were so terrified that they fled to Egypt; only Zeus and Athena remained to fight him. After a terrific battle Zeus succeeded in destroying him with a thunderbolt near Mount Etna, but Typhon continues to spit fire from the volcano to this day. He symbolizes the evil that brute stupidity can achieve in the service of a destructive 'reptilian' passion.

Unicorn A fabulous horse with a single horn sprouting from the middle of his forehead. Since no such beast exists in nature, its ubiquitous appearance in myth and legend is surprising and demonstrates its psychological significance. The single horn is phallic, but because it sprouts from the head it is thought to represent sublimated sex and chastity. According to legend, the unicorn cannot be captured or tamed except by a virgin, whom he will instantly approach in order to lay his horned head in her lap. In Christian iconography this image refers to the Virgin Mary's Immaculate Conception.

Uraeus The terrible sacred cobra which rears up on the heads of gods and kings, hood erect and with the burning eye of Ra, the Egyptian god; it spits fire and destroys all those who oppose the wearer.

v Plants, Fruits, and Trees

To view the plant world as something inanimate and apart from ourselves is a wholly modern aberration that our ancestors would have found incomprehensible. So indispensable a role did trees, fruits, berries, and flowers play in their world view and their survival that the qualities symbolically attributed to them were of a commensurate significance.

The **tree**, for example, holds a central place in the symbolic canon of peoples from all over the world. This fact cannot be unconnected with our long phylogenetic association with trees and a primordial awareness that they are living embodiments of cosmic powers whose life-cycle long outstretches our own, by as many as ten human generations in some cases. That trees can grow to great size, their branches reaching up into the heavens, their roots plunging deep into the earth, implicates them in the symbolism of levels as well as the cycles of generation and regeneration which are the essence of organic life. That they have always been climbed for their fruits and their value as look-out points makes trees obvious symbols of aspiration, development, growth, and consciousness. As with so many other symbols, specialized meanings have been superimposed on the basic symbolism of trees, and these attributes are described in this and other sections of the Thesaurus. The basic symbolic meanings are summarized here:

The symbolism of ascent and descent is associated with the tree's three primary components: foliage (upper world, Heaven, realm of the sky gods and birds); trunk (middle world, Earth, realm of earth goddesses, humans, and animals); roots (underworld, Hell, realm of spirits, demons, devils, monsters, and snakes). As a means of ascent and descent, the tree resembles other symbols, such as the hill, mountain, ladder, and staircase.

The symbolism of centrality In the savannah, individual trees are distinctive landmarks, places for gathering in the shade for meetings, councils of war, story-telling, recital of myths, and religious rituals. Commonly, one special tree may come to hold central importance in the territory of a group, so that the community becomes identified with it. Hence the symbolism of the Cosmic Tree as embodiment of the World Axis, the central point of the cosmos round which all existence revolves. It was often an especially majestic species: for Nordic peoples it was Yggdrasil, the ever-verdant World Ash, for Celts it was the oak, for the peoples of Eastern Islam the olive, for Germans the lime, and in Siberia the larch and the birch. The axial symbolism is also apparent in the centre pole of a Voodoo shrine or a Sioux medicine lodge (round which the sun dance is performed) and the shaman's post in a Siberian yurt. The central symbolism of the *axis mundi* is invariably associated with the symbolism of ascent and descent, since the World Tree is the central bridge or pathway connecting the three cosmic levels of Heaven, Earth, and Underworld.

The symbolism of life, death, and resurrection Deciduous trees, with their annual cycle of death and renewal of foliage, symbolize the triumph of life over death, while evergreen conifers are symbols of immortality (hence, the Djed Pillar, made of pine wood, sacred to Osiris; the wooden herms which marked graves in classical antiquity; and the cypress and yew trees in churchyards. The World Tree is also the Tree of Life at the centre of the Garden of Eden (its twelve fruits symbolizing the cycle of the year, rebirth, and the Heavenly Jerusalem), the Tree of the Golden Apples (guarded by a serpent) in the Garden of the Hesperides, and the Bodhi-Tree under which the Buddha attained enlightenment (its roots representing Brahma, its trunk Shiva, and its branches Vishnu).

The symbol of individuation, the process by which 'everything becomes what it was destined to become from the beginning'. The acorn becomes the best oak tree it can become, given the circumstances influencing its growth – the climate, the soil, the presence of other trees competing for the same resources of water, nutrition, and light. If any of these resources is deficient, the mature tree may be distorted, stunted, or diseased. This is a striking metaphor of human development and human psychopathology.

The symbolism of duality The Tree of Life is compared with the Tree of Death or, in the Garden of Eden, with the Tree of Knowledge of Good and Evil (the *arbor philosophicum* of alchemy), and, at the East Gate of the Babylonian heaven, with the Tree of Truth. This symbolism relates to the dual nature of the Gemini, the two faces of Janus, etc. Moreover, the Tree of Life has bisexual or hermaphroditic associations, the trunk and rising sap symbolizing masculine creative powers, the foliage and seed-bearing fruits carrying feminine connotations. This is reflected in Latin nomenclature, where all words for trees have feminine gender and masculine endings. Such a *coniunctio* accords well with the unifying significance of the Cosmic Tree and its identity with the individuation process in which paired opposites (e.g. masculine and feminine) are transcended.

For an animal that rarely eats **flowers**, it is perhaps surprising that we attach so much value to them. However, their presence in a landscape indicates the existence of good soil and water and can, therefore, provide valuable clues as to good foraging sites. Although different flowers have assumed different nuances of meaning, generally the flower is a symbol of nature's bounty, the transitoriness of life and its delights. The ancient practice of scattering flower petals over the dead expresses this idea. The flower's structure in the form of a mandala has drawn it into the symbolism of the sun, the soul, the Self and the deity. In Eastern symbolism the lotus has been celebrated in this context; in the West, the rose and the lily (*see below*). The allegorical use of flowers is very extensive – they appear as the attributes of spring, youth, the dawn, and of feminine virtue, beauty, and purity. As receptacles of dew and rain, they are worthy recipients of the gifts of Heaven. Plucking or crushing a flower is symbolical of rape (de-flowering). Paul Kugler (1982) has uncovered an archetypal complex of images and words centred on this theme. Some 'invariant or syncretic fantasy', he says, must lie behind the idea of flowers as female symbols and as symbols of violation. If we examine words like violet or carnation we are led inexorably to violence, rape, sex, bloodshed, and rebirth: *viol*-et → *viol*-ent → *viol*-ate; *carn*-ation → *carn*-al → *carn*-age → rein-*carn*-ation. Both sequences reveal the same complex of associations centring on a fantasy of flowers, defloration, and rape from entirely different routes. This phonemic linkage occurs not only in English but in German and French. In German *Blüten* means blossom, *Blüt* means blood, and *bluten* to bleed. In French *violette* is the bluish-purple flower, *viol* means rape, and *violer* means to violate.

If Jung's theory of archetypes and Kugler's linguistic deductions are both valid, then we would expect to find confirmation of this complex in mythology. It exists in the rape of Demeter's daughter, Persephone, by Hades. Persephone is picking violets, roses, and other flowers with the daughters of Okeanos. Gaia, the earth goddess, lures Persephone by showing her a beautiful flower she has never seen before, a rare narcissus. As Persephone reaches out to pick it, the earth opens violently to reveal Hades in his chariot galloping towards her. He seizes her and takes her back to the Underworld, a ravished bride. Eventually Zeus arranges a compromise between Hades and Demeter whereby Persephone comes to her mother in the upper world with the first growth of spring and returns to Hades in the Underworld in autumn once the seed has been sown. The myth therefore links the ideas of flowers, rape, the reproductive cycles of nature, death, and reincarnation.

Much **fruit symbolism** derives from the identification of its smooth, rounded, ripe form with the erotic appeal of the female body: apple cheeks, cherry lips, breasts like peaches, buttocks like melons, teeth like pomegranate seeds, etc. Ripe fruit entices: it is as if it wishes to be plucked, eaten, and digested, for then its progeny (the seeds containing its genes) will pass through the alimentary tract to be eliminated and deposited, healthy and intact, in well-fertilized soil.

As the gift of the fertility goddess, with her overflowing horn of plenty, it is hard to better fruit as a symbol of ripeness, abundance, and earthly pleasures. Because it contains seeds, fruit is a symbolic equivalent of the World Egg, the origin of all creation and all potentiality. In the ancestral environment, fruit would have been much prized as a source of sweetness and nourishing moisture.

If the growing tree is a symbol of the individuation process, then fruit represents its culmination: 'By their fruits ye shall know them.' The forbidden fruit in Paradise, which occurs in myths other than the Judaeo-Christian, symbolizes the temptation to sin, to defy authority, and to fulfil one's heart's desires. The fruit of the Tree of Knowledge is awareness of Good and Evil; the fruit of the Tree of Life is immortality: in Egypt the immortal fruit was the fig or date; in China, the peach. Whatever the fruit and whatever it may symbolize, it is the actual eating that results in transition: Snow White falls into a coma, Adam and Eve are expelled, Persephone is committed for one third of every year to Hades.

The symbolism associated with individual trees, shrubs, fruits, seeds, nuts, and plants is presented alphabetically below.

Acorn The knowledge that 'great trees from little acorns grow', makes this a supreme symbol of maturation, growth, and individuation, as well as providing a model for psychopathology. On the religious plane, the acorn represents the human capacity for spiritual development: it is depicted on the capitals of columns, in coats of arms, and is placed at the end of the red cords of a cardinal's hat. The acorn also carries sexual symbolism, the tip protruding from the cup resembling the glans of the penis, and the child emerging from the mother's womb.

Almond Like all nuts concealed within their husk, the almond symbolizes the secret or special substance hidden within, such as the divine nature concealed within the human 'husk' of Jesus. The Italian for almond, *mandorla*, is the term used for the golden oval shape enclosing the figures of Christ, the Virgin, and the saints in traditional Christian iconography.

Almond tree A sign of the rebirth of nature, since this is one of the first trees to flower in spring. As its blossom is susceptible to late frosts and can quickly fade, it is also a symbol of transience.

Anemone A symbol of transience; the flower identified with Adonis, who was transformed into an anemone by Aphrodite. The anemone has been identified with the 'lily of the fields' celebrated in the Bible. Palestine possessed no white lilies, but the anemone was widely distributed there. 'And why take ye thought for raiment? Consider the lilies of the field, how they grow; they toil not, neither do they spin: And yet I say unto you, That even Solomon in all his glory was not arrayed like one of these' (Matthew 6:28–9).

Apple Embodies the ideas of sensuality, fertility, ripe sexuality, and physical desire. The Golden Apples of the Hesperides (the three daughters of Evening) grew on the tree which had been given as a wedding present to Hera by Gaia to endow her womb with fruitfulness. Eve Jackson (1996) has drawn our attention to the term 'apple' as not being botanically specific. In Greek, and in some modern European languages, it is a generic term which can be applied to a variety of round fruits. Aphrodite's apple may have been a quince. Jewish authorities maintain that the forbidden fruit in the Garden of Eden was a fig. The Biblical 'apple' is a translation of the Latin word *malum*, which means both apple and evil. The image of the forbidden apple that tempts and results in evil is repeated in fairy tales of the poisoned apple, which looks delicious but results in death. The forbidden fruit, like the poisoned fruit, has an irresistible appeal: the one is offered by the Tyrannical Patriarch, the other by the Terrible Mother (step-mother/witch). To remain in thrall to either parent is to remain unconscious, undeveloped, and unrealized, still lost in the uroborus of potential existence. When transected, the core of the apple resembles a five-pointed star or pentagram, a symbol of spirituality, suggesting the embodiment of the spirit in the flesh.

Arbutus An evergreen shrub associated with immortality.

Ash Sacred to Scandinavian and Germanic peoples as the World Tree, Yggdrasil, eternally green and drawing its powers of life and regeneration from the spring Urd, in which it had its roots. Just as the Greek gods assembled on Mount Olympus to administer justice, so the Germanic gods assembled at the foot of Yggdrasil.

Asphodel A member of the lily family, possessing hermaphroditic flowers, it was dedicated to Hades and Persephone and was regarded as a flower of death and the underworld.

Birch Sacred to Siberian peoples as their World Tree. It is of particular importance in shamanic initiation ceremonies and healing practices.

Box-wood Because its wood is hard and close grained and its leaves are evergreen, it is a symbol of perseverance, eternity, and immortality. In classical times it was sacred to both Hades and Cybele. It is thought that all evergreen trees were at some time sacred to Aphrodite, since green was a colour specifically attributed to her.

Cherry Its beautiful, swiftly fading blossom makes it a symbol of rebirth, regeneration, and the transience of life.

Chrysanthemum Its petals arranged in expanding rays about its stamen make this flower a solar symbol associated with notions of longevity and immortality. An autumn flower, it celebrates the full achievement of summer which must soon give way to the cold hand of winter.

Cypress Its longevity, evergreen leaves, and incorruptible resin, have made this tree a symbol of immortality and resurrection as well as identifying it with the Tree of Life. In antiquity it was sacred to Hades, god of the Underworld, and for this reason it was planted, as it still is, in graveyards. Its sweet smell has been identified with the 'odour of sanctity'.

Fig Together with the olive and the vine a symbol of plenty. In East Asia, the imposing *Ficus benghalensis*, or banyan tree, is the everlasting fig tree of the Upanishads and *Bhagavad Gita*, the *axis mundi* linking Earth to Heaven.

First fruits The ancient ritual practice of sacrificing the first fruits to the gods was evidently designed to placate them and to encourage them to guarantee greater abundance in the months to come.

Garlic Because of its powerful and, to many, unpleasant smell, garlic is commonly believed to act as a defence against evil influences and danger. It is thus used as a specific against vampires, serpents, and the evil eye.

Hazel A tree of fertility traditionally associated with sexuality and childbirth. Dowsers of precious metals have always used hazel wands, presumably because metals were believed to develop like embryos in the womb of Mother Earth.

Ivy Another evergreen plant symbolizing the eternal cycle of the natural life, death, and rebirth; sacred to Dionysus as well as to Attis, beloved of Cybele, goddess of the earth.

Larch Like all conifers, a symbol of immortality.

Liana A climbing plant which twines round the trunk of a tree, it is a symbol of love: in India, the liana is Parvati and the tree Shiva in the form of the lingam. Like all entwining creepers it relates to the symbolism of the spiral.

Lily Because of its whiteness it symbolizes purity, innocence, and virginity.

Lotus The tight bud thrusting its way up through the murky depths to open out into a beautiful mandala floating on the surface of the water not only makes this flower a worthy symbol of individuation but also an allegory of the creation of the world. The Egyptians regarded the lotus as the holiest of the flowers, while the Hindus compared the opening of the bud to the hatching of the World Egg and saw it as a symbol of cosmic harmony. Vishnu is depicted sleeping on the surface of the primordial ocean, a lotus growing from his navel, containing within its bloom the sitting figure of Brahma. Thus the lotus expresses the cosmic process itself: 'The water represents the unmanifest, seeds, hidden powers; the floral symbol represents manifestation, the creation of the universe. Varuna, as god of water, rain and fertility, was originally the root of the Tree of Life, the source of all creation' (Eliade, 1958). In addition, the lotus carries erotic meaning throughout the Far East, being compared to a vulva endowed with powers of life-giving and life-regeneration. The most flattering name for a Chinese courtesan was Golden Lotus.

Mandrake A term applied to the root of the MANDRAGON or MANDRAGORA plant, which, according to popular legend, grew beneath gallows trees from the semen of hanged men. Its root is commonly forked, giving it a human appearance. Since antiquity, it has found various uses as a charm, narcotic, and aphrodisiac.

Mushroom A symbol of longevity, particularly in China, presumably because mushrooms keep for a long time when they are dried.

Olive tree Because it bears fruit in arid ground it is of great symbolic importance in countries bordering on the Mediterranean Basin. Sacred to Athena, it was symbolic of intellect and knowledge as well as light, its oil being used in lamps. The cleansing power of olive oil was used in purification rituals connected with the Eleusinian Mysteries, and, because of its value, sacrificial oil libations were poured on to altar stones, usually in supplication of fertility. Since it lives to a great age and its leaves are evergreen, the olive is a symbol of longevity and immortality. Because of the calming influence of its oil, the olive is a symbol of peace and reconciliation, as in the olive branch which the dove brought back to Noah at the end of the Flood. In Islam, the olive is the World Axis, a symbol of the prophet, and the Universal Man.

Orchid Having testicle-shaped bulb roots (*orchis* in Greek means testis), the orchid has been considered both an aphrodisiac and a fertility symbol. Satyrs liked them and they were used in love spells.

Palm tree This symbolism refers mainly to the date palm which grows to more than twenty metres in height, has a powerful but supple trunk resistant to the most powerful gales, and can live to be more than 300 years old. In Babylon and Egypt it carried the symbolic significance of the Tree of Life and provided the model for the shape and decoration of architectural columns. Palm branches are widely regarded as symbolic of ascension, regeneration, immortality, and victory. The palms carried on Palm Sunday as well as those borne by Christian martyrs refer to the Resurrection of Christ.

Peach Because of its shape, colour, and texture, the fruit shares much of the female symbolism of the apple. As the tree flowers early in the year, it is a symbol of spring, regeneration, and immortality.

Pear Because of its shape, sweet taste, and juiciness, it embodies erotic female symbolism similar to that of the apple and peach.

Pine Because of its evergreen foliage and the incorruptible nature of its resin, it is, like other coniferous trees, a symbol of regeneration and immortality. Dionysus was often depicted holding a pine cone in his hand, indicating his lordship over nature. The pine was also sacred to the fertility goddess, Cybele. According to one legend, the pine was originally a nymph who changed herself into a tree in order to escape the unwelcome attentions of Pan.

Pomegranate Its symbolism is related to that of all fruit containing large numbers of seeds (e.g. the orange, lemon, melon, or gourd). It is symbolic of fertility, female generativity, and the archetypal potential of the Self. Like the apple, it also carries negative meanings in the sense that it may be poisoned and capable of inducing a deathlike sleep. When Hades gave a pomegranate seed to Persephone, it sealed her fate: she had to spend the winter of each year in the Under-world.

Rose The Western equivalent of the lotus, its mandala form representing the wholeness of creation, the perfection of the deity, and the individuation of the Self. For Christians, it refers to the chalice, the blood of Christ, the promise of redemption and resurrection, and the certainty of divine love. The rosette (the rose seen from above) and the rose window of medieval churches embody all this symbolism as well as incorporating the symbolism of the circle, the wheel, and the sun. For the ancients, the rose was a symbol of beauty and desire: it was sacred to Aphrodite, as well as to Dionysus, Helios, and Aurora. Aphrodite caused the red rose (some say the red anemone) to grow from the blood of her slain lover Adonis.

Snowdrop This welcome little flower appears at the end of winter and is a portent of spring: it is thus a symbol of hope, optimism, and good things to come. For Christians, an emblem of the Virgin Mary.

Sunflower or **Helianthus** Rich in solar symbolism because of the radiant configuration of its petals and because it turns its face to the sun through the course of the sun's daily journey. In Greece, it became a symbol of Clytie, who turned into a sunflower when her love was spurned by the sun god Apollo.

Sycamore In Egypt, the sycamore fig, which flourished on the banks of the Nile, was sacred to Nut, the sky goddess, and was the Egyptian

Tree of Life. The souls of the deceased were birds resting in its branches. The milky substance produced by its fruit also linked it to the cow goddess Hathor and to the many-breasted Artemis of Ephesus.

Tamarisk A hardy bush or small tree, somewhat pine-like in appearance, adopted as the Tree of Life in both Sumer and Egypt, and sacred to both Tammuz and Osiris. It was created in Heaven (like the date palm); it represents immortality, and manna exudes from its bark.

Thistle Like all spiky plants and THORNS generally, thistles symbolize protectiveness, 'prickliness', and the possibility of vengeance − as in the device of Scotland (whose emblem is the thistle): *Nemo me impune lacessit* (None touches me unharmed).

Vine Sacred to the 'dying gods' of fertility, who taught wine-making as well as agriculture (e.g. Osiris and Dionysus/Bacchus). Its symbolism thus pertains to both sacrifice and fecundity. 'I am the true vine,' said Christ, 'and my Father is the husbandman' (John 15:1). Being one of the first products of agriculture, the vine was also sacred to the Great Mother in her guise of 'Goddess of the Vines'. Identification of the vine with the Tree of Life is very ancient: the Sumerian sign for life was a vine leaf.

Willow Because of its weeping habitus, the willow evokes the symbolism of sadness, lost love, grief, and death. In antiquity it was a graveside tree and Odysseus noticed a willow and a black poplar at the entrance to Hades. However, the rapidity with which its branches grow back again when they are pruned makes the willow a symbol of eternal life. Moreover its beauty and the grace of its movements in the wind gives rise to feminine connotations and the possibility of miraculous birth, as does its association with the banks of rivers, lakes, and streams. So it is that Moses was found floating in a willow basket on the Nile. The symbolism of the willow is thus ambivalent: to the Prairie Indians it was a symbol of rebirth, while the Russians believed that to plant a willow was to dig one's own grave.

Yew tree A hardy evergreen which lives to a great age and produces poisonous berries; it is consequently considered a symbol of death and eternal life, and has been planted in graveyards since classical times.

SECTION 4

THE BODY

4

The Body

As the mobile conveyance on which our experience and personal identity is loaded, the body is the vehicle that carries us (and our genes) through life. The body is also our abode, a citadel in which – for the course of our tenancy until the lease runs out – we preserve our most precious treasure. Our physical form is the *embodi*ment of the Self, living proof that we exist, that we are some*body*. In addition to using the body as a highly evocative means of symbolic communication ('body language'), each part is invested with symbolic implications.

Though mind and body are indivisible, we nevertheless experience each as separate, and we feel that mind is primary because, through exercise of the conscious will, we can control the body, and, up to a point, make it do our bidding. Much of the time we are oddly unaware of it and, except when it is ill, in pain, or hungry, take it almost entirely for granted. Nevertheless, the body's infinitely complex systems go on functioning smoothly without our conscious participation or interference. Provided we service it regularly with food and drink, and keep it clean and warm, it gives remarkably little trouble – until it begins to wear out and malfunction in old age.

Despite this lack of conscious attention – or rather because of it – the body is a ready receptacle for psychological projections, and there is no part of it which has not over the millennia been loaded with symbolic meanings. As repository of the spirit, the body is imbued with spirit in all its parts, and this seems to have generated parallel symbolisms among peoples from widely differing traditions. This greatly impressed Richard Onians in compiling his *magnum opus*, *The Origins of European Thought* (1973): 'It is remarkable that, with slight variations in detail, the same basic conceptions of the body, the

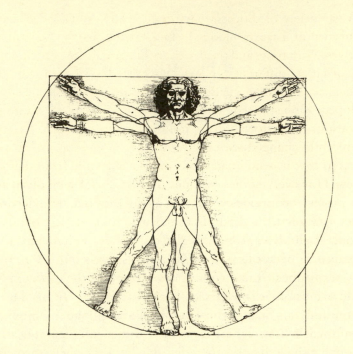

mind and the soul which can be traced in our earliest evidence for the Greeks and Romans and the Celtic, Slavonic, Germanic and other "Indo-European" peoples are to be seen also in early Egypt and Babylonia and among the Jews. Influence cannot be excluded; but the same phenomena probably led the early Semites, the "Indo-Europeans" and other peoples to the same conclusions.' Some of the most significant of these conclusions are summarized here.

i Adornment, Clothes, and Nudity

The symbolism of adornment and dress is extremely rich, for it is inextricably linked with the archetypal dominants of human behaviour – sexuality, status, warfare, religion, healing, etc. The use of covering made from leaves, animal skins, and fleeces to preserve body warmth must have been customary from the time of the earliest human migrations North and East out of Africa, and has been indispensable to the phenomenal capacity possessed by our species for adaptation to a vast variety of different environments, many of them hostile to the survival of a warm-blooded, thin-skinned, hairless mammal like ourselves. With time, and the discovery of agriculture and the development of cities, different types of garments began to assume social significance, defining gender, status, role, and age. The more developed, sophisticated, and organized the society, the more subtle and various the sartorial forms adopted. In our culture this trend has only recently changed with the prevalence of egalitarian, anti-sexist values, so that it is no longer easy to 'place' people from their mode of dress. However, clothes continue to carry social symbolism as well as to protect our modesty or provide us with warmth. In dreams, clothes symbolize the *persona*, namely, how we present ourselves to (or conceal ourselves from) the world.

Because the symbolism of dress is so important in human societies it has always been subject to rules and regulations. Some forms of dress are *de rigueur* on certain occasions or for certain functions (black at funerals, white at weddings, habits for riding, uniforms and warpaint for battle, vestments for praying or preaching, shorts for tennis or football, dresses and tiaras, white ties and tails for banquets, and so on) and for certain people (gowns and wigs for judges, ermine for lords and ladies, purple for bishops, dog-collars for vicars, three pips on the shoulder for a captain, two stripes on the arm for a corporal, etc.). Thus do we code ourselves and advertise our activities, so that others will know who we are and what we are about. Because these signals are so distinctive, and as a species we are so inventive, forms of dress and adornment are open to manipulation and abuse. This has always been of advantage to the unscrupulous and, in order to control potential impostors ('free-riders'), all societies apply sumptuary laws in one form or another. In the rigorously stratified society of medieval times it was a severely punishable offence to ape one's betters in dress or to assume sartorial affectations designed to elevate one's social position above the one allotted by the Almighty. Much of this has changed, though not perhaps as much as we may imagine, for the rigour of sumptuary law has been usurped by the tyranny of fashion. Moreover, our society is still intolerant of those who by their dress attempt to assume a role or status to which they are not entitled – e.g. wearing the uniform of a naval officer, a policeman, or a doctor (the white coat, the stethoscope, and the bleep), and in many countries it is still an offence to appear in public (except at times of carnival) dressed as a member of the opposite sex. All societies remain strict in proscribing the display of primary sexual characteristics in public, except in certain resorts, beach areas, nudist colonies, etc.

In non-equatorial climates, where some covering has to be worn all the time as a necessary preventive against hypothermia, clothes are prone to assume an erotic significance, deputizing for the sexual characteristics which they hide. Herein lies the secret of clothes FETISH-ISM, the silk underwear, suspender belt, and stockings as charged with erotic significance as the pudenda and limbs beneath them – more so in some cases. Young people, everywhere wishing to render themselves attractive to the opposite sex, make artful use of clothing to emphasize rather than conceal their sexuality, females stressing their breasts, hips, and legs, males their shoulders, buttocks and height. The see-through nightie and the codpiece are both blatant manifestations of this practice.

Disguise The use of veils, cloaks, hoods, and masks is to do the opposite of what clothes normally do and disguise one's gender, status, or role, so as to become liberated from socially prescribed functions and responsibilities. For this reason, these forms of dress carry a sinister connotation since they put the wearers outside the provisions of normal society and it is not possible to tell who they are or what they are up to. No good, is the common assumption.

Hairstyle This also reflects status or role: elaborate styles, particularly if they increase the height of the wearer, stress dominant status, while short hair (military recruits), the tonsure (monks), and the shaven head (criminals, concentration camp inmates) indicate lowly status. Haircutting is also an important aspect of initiation (puberty initiation rites, induction into religious orders, etc.).

Headgear and footwear These are particularly linked with status symbolism, the dominance–submission archetypal system, and with the fetishes and practices of sado-masochism, as the notions of 'high-ness' and 'lowness' are clearly implicated. All forms of dress which emphasize the head and the height of the wearer stress his or her dominant status, whilst modest headgear or bareheadedness is associated with the lowly status. Similarly, elaborate, handsome boots or shoes emphasize dominance, while poor, inadequate footwear and bare feet symbolize subdominance. Doffing one's headgear, pulling one's exposed forelock, licking the boots or washing the feet of a superior is an unmistakable sign of submission or obeisance.

Jewellery Jewels, in the form of rings, necklaces, bracelets, etc., are similarly symbols of dominant status, especially when worn on the head in the form of a tiara or crown.

Nudity To appear naked in a dream is to be stripped of one's persona characteristics and conventional social role and to be exposed as vulnerable, guileless, and 'as nature intended'. Nudity may be associated with shame and embarrassment or with feelings of being socially inept and inadequately prepared. The context is important: finding oneself naked at a public event gives rise to one set of responses; being naked in bed with a lover another. Why civilized society should insist that nudity be covered up in the name of decency is because the powerful urges it engenders cannot be readily controlled by will-power and can thus be a potent cause of social disruption.

This is not true of all cultures, however. Western attitudes to nudity are heavily influenced by the doctrine of Original Sin, the Fall of Adam and Eve, and their expulsion in shame from the Garden of Eden. Even so, medieval Christians made a distinction between *nuditas virtualis* (pure, innocent nudity) and *nuditas criminalis* (culpable, lascivious nudity). What frightened Christians were the deeply irrational passions that the nude figure could conjure up, releasing desires so powerful as to be beyond the control of the conscious mind. For this reason, nudity itself stands as an evocative image of sexuality, capable of creating the very passion that it symbolically represents.

Skin adornment This is also linked to the archetypes of sex, status, and initiation. The use of make-up to enhance sex appeal, especially by females, is common to most societies. Males use it as a preparation for battle (in the form of warpaint). This use is by no means confined to primitive warriors; modern soldiers still make copious use of it in the form of 'cam cream'. Various forms of tattooing, piercing, branding, scarification, ring insertion through ears, nose, and nipples, etc. have been associated with rites of initiation since time immemorial, and are still highly fashionable among the young of our own society (which no longer practises initiation). The occurrence of such symbolism in dreams is usually associated with the dreamer's need to be initiated into some role or to acquire status as a member of his or her peer group.

Uniform As the name implies, uniform stresses uniformity and identification with a specific group. Hence uniform is a symbol of initiation, or of having been initiated (e.g. as a soldier, a sailor, a monk, a nurse, or a nun). To wear a uniform, therefore, is to negate one's individuality and to assert one's conformity to an ideal or a role. Uniforms are also unmistakably linked to the two great archetypal systems: sexuality and dominance–submission. Until very recently, all uniforms were

gender specific – military uniforms masculine, nurses' uniforms feminine, etc. – and thus stood as a symbol for the sex of the wearer. As
a result uniforms can function as erotic fetishes and as enhancers of
sex appeal. In fact, military uniforms are specifically designed, either
consciously or unconsciously, to perform this function through their
emphasis on the shoulders (epaulets carrying insignia of rank, gold
braid), the head (peaked caps, helmets, plumed or otherwise, bearskins
to increase height), and the feet (heavy, brightly polished boots,
jackboots, riding boots with spurs). More than any other form of
dress, uniforms display status dominance, as well as sex appeal and
a prestigious social role, and this would explain why men have always
loved to dress up in them. The higher the rank the more splendid the
uniform, insignia, and accoutrements.

ii Parts of the Body

Ankle The part of the body to which Hermes' wings are attached.
Since the means of elevation are attached to the lowest part of the body,
this emphasizes the symbolism of ascension and also the possibility of
higher consciousness.

Arm A symbol of activity, power, aggression, and self-defence. The
multiple arms of some Indian gods (e.g. the four arms of Brahma and
Ganesha, and the numerous arms of the dancing Shiva) symbolize
their omnipresent power. To raise the arms in surrender is a gesture
both of submission and supplication: the defeated man renounces his
capacity for self-defence and puts himself at the mercy of the victor.
One arm is raised in greeting and in taking an oath. Outstretched
arms indicate readiness to give or receive affection.

Back That which is hidden, out of view, and therefore unconscious.
Since it is not readily accessible, the back has always been an area for
mutual grooming and consequently provides a means for mutual
exchange: 'You scratch my back, and I'll scratch yours.' It is a symbol
of strength in the sense that if a job has to be done one must put one's

back into it, though it may prove back-breaking. An upright man is one who has backbone, whereas a bent back is one that has been over-burdened and thus indicates lower status – possibly the result of having too many people on one's back.

Beard Symbol of mature manhood, courage, and wisdom. The sky gods of the Greeks, the one God of the Christians and Jews, as well as the Vedic god Indra, are all bearded. Semitic peoples attached particular importance to the beard. When two men greeted one another they grasped each other's beard and kissed it. In the Old Testament the beard is cut off or covered as a form of penance, mourning, or punishment. To shave off the beard of a captured enemy was to degrade him, and he would hide away in shame until it had grown again. Slaves were shaved to emphasize their servility. Facial hair can be formally regulated as part of a uniform – full beards for sailors, moustaches for soldiers, etc.

Blood The most precious life substance (life's blood); to give one's blood is the most significant sacrifice one can make. Wounds carry similar significance. Blood symbolism is closely associated with that of the colour red. Thus the Red Knight has come through war and sacrificed his blood in the service of the highest ideal. He has mastered his steed, destroyed the monster, and controlled men. The Holy Blood of Christ is symbolized by the red wine of the Eucharist.

Bone The enduring, 'indestructible' part of the human being; because it contains the marrow it embodies the essence of the person. Bones are also symbols of the dead and of the ancestors. The Biblical myth of Eve being fashioned out of Adam's rib means that she is the most precious part of him – 'Bone of my bones' (Genesis 2:23). Bones are particularly important in making spells: in some African tribes 'to point the bone' at someone ('boning') is tantamount to a sentence of death. The SKULL has special meaning as the seat of the departed person's soul. To drink from the skull of an enemy is to absorb his warlike power; to drink from the skull of a saint is to be healed and made holy. The **thigh** is a common euphemism for the phallus and thus symbolizes procreative power: the skull and crossed thigh-bones therefore represents the seat of the intellectual and generative powers of a dead person. Dionysus emerged from the thigh of Zeus.

Bowels Formerly considered to be the seat of the emotions – hence the 'bowels of compassion'. 'I beseech ye in the Bowels of Christ consider that ye may be wrong' (Cromwell).

Breast Because of their reproductive significance, full, well-shaped breasts carry a high erotic charge for male sexual responsiveness. Generally, breasts represent maternity, fertility, nurturance, comfort, consolation, and plenty. The act of taking an infant to the breast is ritualized into an adult gesture of comfort and attains religious funerary significance when the rite of burial is described as being taken to Abraham's Bosom, where there is 'no pain, suffering, nor sighs'.

Deformity Unfairly, deformity induces moral condemnation and even mockery for the 'sin' of nonconformity. The deformed are felt to be different, uncanny, sinister, and potentially dangerous or evil. There is, it seems, in all of us a deep-seated prejudice in favour of the ordinary: we do not like people to have less than the usual number of limbs, eyes, teeth, and so on and we are intolerant – not least in ourselves – of irregular or asymmetrical features. Those possessing such irregularities have to develop a strategy for compensating for them if their lives are not to be blighted by feelings of worthlessness and fears of rejection. Although prevailing social attitudes can increase suffering, they can also facilitate the development of a compensatory role. Thus, the blind have commonly been attributed with second sight, with possessing the clairvoyance of the seer; the deaf may be attributed with clairaudience, the mentally 'simple' may be thought especially loved of the gods, and the stammerer deemed capable of great eloquence. For some, the image of a person with an amputated limb can render him or her sexually desirable. This may have to do with a compensation for castration fears, may carry initiatory symbolism, or may indicate feelings of sexual inadequacy. But it can possess great erotic and symbolic power for those who experience it.

Eye As the organ through which we perceive light and the visual world, the eye symbolizes consciousness, intelligence, knowledge, and understanding ('*I see*'). The third eye is the eye of insight, clairvoyance, and superhuman or divine awareness. Eyes in profusion are linked with the symbolism of stars, celestial consciousness, and 'multiple luminosities'. A single eye, represented on its own, connotes divinity, the sun god Ra; the single eye can also represent primitive, destructive consciousness as in the case of the Cyclops. Staring eyes are experienced as a threat (as from a predator) or a put-down (as from a high-ranking superior). The staring eye is also the EVIL EYE, the eye that inflicts actual harm on the person it looks at. Defence against the evil eye can be derived from the use of amulets and protective gestures and signs. The eyes are the most expressive part of the face ('the windows of the soul') and consequently receive close attention during social interactions so as to read the mental and emotional state of the other person.

Whereas sight is equated with consciousness, BLINDNESS is symbolically associated with unconsciousness – our inability (or unwillingness) to see something: 'I don't see how ...' 'I can't see that.' 'There's none so blind as those who will not see'; they too readily become the 'blind who lead the blind', etc. However, perceptual blindness can be associated with clearer inner vision, as if one capacity may be exchanged for the other, as in the case of the Greek seer Tiresias, or the poet Milton. To be one-eyed like the Cyclops is to possess limited, narrow, one-track consciousness, while to have a third eye is to be intuitive, clairvoyant, possessing 'second sight'.

Face Because of the richly complex musculature surrounding our eyes and mouths and underlying the skin of our foreheads, we have the most expressive faces of all members of the animal kingdom. This anatomical equipment enables us to adopt expressions which symbolize our emotional and mental state, such as smiling when we are happy, frowning when annoyed, pulling back the lips to expose the canine teeth in a snarl when very angry, raising the eyebrows in surprise or in recognition of a friend, and so on. All these expressions transcend differences of language and culture and make it possible to achieve some degree of communication with foreigners without the use of words. To a certain extent, we also share them with our primate ancestors.

In line with our distinction of two basic archetypal modes of social interaction, the hedonic and agonic (p. 55), cross-cultural evidence indicates that certain facial expressions involved in these characteristic interactions, such as smiling, frowning, and disdain, are genetically determined. They first become apparent in sleeping infants in the REM (rapid eye movement 'dreaming') state. REM-state smiling, sometimes called 'smiling at the angels', can be observed in human infants before the development of social smiling in wakefulness. Similarly, complex expressions normally associated with anger, perplexity, and disdain also first appear in the REM state. These behaviours evidently rehearse and anticipate those social capacities which will appear in wakefulness some weeks later. Evidence such as this lends weight to the theory that the REM state plays a crucial role in the maturation of species-specific instinctual behaviour.

Fat All carnivores place high value on fat, not only relishing its taste but prizing it as a long-lasting form of concentrated energy, a form of nutritional credit to be banked in the adipose tissues against hard times of drought or famine. For most of our existence as a species, OBESITY has probably functioned as a status symbol, its significance being determined by cultural attitudes and by the availability of food. At times when food is scarce, 'fatness' symbolizes high social status, and human cultures still survive in which desirable women are too fat to stand up. In these cultures, 'thinness' symbolizes low resource-holding potential and, therefore, indicates low social standing.

In cultures where food is consistently abundant, however, low-ranking individuals can acquire sufficient resources to become as fat as persons of high rank, and 'fatness' loses its status appeal. As a result, the symbolism is reversed, and it becomes a symbol of high rank to be thin. When this reversal occurs, a new factor is introduced into the situation: to keep thin in the presence of abundant supplies demands the acquisition of self-control. This might help to explain why it is affluent families that place great store on diet, health, fitness, appearance, and self-presentation, and why the education of rich children is more demanding than that of poor children. The extreme dietary abstinence of young women with anorexia nervosa caricatures the world-denying asceticism which mystics have everywhere practised in the name of spiritual development. While such behaviour may be a compensation for feelings of low self-esteem, it also derives from the age-old dichotomy between the flesh and the spirit, and the belief that the one is the enemy of the other. For the anorexic, the body image is a replica of the self-image, and the obsession to refine the former is identical with the compulsion to enhance the latter. The symbolic conflict between the flesh and the spirit is as alive in the young of today as ever it was among the saintly mystics of the past.

Interesting Palaeolithic examples of fat symbolism are provided by the VENUS FIGURINES dating from the Ice Age, about 25,000 years ago. They are beautifully carved in stone, bone, or ivory, small enough to be readily portable, and display remarkable stylistic similarities across the vast geographical area, stretching from Russia to the Pyrenees, in which they have been found. The most striking thing about them is that they are usually very fat – as is the famous Venus of Willendorf – and represented as naked at a time of extreme cold. They have small heads and feet, large pendulous breasts, and enormously fat hips, buttocks, and abdomens. Whether they were Celtic representations of the Great Mother, erotic images cherished by men, gynaecological charms, or simply ornamental toys, is open to conjecture. Whatever their purpose, their wide distribution and preservation indicate that considerable value was placed on them and that they represented qualities perceived as highly desirable at the time – such as high status, female fecundity, sex appeal, and religious significance. The fact that many were originally painted red suggests the association between femininity, fertility, and blood, as when a contemporary Igbo woman, wishing to conceive a child, will rub her belly with ochre from a pregnant woman's doll.

Foot The lowest part of the body through which one is related to the ground (to fundamental reality). A single foot is phallic, as when fitting into a shoe. Kissing or washing someone's feet indicates reverence and self-abasement.

Hand and **Fingers** The human hand is a supreme evolutionary achievement which has made civilization possible: tool, utensil, and weapon-making; spear-throwing, shooting, cooking, ploughing, sewing, harvesting, butchering, building and so on – all depend on the advanced human capacity for 'manipulation' in the service of the dominant left cerebral hemisphere. The hand is also indispensable to social interactions such as hand-shaking, waving, gift-giving, gift-receiving, measuring, weighing, calculating, and counting (the metric system being based on the possession of ten fingers). It is through the hand, therefore, that the brain manifests its intentions (the word manifest, like the word manipulate, comes from *manus*, the Latin word for hand).

Because 90 per cent of every human population is right-handed, it follows that the left/right symbolism associated with this fact is universal (pp. 121–3).

Desmond Morris (1977) has estimated that we make 3,000 different gestures using our hands and fingers, and that does not include the stylized sign language used by the deaf. Many of the gestures we make as we talk are unconscious, but others are more deliberate and conventionalized – e.g. clenching the fist in anger, punching the air in victory, thumbs up for feeling good, thumbs down in condemnation or disapprobation, finger and thumb closed together in a circle to make a delicate point, turning the palm downwards towards the ground to induce calm, palm up and extended to implore or beg, shaking hands or touching palms in greeting, wagging the forefinger in admonition as if it were a small club, or pointing directly at

someone with stiff and steady forefinger as in the 'Kitchener needs YOU!' gesture. Such is the universality of the begging and hand-touching gestures that even chimpanzees use them.

Since the hand is supremely valuable to its owner, it, or part of it, is deemed a worthy object of sacrifice – as an act of propitiation, atonement, or punishment – on the *pars pro toto* principle. As Walter Burkert (1996) has shown, FINGER SACRIFICE is a worldwide phenomenon which makes its appearance at times of crisis, such as illness, ill fortune, or threatened catastrophe. It seems to be a generally accepted thing to do to placate the gods and buy off a hostile fate. The forms of self-mutilation common in 'borderline' patients, as well as the more drastic physical sacrifices sometimes made by psychotic people, may well have a similar underlying aetiology. One schizophrenic patient who walked into a crowded butcher's shop, picked up a cleaver and hacked off his arm, announced that his voices had told him it was a 'necessary sacrifice'. According to Pausanias, there was a sanctuary in Arcadia marked by a Finger Memorial carved in stone. Here, Orestes was said to have been driven mad by the Furies for the murder of his mother: he recovered his sanity by biting off one of his fingers.

A number of sanctuaries would accept symbolic substitutes for actual finger sacrifice – for example, the sacrifice of a ring, or a specially made finger carved in stone. In India, where finger sacrifice was forbidden by the British Imperial Government, a finger fashioned out of dough was acceptable. Similarly, cutting off or shooting off the index finger has been a modern sacrificial means of avoiding death on the battlefield. Biological analogies to finger sacrifice are a lizard relinquishing its tail to a predator's grasp, a spider sacrificing a leg, and the terror moult of a bird, leaving its attacker with a mouthful of feathers. Similarly, in wartime, a general, working on the *pars pro toto* principle, will sacrifice a portion of his army in the interests of some higher strategic purpose or in order to facilitate a withdrawal and preserve his army as a whole.

Though many gestures involving the fingers are universal, many are culturally relative. An example is the V-sign. In many countries this signifies 'victory', irrespective of the direction in which the palm is facing, and it carries no insulting or aggressive connotations. In

Britain, however, the V-sign means victory *only* if the palm is facing forward. If it is made with the back of the hand foremost, it means something quite different. When people are asked to explain the meaning and origin of this very insulting gesture, they suggest that it means 'up yours' and guess that it represents such things as a double phallus, a receptive vagina, open female legs, the female pubic triangle, and so on. In fact, the origin seems to have been historical. In 1415, before the Battle of Agincourt, the French declared that when they had won, they would cut off the bow fingers (the first and second fingers used to draw back the bowstring) of every surviving British bowman. Wisely, Henry V warned them of this threat before the battle began. When they had prevailed over the French, the victorious British bowmen derisively stuck their two fingers up, back of the hand foremost, in the faces of the defeated Frenchmen. That the gesture has survived so long after its original meaning had been forgotten is probably due to the essentially phallic suggestiveness of jerking the fingers upwards. Accordingly, the phallic middle finger gesture is one of the most ancient insults known to history and is found in a large number of countries. The ancients called it the 'infamous digit'.

Hair In all cultures, hair is both a private asset and a public symbol (Firth, 1973). A full head of hair symbolizes youthful vigour, sex appeal, and abundant vitality. In dreams, loss of hair symbolizes the loss of these things, or the fear of losing them. To shave one's head is to renounce them in the service of asceticism or of some high ideal (religious, military, etc.). To cut off someone's hair is to deprive him of power, as Delilah did to Samson. Golden hair refers to the sun and the sun gods, particularly Apollo. Grey hair indicates wisdom as well as ageing and the ending of life. In addition, hairstyles are indicators of age, sex, and social status. The way in which the hair is worn is not just a matter of individual preference but is subject to strong social, conventional, or peer group pressures.

As Desmond Morris (1977) and many others have pointed out, 'we are naked apes' in that we are differentiated from other animals by our lack of hair. As a result, people with an unusual amount of hair are commonly attributed wild or feral qualities. Hence the Biblical distinction between Esau, who was a rough and hairy man, and Jacob, who was in all senses a smooth man. 'A hairy body and arms stiff with bristles, give promise of a manly soul' (Juvenal, *Satires*, ii, 11).

Deliberate shaving or close cropping of the head usually has a ritual or initiatory quality, marking the transition from one social state and one identity to another, as when a young man gives up his civil status to become a soldier or a monk, or a young woman becomes a nun. As various commentators have suggested, the shaved head carries both the appearance of a death's head, as well as that of a new-born infant. This serves to heighten the initiatory symbolism of head-shearing since it strengthens the implications of death and rebirth. Shaving the pate as a matter of personal choice can be used as a *demarcation sign* as by skinheads, punk rockers, etc. At many periods, women have cut their hair short either to demonstrate equality with men or as a gesture of repudiation of the traditional female role.

Generally, hair-loss or head-shaving represents loss, renunciation, subordination, and a lowering of status, as when a monk takes vows of obedience, chastity, and poverty. The tonsure probably originated in the Babylonian custom of shaving part of the head of slaves.

As with fingers, hair can be used in accordance with the *pars pro toto* principle, for it can represent the 'macrocosmic' individual in microcosm, so to speak. Thus, a lock of hair from the beloved can render her symbolically present when she is absent; hair can also be used for magical or therapeutic procedures directed at its owner.

Head The head is the seat of the spirit, the quintessence of the individual, his or her power, intellect, and virtue. As a sphere it represents the world in microcosm and is the symbol of the total personality, hence the importance of head-hunting (annexing the power and heroic virtue of the warrior from whom the head has been taken), and the significance of decapitation (depriving the victim of his spirit forever).

All mythologies have many-headed animals, men, and gods. Janus, the Roman god with two faces, was the Guardian of the Gate, separating the sacred from the profane. He watched over both entrances and exits, and was the deity presiding over the beginning and ending of things. Creatures with three heads may symbolize the three stages of life (as in Titian's self-portrait in the National Gallery in London), the three cosmic levels (Heaven, Earth, and the Underworld), the Trinity or its infernal inversion (as in Cerberus, the three-headed dog guarding the Gates of Hell). Four heads share in the symbolism of the tetramorph (as in the four-headed image of Brahma).

Gestures with the head, such as shaking it to indicate a 'No' and nodding to indicate 'Yes', are ritualizations of innate prospensities, and not, as was once thought, purely the result of learning and mimicry. Head shaking is a ritualization of the movements babies make when they reject the breast, having fed and consumed enough. They either turn the face away to the side or tilt it upwards and backwards away from the nipple. Sated infants make similar rejecting movements when parents try to spoon-feed them. In most cultures people signify negation by shaking their heads from side to side, but in Greece 'No' is conveyed by an upward toss of the head – as it is, indeed, in Naples, which the Greeks colonized 2,500 years ago. This is an intriguing example of how an innate pattern of response can be subjected to cultural influences and become a conventional sign. Moreover, on progressing northwards from Naples towards Rome, an invisible frontier is reached where people no longer toss their heads in negation but shake them from side to side. This is at the Massico mountain range, and it happens to be the northernmost point of ancient Greek penetration!

Nodding the head in affirmation is a universal gesture: it was observed on first contact with remote tribes such as the Aborigines of Australia and New Guinea. Of the upward and downward vertical movements made by the head in nodding, the downward element is the stronger. While this could be a ritualization of the hungry baby's head movement as it latches on to the breast, it is more probably an incipient bowing action. Bowing is a form of submissive body-lowering observed not only in human communities but in primate groups as well. In nodding, the head begins to make a bow and then stops short in a polite form of agreement: 'I submit (acquiesce) to your opinion.'

Heart Being at the 'heart' of the body, the heart shares in the symbolism of the **centre**. Thus, in churches erected on the cruciform configuration to represent the body of Christ, the altar is placed at the heart (centre) of the church. The Holy of Holies was placed at the heart of the

Temple at Jerusalem, at the heart of Zion, which, in common with all other sacred centres, was at the heart of the world.

While modern Western thought has located spirit and intellect in the head, traditional cultures have attributed greater importance to the heart, seeing it as the seat of wisdom, understanding, and the soul, the 'Abode of Brahma' (India), the 'Throne of God' (Islam), the 'Kingdom of God' (Christendom). The heart of the organ through which God relates to us and fills us with His love: it is the 'sacred heart', the Grail containing the Blood of Christ, from which love, forgiveness, and compassion flow. The regular contraction (systole) and expansion (diastole) of the heart make it a symbol of the rhythms of nature and of the universe.

In Egypt, the heart was the only visceral organ to be embalmed together with the rest of the body, since, as the central organ of life, it would be indispensable to the departed soul in eternity.

In everyday speech the heart is used as a metaphor for a person's essential nature or personality: we say that someone is hard-hearted, tender-hearted, warm-hearted, cold-hearted, or heartless; one's heart can be in one's mouth, one's boots, or in the right place. The location and condition of one's heart, therefore, describes how and where one is placed emotionally.

Heel Indispensable to the upright posture, the heel is most vulnerable to the snake's bite and the scorpion's sting. Achilles was not the only man to experience it as his most vulnerable spot. If the heel is severely damaged, and certainly if the tendon connecting it to the calf is severed, then one cannot stand, walk, or run, and one is at the mercy of whatever hostile influence fate chooses to fling at one.

Joints Symbols of communication, articulation, and coordinated action.

Knee Because the knees are indispensable to athletic action, they have always symbolized masculine strength. On the other hand, they are the means of indicating submission or subordination, for 'to bend the knee' to someone, or to be 'brought to one's knees' is to make oneself lower to the ground, thus representing oneself as of inferior status to the one to whom one kneels. To 'clasp someone's knees' is to beg them for protection.

Lap The secure base of maternity, the safe refuge to which one longs to return in times of crisis; a sanctuary of containment and peace. It can also be a trap, as when the unicorn lays his head in a virgin's lap only to make himself vulnerable to the huntsman. Regression to the mother can make a young person similarly defenceless in facing threats imposed by life.

Leg Participates in the symbolism of the knee, ankle, heel, and foot.

Liver Because it is a large organ, engorged with bood, it has variously been considered the seat of life and of the passions – especially wrath (BILE). The Greek words for wrath and bile are *cholos* and *choli* respectively. Hence the choleric temperament.

Mouth The body's portal of entry and exit for breath, food, and, according to many traditions, the soul. The mouth is symbolic of its functions – speech, eating, devouring, and predation. The mouth of a monster or dragon represents the jaws of Hell, the organ responsible for swallowing the sun at dusk and vomiting it up again at dawn. As the 'mouthpiece' of the soul, it has the power to praise or blame, create or destroy, to lie or tell the truth. When gagged it is a symbol of secrecy: the lips are sealed.

Neck The vulnerable channel of communication between the soul and body: its severance means death. It can thus be a symbol of risk-taking, 'to stick one's neck out' one has the 'neck' (nerve or courage) to do something.

Nose A symbol of intuition or clairvoyance by which one can 'sniff' something out. The idea of being nosey, of sticking one's nose into other people's affairs, seems to be a fairly widespread metaphor of intrusiveness. In Japan, for example, such people are supposed to have long noses and evil spirits called *tengu* are depicted as mountain demons with very long noses or greedy beaks. That the nose is a single organ jutting out from the midline of the body lends it phallic significance.

Shoulders Symbolical of strength and the capacity to bear the burdens of life.

Skeleton Like the skull, a symbol of death and the spirits of the ancestors; as a subject of contemplation, a *vanitas*, a reminder of the transitoriness of life in this world and the inevitability of its termination.

Stomach A symbol of the capacity for assimilation and endurance, in the sense of being able 'to stomach something' (to accept it, cope with it, hold it down, and digest it), and 'to have the stomach to do something' (to have the courage and determination necessary to do it).

Thigh A euphemism for sexuality in view of its proximity to the genitalia. Thighbones were offered as sacrifice to the gods because they are rich in marrow, the immortal essence of the animal.

Tongue Its symbolism has to do with its physiological and anatomical functions. It provides a synonym for language, as in 'to give tongue', or 'to speak in tongues' (glossolaly). As an organ of taste, it can be used in association with the lips in gestures of pleasurable anticipation – to lick or smack one's lips. Sticking out the tongue past the lips can be either an insult or a sexual invitation, depending on the social context. In kissing and oral sex it is a phallic substitute.

Tooth The symbolism of teeth relates to their functions in biting, chewing, and social signalling. Together with claws, teeth are natural weapons. That humans have small teeth and no claws to speak of means that they have had to manufacture weapons to make good these deficiencies. We still display our pathetically small canine teeth, however, when we draw back our lips and snarl in the course of an argument (a phylogenetic residue from times when, like other primates, we had larger, more lethal canines). We also use intellectual teeth in the process of chewing things over in order to reflect on them and consider their implications. To draw someone's teeth is to render him impotent; to lose one's teeth is a sign of personal disintegration and ageing. Loss of teeth is considered by Freudian analysts to be a symbol of castration. When teeth are exposed in a smile, their relative whiteness and structural integrity act as signs of youth, attractiveness, and sex appeal.

iii Physical Activities

Breathing Self-evidently a symbol of life; 'And the Lord God formed man of the dust of the ground, and breathed into his nostrils the breath of life; and man became a living soul'(Genesis, 2:7); 'And they went in unto Noah into the ark, two and two of all flesh, wherein is the breath of life' (Genesis, 7:15). The Taoists of the Han Dynasty understood the space between Heaven and Earth to be filled with 'breath' in which people lived 'like fish in the water'. In India, the wind is the breath of life and *ātman*, the Universal Spirit, literally means breath. The Hebrew word *ruah* (*Ruah-Elohim* = the Breath of God) means spirit, as does the Greek *pneuma* and the Latin *spiritus*. Inspiration and expiration are equated with the Yang and Yin of Taoist philosophy and with the *kalpa* and *pralaya* of Indian philosophy, with evolution and involution, with the expansion and contraction of the universe. The Taoists also referred to the two phases of respiration as 'the opening and the closing of the Gates of Heaven'. The equation of 'inspiration' with poetic and artistic creativity is so widespread as to be universal. The use of breath in healing practices is also extremely widespread: Zulu healers breathe into the sick person's ear through a bull's horn, so as to drive evil spirits out of the body, while Siberian shamans are much given to blowing in the course of their healing rituals. Breathing is, of course, attributed great importance in yogic and other spiritual exercises. SNEEZING, the momentary forceful expulsion of spirit or soul, invokes 'Bless you!' from others so as to guarantee the return of the spirit to the body before fiendish harm can befall it.

Checking A means of verification to ensure that something is the way one thinks it is or wishes it to be. Checking behaviour is apparent in many animals and evidently contributes to survival. In humans it is particularly apparent and can result in the form of compulsive checking that occurs in obsessional disorders. Checking probably arose in relation to the defence of resources – food supplies, territory, and mates. When human communities began to store surplus food and to make tools, weapons, and utensils these valuable possessions had to be protected from those who might have wishes to appropriate them. Security arrangements had to be frequently and thoroughly checked to ensure that they were in effective operation. Such activity commonly occurs in dreams and can be expressive of a fear that things could be getting out of control.

Dancing An activity of great phylogenetic antiquity: the 'goose-step' of lizards engaged in ritual agonistic combat and the ritual steps of courting birds are examples of the dance in nature. Among humans, dancing is perhaps the most ancient social activity, having profound influences on the mood and psychology of the dancers as in hunting dances (the participants wearing animal skins), fertility dances (round a phallic pole, obelisk, or stone), leap dances (the higher the dancers leap, the higher the corn will grow), marriage-fertility dances (male and female dancers approach, separate, and reunite), round dances (imitating the movements of the sun and stars, dancing round bonfires at the winter solstice), war dances (to inflame passions and strengthen valour before battle), celebration dances (to enhance group solidarity), therapeutic dances (to drive away evil spirits), sex dances (a relatively late-Roman invention), and so on.

Dancing mobilizes energy and produces transformation – the dancer turns into god, demon, healer, hunter, warrior, preparing him for certain activities of crucial importance to the community. Everywhere, dancing has been endowed with religious as well as secular meaning.

Above all, synchronized body movements in a group – dancing or marching or performing a ritual – have a powerful social bonding effect. This can be observed in arm-waving and rhythmic clapping or chanting at football matches, pop concerts, evangelical church services, and political rallies. The arm raised in fascist salute at vast parades of goose-stepping troops had a similar bonding effect among German and Italian crowds in the 1930s. Such synchronized behaviour promotes a 'feel-good factor' of being one of the gang. Those who do not, or feel they cannot, join in such group activities experience themselves as cast in the role of 'outsider'.

Eating Since food and drink are essential to survival, it is not surprising that both have been charged with symbolic meanings which reach far beyond their nutritional significance. The idea that we are what we eat has a psychological as well as a physiological validity: when we ingest something, take it in and absorb it, we subject ourselves to its influence and assume something of its quality. It becomes integrated with what we already are. The lips and teeth of the mouth are guardians, like *nagas* or dragons, of the threshold. When food crosses the threshold, it enters the underworld of the stomach and the gut. There transformation occurs: it is assimilated, incorporated, em-bodied (Jackson, 1996).

The Latin *digerere* means 'to take apart' and the process of digestion is a form of Osirian dismemberment and 'scattering far and wide' throughout the body to renew its structure and maintain its functions. What is eaten is taken apart by chewing and mixing with enzymes, broken into smaller molecules, and assimilated from the gut; what is unassimilable is excluded and expelled. This is an apt metaphor for how the psyche processes the events of life, assimilating new information into the old. 'Some books are to be tasted,' wrote Francis Bacon, 'others are to be swallowed, and some few to be chewed and digested.' Most of the assimilation proceeds out of sight and out of mind in the processing plant of the unconscious.

Because food can be poisonous as well as nourishing, all organisms have evolved defence mechanisms to detect and reject food that could be harmful: hence the gastronomic conservatism of children and the aesthetic rejection by adults of things that are in bad taste. One may start to assimilate something only to discover that one has bitten off more than one can chew: it sticks in the gullet and one cannot stomach it.

Neumann (1954) associates the symbolism of eating and assimilation with the generation of consciousness. In childhood the development of conscious awareness goes hand-in-hand with 'a fragmentation of the world continuum into separate objects, parts, figures, which can only be assimilated, taken in, introjected, made conscious – in a word, 'eaten'. When the sun-hero, having been swallowed by the dragon of darkness, cuts out its heart and eats it, he is taking into himself the essence of this object. Consequently aggression, destruction, dismemberment, and killing are intimately associated with the corresponding bodily functions of eating, chewing, biting, and particularly with the symbolism of the teeth as instruments of these activities, all of which are essential for the formation of an independent ego. In this lies the deeper meaning of aggression during the early phases of development. Far from being sadistic, it is a positive and indispensable preparation for the assimilation of the world.'

EXCREMENT, the unassimilated, undigested, and rejected matter, carries all the stigmata of dirt, lowliness, and worthlessness. It is literally untouchable. To identify someone with it is the ultimate catathetic ('down-putting') signal. Yet, through the principle of opposites, excrement is also of potential value: not only is it a fertilizing agent but it may conceal gold. Paracelsus saw it as the *prima materia*, the starting point of the alchemical *opus*, the matrix of the Philosopher's Stone. Excrement is also personal – a poor thing, but one's own. Animals use it as a personal marker – in the guise of Kilroy – to denote the fact that *I* – and no other – *was here*. In Freudian psychology, children who hoard their faeces (self-induced constipation), or delight in playing with them, are either misers or potters in the making.

Falling A natural calamity much featured in dreams. For a creature that has spent much of its evolutionary history living in trees, it is appropriate to fear such a hazard and to receive regular warnings of it as a fearful possibility. Falling is also a common event in childhood and old age. Symbolically, it represents loss of social, spiritual, or moral status – as in fall from grace, pride going before a fall, a fallen woman, etc. Examples of epic falls are those of Adam, Lucifer, Icarus, and Humpty-Dumpty. The Fall of Adam and Eve from Paradise into mortal existence is an allegory of the incarnation of an archetype.

Something transpersonal becomes embodied in the here and now: God becomes Christ; the Divine Child becomes the human child at its mother's breast; the archetypal enemy becomes reality in the Nazi bombers flying overhead; the Original Man, the Anthropos, the supreme achievement of the Creator becomes the mortal peasant labouring in the fields. 'How are the mighty fallen!' To fall into reality is the *sine qua non* of existence.

The Fall is thus a mythic representation of humanity's transformation from hunter to farmer. As hunter-gatherers, we obeyed nature, we adapted to our ecological niche, we accepted our lot as the dependents of God, grateful for whatever it pleased him to provide. Such was the primordial 'Paradise' in which our species lived out 99 per cent of its existence. Then we sampled the forbidden fruit: we learned the secrets of agriculture and animal husbandry, relinquished our dependence on God, and started to bend nature to our will – with incalculable consequences.

Fasting Abstinence, especially refraining from meat, has regularly been associated with asceticism and the higher spirituality derived from renunciation of all that is 'carnal' – e.g. sex, gluttony, and greed. The extreme abstinence encountered in people with anorexia nervosa is a caricature of such ascetic renunciation. It comes of the age-old dichotomy between the flesh and the spirit which conceives one as the enemy of the other.

Flying Dreams of flying are invariably pleasant, often elating, giving rise to feelings of freedom and self-mastery, a sense of transcending the constraints of mundane reality. Flying is clearly linked to the symbolism of ASCENT and DESCENT, of rise and fall in all their spiritual, emotional, and social implications. Flying is a momentary and intoxicating awareness of what it is to be in the transcendent state, to be absolutely and uncompromisingly free and beyond all restriction. Such a condition can never last, but it is nonetheless intensely agreeable while it does.

The capacity for MAGIC FLIGHT is commonly considered to be the attribute of shamans and witches.

Food-sharing This is a legacy of our hunter-gatherer past. It is a bonding ritual which symbolizes our entitlement to share in the resources of the group, by virtue of being one of its members and being accepted and valued as such. A com*pan*ion is one with whom one shares bread (*pain*). Food-sharing is the celebration of a common interest, the recognition of a shared identity, and the forgetting of all differences: hence the taboo against raising controversial topics during meals. Offering someone food is more than a gesture of goodwill: it is an invitation to enter into a reciprocal obligation. Laws of hospitality are universally propounded and observed and stress the underlying reciprocity of the host–guest relationship (French *hôte* = host and guest).

As in all social interactions, the question of hierarchy enters the etiquette of food-sharing, higher ranking individuals being given places closest to the host, being served before everyone else with the best cuts, and so on. Meals are a major focus of socialization for children, where they learn 'table manners' – proper deportment, self-restraint, deference to elders and people of rank, polite forms of address, how to make requests and return thanks, etc. Food-sharing is, therefore, a microcosmic exemplar of the social macrocosm.

Playing By ensuring that all young animals play, nature provides the means of training the behavioural systems which are vital to life. Through play a young child acquires those basic skills which will guarantee its autonomy and its survival. For this reason, the hero archetype is implicated in all games. However spontaneous they may appear, they are all about the struggle to break free from infantile dependence and to achieve greater competence. Social cooperation and conflict, intimacy with peers, physical combat, the control of aggression, hunting, sexuality, marital relations, and child-rearing are all activities which feature in childhood games, where imagination is given free rein to complement the realities or compensate for the deficiencies of everyday existence. Although opportunities for playing dwindle with age, the capacity to delight in games persists far into adult life, where through the exercise of intelligence and ingenuity we can achieve the elaborate intricacies of chess, cricket, and association football. To become a serious participant in such games is to enter a peculiar universe with its own rules, regulations, and etiquette.

The earliest organized games were sacred in intent: they had a ritual quality which turned them into an offering to as well as a celebration of the power and bounty of sky gods and earth goddesses. The Olympic Games, dedicated to Zeus, were an all-male affair: the only woman admitted to them was the priestess of Demeter, for whom a place of honour was reserved.

Organized men's team games are, in fact, symbolic wars. They provide an opportunity for males to band together into squads which then go off to play ('do battle') against one another on a pitch ('battlefield') divided into opposite ends ('territories'). Games are ritual expressions of physical conflict between individuals (status conflicts or tournaments) or between groups (wars): tennis, billiards, pool, squash, chess, draughts (chequers), and backgammon are essentially ritualized dominance struggles between individual members of an in-group; whereas football, rugby, ice-hockey, and basketball are rituals of territorial conflict and war. Gambling large sums of money on the outcome adds to the excitement by augmenting the joy of victory and the despair of defeat. In this way supporters identify themselves with the performance of their team, just as in wartime the civil population identifies with the fate of its troops on the battlefield.

Running Running away, being pursued by a predator or savage warrior, is a common happening in our dreams – as it presumably was for our ancestors in the evolutionary past. Running in dreams can also be enjoyable – delight in the animal state of covering distance effortlessly and at speed, feeling full of energy, vitality, and 'animal spirits'. This can be associated with the same feelings of freedom as experienced in dreams of flying. A similar state of animal well-being is commonly reported by athletes and experienced joggers.

Swimming Dreams of swimming can express the state of one's ego relationship with the unconscious psyche. Such dreams can vary from the agreeable to the terrifying – from feeling at home in the matrix of one's psychic being to the horror of being overwhelmed by tempestuous seas or being attacked by monsters of the deep. Swimming dreams are fairly common at the commencement of an analysis and can convey valuable prognostic as well as diagnostic information.

Washing The removal of dirt by washing it away with water is a universal symbol of purification – the removal of guilt, sickness, or contamination. Hence ritual washing before entering a sacred precinct, participating in a religious ritual, performing a surgical operation, or preparing to cook a meal. Washing, cleaning, and grooming behaviours are apparent in all animals and birds. It evolved as a defence against micro-organisms. Since germs cannot be seen or easily conceptualized, notions such as 'contamination' and 'purification' emerged to organize the appropriate defensive behaviour: those who feel compelled to indulge in obsessive washing rituals have carried this symbolism too far.

Bibliography

Note: In the text the author/date system of reference is used with the exception of: *CW Collected Works* (Jung).

Adler, A. (1932), *What Life Should Mean to You*, Allen & Unwin, London.

Alain-Fournier (1913), *Le Grand Meaulnes* (trans. Frank Davison), Penguin Books, London.

Appleton, Jay (1990), *The Symbolism of Habitat: An Interpretation of Landscape in the Arts*, University of Washington Press, Seattle and London.

Apuleius (trans. 1910), *The Metamorphoses or the Golden Ass of Apuleius of Madaura*, Clarendon Press, Oxford.

Atran, Scott (1990), *Cognitive Foundations of Natural History: Towards an Anthropology of Science*, Cambridge University Press, Cambridge.

Axelrod, R. (1984), *The Evolution of Co-operation*, Basic Books, New York.

Bachofen, J. J. (1967), *Myth, Religion, and Mother Right*, Routledge & Kegan Paul, London.

Bailey, K. (1987), *Human Paleopsychology: Applications to Aggression and Pathological Processes*, Lawrence Erlbaum Associates, Hillsdale, N. J.

Balling, J. D. and Falk, J. H. (1982), 'Development of Visual Preference for Natural Environments', *Environment and Behaviour*, 14, pp. 5–28.

Barkow, Jerome H., Cosmides, Leda, and Tooby, John (eds.) (1992), *The Adapted Mind: Evolutionary Psychology and the Generation of Culture*, Oxford University Press, Oxford and New York.

Becker, Udo (ed.) (1994), *The Element Encyclopedia of Symbols*, Element Books, Shaftesbury, Dorset; Brisbane, Queensland.

Berlin, Isaiah (1980), *Concepts and Categories: Philosophical Essays*, Oxford University Press, Oxford.

Bettelheim, Bruno (1955), *Symbolic Wounds*, Thames & Hudson, London.

Bowlby, John (1958), 'The Nature of the Child's Tie to His Mother', *International Journal of Psycho-Analysis*, 39, pp. 350–73.

Bowlby, John (1969), *Attachment and Loss, Volume 1, Attachment*, Hogarth Press and Institute of Psycho-Analysis, London.

Bowlby, John (1973), *Attachment and Loss, Volume 2, Separation: Anxiety and Anger*, Hogarth Press and Institute of Psycho-Analysis, London.

Boyd, Robert and Richerson, Peter (1985), *Culture and the Evolutionary Process*, Chicago University Press, Chicago.

Boyer, Pascal (1994), *The Naturalness of Religious Ideas: A Cognitive Theory of Religion*, University of California Press, Berkeley.

Burkert, Walter (1996), *Creation of the Sacred: Tracks of Biology in Early Religions*, Harvard University Press, Cambridge, Mass., London.

Campbell, Joseph (1949), *The Hero with a Thousand Faces*, Pantheon, New York.

Campbell, Joseph (1959), *The Masks of God, Volume 1, Primitive Mythology*, Viking, New York.

Campbell, Joseph (1990), *The Hero's Journey*, Harper & Row, San Francisco.

Cassirer, Ernst (1944), *An Essay on Man*, Yale University Press, New Haven.

Cassirer, Ernst, (1953–7), *The Philosophy of Symbolic Forms*, 3 volumes (trans. Ralph Manheim), Yale University Press, New Haven.

Cawson, Frank (1995), *The Monsters in the Mind*, Book Guild, London.

Chance, M. R. A. (ed.) (1988), *Social Fabrics of the Mind*, Lawrence Erlbaum Associates, Hove and London.

Chance, M. R. A., and Jolly, C. (1970), *Social Groups of Monkeys, Apes and Men*, Jonathan Cape/E. P. Dutton, New York and London.

Cheney, D. L., and Seyfarth, R. (1990), *How Monkeys See the World*, University of Chicago Press, Chicago.

Chevalier, Jean, and Gheerbrant, Alain (1996), *A Dictionary of Symbols* (trans. John Buchanan-Brown), Penguin, London.

Chomsky, Noam (1965), *Aspects of the Theory of Syntax*, MIT Press, Cambridge, Mass.

Cirlot, J. E. (1971), *A Dictionary of Symbols*, Routledge & Kegan Paul, London.

Cohn, Norman (1996), *Noah's Flood: The Genesis Story in Western Thought*, Yale University Press, New Haven and London.

Coleridge, Samuel Taylor (1816), *The Statesman's Manual*, Gale and Fenner, Pater Noster Row, J. M. Richardson, Royal Exchange, and Hatchard, Piccadilly, London.

Cooper, J. C. (1978), *An Illustrated Encyclopaedia of Traditional Symbols*, Thames & Hudson, London.

Cosmides, L., and Tooby, J. (1989), 'Evolutionary Psychology and the Generation of Culture, Part 1: Case Study: A Computational Theory of Social
Exchange', *Ethology and Sociobiology*, 10, pp. 51–97.

Darwin, Charles (1859), *On the Origin of Species by Means of Natural
Selection*, John Murray, London.

Davies, Michael, Davies, Henry, and Davies, Kathryn (1992), *Humankind,
the Gatherer-Hunter: From Earliest Times to Industry*, Myddle-Brockton,
Swanley, Kent.

Dawkins, Richard (1976, 1989), *The Selfish Gene*, Oxford University Press,
London.

Dawkins, Richard (1995), *River out of Eden: A Darwinian View of Life*,
Weidenfeld & Nicolson, London.

Diamond, Jared (1991), *The Rise and Fall of the Third Chimpanzee*, Vintage,
London.

Douglas, Mary (1970), *Natural Symbols: Explorations in Cosmology*, Barrie
& Rockliff, Cresset Press, London.

Durham, William (1991), *Coevolution*, Stanford University Press, Stanford.

Edelman, Gerald (1989), *The Remembered Present: A Biological Theory of
Consciousness*, Basic Books, New York.

Edinger, E. F. (1985), *Anatomy of the Psyche: Alchemical Symbolism in
Psychotherapy*, Open Court, La Salle, Illinois.

Edinger, E. F. (1992), *Ego and Archetype*, Shambhala, Boston and London.

Eibl-Eibesfeldt, I. (1971), *Love and Hate*, Methuen, London.

Eliade, Mircea (1954), *The Myth of the Eternal Return* (trans. Willard R.
Trask), Bollingen Series XLVI, Pantheon Books, New York; Routledge
& Kegan Paul, London.

Eliade, Mircea (1958), *Patterns in Comparative Religion* (trans. Rosemary
Sheed), Sheed & Ward, London and New York.

Eliade, Mircea (1960), *Myths, Dreams and Mysteries: The Encounter between
Contemporary Faiths and Archaic Realities* (trans. Philip Mairet), Harvill
Press, London.

Eliade, Mircea (1964), *Shamanism: Archaic Techniques of Ecstasy* (trans.
Willard R. Trask), Routlege & Kegan Paul, London.

Eliade, Mircea (1971), *The Forge and the Crucible: The Origins and Structures
of Alchemy* (trans. Stephen Corrin), Harper Torchbooks, Harper & Row,
New York and Evanston.

Firth, Raymond (1973), *Symbols, Public and Private*, George Allen & Unwin
Ltd, London.

Fox, Robin (1975), 'Primate Kin and Human Kinship', *Biosocial Anthropology*, ed. R. Fox, pp. 9–35, Malaby Press, London.

Fox, Robin (1989), *The Search for Society: Quest for a Biosocial Science and Morality*, Rutgers University Press, New Brunswick and London.

Frazer, Sir James G. (1926), *The Worship of Nature: The Gifford Lectures*, University of Edinburgh, Edinburgh and New York.

Freud, Sigmund (1900; 1976), *The Interpretation of Dreams*, Pelican Books, London.

Gebser, J. (1966), *Ursprung und Gegenwart*, Deutsche Verlags-Anhalt, Stuttgart.

Hall, Calvin S., and Nordby, Vernon J. (1972), *The Individual and His Dreams*, New American Library, New York.

Hannah, Barbara (1992), *The Cat, Dog and Horse Lectures*, Chiron Publications, Wilmette, Illinois.

Helman, C. G. (1978), ' "Feed a Cold; Starve a Fever" – Folk Models of Infection in an English Surburban Community, and Their Relation to Medical Treatment', in *Culture, Medicine and Psychiatry*, 2, pp. 107–37.

Hirschfeld, Lawrence (1996), *Race in the Making: Cognition, Culture, and the Child's Construction of Humankinds*, Bradford Books.

Hirschfeld, Lawrence and Gelman, Susan (1994), *Mapping the Mind: Domain-Specificity in Cognition and Culture*, Cambridge University Press, Cambridge.

Hobson, J. Allan (1990), *The Dreaming Brain*, Penguin Books, London.

Homer, *The Iliad* (1950, trans. E. V. Rieu), Penguin Books, Harmondsworth.

Hoult, Janet (1990), *Dragons: Their History and Symbolism*, Second Edition, Gothic Image Publications, Glastonbury.

Ingold, Tim (1992), Comment on 'Beyond the Original Affluent Society' by N. Bird-David, *Current Anthropology*, 33, pp. 34–47.

Jackson, Eve (1996), *Food and Transformation: Imagery and Symbolism of Eating*, Inner City Books, Toronto.

Jaynes, Julian (1976), *The Origin of Consciousness in the Breakdown of the Bi-cameral Mind*, Houghton Mifflin, Boston.

Jung, C. G. The majority of quotations in the text are taken either from *The Collected Works of C. G. Jung* (1953–78), ed. H. Read, M. Fordham and G. Adler and published in London by Routledge, in New York by Pantheon Books (1953–60) and the Bollingen Foundation (1961–7) and in Princeton, New Jersey by Princeton University Press (1967–78), or from *Memories, Dreams, Reflections* (1963), published in London by Routledge & Kegan Paul and in New York by Random House. Sources of quotations from *The Collected Works* are indicated by the volume number followed by the number of the paragraph from which the quotation is taken, e.g. CW9i, para. 260.

Jung, C. G. (1933), *Modern Man in Search of a Soul*, Kegan Paul, London.

Jung, C. G. (1959), *Flying Saucers: A Modern Myth of Things Seen in the Skies*, Routledge & Kegan Paul, London.

Jung, C. G., and von Franz, M.-L. (eds.) (1964), *Man and His Symbols*, Aldus Books, London.

Kaplan, Stephen (1992), 'Environmental Preference in a Knowledge-Seeking, Knowledge-Using Organism', in *The Adapted Mind*, ed. Jerome H. Barkow, Leda Cosmides, and John Tooby, Oxford University Press, New York and Oxford.

Kast, Verena (1992), *The Dynamics of Symbols: Fundamentals of Jungian Psychotherapy* (trans. Susan A. Schwarz), Fromm International, New York.

Kirk, G. S. (1974), *The Nature of Greek Myths*, Penguin Books, London.

Knight, Chris (1996), *Blood Relations: Menstruation and the Origins of Culture*, Yale University Press, Newhaven and London.

Koepping, Klaus-Peter (1983), *Adolf Bastian and the Psychic Unity of Mankind*, University of Queensland Press, St Lucia.

Kugler, Paul (1982), *The Alchemy of Discourse: An Archetypal Approach to Language*, Bucknell University Press, Lewisburg Pa.

Larousse Encyclopedia of Mythology (1959) (trans. Richard Aldington and Delano Ames), Batchworth Press, London.

Langer, Suzanne (1967), *Mind: An Essay on Human Feeling*, Johns Hopkins University Press, Baltimore.

Langer, Suzanne (1969), *Philosophy in a New Key: A Study in the Symbolism of Reason, Rite and Art*, Third Edition, Harvard University Press, Cambridge, Mass.

Leach, Maria and Fried, Jerome (eds.) (1972), *Funk & Wagnalls Standard Dictionary of Folklore, Mythology and Legend*, Funk & Wagnalls, New York.

Leakey, Richard E. (1981), *The Making of Mankind*, Michael Joseph, London.

Leff, Julian (1981), *Psychiatry around the Globe: A Transcultural View*, Gaskell (Royal College of Psychiatrists), London.

Leroi-Gourhan, André (1982), *The Dawn of European Art: An Introduction to Palaeolithic Cave Painting* (trans. Sara Champion), Cambridge University Press, Cambridge and New York.

Lévi-Strauss, Claude (1968), *The Savage Mind*, University of Chicago Press, Chicago.

Lévy-Bruhl, Lucien (1938), *L'Expérience Mystique et les Symboles chez les Primitifs*, Alcan, Paris.

Lindholm, Charles (1990), *Charisma*, Basil Blackwell, Cambridge, Mass., and Oxford.

Lopreato, Joseph (1984), *Human Nature and Biocultural Evolution*, Allen & Unwin, Boston, London and Sydney.

Lorenz, Konrad (1970), *The Enmity between Generations and its Possible Causes*, Nobel Foundation, Stockholm.

Lovelock, James (1987), 'Gaia: A Model for Planetary and Cellular Dynamics', in *Gaia: A Way of Knowing: Political Implications of the New Biology*, ed. William Irwin Thompson, Lindisfarne Press, Great Barrington, Mass.

Lumsden, Charles J., and Wilson, Edward O. (1981), *Genes, Minds and Culture*, Harvard University Press, Cambridge, Mass.

Lumsden, Charles J., and Wilson, Edward O. (1983), *Promethean Fire: Reflections on the Origin of Mind*, Harvard University Press, Cambridge, Mass. and London.

MacLean, P. D. (1973), *A Triune Concept of the Brain and Behavior*, University of Toronto Press, Toronto.

MacLean, P. D. (1976) 'Sensory and Perceptive Factors in Emotional Function of the Triune Brain', in *Biological Foundations of Psychiatry*, ed. R. G. Grennell and S. Gabay (Vol. 1, pp. 177–98), Raven, New York.

MacLean, P. D. (1985) 'Evolutionary Psychiatry and the Triune Brain', *Psychological Medicine*, 15, pp. 219–21.

Mahdi, Louise Carus (1987), *Betwixt and Between: Patterns of Masculine and Feminine Initiation*, ed. Louise Carus Mahdi, Steven Foster and Meredith Little, Open Court, La Salle, Illinois.

Mahdi, Louise Carus (1996), *Crossroads: The Quest for Contemporary Rites of Passage*, ed. Louise Carus Mahdi, Nancy Geyer Christopher and Michael Meade, Open Court, Chicago and La Salle, Illinois.

Mallon, Brenda (1989), *Children Dreaming*, Penguin, London.

Marshack, Alexander (1972), *The Roots of Civilization: The Cognitive Beginnings of Man's First Art, Symbol and Notation*, Weidenfeld & Nicolson, London.

Maslow, Abraham (1968), *Towards a Psychology of Being*, Van Nostrand, Princeton.

McFarland, David (ed.) (1987), *The Oxford Companion to Animal Behaviour*, Oxford University Press, Oxford and New York.

Mead, G. R. S. (1960), *Fragments of a Faith Forgotten*, University Books, New Hyde Park, New York.

Mithen, Steven (1996), *The Prehistory of the Mind: A Search for the Origins of Art, Religion and Science*, Thames & Hudson, London.

Monick, Eugene (1987), *The Phallos: Sacred Image of the Masculine*, Inner City Books, Toronto.

Moon, Beverly (ed.) (1991), *An Encyclopaedia of Archetypal Symbolism*, Shambhala, Boston and London.

Morgan, Elaine (1990), *The Scars of Evolution: What Our Bodies Tell Us about Human Origins*, Penguin Books, London.

Morris, Desmond (1977), *Manwatching: A Field Guide to Human Behaviour*, Jonathan Cape, London.

Mumford, Lewis (1966), *The Myth of the Machine: Technics and Human Development*, Harcourt, New York.

Murdock, G. P. (1945), 'The Common Denominator in Culture', in *The Science of Man in the World Crisis*, ed. R. Linton, Cambridge University Press, New York.

Nadel, S. F. (1951), *Foundations of Social Anthropology*, Cohen & West, London.

Neumann, Erich (1954), *The Origins and History of Consciousness*, Bollingen Series XLII, Pantheon Books, New York.

Neumann, Erich (1955), *The Great Mother: An Analysis of the Archetype*, Routledge & Kegan Paul, London.

Neumann, Erich (1956) *Amor and Psyche: The Psychic Development of the Feminine: A Commentary on the Tale by Apuleius*, Routledge & Kegan Paul, London.

Onians, Richard Broxton (1973), *The Origins of European Thought*, Arno Press, New York.

Orians, Gordon H. (1985), 'An Ecological and Evolutionary Approach to Landscape Esthetics', Unpublished manuscript, University of Washington, Seattle. Cited by Kaplan (1992).

Orians, Gordon H., and Heerwagen, Judith H. (1992), 'Evolved Responses to Landscapes', in *The Adapted Mind: Evolutionary Psychology and the Generation of Culture*, ed. Jerome H. Barkow, Leda Cosmides, and John Tooby, Oxford University Press, New York and Oxford.

Peers, E. Allison (1927), *Studies of the Spanish Mystics*, The Sheldon Press, London.

Plato, *Timaeus* (1921, trans. R. G. Bury), Loeb Classical Library, Harvard University Press, Cambridge, Mass.

Propp, Vladimir (1968), *Morphology of the Folktale*, Second Edition, Austin, Texas.

Radcliffe-Brown, A. R. (1922), *The Andaman Islanders*, Cambridge University Press, Cambridge.

Rank, Otto (1961), *Psychology and the Soul*, Perpetua, New York.

Ricoeur, Paul (1970), *The Symbolism of Evil*, Beacon Press, Boston.

Riddington, R. (1982), 'Technology, World View and Adaptive Strategy in a Northern Hunting Society', *Canadian Review of Sociology and Anthropology*, 19, pp. 469–81.

Ridley, Matt (1994), *The Red Queen: Sex and the Evolution of Human Nature*, Macmillan, New York.

Ridley, Matt (1996), *The Origins of Virtue*, Viking, London.

Rosen, David H. (1992), 'Inborn Basis for the Healing Doctor–Patient Relationship', *Pharos*, 55, pp. 17–21.

Rosenberg, John (1963), *The Darkening Glass*, Routledge & Kegan Paul, London.

Ryce-Menuhin, Joel (ed.) (1994), *Jung and the Monotheisms: Judaism, Christianity and Islam*, Routledge, London and New York.

Sagan, Carl (1977), *The Dragons of Eden*, Hodder & Stoughton, London.

Sears, E. (1986), *The Ages of Man: Mediaeval Interpretations of the Life Cycle*, Princeton University Press, New Jersey.

Serpell, James (ed.) (1995), *The Domestic Dog: Its Evolution, Behaviour and Interactions with People*, Cambridge University Press, Cambridge.

Sinclair, Andrew (1991), *The Naked Savage*, Sinclair-Stevenson, London.

Smith, W. Robertson (1889), *Lectures in the Religion of the Semites*, Black, Edinburgh.

Sperber, Dan (1975), *Rethinking Symbolism* (trans. Alice L. Morton), Cambridge University Press, Cambridge and New York.

Sperber, Dan (1996a) *Explaining Culture: A Naturalist Approach*, Blackwell, Oxford.

Sperber, Dan (1996b) 'Learning to Pay Attention: How a Modular Image of the Mind Can Help to Explain Culture', *Times Literary Supplement*, 27 December 1996.

Steele, James and Shenan, Stephen (eds.) (1996), *The Archaeology of Human Ancestry: Power, Sex and Tradition*, Routledge, London and New York.

Stein, Murray (1994), 'The Dream of Wholeness', in *Jung and the Monotheisms: Judaism, Christianity and Islam*, ed. Joel Ryce-Menuhin, Routledge, London and New York.

Stevens, Anthony (1982), *Archetype: A Natural History of the Self*, Routledge & Kegan Paul, London; William Morrow & Co., New York.

Stevens, Anthony (1986), 'Thoughts on the Psychobiology of Religion and the Neurobiology of Archetypal Experience', in *Zygon: Journal of Religion and Science*, 21 March, pp. 9–29.

Stevens, Anthony (1991), *On Jung*, Penguin Books, London.

Stevens, Anthony (1993), *The Two-Million-Year-Old Self*, Texas A. & M. University Press, College Station, Texas.

Stevens, Anthony (1996), *Private Myths: Dreams and Dreaming*, Penguin Books, London.

Stevens, Anthony and Price, John (1996), *Evolutionary Psychiatry: A New Beginning*, Routledge, London.

Storr, Anthony (1992), *Music and the Mind*, HarperCollins, London.

Storr, Anthony (1996), *Feet of Clay: A Study of Gurus*, HarperCollins, London.

Stravinsky, Igor (1947), *Poetics of Music* (trans. Arthur Knodel and Ingolf Dahl), Vintage Books, New York.

Stringer, Chris and McKie, Robin (1996), *African Exodus: The Origins of Modern Humanity*, Jonathan Cape, London.

Tattersall, Ian, Delson, Eric, and Van Couvering, John (1988), *Encyclopaedia of Human Evolution and Prehistory*, St James Press, Chicago and London.

Tinbergen, Niko (1951), *The Study of Instinct*, Oxford University Press, Oxford.

Trinkaus, Eric (ed.) (1989), *The Emergence of Modern Humans: Biocultural Adaptations in the Latter Pleistocene*, Cambridge University Press, Cambridge, New York, Port Chester, Melbourne, Sydney.

Tripp, Edward (1970), *A Dictionary of Classical Mythology*, Collins, London and Glasgow.

Turner, Frederick, and Poppel, Ernst (1983), 'The Neural Lyre: Poetic Meter, the Brain and Time', *Poetry*, August, pp. 277–309.

Turner, Victor (1969), *The Ritual Process*, Routledge & Kegan Paul, London.

Turner, Victor (1983), 'Body, Brain, and Culture in the Ritual Process', in *Zygon: Journal of Religion and Science*, 18 (September), pp. 221–45.

Turner, Victor, and Turner, Edith (1978), *Image and Pilgrimage in Christian Culture: Anthropological Perspectives*, Columbia University Press, New York.

van Gennep, Arnold (1960), *The Rites of Passage*, Routledge & Kegan Paul, London.

von Franz, Marie-Louise (1970), *A Psychological Interpretation of the Golden Ass of Apuleius*, Spring Publications, New York.

von Franz, Marie-Louise (1972), *Patterns of Creativity Mirrored in Creation Myths*, Spring Publications, Zurich.

von Franz, Marie-Louise (1975), 'Individual and Social Contact in Jungian Psychology', *Harvest*, 21, pp. 12–27.

de Vries, Ad (1984), *Dictionary of Symbols and Imagery*, North-Holland Publishing Company, Amsterdam and London.

Wallace, Anthony F. C. (1966), *Religion: An Anthropological View*, Random House, New York.

Warner, Marina (1994), *From the Beast to the Blonde: On Fairy Tales and Their Tellers*, Chatto & Windus, London.

Wenegrat, Brant (1990), *The Divine Archetype: The Sociobiology and Psychology of Religion*, Lexington Books, Lexington, Mass.

Whitmont, E. C. (1969), *The Symbolic Quest*, Barrie & Rockliff, London.

Wickler, Wolfgang (1968), *Mimicry in Plants and Animals* (trans. R. D. Martin), McGraw-Hill, New York.

Wilber, Ken (1983), *Up from Eden: A Transpersonal View of Human Evolution*, Routledge & Kegan Paul, London.

Wilhelm, Richard (1951), *The I Ching or Book of Changes* (trans. Richard Wilhelm, rendered into English by Cary F. Baynes), Routledge & Kegan Paul, London.

Wilson, Glen (1989), *The Great Sex Divide: A Study of Male–Female Differences*, Peter Owen, London.

Woley, Eleanora M. (1990), *The Symbol of the Dog in the Human Psyche: A Study of the Human–Dog Bond*, Chiron Publications, Wilmette, Illinois.

Wolff, A. (1956), *Structural Forms of the Feminine Psyche*, privately printed in Zurich, quoted by Whitmont (1969).

Wright, Robert (1995), *The Moral Animal: Why We Are the Way We Are*, Little, Brown & Co., London.

Ziegler, Alfred J. (1988), 'Morbistic Rituals', in *The Meaning of Illness*, ed. Mark Kidel and Susan Rowe-Leet, Routledge, London.

Glossary

agonic mode: a mode of social interaction characteristic of hierarchically organized societies where individuals are concerned with warding off threats to their status and inhibiting overt expressions of aggressive conflict.

allegory: a sustained metaphor in narrative form.

ancestral society: the kind of intimate community characteristic of human beings living in the environment in which our species evolved; the kind of society which we are probably best adapted to live in.

apotheosis: the exaltation of a person to rank among the gods.

archetypes: innate neuropsychic centres possessing the capacity to initiate, control, and mediate the common behavioural characteristics and typical experiences of all human beings irrespective of race, culture, or creed. Archetypes are the components of the **collective unconscious**. 'The concept of the archetype . . . is derived from the repeated observation that, for instance, the myths and fairy tales of world literature contain definite motifs which crop up everywhere. We meet these same motifs in the fantasies, dreams, deliria, and delusions of individuals living today. These typical images and associations are what I call archetypal ideas. The more vivid they are, the more they will be coloured by particularly strong feeling-tones' (Jung, CW10, para. 847).

arousal: a neurophysiological state which accompanies intense emotions such as sex, anger, and aggression or the perception of actual or potential threat; it is mobilized by hypothalamic structures in the **limbic system** (q.v.), acting through the sympathetic nervous system and its connections with the endocrine glands.

avatar: a Sanskrit word meaning descent and applied specifically to the descent of a deity to earth in incarnate form.

axis mundi: the world axis; a concept common to many peoples of a central cosmic axis connecting Heaven, Earth, and Underworld, round which all things revolve; often symbolized by the Cosmic Tree or Sacred Mountain.

charisma: a term derived from New Testament Greek meaning the gift of grace; introduced into sociology by Max Weber to describe an 'extraordinary quality' possessed by persons or objects which is thought to give them a unique, magical quality.

chthonic: dwelling in or below the earth; from the Greek *chthon*, meaning the earth; occasionally used as an alternative name for Gaia or Ge, Mother Earth.

collective unconscious: a term introduced by C. G. Jung to designate the phylogenetic psyche (those aspects of the psyche which are inherited and common to all humanity).

ego: the part of the personality which one consciously recognizes as I or me.

enantiodromia: the propensity of all polarized phenomena to go over to their opposite.

epiphany: the manifestation or appearance of some divine or supernatural being.

exogamy: the custom whereby a man or woman is bound to take a spouse from outside their own clan or group.

free-rider: an individual who seeks to acquire an undue proportion of the group's resources without first satisfying the usual requirement of achieving appropriate social rank.

gene: the basic unit of heredity, made up of DNA.

genome: the complete genetic constitution of an organism; the entire genetic programme characterizing the species.

Gestalt: a German word meaning form, pattern, or configuration; used in psychology to designate an integrated whole that is greater than the sum of its parts.

hedonic mode: a mode of social interaction in which underlying dominance relations are not being challenged and agonic tensions are consequently absent, permitting individuals to be affiliative and to give their attention to recreational or task-oriented activities.

hierophany: a sacred revelation; derived from Greek *hieros* meaning sacred and *phanien*, to reveal.

homeostasis: the maintenance of balance between opposing mechanisms or systems.

hubris: an act of outrage or contempt, especially against the gods.

icon: a picture or a statue that represents its object by resembling it, as when the statue of a lion represents the lion and its leonine attributes.

individuation: the term used by C. G. Jung to designate the process of personality development which leads to the fullest possible actualization of the archetypal endowment of an individual.

in illo tempore: the term used by Mircea Eliade (1958) to designate the 'original time' when the cosmos and humanity were created, and when the rules, rituals, and customs of the tribe were formulated; known to Australian Aborigines as the 'Dreaming Time'.

innate releasing mechanism (IRM): the postulated neuronal centre responsible for the release and coordination of instinctively determined patterns of behaviour when appropriate **sign stimuli** are encountered by an organism in the environment.

kratophany: a revelation through power; from Greek *kratos* meaning power and *phanein* to reveal.

limbic system: part of the old mammalian brain, consisting of the hippocampus, hypothalamus, thalamus, and pituitary gland. The limbic system is involved in memory storage, the mediation of basic archetypal patterns of behaviour and experience, and the maintenance of **homeostasis**.

liminality: derived from the Latin *limin*, meaning threshold or doorway; used in psychology to refer to psychic states experienced on the threshold between conscious and unconscious levels of awareness; hence, subliminal, referring to psychic processes occurring below the threshold of consciousness.

liminoid: a term applied by Victor and Edith Turner (1978) to rituals which go beyond or break the pattern of the conventional rituals practised in a society.

mana: a Melanesian word describing the exceptional power perceived as emanating from certain people, objects, or events; approximately equivalent to the Western sociological term **charisma**.

module: a term introduced by evolutionary psychologists to describe a specialized component of the mind which equips it with the necessary 'intelligence' to deal with a specific 'cognitive domain' or a certain type of behaviour pattern. Examples are modules for acquiring language, intuiting the psychological state of others, classifying plants and animals, making and using tools, and dealing with the physical properties of the inanimate world.

mysterium tremendum et fascinans: see **numinosity**.

natural selection: the principal mechanism of evolutionary change, originally proposed by Charles Darwin (1859). The theory holds that of the range of different individuals making up the population of a given species those individuals possessing certain advantageous characteristics will contribute more offspring to the succeeding generation than those lacking these characteristics. Provided these advantageous attributes have an inherited basis, they will eventually become established as standard components of the genetic structure of the species (i.e. they will be selected by a natural process).

neocortex: the cerebral cortex; the new mammalian brain responsible for cognition and sophisticated perceptual processes as distinct from the instinctive and affective behaviour patterns mediated by the old mammalian brain and the reptilian brain.

neolithic: pertaining to the later part of the prehistoric Stone Age (Greek *neos* = new + *lithos* = stone); the era which saw the beginning of agriculture.

nemesis: retribution; the punishment for **hubris**.

numinosity: a term introduced into psychology by C. G. Jung, who borrowed it from the German theologian, Rudolf Otto. Otto used it to describe what he regarded as the fundamental experience common to all religions – namely, the sense of awe and exaltation generated by the feeling of being in the presence of the Creator, an experience which Otto designated the *mysterium tremendum et fascinans*.

objective psyche: Jung sometimes referred to the **collective unconscious** as the objective psyche in order to stress its conaturality with all existence: it is as *real* and as *existent* as anything in nature. This is why fundamental natural laws, like the principles of adaptation, homeostasis, and growth, apply to the psyche just as surely as to any other biological phenomenon.

omphalos: the navel or exact centre of the earth, believed by the Greeks to be at Delphi where it was represented in the form of a beehive-shaped stone. Two eagles (or swans, or crows) flying from the opposite ends of the earth were believed to have met at this point. The omphalos was Apollo's seat, and the Pythia sat on a tripod near by in order to pronounce her oracles.

ontogeny: the development of the individual, as opposed to **phylogeny**, which refers to the evolution of the species.

orientation response: this was termed by Pavlov the 'what is it?' reflex. It serves to focus an animal's attention when it is presented with a stimulus. The orientation response is commonly associated with increased heart rate and other signs of **arousal**, which have the function of preparing the organism for an emergency reaction.

palaeolithic: pertaining to the earlier part of the prehistoric Stone Age (Greek *palaeo* = old + *lithos* = stone); the pre-agricultural era.

palaeontology: the study of prehistoric animal and plant life.

participation mystique: a term borrowed by C. G. Jung from the anthropologist, Lucien Lévy-Brühl, to describe the psychic state in which a subject experiences a sense of identification with an object. It approximates to the modern psychoanalytic term 'projective identification'.

persona: the mask worn by an actor in classical times; C. G. Jung used the term to describe the 'packaging' with which we present ourselves to the world.

Philosopher's Stone: a symbol of the realization of the alchemical goal of transforming base metal, the *prima materia*, into gold; identified by C. G. Jung as a symbol of the realization of the psychological goal of **individuation**.

phylogeny: the evolutionary history of the species, as opposed to **ontogeny**, the developmental history of the individual.

prima materia: an alchemical term meaning 'original matter'; also referred to as the *massa confusa*, the original elements existing in a state of chaos at the beginning of the alchemical *opus*.

projection: the unconscious process by which aspects of the **Self**, or feelings or ideas associated with those aspects, are experienced as if they were located in someone or something external to oneself. Projection commonly functions in association with another ego-defence mechanism, denial, whereby one denies the existence in oneself of the beliefs, motives, or intentions that one attributes to the person, animal, or thing on to whom or on to which one projects them.

psyche: the totality of all mental processes, unconscious as well as conscious; as opposed to mind, which is conventionally applied to conscious processes only. 'The psyche is not of today,' wrote Jung; 'its ancestry goes back many millions of years. Individual consciousness is only the flower and the fruit of a season, sprung from the perennial rhizome beneath the earth . . .' (CW 5, p. xxiv).

repression: the ego-defence mechanism by which an impulse or psychic component unacceptable to the **superego** is rendered unconscious.

resource holding potential (RHP): an estimate of fighting capacity defined on the input side by size, strength, skill, weapons, allies, and other resources, and on the output side by the probability of escalating **ritual agonistic behaviour (RAB)**.

reverted escape: the subsequent return after an initial withdrawal by a threatened subdominant animal to the proximity of a dominant animal that has threatened him or her.

ritual agonistic behaviour (RAB): a process of signalling between two individuals that converts a symmetrical relationship into an asymmetrical complementary relationship.

the Self: the term introduced by C. G. Jung for the dynamic nucleus at the core of the personality responsible for the process of **individuation**; the Self incorporates the entire archetypal potential of the phylogenetic psyche.

shadow: the term introduced by C. G. Jung for that aspect of the **Self** which remains unconscious because it is repressed by the **superego** or is unactualized because of deficiencies in the life experience of the individual.

sign stimulus: a specific perceptual stimulus possessing the capacity to trigger a specific **innate releasing mechanism (IRM)**.

superego: the term introduced by Freud to designate the inner moral authority which monitors individual behaviour in such a way as to make it acceptable first to the parents and later to society.

tellurian: of or pertaining to the earth (from Latin *tellus* earth).

transcendent function: Jung's term for the mutual influence which is exerted between the **ego** and the **Self** in the course of **individuation**.

unus mundus: the 'unitary world', the 'eternal ground of all empirical being'.

uroboros: ancient symbol of a serpent bent in a circle and biting its own tail; it incorporates the notion of self-regeneration, the eternal cycle of nature, and the food chain, as well as standing as an image of the primordial **Self** (q.v.) out of which ego-consciousness develops.

General Index

Names of ordinary places and people, as well as ideas, concepts, and facts discussed in the text, are included in this index. Names of mythic, legendary or religious places or figures, as well as individual symbols, are included in the Symbol Index.

Symbol Index

Names of mythic, legendary or religious places or figures, as well as individual symbols, are included in this index. Names of ordinary places and people, as well as ideas, concepts, and facts discussed in the text, are included in the General Index.